MAJOR LAW AND POLICY ISSUES IN THE SOUTH CHINA SEA

Contemporary Issues in the South China Sea

The South China Sea involves a wide array of complex issues covering sovereignty over islands and reefs, maritime delimitation, maritime security, cooperation against piracy and terrorism, resource development and environmental protection, all of which require extensive research. The area's importance largely results from one-third of the world's shipping transiting through its waters and that it is believed to hold huge oil and gas reserves beneath its seabed. Several countries have made competing territorial claims over the South China Sea with such disputes being regarded as Asia's most potentially dangerous source of conflict. This series seeks to provide thoughtful consideration of these issues from a variety of interdisciplinary perspectives. It provides an opportunity for early career researchers as well as established scholars to publish theoretically informed monographs and edited volumes that engage with key issues in this region.

Others titles in this series:

Non-Traditional Security Issues and the South China Sea
Shaping a New Framework for Cooperation
Edited by Shicun Wu and Keyuan Zou

Major Law and Policy Issues in the South China Sea

European and American Perspectives

Edited by

YANN-HUEI SONG
Academia Sinica, Taiwan

KEYUAN ZOU
University of Central Lancashire (UCLan), UK

Routledge
Taylor & Francis Group
LONDON AND NEW YORK

First published 2014 by Ashgate Publishing

Published 2016 by Routledge
2 Park Square, Milton Park, Abingdon, Oxfordshire OX14 4RN
711 Third Avenue, New York, NY 10017, USA

First issued in paperback 2016

Routledge is an imprint of the Taylor & Francis Group, an informa business

British Library Cataloguing in Publication Data
A catalogue record for this book is available from the British Library

The Library of Congress has cataloged the printed edition as follows:
Major law and policy issues in the South China Sea : European and American perspectives / edited by By Yann-huei Song and Keyuan Zou.
pages cm. -- (Contemporary issues in the south china sea)
Includes bibliographical references and index.
ISBN 978-1-4094-5594-3 (hardback)
1. Law of the sea--South China Sea. 2. Pacific settlement of international disputes. 3. National security--South China Sea--International cooperation. 4. South China Sea--Safety measures--International cooperation. 5. Territorial waters--South China Sea Region. 6. Security, International--South China Sea Region. I. Song, Yann-huei, editor of compilation. II. Zou, Keyuan, editor of compilation.
KZA1146.C6M35 2013
341.4'50916472--dc23

2013025913

ISBN 13: 978-1-138-24765-9 (pbk)
ISBN 13: 978-1-4094-5594-3 (hbk)

This book is dedicated to the late Professor Jon M. Van Dyke for his significant contributions to the law of the sea studies and discipline developments with a particular reference to the Asia-Pacific region

Contents

List of Figures and Tables

Figures

Tables

List of Editors and Contributors

Editors

Yann-huei Song received his undergraduate degree from National Chengchi University, Taipei, Taiwan, a Master's degree in Political Science from Indiana State University, Indiana, USA, a LL.M. degree from the University of California School of Law (Boalt Hall), Berkeley, California, USA, a doctoral degree in International Relations from Kent State University, Kent, Ohio, USA, and a JSD degree from the University of California School of Law.

Following graduation from Kent State University, Dr. Song taught at Department of Political Science, Indiana State University as Assistant Professor in 1988. He then returned to his country and taught as an Associate Professor at Institute of Maritime Law, National Taiwan Ocean University, Keelung, Taiwan in 1990. Currently, Dr. Song is a research fellow at the Institute of European and American Studies, Academia Sinica, Nangang, Taipei, Taiwan.

Dr. Song's research interests are in the fields of International Law of the Sea, International Fisheries Law, International Environmental Law, National Ocean Policy Study, Naval Arms Control and Maritime Security. He has published articles in journals such as *Political Geography Quarterly*, *Asian Survey*, *Marine Policy*, *Chinese Yearbook of International Law and Affairs*, *Issues and Studies*, *The American Asian Review*, *Ocean Development and International Law*, *EurAmerica*, *Ecology Law Review*, *the International Journal of Coastal and Marine Law*, *The Indonesian Quarterly* and others.

Keyuan Zou is Harris Professor of International Law at the Lancashire Law School of the University of Central Lancashire (UCLan), United Kingdom. He specializes in international law, in particular law of the sea and international environmental law. Before joining UCLan, he worked at Dalhousie University, Canada, Peking University, China, University of Hannover, Germany and National University of Singapore.

He has published over 60 refereed English papers in nearly 30 international journals including *Asian Yearbook of International Law*, *Asia-Pacific Journal of Environmental Law*, *Chinese Journal of International Law*, *Columbia Journal of International Affairs*, *Criminal Law Forum*, *International Journal of Marine and Coastal Law*, *International Lawyer*, *Journal of Environmental Law*, *Journal of International Maritime Law*, *Journal of International Wildlife Law and Policy*, *Journal of Maritime Law and Commerce*, *Lloyd's Maritime and Commercial Law Quarterly*, *Marine Policy*, *Maritime Policy and Management*, *Netherlands*

International Law Review, *Ocean Development and International Law*, *Ocean Yearbook*, *Singapore Journal of International and Comparative Law*, *Ocean and Coastal Management* and *Yearbook Law and Legal Practice in East Asia*.

His recent single-authored books include *Law of the Sea in East Asia: Issues and Prospects* (London/New York: Routledge, 2005), *China's Marine Legal System and the Law of the Sea* (Leiden/Boston: Martinus Nijhoff, 2005), *China's Legal Reform: Towards the Rule of Law* (Leiden/Boston: Martinus Nijhoff, 2006), and *China-ASEAN Relations and International Law* (Oxford: Chandos, 2009).

He is member of Editorial Boards of the *International Journal of Marine and Coastal Law* (Martinus Nijhoff), *Ocean Development and International Law* (Taylor & Francis), *Journal of International Wildlife Law and Policy* (Taylor & Francis), *The Polar Journal* (Routledge), and *Chinese Journal of International Law* (Oxford University Press), and of Advisory Boards of the *Chinese Oceans Law Review* (Hong Kong: China Review Culture Limited), *Korean Journal of International and Comparative Law* (Brill) and *Global Journal of Comparative Law* (Brill).

Contributors

Sam Bateman, retired from the Royal Australian Navy as a Commodore, is now a Professorial Research Fellow at the Australian National Centre for Ocean Resources and Security (ANCORS), University of Wollongong, NSW 2522, and currently also an Adviser to the Maritime Security Programme at the S. Rajaratnam School of International Studies (RSIS), Nanyang Technological University, Singapore. He was awarded his PhD from the University of NSW in 2001 for a dissertation on "The Strategic and Political Aspects of the Law of the Sea in East Asian Seas." He has written extensively on defence and maritime issues in Australia, the Asia-Pacific and Indian Ocean, including numerous articles on law of the sea issues. He has co-authored several reports for the Australian Strategic Policy Institute (ASPI), including Sea Change: Advancing Australia's ocean interests (2009) and Our Western Front: Australia and the Indian Ocean (2010), as well as the Policy Paper Good Order at Sea in Southeast Asia—Policy Recommendations for RSIS (2009).

Sherry P. Broder is Attorney at Law and concentrates on complex civil litigation—trials and appeals, class actions, international human rights law, international environmental law, ocean law and law of the sea, climate change issues, and rights, claims and entitlements of Native Hawaiians and other indigenous people. Broder graduated in 1970 from Wellesley College as a Wellesley Scholar and in 1975 from U.C. Berkeley Law School with highest honors, Order of the Coif. She was the first woman President of the Hawaii State Bar Association. She also teaches International Law and Ocean Law at the William S. Richardson School of Law, University of Hawaii at Manoa. She has written extensively and her recent publications include *Governing Ocean Resources: New Challenges and Emerging*

Regimes: A Tribute To Judge Choon-Ho Park (co-edited with Jon M. Van Dyke †, Jin-Hyun Paik and Seokwoo Lee) (Martinus/Nijhoff, 2013); "Geoengineeering: Ocean Iron Fertilization and the Challenges for International Regulatory Action", a chapter coauthored with Marcus Haward; and "Shipping Industry and the Imperative to Reduce its Air Pollution and Black Carbon Emissions", co-authored with Jon Van Dyke, in *The Regulation of International Shipping: International and Comparative Perspectives: Essays in Honor of Edgar Gold*, edited by Aldo Chircop et al. (Martinus/Nijhoff, 2012).

Peter A. Dutton is a Research Professor in and Director of the China Maritime Studies Institute at the U.S. Naval War College in Newport, Rhode Island. Professor Dutton's current research focuses on Chinese and Southeast Asian views of maritime sovereignty and jurisdiction in the South China Sea. He also researches and writes on international law of the sea and maritime strategy. He is a retired Navy Judge Advocate with the rank of Commander.

Theresa Fallon was educated at Loyola University, University of Chicago and the London School of Economics and Political Science. Her area of specialization is energy and her current research areas are EU-Asia relations and Asian maritime disputes. In the 1990s she contributed to the Centre for Global Energy Studies in London, and to Cambridge Energy Research Associates, Paris. She wrote on energy and current affairs for Saudi Arabia's *Al Eqtisadiah*, the International Arab Business Daily. From 1998 to 2003 she was the Moscow representative of PlanEcon, a research and consulting firm. She lectured at the American Institute of Business and Economics in Moscow. From 2003 to 2007 she worked in Beijing as a researcher and consultant. Inter alia, she delivered presentations at the Chinese Academy of Social Sciences and participated in scenario simulations at the Central Party School. She gave several interviews to the international media including BBC and CNN. Now based in Brussels, she is a Senior Associate with the European Institute of Asian Studies. She has briefed NATO, the EU Council Working Group on Asia (COASI) and U.S. Army Headquarters Europe (USAREUR) on the evolving situation in the South China Sea.

Erik Franckx is Research Professor, President of the Department of International and European Law and Director of the Centre for International Law at the Vrije Universiteit Brussel, Brussels, Belgium. He holds teaching assignments at the Vesalius College (V.U.B.), Université Libre de Bruxelles, the Brussels School of International Studies (University of Kent at Canterbury), the Program on International Legal Cooperation (Institute of European Studies, V.U.B.), and the Université Paris-Sorbonne Abu Dhabi. He has been appointed by Belgium as a member of the Permanent Court of Arbitration, The Hague, The Netherlands; as an expert in marine scientific research for use in special arbitration under the 1982 United Nations Convention on the Law of the Sea; as a legal expert in the Advisory Body of Experts of the Law of the Sea of the Intergovernmental

Oceanographic Commission of the United Nations Educational, Scientific and Cultural Organization; and as an expert in maritime boundary delimitation to the International Hydrographic Organization.

Cheng-yi Lin has been Research Fellow/Professor, Institute of European and American Studies, Academia Sinica, Taipei, Taiwan since 1994. He was also Director of that Institute between March 1998 and August 2003. He obtained PhD from University of Virginia in 1987 and is specialized in International Relations, National Security Policy and Sino-American Relations. His recent publications include "A Status Quo with Different Interpretations: Taiwan, China, the U.S. and Security in the Taiwan Strait," in Cheng-yi Lin and Denny Roy (eds), *The Future of U.S., China and Taiwan Relations* (New York: Palgrave Macmillan, 2011), pp. 71–100; and "The Security Implication of Cross-Strait Competition in the South Pacific from a Taiwanese Perspective," in Anne-Marie Brady (ed.), *Looking North, Look South: China, Taiwan, and South Pacific* (Singapore: World Scientific, 2010), pp. 113–33.

General (rtd) Daniel Schaeffer is currently an International Business Consultant with French think tank Asie 21, and former French defense attaché in Thailand, Vietnam and China. Graduate from the French Cadet school of Saint-Cyr in 1965, from the French Staff college/International relations—languages branch (Chinese) in 1982, and from the French National Institute of Foreign Languages and Civilizations in 1986 at the level of Master degree, General Daniel Schaeffer was an engineer officer in the first part of his carrier. In the second part he held different positions of responsibilities related to the international military relations (operational logistics, military cooperation, crises management, intelligence). In that frame, he served thrice as a defence attaché, in Thailand (1986–89), in Vietnam (1991–95) where he opened the office and therefore became the first French defence attaché in that country, and in China (1997–2000). When he retired he decided to bring his experience on Asia and in the international relations with the Asian countries to the service of the French companies. On that purpose, as of the 1rst of July 2000, he settled himself as an international business consultant for China and South East Asia.

Carlyle A. Thayer is Emeritus Professor, University of New South Wales at the Australian Defence Force Academy (ADFA), Canberra. He was educated at Brown, holds an M.A. in Southeast Asian Studies from Yale and a PhD in International Relations from The Australian National University. He has spent his entire career teaching in a military environment, first at The Royal Military College-Duntroon (1979–85) and then at ADFA. He is the author of over 400 publications dealing with politics and security issues in Southeast Asia including *Southeast Asia: Patterns of Security Cooperation* (Australian Strategic Policy Institute 2010).

Geoffrey Till, Professor of Maritime Studies at the Joint Services Command and Staff College and a member of the Defence Studies Department, part of the War Studies Group of King's College, London. In addition to many articles and chapters on various aspects of defense, he is the author of a number of books including *Air Power and the Royal Navy 1979*; *Maritime Strategy and the Nuclear Age* (2nd ed., London: Macmillan, 1984), *Modern Sea Power* (London: Brassey's, 1987), and, with Bryan Ranft, *The Sea in Soviet Strategy* (2nd ed., London: Macmillan, 1989). More recently he has edited *Coastal Forces* (London: Brassey's 1994), *Sea Power: Theory and Practice* (London: Frank Cass, 1994), and *Seapower at the Millennium* (Stroud: Suttons Publishing, 2001). *The Challenges of High Command: The British Experience* with Gary Sheffield followed, and, with the aid of a research grant from the British Academy, he has completed a major study, *Seapower: A Guide for the 21st Century* (London: Frank Cass, 2004). *The Development of British Naval Thinking* (London: Routledge, 2006) followed. Forthcoming are *On Naval Transformation* (London: Praeger, 2008) and a major study of the impact of globalization on naval development. His works have been translated into nine languages, and he regularly lectures at staff colleges and conferences around the world.

Stein Tønnesson is Research Professor at the Peace Research Institute Oslo (PRIO), Norway and Adjunct Professor at the Department of Peace and Conflict Research, Uppsala University, Sweden. He has done research on decolonization, revolution, war and nation-building in Southeast Asia, and the disputes in the South China Sea. His publications include "Vietnam's Objective in the South China Sea: National or Regional Security," *Contemporary Southeast Asia*, 22(1), April 2000: 199–220; "China and the South China Sea: A Peace Proposal," *Security Dialogue* 31(3), September 2000: 307–26; "The Paracels: The 'Other' South China Sea Dispute," *Asian Perspective*, 26(4), 2002: 145–69; "The South China Sea in the Age of European Decline," *Modern Asian Studies* 40(1), 2006: 1–57, and "China's Changing Role in the South China Sea: Reflections on a Scholar's Workshop," *Harvard Asia Quarterly*, XII (3&4), 2010: 18–30.

Ian Townsend-Gault is Associate Professor of Law and Director, Southeast Asian Legal Studies at the Faculty of Law, University of British Columbia, Vancouver, Canada. Before joining UBC in 1989, he taught at Dalhousie University and the University of Calgary, was Visiting Assistant Professor at the University of Oslo, and Assistant Director of the Centre for Petroleum and Mineral Law Studies at the University of Dundee. He taught in the LL.M. Business Law program at Chulalongkorn University, Bangkok, July–August 2010. He is currently Co-Investigator of a seven-year international and interdisciplinary project examining the linkages between trade and human rights in selected jurisdictions in the Asia-Pacific which is supported by a major grant from Canada's Social Science and Humanities Research Council. He is also a Senior Advisor to the Asia-Pacific Energy Resources Project of the National Bureau for Asian Research.

Jon M. Van Dyke was formerly Professor at the William S. Richardson School of Law, University of Hawaii at Manoa since 1976. Previously he taught at the Hastings College of the Law (University of California) in San Francisco (1971–76) and Catholic University Law School (1967–69) in Washington, D.C. In the spring of 2011, he was a Visiting Professor of Law at the University of California at Berkeley. Professor Van Dyke has written or edited 11 books, including *Who Owns the Crown Lands of Hawai`i?*, *Maritime Boundary Disputes, Settlement Processes, and the Law of the Sea* (Martinus Nijhoff 2009), *International Law and Litigation in the U.S.* (West, 3rd ed. 2009), *Updating International Nuclear Law* (2007); *Sharing the Resources of the South China Sea* (Martinus Nijhoff 1997; paperback edition, University of Hawai`i Press 1999), and *Freedom for the Seas in the 21st Century: Ocean Governance and Environmental Harmony* (Island Press 1993) (which received the Harold and Margaret Sprout Award from the International Studies Association for excellence in the field of international environmental policy). In 1987, he received the University of Hawai`i Presidential Citation for Excellence in Teaching; in 1984, 1993, 1996, and 2002 he was selected as the "Outstanding Professor" at the Law School; in 2006 and 2008 he was selected by the students to give the faculty address at the graduation ceremony; and in 2009 he received the Regents' Medal for Excellence in Research.

Acknowledgments

We would like to express our thanks to the Institute of European and American Studies (IEAS) and the Center for Asia-Pacific Area Studies (CAPAS), Academia Sinica for organizing the international conference with the theme of "Major Law and Policy Issues in the South China Sea: European and American Perspectives," which was convened on October 6-9, 2011 in Taipei, Taiwan. We would also like to thank all of the paper presenters in the conference and the contribution they have made in the study of the complex South China Sea issues that cover sovereignty over islands and reefs, maritime delimitation, maritime security, cooperation against piracy and terrorism, and resource development and environmental protection.

Acknowledgments

PART I
Introduction

Chapter 1
South China Sea Issues in European and American Perspectives: An Introduction

Yann-huei Song and Keyuan Zou

Background and Purposes

A new round of conflicts in the waters around the Paracel and Spratly Islands of the South China Sea between the claimants, in particular China, Vietnam and the Philippines, over the right to develop oil and gas resources has been seen since 2011. In January, the Vietnam-controlled media, citing Japanese newspaper *Asahi Shinbum*, reported that China had drawn up a military plan to seize control of islands in the South China Sea that are under effective control of other nations.[1] In March, the Vietnamese Foreign Ministry raised a protest against an anti-piracy exercise conducted by China's eighth naval escort flotilla in the waters near the Spratly Islands, claiming that the exercises "seriously violated Vietnam's sovereignty over the archipelago" and was in violation of the 2002 ASEAN–China Declaration on the Conduct of Parties in the South China Sea (DOC).[2] Again, in the same month, the Vietnamese Foreign Ministry registered its protest against China's 12th Five-Year Socio-economic Development Plan, which mentioned creating plans for exploitation of resources in the Paracel and Spratly Islands and the surrounding waters in the South China Sea. It also planned to strengthen tourism development for the Paracel Islands.[3]

In February 2011, the Energy Department of the Philippines gave the go signal to the Forum Energy plc (FEP) of the United Kingdom to proceed with the exploration of the Reed Bank Basin near the disputed Kalayaan Island Group of the Spratly archipelago. In March, two Chinese marine surveillance vessels ordered MV *Veritas Voyager*, an FEP survey vessel[4] operating at the area near Reed Bank, to leave.

---

1 Adm. James A. Lyons, "China's imperialism on full display; PLA weapons upgrades signal goal of Pacific hegemony," *The Washington Post*, January 12, 2011, Section B, Commentary, p. 1.

2 "Vietnam protests against Chinese naval exercise near disputed islands," *BBC Monitoring Asia Pacific—Political*, March 4, 2011 (LEXIS).

3 "Vietnam protests Chinese, Taiwanese moves in South China Sea," *BBC Monitoring Asia Pacific—Political*, March 13, 2011 (LEXIS).

4 The survey ship was chartered by Forum Energy plc, a UK-based oil and gas company, which had been awarded a contract by the government of the Philippines to conduct seismic

The government of the Philippines lodged a protest against the Chinese action, and dispatched an OV-10 bomber plane and a naval Islander light aircraft to Reed Bank area to protect its survey activities.[5] The Philippine President, Aquino III, also sent Commission on Maritime and Ocean Affairs Secretary Henry Bensurto to China to discuss the incident.[6] Moreover, officials of the armed forces of the Philippine Western Command recommended that the Latag (Lawak) and Patag Islands (Flat Island) in the Philippine-occupied Kalayaan Island Group be turned into tourist sites to strengthen the country's territorial claims.[7] Top Philippine military officials urged Senate President Pro Tempore Jinggoy Estrada to help pass legislation that would support the proposed revision of President Proclamation 72 to expand the security coverage to all service contracts.[8] Furthermore, the Philippines bought a large *Hamilton*-class patrol craft from the United States to help guard its waters amid tensions over territorial claims in the South China Sea. The Philippines planned to acquire more patrol ships, aircraft and an air defense radar system, and to repair its worn-out airstrip on Pag-asa (Thitu Island) in the Spratly archipelago.[9]

In March 2011, China's foreign ministry warned that "[o]il and gas exploration activities by any country or company in the waters under China's jurisdiction without permission of the Chinese government constitute a violation of China's sovereignty, rights and interests."[10] In May and June 2011, Chinese vessels were spotted in the area near Bombay Shoal, Reed Bank and Amy Douglas Bank, reportedly unloading building materials, erecting posts, installing plastic buoys and placing markers. It was also reported that China planned to install its most advanced oil rig in the disputed areas in the South China Sea.[11] Actions have also been taken by China to support its claim to sovereign right for the exploration

studies in the Sampaguita gas field located in the Reed Bank basin in the South China Sea.

5 Tom Grioder, "Sino–Philippine Tensions Rise in South China Sea as Chinese Patrol Boats Threaten Seismic Vessel," *Global Insight*, March 8, 2011 (LEXIS) and Ian Storey, "China and the Philippines: Implications of the Reed Bank Incident," *China Brief*, Vol. 11, Issue 8, May 6, 2011, pp. 6–8, available at: http://www.jamestown.org/uploads/media/cb_11_8_03.pdf.

6 "Manila sends maritime expert to Beijing to discuss harassment of research ship," *BBC Monitoring Asia Pacific—Political*, March 6, 2011 (LEXIS).

7 "Indonesia hopes Spratlys to become 'zone of cooperation'," *BBC Monitoring Asia Pacific—Political*, March 9, 2011 (LEXIS).

8 Ibid.

9 "Philippines to restore military airfield in Spratlys," *BBC Monitoring Asia Pacific—Political*, March 24, 2011 (LEXIS).

10 "Foreign Ministry Spokesperson Jiang Yu's regular press conference on March 24, 2011," *State News Service*, March 25, 2011 (LEXIS).

11 Carlyle A. Thayer, "Security Cooperation in the South China Sea: An Assessment of Recent Trends," paper presented at the First Manila Conference on the South China Sea: "The South China Sea: Toward a Regional of Peace, Cooperation, and Progress," July 5–6, 2011, Dusit Thani Hotel, Makati City, the Philippines, pp. 16–17. See also Michaela P. del Callar and Mario J. Mallari. "RP gov't protests China's planned oil rig, constructions in

and exploitation of nonliving resources in the waters encircled by the U-shaped line in the South China Sea. In May 2011, a Chinese marine surveillance vessel cut exploration cables of the *Binh Minh 02* of the Vietnam National Oil and Gas Corporation that was operating in a contracted area called Block 148, which is located about 120 km (75 miles) off the south-central coast of Vietnam from the beach town of Nha Trang, and some 600 km (373 miles) south of China's Hainan island.[12] This was followed by another cable-cutting incident that occurred in the contracted area called Block 136-03 in the vicinity of Vanguard Bank, which is one of the features in the Spratly archipelago, in June 2011.[13]

The rising tensions in the South China Sea could disrupt peace and stability, and therefore not only the countries in the region but also a number of non-South China Sea-bordering states such as the United States, India, Australia, Japan and even some European countries had raised concerns about the development of the situation in the South China Sea. These concerns were discussed at a series of meetings hosted by ASEAN, including the ASEAN Foreign Ministers Meeting (AMM),[14] ASEAN Summit, ASEAN Regional Forum (ARF) and East Asia Summit (EAS), and can also be found in the official statements issued after these meetings, which include the 44th AMM (July 2011), the 18th ASEAN Regional Forum (July 2011),[15] the 19th ASEAN Summit (November 2011),[16] the 14th ASEAN–

Reeds, Spratlys," *The Daily Tribune*, June 2, 2011, available at: http://www.tribuneonline.org/headlines/20110602hed4.html.

12 "Vietnam demands China stop sovereignty violations," *Thanh Nien Daily*, May 29, 2011, available at: http://www.thanhniennews.com/2010/Pages/20110530011353.aspx.

13 "Vietnam Navy Drills Roil China Sea Waters," *International Oil Daily*, June 14, 2011 (LEXIS).

14 Joint Communique of the 44th ASEAN Foreign Ministers Meeting, Bali, Indonesia, July 19, 2011, available at: http://www.aseansec.org/documents/44thAMM-PMC-18thARF/44thAMM-JC.pdf.

15 Paragraph 11 of the 18th ASEAN Regional Forum's Chair's Statement on July 23, 2011 reads inter alia: " The Ministers welcomed the recent finalization and adoption of the Guidelines for the Implementation of the Declaration on the Conduct of Parties in the South China Sea (DOC) at the recent ASEAN PMC+1 with China. The Ministers further reaffirmed the importance and continued relevance of the Declaration on the Conduct of Parties in the South China Sea (DOC) of 2002, as a milestone document between ASEAN Member States and China, embodying their collective commitment to promoting peace, stability and mutual trust and to ensuring the peaceful resolution of disputes in the area, in accordance with universally recognized principles of international law, including the 1982 United Nations Convention on the Law of the Sea (UNCLOS)." For the text, visit http://www.asean.org/documents/44thAMM-PMC-18thARF/18thARF-CS.pdf.

16 Paragraph 147 of the 19th ASEAN Summit's Chair's Statement on November 17, 2011 reads inter alia: "We reaffirmed the importance of the Declaration on the Conduct of the Parties in the South China Sea (DOC) as a milestone document signed between ASEAN and China embodying the collective commitment to promoting peace, stability, and mutual trust in the South China Sea and to ensuring the peaceful resolution of disputes in this area in accordance with international law, including the 1982 United Nations Convention on the

China Summit (November 2011)[17] and the 6th East Asia Summit (November 2011).[18] Paragraph 22 of the Joint Communique of the 44th AMM provides that the ASEAN Foreign Ministers "discussed in depth the recent developments in the South China Sea and expressed serious concern over the recent incidents."[19] Accordingly, they "stressed the importance of maintaining peace and stability in the South China Sea, the continued exercise of self-restraint by all parties concerned, and the promotion of confidence-building measures in this area."[20] In addition, they also "further reaffirmed the importance and continued relevance of the Declaration on the Conduct of Parties in the South China Sea (DOC) of 2002, as a milestone document between ASEAN Member States and China, embodying their collective commitment to promoting peace, stability and mutual trust and to ensuring the peaceful resolution of disputes in the area, in accordance with universally recognized principles of international law, including the 1982 United Nations Convention on the Law of the Sea (UNCLOS)."[21] Moreover, they "called on all parties to respect the freedom of navigation in and over-flight above the South China Sea as provided for by the universally recognized principles of international law, including the 1982 UNCLOS."[22]

The United States was also concerned about the escalation of tensions in the South China Sea. In July 2011, Secretary of State Clinton, when attending the 18th ASEAN Regional Forum held in Bali, Indonesia, expressed US concern about a number of naval incidents in the South China Sea that threatened peace and stability in the Asia-Pacific because these incidents "endanger the safety of life at sea, escalate tensions, undermine freedom of navigation, and pose risks to lawful unimpeded commerce and economic development."[23] In October 2011, during his visit to Indonesia, U.S. Defense Secretary Leon Panetta asked the member states of ASEAN to continue working towards a binding code of conduct. He reiterated that the United States has a national interest in freedom of navigation and overflight, in unimpeded economic development and commence, and in respect for international

---

Law of the Sea (UNCLOS)." For the text of the statement, visit http://www.aseansec.org/documents/19th%20summit/CS.pdf.

17 Paragraph 10 of the Joint Statement of the 14th ASEAN–China Summit to Commemorate the 20th Anniversary of Dialogue Relations, November 18, 2011 reads: "We will cooperate to enhance maritime security, including to ensure freedom of commerce, safety of navigation and maritime traffic, in accordance with international law, including the 1982 United Nations Convention on the Law of the Sea (UNCLOS)." For the text of the joint statement, visit http://www.aseansec.org/26739.htm.

18 Chairman's Statement of the 6th East Asia Summit, Bali, Indonesia, November 19, 2011, available at: http://www.aseansec.org/documents/19th%20summit/EAS-CS.pdf.

19 *Supra* note 14.

20 Ibid.

21 Ibid.

22 Ibid.

23 For the remarks made on July 22, 2011, visit the website of the U.S. Department of State at http://www.state.gov/secretary/2011/07/168989.htm.

law. In addition, he said, although the United States does not take a position on competing territorial claims, it hopes that in the interest of peaceful resolution all parties concerned need to clarify their maritime claims in terms consistent with customary international law, as reflected in the Law of the Sea Convention.[24] In November 2011, US President Obama stated at the 6th East Asia Summit, held in Bali, Indonesia, that the United States strongly opposes the threat or use of force by any party to advance its territorial or maritime claims or interfere in legitimate economic activity.[25]

Taiwan is one of the claimants to sovereignty and maritime rights in the South China Sea and has effectively controlled the Pratas Islands and Taiping Dao (Itu Aba), the largest island in the Spratly archipelago, since 1956. However, due to the policy consideration of the so-called "One China" principle by the ASEAN member states and China, Taiwan has been barred from attending the regional security dialogue process that deals with the South China Sea issue, such as ARF, the expanded ASEAN Defense Ministers Meeting (ADMM+) and EAS. Although Taiwan has been participating in the Council for Asia-Pacific Security Cooperation (CSCAP), and the Indonesia-sponsored Informal Workshop on Managing Potential Conflicts in the South China Sea, the nature, status and functions of Taiwan's participation in these Track II-level meetings had been constrained. In particular, since the signing of the DOC in November 2002, seven ASEAN–China joint working group meetings for the implementation of the declaration had been held, but Taiwan had never been invited to participate in the discussion.

Recent developments in the South China Sea give rise to a number of policy questions that need to be answered carefully by Taiwan's Ma Ying-jeou administration. These include the following: (1) what actions should be taken by Taiwan with a view to pushing China and ASEAN member states to consider it necessary to include Taiwan in the regional dialogue process that deals with the implementation of the DOC and the formulation of a regional code of conduct in the South China Sea in the years ahead and (2) what actions could be taken by Taiwan to obtain the support of the US government so that Taiwan could be invited to participate in the "collaborative diplomatic process by all claimants for resolving the various disputes in the South China Sea" that were referred to in the statement made by the US Secretary of State at both the 17th and 18th ARF meetings.

In order to avoid being further marginalized and being excluded from the regional mechanisms that deal with the South China Sea issue, it is necessary for Taiwan to raise its voice internationally and take actions to increase its

---

24 US Defense Secretary Leon Panetta, Statement to ASEAN Defense Ministers, Bali, Indonesia, October 23, 2011, available on the website of the U.S. Department of Defense at http://www.defense.gov/speeches/speech.aspx?speechid=1624.

25 See White House Fact Sheet: East Asia Summit, Office of the Press Secretary, November 19, 2011, available at: http://iipdigital.usembassy.gov/st/english/texttrans/2011/11/20111119151041su0.2769434.html#axzz1eDErWMlR.

participation in the international and regional dialogue processes, at both the Track I and Track II levels. One of the actions that was proposed and adopted by Taiwan's government is to convene international conferences or workshops in Taiwan by inviting eminent international scholars who are experts on the South China Sea issues.

These complex issues include disputes over territorial sovereignty, disputes over maritime claims to sovereign and jurisdictional rights over waters and seabed, and disputes over the rights and duties of the countries that border the South China Sea and other countries that use the seas, including for military purposes, in accordance with generally recognized rules and principles under international law, as reflected in the 1982 UNCLOS. Over the past three years, there have been several incidents at sea between the claimants, and between the claimants and non-claimants, in the South China Sea over fisheries, collection of seismic data, exploration for oil and gas resources, and exercise of freedom of navigation. Third parties' concerns and involvement in the South China Sea disputes have been increasing, as manifested in actions taken by the United States, India and Japan. It is therefore important to examine the South China Sea dispute from legal and political perspectives and from the viewpoints of American and European experts who have been studying the South China Sea issues for years.

Structure and Contents

The book is divided into six parts and 15 chapters. The first part is the Introduction, with the introductory chapter prepared by the editors. The second part deals with the general assessment of South China Sea issues, including two chapters written by lawyers and political scientists.

Chapter 2 introduces the regional maritime cooperation in the South China Sea. This chapter serves as a tribute from all the contributors of this book to Jon M. Van Dyke who sadly and unexpectedly passed away in his sleep while attending a law of the sea conference in Australia on November 29, 2011. Van Dyke was there to give the keynote address for the Law of the Sea Institute, an organization which he helped to create. This chapter begins with a reminder to the bordering countries in the South China Sea that under Article 123 of the Law of the Sea Convention, they are obligated to cooperate in the sea, which is a semi-enclosed sea governed by Part IX of the Convention. This is followed by the discussion of the two existing institutions that deal with the management, conservation, exploration and exploitation of the fisheries resources, as well as the protection and preservation of the marine environment, namely the Coordinating Body on the Seas of East Asia (COBSEA) and the Partnerships in Environmental Management for the Seas of East Asia (PEMSEA). The chapter ends by calling the countries of the region and those with interests in the region to work together to manage and protect the shared ocean spaces in the South China Sea for the benefit of present and future generations.

Chapter 3 reviews political and military developments related to the South China Sea in 2011. It discusses Chinese assertiveness directed at the Philippines, the responses by the Philippines, Chinese assertiveness directed at Vietnam, Vietnam's responses, the adoption of guidelines for the Declaration on Conduct of Parties in the South China Sea, relations between China and the Philippines in the post-DOC Guidelines period, and relations between China and Vietnam.

Part III contains five chapters dealing with legal issues in the South China Sea. Chapter 4 looks into relevant Chinese state practice and examines authoritative scholarly writings to better understand the nature of China's claim to historic rights within the U-shaped line in the South China Sea. It also discusses the relevant international law regarding historic rights to islands and historic rights to water space, and draws some conclusions and presents key questions for further analysis.

Chapter 5 analyzes recent development in US efforts to accede to the 1982 Law of the Sea Convention and the potential impact of US accession to the Convention on state practices and maritime claims in the South China Sea. Chapter 6 postulates that due to the complex geography of the South China Sea and the multiple bordering states, a conventional system of straight-line maritime boundaries will be impossible to achieve in parts of the sea. This situation is aggravated by the difficulties of resolving the sovereignty disputes over most features in the sea, as well as by the need for agreement on whether any of these features qualify as "islands" entitled to a full set of maritime zones. This chapter claims that by international precedent, there are features in the sea that qualify as islands, and thus the whole sea is potentially closed off as an exclusive economic zone (EEZ) of one bordering country or another. These considerations suggest the importance of the bordering countries changing their mind-set from one of sovereignty, sole ownership of resources and seeking "fences in the sea" to one of functional cooperation and cooperative management of the sea and its resources.

Chapter 7 takes the approach to functionalism by examining relevant legal principles and norms embodied in the Antarctic Treaty System which could be borrowed to apply to other contested regions. More importantly, the topic is worth exploring further, particularly under the current circumstances of high tension and even confrontation in the South China Sea. Chapter 8 attempts to compare the legal phenomenon in the North Pole with the South China Sea. While the Arctic Ocean and the South China Sea do not seem to have much in common at first sight, the legal technique of drawing imaginary lines in the oceans has been relied upon by China as well as Russia in order to try to extend their respective influences over the region in question. By first looking at the physical differences, and subsequently at the legal similarities, the chapter tries to evaluate the relevance of the drawing of such imaginary lines at sea under contemporary international law.

Part IV also contains four chapters but particularly discusses policy issues in the South China Sea. Chapter 9 looks into the impact of competing conceptions of the freedom of navigation on the problems of working towards a sustainable way of handling the dispute over the South China Sea, whether that aspires to actually resolving the dispute or more immediately to managing away its more dangerous aspects.

Chapter 10 examines the positions of the main players in the South China Sea. In particular, it looks at China's increasingly assertive stance and at recent bellicose statements in China's official media. It argues that such statements are counterproductive from a strategic and military point of view, but aim to deter international oil companies from drilling in waters claimed by Vietnam and the Philippines. It also examines the position of the European Union (EU), perceptions of EU action in the region and the possible role the EU could play in connection with this dispute. Finally, it briefly sets out some possible future scenarios of conflict or cooperation in the South China Sea.

Chapter 11 discusses the interests and claims of China and Vietnam, the two communist partners and adversaries in the South China Sea, as well as the tensions in their asymmetric relationship. It also seeks to point out a possible way forward for long-term conflict resolution between Beijing and Hanoi. Chapter 12 analyzes China's global naval encirclement strategy, in which the South China Sea is used as a sanctuary to ensure its full defense scheme against the presumed hostile forces that could be those of the United States and its allies, especially Japan.

The final part of the book contains two chapters dealing with Taiwan's role in the resolution of South China Sea issues. Chapter 13 analyzes the confidence-building measures in the South China Sea, Taiwan's participation in the South China Sea workshop process, and the implication of the South China Sea issue for the development of US–China–Taiwan relations. The chapter argues that although the United States has encouraged cross-Strait confidence-building measures in the Taiwan Strait for some time, it has no justification for blocking similar measures in the South China Sea. However, the United States has remained vigilant because cooperation between China and Taiwan often has security ramifications for ASEAN and the United States, be they in the Taiwan Strait or in the South China Sea.

Chapter 14 examines several aspects of the past, present and future roles of Taiwan in a variety of South China Sea issues. It begins by considering the objectives and accomplishments of the Track-II informal diplomacy initiative "Managing Potential Conflicts in the South China Sea." It goes on to investigate the appropriate role for Taiwan in the larger question of South China Sea ocean governance, and concludes with suggestions as to how all governing authorities bordering those waters should proceed in the interests of human security, marine environmental protection and preservation, the preservation of biological diversity, and the appropriate exploitation of living and nonliving resources.

By presenting the above chapters with a concluding chapter written by the editors of this book, the editors strongly hope that the book can contribute to the existing literature on the South China Sea, in particular from legal and policy perspectives, assisting law and policy makers in their deliberations of the relevant policies and legislation as well as providing interested readers with a substantial knowledge and understanding of South China Sea issues.

Prospect and Conclusions

Since April 2012, countries outside the South China Sea, such as the United States, Australia and member states of the EU, have expressed their concerns about the escalation of tensions and possible conflicts in the South China Sea. These concerns were triggered by a series of actions and counteractions taken by China, the Philippines and Vietnam respectively in support of their claims to sovereignty and maritime rights in the South China Sea. In early April 2012, the Philippines' biggest warship, BRP *Gregorio del Pilar*, was locked in a standoff with two Chinese surveillance vessels in the waters near Scarborough Shoal (Huangyan Dao in Chinese and Bajo de Masinloc or Panatag Shoal in Filipino), which is located in the area enclosed by the Chinese U-shaped line and in the Philippines-claimed EEZ in the South China Sea. The shoal is claimed by China, Taiwan and the Philippines. The Philippine warship attempted to arrest Chinese fishermen but was blocked by the Chinese surveillance vessels.[26] Following the incident, tensions quickly escalated not only between China and the Philippines but also between China and Vietnam, and between Vietnam and Taiwan.

In April 2012, a number of Taiwanese lawmakers visited Taiping Dao (Itu Aba), aiming to reaffirm Taiwan's sovereignty over the Spratly Islands. Vietnam lodged a protest against the visit.[27] In June 2012, in response to Vietnam's passage of a new sea law asserting its sovereignty over the Paracel and Spratly Islands, China approved a plan to establish Sansha City to administer the Paracel Islands, Macclesfield Bank and the Spratly Islands.[28] In addition, China National Offshore Oil Corporation (CNOOC) announced that nine offshore areas in the South China Sea are available for exploration through cooperation with foreign companies. The nine areas collectively total more than 160,000 km^2 in size and are located within the EEZs unilaterally claimed by Vietnam.[29] On July 24, 2012, Sansha City was officially set up.[30] Simultaneously, China approved the formal establishment of a military garrison on Woody Island, which is the seat of Sansha City and the largest feature in the Paracel archipelago. Both Vietnam and the Philippines lodged protests immediately.[31]

26 Jim Gomez, "Philippine warship in standoff with China vessels," *Associated Press Online*, April 11, 2012.

27 "VN opposes Taiwanese officials' visit to Spratly," *States News Service*, May 10, 2012.

28 Teddy Ng, "New city to run disputed island chains," *South China Morning Post*, June 22, 2012.

29 "CNOOC to offer 9 blocks in S. China Sea for joint exploration," *Global Times*, June 27, 2012, available at: http://www.globaltimes.cn/content/717464.shtml.

30 "China establishes Sansha City," *China News*, July 24, 2012, available at: http://news.xinhuanet.com/english/china/2012-07/24/c_131734893.htm.

31 "Philippines Slams China's Establishment of Sansha City in South China Sea," *VOA News*, July 23, 2012, available at: http://www.voanews.com/content/philippines-slams-chinese-establishment-of-city-in-south-china-sea/1443944.html.

In response to the rising tensions in the South China Sea, a prominent Australian think tank, the Lowy Institute for International Policy, suggested that Australia should try to broker a solution to the South China Sea dispute. Michael Wesley, the executive director of the Institute, stated that:

> None of the options for managing and resolving the competition currently on the table have any chance of working, and so new initiatives must be found. While Australia has no direct interest in the territorial disputes, it should be extremely concerned about the prospects for the disruption of its own trade flows within the region, and more broadly about the possible impacts on the strategic balance in the Pacific. Canberra is not a party to the dispute nor a great power, and therefore is well placed to play a significant role in proposing and brokering a solution.[32]

On September 10, 2012, Australia and Singapore stated in a Joint Communique issued after convening the 7th meeting of the Singapore–Australia Joint Ministerial Committee in Canberra that "neither Australia nor Singapore took a position on the merits of the various territorial claims, but had an interest in the maintenance of peace and stability, respect for international law, unimpeded trade and the freedom of navigation in the South China Sea."[33]

The European Union has also raised its concerns about the developments in the South China Sea. On July 12, 2012, Catherine Ashton, High Representative for Foreign Affairs and Security Policy and Vice President of the European Commission, signed in Phnom Penh, Cambodia the Instrument of Accession of the EU to the Treaty of Amity and Cooperation in Southeast Asia. Simultaneously the ten ASEAN Foreign Ministers signed the Instrument of Extension to agree to the EU's accession from the ASEAN side. The EU High Representative stated that it was an important step in acceding to the Treaty because it commits the EU to working together in tackling issues in a peaceful way, issues that certainly include the South China Sea. The signing of the instrument also confirmed that the EU and ASEAN member states will work to address some of the security and political concerns of the region.[34] On the same day, the EU and United States issued a joint statement on the Asia-Pacific region, in which the two sides committed to work together continuously to encourage China and ASEAN to advance a regional code

32 Michael Wesley, "What's at stake in the South China Sea?" Strategic Snapshots, Snapshot 11, the Lowy Institute for International Policy, July 2012, p. 3. However, Australian Foreign Minister Bon Carr rebuffed this suggestion, stating that Australia should stay out of the South China Sea dispute.

33 See "Australia should stay out of South China Sea dispute, says Carr," ABC Radio Australia, available at: http://foreignminister.gov.au/releases/2012/bc_mr_120910.html.

34 "The EU accedes to Treaty of Amity and Cooperation in Southeast Asia," Press Release, European Commission, July 12, 2012, available at: http://europa.eu/rapid/pressReleasesAction.do?reference=IP/12/781&type=HTML.

of conduct for the South China Sea and to resolve territorial and maritime disputes through peaceful, diplomatic and cooperative solutions.[35]

The increasing American concerns about and involvement in the South China Sea issue are manifested in the actions taken by the US Congress and Department of State. In July 2012, a resolution was introduced by U.S. Senator John F. Kerry to express US concerns about the rising tensions in the South China Sea and to reaffirm the strong US support for the 2002 DOC and peaceful resolution of the disputes in the region. The resolution was co-sponsored by Senators Richard Lugar (R-IN), Jim Webb (R-VA), James Inhofe (R-OK), Joe Lieberman (I-CT) and John McCain (R-AZ), and unanimously passed on August 2, 2012. It is stated in the resolution that the US Senate supports the implementation of the DOC and the adoption of a legally binding code of conduct of parties in the South China Sea. In addition, the Senate urges that, pending adoption of a code of conduct, all parties concerned, consistent with their commitments under the DOC, "exercise self-restraint in the conduct of activities that would complicate or escalate disputes and stability." Moreover, the Senate gives its support for "a collaborative diplomatic process by all claimants for resolving outstanding territorial and jurisdictional disputes, allowing parties to peacefully settle claims and disputes using international law."[36] On September 12 and 20, 2012 respectively, an oversight hearing on "Beijing as an Emerging Power in the South China Sea" was held by the US House Committee on Foreign Relations, and a hearing was held by the Senate Foreign Relations Committee, Subcommittee on East Asian and Pacific Affairs on "Maritime Territorial Disputes and Sovereignty Issues in Asia."[37]

On August 3, 2012, the U.S. Department of State issued a statement on the South China Sea, in which the Obama administration expressed its concerns about the escalation of tensions in the South China Sea and stated that it is monitoring the situation closely. The United States is worried by recent developments in the South China Sea, including "an uptick in confrontational rhetoric, disagreements over resource exploitation, coercive economic actions, and the incidents around the Scarborough Reef, including the use of barriers to deny access."[38] In particular, it is the view of the United States that China's upgrading of the administrative level of Sansha City and establishment of a new military garrison there covering

35 Joint EU–US statement on the Asia-Pacific region, Press, European Union, July 12, 2012, available at: http://www.eu-un.europa.eu/articles/en/article_12417_en.htm.

36 For US Congress SR 524, visit http://legiscan.com/gaits/view/432174.

37 For the information about the oversight hearing, visit http://foreignaffairs.house.gov/hearings/views/?1467. For the Senate hearing, visit http://www.foreign.senate.gov/hearings/maritime-territorial-disputes-and-sovereignty-issues-in-asia.

38 For the press statement by Patrick Ventrell, Acting Deputy Spokesperson, Office of Press Relations, U.S. Department of State, August 3, 2012, visit http://www.state.gov/r/pa/prs/ps/2012/08/196022.htm.

disputed areas of the South China Sea run counter to collaborative diplomatic efforts to resolve differences and risk further escalating tensions in the region.[39]

It is acknowledged that the maritime issues in East Asia are intertwined with one another and the issues in the South China Sea have strong implications for the East China Sea. Ideally this book should address the issues in the East China Sea as well. However, due to the space as well as focus of the book, the editors could not accommodate any chapter discussing East China Sea issues.[40] Despite that, the editors wish to make efforts in a future book specifically on the East China Sea when an opportunity arises.

Finally, if the potential conflicts in the region cannot be managed effectively in the years to come, more concern, responses and involvement can be expected from the United States, the EU and other countries that are non-claimants to the land territories and do not border the South China Sea. It is therefore probable that the South China Sea dispute will continue as a main theme and subject for examination and study not only by Asian experts but also by American and European experts, particularly from legal and political perspectives, both today and tomorrow.

39 Ibid.

40 For details on East China Sea issues, see International Crisis Group, *Dangerous Waters: China–Japan Relations on the Rocks*, Asia Report No.245, April 8, 2013, available at: http://www.crisisgroup.org/~/media/Files/asia/north-east-asia/245-dangerous-waters-china-japan-relations-on-the-rocks.

PART II
General Assessment of South China Sea Issues

Chapter 2

Regional Maritime Cooperation in the South China Sea: COBSEA and PEMSEA

Jon M. Van Dyke and Sherry P. Broder

Introduction

The South China Sea is a semi-enclosed sea governed by Part IX of the Law of the Sea Convention,[1] which says in Article 123 that countries bordering such seas "should co-operate with each other in the exercise of their rights and in the performance of their duties under this Convention." More specifically, they are instructed to "endeavor, directly or through an appropriate regional organization: (a) to co-ordinate the management, conservation, exploration, and exploitation of the living resources of the sea" and also to co-ordinate their activities "with respect to the protection and preservation of the marine environment." The countries bordering on the South China Sea have failed to create an effective regional organization, and their cooperation "directly" has been generally unsuccessful as well. The Coordinating Body on the Seas of East Asia (COBSEA) has been mostly dysfunctional and the Partnerships in Environmental Management for the Seas of East Asia (PEMSEA) has been modest in its accomplishments. No effective organization to manage the shared fisheries has been established.

The UNEP Regional Seas Programmes

The UNEP Regional Seas Programme was launched in 1974 and currently consists of 13 regional programmes,[2] six of which are administered directly by UNEP,[3] and it has links to five "partner" regional environmental bodies.[4] These

1 United Nations Convention on the Law of the Sea, December 10, 1982, Montego Bay, Jamaica, 1833 U.N.T.S. 397, 2 I.L.M. 1261 (1982), entered into force on November 16, 1994.

2 Black Sea, Wider Caribbean, East Asian Seas-COBSEA, Eastern Africa, South Asian Seas, Persian/Arab Gulf-ROPME Sea Area, Mediterranean, Northeast Pacific, Northwest Pacific-NOWPAP, Red Sea and Gulf of Aden, Southeast Pacific, Pacific-SPREP, and Western Africa.

3 Wider Caribbean, East Asian Seas, Eastern Africa, Mediterranean, Northwest Pacific-NOWPAP, and Western Africa.

4 Antarctic, Arctic, Baltic Sea, Caspian Sea, and Northeast Atlantic-OSPAR.

programmes emerged from the recognition that ocean regions differ dramatically and that unique ecosystems require individual conservation approaches, but it has also been recognized that many sources of marine pollution are global in nature and frequently uniform global standards and approaches are needed.[5] Although some of these programs have thrived, others have stumbled because of a lack of interest, political disputes, mission uncertainty, and modest funding. The goal of these programs has also been questioned, because they were established with a single-sector focus on pollution, and today attention is given to multi-sector, integrated coastal and ocean management strategies.[6]

COBSEA

The Coordinating Body on the Seas of East Asia (COBSEA) was established pursuant to an Action Plan which was adopted in 1981 and revised in 1994.[7] Its website states optimistically that "[t]here is no regional convention, but instead the programme promotes compliance with existing environmental treaties and is based on member country goodwill."[8] The participating states are Australia, Cambodia, China, Indonesia, Malaysia, the Philippines, Singapore, South Korea, Thailand, and Vietnam.[9]

From 2001 to 2006, COBSEA undertook projects such as a study of the impact of sewage on the marine environment in preparation for the 2001 "Regional Workshop on Protecting Coastal and Marine Ecosystems from Land-based Activities in the Asia-Pacific Region" in Toyama, Japan. This project was designed

5 See for example, J.G.B Derraik, *The Pollution of the Marine Environment by Plastic Debris: A Review*, 44:9 Marine Pollution Bulletin 842 (September 2002); M.S. Islam and M. Tanaka, *Impacts of Pollution on Coastal and Marine Ecosystems including Coastal and Marine Fisheries and Approach for Management: A Review and Synthesis*, 48:7–8 Marine Pollution Bulletin 624 (April 2004); and D.A. Holdway, *The Acute and Chronic Effects of Wastes Associated with Offshore Oil and Gas Production on Temperate and Tropical Marine Ecological Processes*, 44:3 Marine Pollution Bulletin 185 (March 2002).

6 See, for example, Biliana Cicin-Sain and Robert Knecht, *Integrated Coastal and Ocean Management: Concepts and Practices* (Island Press, 1998).

7 UNEP, *New Strategic Direction for COBSEA (2008–2012)*, UNEP EAS/RCU, Coordinating Body for the Seas of E. Asia Secretariat [COBSEA] (23 January 2008), available at: http://www.cobsea.org/documents/Meeting_Documents/19COBSEA/New%20Strategic%20Direction%20for%20COBSEA%202008-2012.pdf.

8 UNEP, http://www.unep.org/regionalseas/programmes/unpro/eastasian/default.asp.

9 The island of Taiwan is included in the map on the cover of the most recent governance document showing the member states, but the Republic of China (Taiwan) is not listed as a member, and Taiwan has not been able to participate directly in regional environmental programmes.

to raise awareness of the needs for regional guidelines and standards, innovative solutions, and state partnerships for sewage management.[10]

At the 2001 Regional Workshop on Identification of Pollution Hot Spots in the East Asian Seas Region in Hua Hin, Thailand, catchments and major pollution sources were nominated as hot spots by the member countries. The participants at this meeting also confirmed the need for further regional cooperation for data and information sharing to identify major pollution sources, their management, and the use of modeling to predict pollution effects. This recognition resulted in the development of a project called "Determination of Pollution Loading Using Modeling and GIS," which focused on collection of data from selected catchments in the member countries, modeling pollution-loading from the major pollution sources, the establishment of a geographic information systems database of land-based nutrient pollution, and capacity-building. Through this activity, member countries were to be provided with a quantitative modeling tool for the estimation of nutrient pollution loading in catchment areas with no or limited data availability.[11]

The COBSEA Action Plan was superseded in 2008 by the New Strategic Direction for COBSEA (2008–2012), which was adopted at the 19th meeting of the members in Siem Reap, Cambodia. That document includes an assessment of challenges, as well as objectives and strategies to:

1. Establish a knowledge base to provide information on programmes and projects, and the state of the coastal and marine environment in the East Asian Seas region, with information synthesis and reporting activities under the COBSEA Coordinating Centre;
2. Strengthen member capacity in responding to the growing pressures exerted on the coastal and marine environment, and the increasing need for sustainable management of their natural resources;
3. Assist members in identifying and addressing upcoming issues of priority to the East Asian Seas region; and
4. Implement a new strategic direction in collaboration with member countries and regional partners, and work to prevent duplication of efforts.[12]

---

10 UNEP, *Regional Workshop on Protecting Coastal and Marine Ecosystems from Land-Based Activities in the Asia-Pacific Region*, September 2001, UNEP(DEC)/EAS/GPA-Toyama (September 2001), available at: http://www.cobsea.org/documents/report_landbased/Protecting_Coastal_and_Marine_Ecosystems_from_Land-based_Act.pdf.

11 S. Jarayabhand, The Regional Programme of Action for the Protection of the Marine Environment of the East Asian Seas from the Effects of Land-based Activities and related actions, in *Report of The East Asian Seas IGR-2 Preparatory Workshop, Partnership Opportunities for Enhanced GPA Implementation* 177, September 4–5, 2006, UNEP(DEC)/EAS.IGR2.WS.3 (August 31, 2006), available at: http://www.cobsea.org/documents/Meeting_Documents/EAS%20IGR2%20Prep/Final%20Report%20of%20the%20EAS%20IGR2%20Prep%20Workshop.pdf.

12 *New Strategic Direction for COBSEA (2008–2012)*, *supra* note 7, at 5.

COBSEA has been relatively inactive since the adoption of the New Strategic Direction document in 2008, apparently because of a combination of insufficient funding, competition for professional expertise, member state inertia, and other factors. Current activity categories are listed as Information Management, Strategic and Emerging Issues, Regional Cooperation, and National Capacity Building. As of August 2011, the most recent event documented on the COBSEA website was the "COBSEA Forum on Marine Pollution-Related Multilateral Environmental Agreements (MEAs)," which took place in Guangzhou, China in June 2008.[13] China was slated to take the lead on the resulting project, called "Understanding the Status of Implementation of These MEAs,"[14] designed to enable COBSEA to identify capacity building needs and propose solutions that will lead to more effective MEA implementation in member countries."[15] COBSEA Coordinator Dr. Ellik Adler explained at a workshop held during the East Asian Seas Congress in 2009 in Manila, Philippines that his organization has "been actively implementing the [marine litter] programs covering the organization of workshops, meetings and International Coastal Cleanup campaigns, establishing data bases, developing monitoring guidelines and producing publications such as regional overviews on [marine litter], posters and brochures."[16]

Over the last 15 years, COBSEA has been faced with major financial challenges.[17] The organization operates and carries out activities and programs from contributions by member countries into a trust fund. Each member was originally required to contribute a set amount, based on the economic status of that country, toward a total of US$170,000 per year. Even if that goal had been met completely, it would fall far short of the amount required to sustain the secretariat and carry out regional activities.[18] UNEP also assisted with funding until 2006,

13 COBSEA Forum on Marine Pollution-Related Multilateral Environmental Agreements (MEAs), June 10–11, 2008, *Report of COBSEA Forum on Marine Pollution Related Multilateral Environmental Agreements (MEAs)*, UNEP (DEPI)/MEAs1 WS.1 (July 25, 2008).

14 The MEAs are: the Global Programme of Action on the Protection of the Marine Environment from Land-based Activities (GPA); the International Convention for the Control and Management of Ship's Ballast Water and Sediments; the International Convention on Oil Pollution Preparedness, Response and Co-operation (OPRC); the 1972 London Convention: Convention on Prevention of Marine Pollution by Dumping of Wastes and Other Matter (LDC); the MARPOL Convention: International Convention for the Prevention of Pollution from Ships; and the United Nations Convention on the Law of the Sea.

15 COBSEA website: http://www.cobsea.org/activities/activities_national%20capacity%20building.html.

16 East Asian Seas Congress, November 23–26, 2009, *Addressing the Transboundary Challenge in East Asia by Two UNEP Regional Seas Programs*, in *Proceedings of the International Conference on Sustainable Coastal and Ocean Development*, Workshop 4, at 5, EAS Congress/WP/2010/01 (2010).

17 Ellik Adler, Coordinator, COBSEA (telephone interview, August 15, 2011).

18 *Id.*

when the UNEP Secretariat "decided that members should carry the financial burden if they wanted a viable organization."[19] This UNEP decision was based on the growing economies of member states such as China, Singapore, and South Korea, which increased abilities to contribute higher sums to the organization's trust fund.[20] Dr. Adler reported at the November 2009 meeting of COBSEA that "if no substantial change will occur in the support given to the Trust Fund either by UNEP or by increased contributions from the member countries, the Trust Fund will become completely depleted at the beginning of 2011."[21]

In addition to funding shortfalls, other significant challenges for COBSEA include the diminishing interest among member countries for the organization, territorial disputes between the members,[22] competition with other marine environmental organizations for funding and donor attention, and difficulties with the focal ministries in some of the member governments.[23] Little progress has been made toward fulfilling the objectives of the New Strategic Direction document under these circumstances.[24]

PEMSEA

Another challenge facing COBSEA is that it appears to be in competition with another East Asian marine conservation organization—the Partnerships in Environmental Management for the Seas of East Asia (PEMSEA)[25]—which was established in 1993 with funding from the Global Environment Facility (GEF) to promote coastal conservation:

---

19 *Id.*

20 *Id.*

21 UNEP, *Report of the Twentieth Intergovernmental Meeting of the Coordinating Body on the Seas of East Asia (COBSEA)*, UNEP/DEPI/COBSEA IGM 20/15 (November 5, 2009), at 3, ¶12.

22 China, Vietnam, Malaysia, and the Philippines have, for instance, a major dispute over the sovereignty of the Spratly Islands in the South China Sea and over the governance of the waters of the South China Sea. See, for example, Mark J. Valencia, Jon M. Van Dyke, and Noel Ludwig, *Sharing the Resources of the South China Se*a (Kluwer Law International/Martinus Nijhoff, 1997), reprinted in paperback form in 1999 by the University of Hawaii Press.

23 Adler Interview, *supra* note 17. Countries are members of COBSEA through their respective foreign ministries, but other interested ministries with power over marine issues confuse or dilute authority.

24 *Id.*

25 Partnerships in Environmental Management for the Seas of East Asia [PEMSEA], http://beta.pemsea.org/; see also *PEMSEA Accomplishment Report 2008–2010* (A GEF/UNDP Regional Programme, 2010).

> PEMSEA is a partnership arrangement involving various stakeholders of the Seas of East Asia, including national and local governments, civil society, the private sector, research and education institutions, communities, international agencies, regional programmes, financial institutions and donors. It is also the regional coordinating mechanism for the implementation of the Sustainable Development Strategy for the Seas of East Asia.[26]

PEMSEA's members are Cambodia, China, Indonesia, Japan, Laos, North Korea, Philippines, South Korea, Singapore, Timor-Leste, and Vietnam. Seven countries are thus in both COBSEA and PEMSEA, and each organization has several members that do not belong to the other.

The mission of PEMSEA overlaps with the goals of COBSEA, particularly relating to regional capacity building and partnership formation.[27] In 2010, PEMSEA moved from the UN Development Program (UNDP) to become an international organization with legal and financial status separate from the UNDP.[28] There appears to be competition for funding and professional expertise between the two organizations, as they both receive support from the Global Environment Facility (GEF).[29]

COBSEA has engaged an external, neutral consultant to investigate the organization's condition and to make recommendations to the members regarding its sustainability.[30] At the next Intergovernmental Meeting of the member states, to take place in late 2011 or early 2012, the members will consider the recommendations and decide on a course of action.[31] One of the options for the future could be to merge COBSEA with PEMSEA, giving the combined organization a platform under international law that PEMSEA no longer enjoys since its break with UNDP. Among the challenges to that solution are differences in the membership of the two organizations are different and the unanimous agreement of all countries that would be required for such a merger.[32]

Conclusion

Neither COBSEA nor PEMSEA govern the exploitation of living or nonliving resources, and it is necessary to think harder about how best to undertake these shared responsibilities. No robust fishery management organization exists for this

26 PEMSEA website, http://beta.pemsea.org/about-pemsea.

27 *Id.*

28 Adler Interview, *supra* note 17.

29 *Id.* For information about the GEF, see Global Environment Facility (GEF), http://www.thegef.org/gef/whatisgef.

30 *Id.*

31 *Id.*

32 *Id.*

region. The Southeast Asian Fishery Development Center (SEAFDEC) has limited scientific competence, and illegal, unreported, and unregulated (IUU) fishing is a major problem in the South China Sea. Navigational freedoms have also become complicated, particularly regarding military activities, as China has challenged the United States on three occasions in the past decade. These challenges have concerned US aerial surveillance (with the collision between the US surveillance plane and a Chinese fighter jet in April 2001), US maritime surveillance (in the *Impeccable* Incident of March 8, 2009), and US hydrographic surveying (China challenged the surveying of the *USNS Bowditch* in September 2002) in the South China Sea.[33] These incidents may continue until a clear understanding regarding governance is established.

Governance of the South China Sea presents challenges. The countries of the region as well as those with interests in these regions must work together to manage and protect these shared ocean spaces for the benefit of present and future generations.

33 See, for example, Jon M. Van Dyke, *The Disappearing Right to Navigational Freedom in the Exclusive Economic Zone*, 29 Marine Policy 107–21 (2005).

Chapter 3
China-ASEAN and the South China Sea: Chinese Assertiveness and Southeast Asian Responses

Carlyle A. Thayer

Introduction

During the first half of 2011 China embarked on pattern of aggressively asserting its sovereignty claims in the South China Sea by targeting the commercial operations of oil exploration ships in waters claimed by the Philippines and Vietnam. China's actions not only raised regional tensions but also provoked the Philippines to align more closely with the United States and take steps to beef up its capacity for territorial defence. Vietnam responded by calculated displays of resolve to defend national sovereignty.

During the second half of the year tensions over the South China Sea began to subside. China and the Association of Southeast Asian Nations (ASEAN) finally agreed to guidelines to implement the 2002 Declaration on Conduct of Parties in the South China Sea (DOC). China also initiated a round of diplomacy with the Philippines by inviting President Benigno Aquino III to Beijing. Vietnam sent a special envoy to China and both sides exchanged a flurry of high-level delegations. In October 2011, the Secretary General of the Vietnam Communist Party visited China.

This chapter reviews political and military developments related to the South China Sea during the first nine months of 2011. It is organised into eight parts. Part one discusses Chinese assertiveness directed at the Philippines in the first half of the year. Part two reviews the responses by the Philippines. Part three discusses Chinese assertiveness directed at Vietnam during the first half of the year. Part four reviews Vietnam's responses. Part five considers the adoption of guidelines for the Declaration on Conduct of Parties in the South China Sea. Part six analyses relations between China and the Philippines in the post-DOC Guidelines period. Part seven analyses relations between China and Vietnam in the same period. Part eight offers some concluding observations.

Chinese Assertiveness and the Philippines (January–June)

According to the Philippines Department of Foreign Affairs, China increased its presence and activities in the Spratly Islands in the fourth quarter of 2010.[1] This increased presence led to six incursions into waters claimed by the Philippines in the first five months of 2011.[2] Chinese actions led the Philippines to officially declare its waters the West Philippine Sea. This section reviews these incidents and the diplomatic responses by the Philippines.

Major Incidents of Chinese Assertiveness

Three major incidents stand out. On February 25, three Philippines fishing vessels, F/V *Jaime* DLS, F/V *Mama Lydia* DLS and F/V *Maricris* 12, were operating in the waters off Jackson Atoll 140 nautical miles west of Palawan. According to a report prepared by the Armed Forces of the Philippines (AFP), the fishing vessels were approached by a Jianghu-V Class missile frigate, *Dongguan* 560, which broadcast over its marine band radio, "This is Chinese Warship 560. You are in the Chinese territory. Leave the area immediately." Then the frigate repeatedly broadcast, "I will shoot you."[3] As the fishing vessels began to withdraw, the Chinese frigate fired three shots that landed 0.3 nautical miles (556 meters) from F/V *Maricris* 12. The F/V Maricris 12 left the area but then returned three days later to recover its anchor that it cut in its hasty departure. The F/V *Maricris 12* spotted three Chinese fishing vessels exploiting marine resources in the area. The Philippine government reportedly did not file a protest with the Chinese Embassy over this incident.[4] The Chinese Ambassador to the Philippines, Liu Jianchao later denied that any Chinese vessel had fired on Filipino fishermen.[5]

The second major incident took place on March 2 when two Chinese white-painted patrol boats, No. 71 and No. 75, ordered MV *Veritas Voyager*, a Forum Energy Plc survey vessel operating in the Reed Bank area off Palawan Island, to leave and twice manoeuvred close in what appeared a threat to ram the MV *Veritas*

1 Max De Leon and Estrella Torres, "Business steps in to end Spratlys row," ABS-CBN News, June 3, 2011.

2 Jerry E. Esplanada and Tara Quismundo, "Abide by UN pact, China told," *Philippine Daily Inquirer*, June 3, 2011. The Philippines has not officially released its list. Government officials initially referred to six or seven incidents and currently they claim nine incidents.

3 Tessa Jamandre, "China fired at Filipino fishermen in Jackson atoll," ABS-CBN News, June 3, 2011.

4 Aurea Calica, "PHL to take Chinese incursions to the United Nations," *The Philippine Star*, June 4, 2011.

5 Jim Gomez, "China warns neighbors: Stop oil search in Spratlys," Associated Press, June 9, 2011.

Voyager.[6] The survey ship was French-owned and registered in Singapore. It was forced to suspend operations and leave the area.

The Philippines responded by dispatching two OV-10 aircraft to investigate. The Chinese boats departed without further incident. Foreign Affairs Undersecretary Erlinda Basilio lodged a protest with Chinese Charge d'Affairs, Bai Tian, on March 4. According to one report the note "raised four points to prove that Reed Bank is not part of the disputed area by projecting eighty-five nautical miles from the base point in the northern part of Palawan and not from the Kalayaan Island Group (KIG). China questioned this during a meeting with the Philippines, but did not reply in a diplomatic note."[7]

After the incident, the Philippines announced a temporary halt to seismic testing and ordered the Philippine Navy and Philippines Coast Guard to escort the survey ship when testing resumed.[8] Later, President Aquino instructed the Philippine Coast Guard to provide security for oil and gas exploration activities in the KIG.[9]

The third major incident took place on May 24 when Filipino fishermen witnessed a China Maritime Surveillance vessel and People's Liberation Army Navy (PLAN) ships unloading steel posts, building materials and a buoy near Likas and Patag islands, near Iroquois Reef-Amy Douglas Bank one hundred nautical miles off Palawan.[10] The fishermen reported their sighting to the AFP the next day. Navy Headquarters in Manila ordered a ship to verify the sighting

---

6 British Broadcasting News (BBC) News, Asia-Pacific, "Philippines halts tests after China patrol challenge," March 8, 2011; Nicholas Heath and Daniel Ten Kate, "Vietnam Says Chinese Boat Harassed PetroVietnam Survey Ship," Bloomberg Businessweek, June 9, 2011; Aurea Calica, "Palace in no hurry to file China protest," *The Philippine Star*, May 21, 2011 and Tessa Jamandre, "China fired at Filipino fishermen in Jackson atoll," ABS-CBN News, June 3, 2011. The Sampaguita gasfield in the Reed Bank is estimated to contain between 3.4 trillion to twenty trillion cubic feet of natural gas"; "Carps among the Spratlys," *The Economist*, March 10, 2011, online edition.

7 Tessa Jamandre, "China fired at Filipino fishermen in Jackson atoll," ABS-CBN News, June 3, 2011

8 AFP, "China stakes claim on disputed islands after spats," March 9, 2011 and Aurea Calica, "Palace in no hurry to file China protest," *The Philippine Star*, May 21, 2011.

9 "Coast Guard to secure oil exploration in Kalayaan island group," GMA News TV, April 19, 2011. The KIG contains nine geological features: Balagtas (Irving Reef), Kota (Loaita), Lawak (Nanshan), Likas (West York), Pag-asa (Thitu), Panata (Lankiam), Parola (Northeast Cay), Patag Island (Flat Island is also considered a part of the Spratlys) and Rizal (Commodore Reef).

10 Jun Pasaylo, "China surveillance ships roam Phl waters," *The Philippine Star*, June 1, 2011; Simone Orendain, "Philippines Seeks Answers About Latest South China Sea Incident," Voice of America News, June 1, 2011; Katherine Evangelista, "Philippines military to act with diplomacy over Spratlys dispute—defense chief, *Philippine Daily Inquirer*, June 1, 2011; Johana Paola d. Poblete, "Philippines preparing issues for UN about China 'intrusions'," *Business World*, June 2, 2011 reports; "China denies 'invasion' of South China Sea," ABS-CN News, June 2, 2011; AFP, "Philippines gov't protests to China over oil plans in South China Sea," *The China Post*, June 2, 2011 and Jerry E. Esplanada

but bad weather delayed its arrival until May 29 by which time the Chinese ships had departed. Local fishermen removed the steel polls and handed them over to authorities.

The AFP reported this incident on May 27, four days later the Department of Foreign Affairs summoned the Chinese Charge d' Affaires to seek a clarification of the incident. On June 1, the Philippines conveyed "serious concerns" in a Note Verbale to the Chinese Embassy. The note stated, "These ships reportedly unloaded building materials, erected an undetermined number of posts, and placed a buoy near the breaker of the Iroquois Bank."[11] The Chinese Embassy responded, "The reported 'incursion of Chinese ships' is not true … It's only China's marine research ship conducting normal maritime research activities in the South China Sea."[12] Speaking on a TV forum that same day, Defense Secretary Voltaire Gazmin observed, "It's alarming in the sense that the intrusions are increasing. They are staking claim on the areas where we do not have a presence. They want to hoist their flag so they can claim the area."[13] Foreign Affairs Secretary Albert del Rosario charged that "any new construction by China in the vicinity of the uninhabited Iroquois Bank is a clear violation of the 2002 Association of Southeast Asian Nations (ASEAN)-China Declaration on the Conduct of Parties (DOC) in the South China Sea."[14]

The other three incidents were relatively minor in comparison:

- Incident on May 6: a Chinese marine vessel with a flat bed was sighted in Abad Santos (Bombay) Shoal.[15]
- Incident on May 11: the AFP claimed that two Chinese jet fighters allegedly flew into Philippines' air space near Palawan.[16]

---

and Tarra Quismundo, "Abide by UN pact, China told," *Philippine Daily Inquirer*, June 3, 2011.

11 Quoted by GMA News, "DFA conveys protest to Beijing over Chinese vessels," GMA News TV, June 4, 2011. See also: Pia Lee-Brago, "China Building in PHL Waters; DFA Summoned Envoy," *The Philippine Star*, June 2, 2011. Tessa Jamandre, "China fired at Filipino fishermen in Jackson atoll," ABS-CBN News, June 3, 2011 reported no Note Verbale was given to the Chinese Charge d'Affaires at the May 31 meeting.

12 GMA News, "DFA: Stronger sea code to prevent 'repeat of Mischief Reef'," GMA News TV, June 2, 2011 and "China denies incursion into West Philippine Sea," *The Philippine Star*, June 3, 2011.

13 Dona Z. Pazzibugan, "Chinese intrusions in PH-claimed parts of Spratlys 'alarming,' says Gazmin," *Philippines Daily Inquirer*, June 2, 2011

14 Pia Lee-Brago, "China Building in PHL Waters; DFA Summoned Envoy," *The Philippine Star*, June 2, 2011.

15 Tessa Jamandre, "China fired at Filipino fishermen in Jackson atoll," ABS-CBN News, June 3, 2011.

16 This initial report was never confirmed and appears the least substantiated of the six incidents of reported Chinese incursions. "Chinese jets intruded into PH space—AFP," *Philippine Daily Inquirer*, May 20, 2011; "Two unidentified aircraft seen over Spratlys—

- Incident on May 21: Chinese Marine Surveillance ship No. 75 and Salvage/ Research Ship No. 707 were observed heading toward Southern Bank.[17]

China Launches Mega Drilling Platform

In addition to the above incidents, in March 2011 China launched a mega oil and gas-drilling platform to be used by the China National Offshore Oil Corporation (CNOOC) in the South China Sea. The rig frees China of dependence on foreign-owned contractors for deep-sea drilling. The rig is capable of exploring waters up to 3,000 metres in depth, a capability that neither the Philippines nor Vietnam possesses.[18] Chinese sources indicated that the rig would begin operations in the South China Sea later in the year and thereby enable China to establish a major presence in the area. On May 27, the Philippines' Department of Foreign Affairs (DFA) summoned Chinese officials to convey its concern about the planned location of the mega rig. Philippines officials asked the Chinese diplomats the exact planned location of the new oil rig and stated that it should not be placed in Philippine territory or waters.[19]

Submission to the United Nations

On April 5, the Philippine Mission to the United Nations submitted a letter in response to China's Notes Verbales of May 7, 2009 (CML/17/2009 and CML/18/2009) restating the Philippines' claim to sovereignty over the Kalayaan Island Group, adjacent waters and geological features (relevant waters, seabed and subsoil).[20] China responded on April 14 with a Note Verbale to the United Nations that accused the Philippines of invading and occupying "some islands and reefs of China's Nansha Islands … The Republic of the Philippines' occupation of some islands and reefs of China's Nansha islands as well as other related acts constitutes an infringement upon

---

AFP," GMA News TV, May 21, 2011; "AFP validates Kalayaan islands aircraft sighting incident," Philippine Information Agency Press Release, May 23, 2011 and Jim Gomez, "China, Philippines warn rivals on Spratlys," *The China Post*, May 24, 2011.

17 Tessa Jamandre, "China fired at Filipino fishermen in Jackson atoll," ABS-CBN News, June 3, 2011.

18 Michael Richardson, "China brings out the big rig in energy race," *The Australian Financial Review*, June 1, 2010 and Michael Richardson, "China steps up drilling, intimidation" *The Japan Times*, June 1, 2011.

19 Pia Lee-Brago, "China Building in PHL Waters; DFA Summoned Envoy," *The Philippine Star*, June 2, 2011.

20 Philippine Mission to the United Nations, letter to the Secretary General of the United Nations, 11-00494, No. 000228, New York, April 5, 2011. See also: AFP, "Philippines protests China's Spratlys claim at UN," April 13, 2011; Tessa Jamandre, "PHL protests Chinese map claiming Spratly Islands," GMA News TV, April 13, 2011 and Jerry E. Esplanada, "PH runs to UN to protest China's '9-dash line' Spratlys claims," *Philippine Daily Inquirer*, April 15, 2011.

China's territorial sovereignty."[21] The Chinese Note Verbale also argued that on the basis of domestic legislation "China's Nansha Islands is fully entitled to Territorial Sea, EEZ [Exclusive Economic Zone] and Continental Shelf."[22]

Responses by the Philippines to Chinese Assertiveness (January–June)

In addition to the diplomatic protests lodged with China discussed above, President Aquino responded to Chinese assertiveness by allocating increased funds to modernize the Armed Force of the Philippines, lobbying his ASEAN colleagues to form a united front behind a South China Sea Code of Conduct as the best way to approach relations with China, increasing defence cooperation with the United States and continued diplomatic pressure on China.

Force Modernization for Territorial Defence

In 2011 the Philippines defence and military agencies began drawing up a new defence strategy in response to developments in the South China Sea. The new strategy is focused on both internal security operations and external territorial defence. AFP chief General Eduardo Oban said the military was planning to set up a coast watch system on the western seaboard in the next two to three years to monitor and secure maritime borders and natural resources.[23]

On March 28, General Oban announced that the Philippines had increased air and naval patrols in the South China Sea and had plans to upgrade Rancudo Air Field on Pag-Asa (Thitu) island and repair barracks.[24] The AFP was allocated US $183 million in funds from the US $1 billion Capability Upgrade Program to purchase two offshore fast patrol boats, long-range maritime aircraft, surveillance and communication equipment including air defence and coastal radars to better protect its territory.[25] President Aquino had earlier released US $255 million to the armed forces.

---

21 Quoted by Tessa Jamandre, "China accuses PH of 'invasion'," ABC-CBN News, April 19, 2011 and Teresa Cerojano, "Beijing counters Manila's UN protest, says Philippines 'started to invade' Spratlys in 1970s," Associated Press, April 19, 2011.

22 The Chinese Note Verbale specifically mentioned the Law of the People's Republic of China on Territorial Sea and Contiguous Zone (1992), the Law on the Exclusive Economic Zone and the Continental Shelf of the People's Republic of China (1998) as well as the 1982 UN Convention on Law of the Sea.

23 China denies incursion into West Philippine Sea," *The Philippines Star*, June 3, 2011.

24 Jaime Laude, "AFP to maintain presence in Spratlys," *The Philippine Star*, March 29, 2011.

25 Jon Grevatt, "Philippines to invest USD183 million in defence of Spratly Islands," *Jane's Defence Weekly*, March 30, 2011; Reuters, "Philippines steps up presence in South

In May, a Philippine navy study recommended the acquisition of submarines as a "deterrent against future potential conflicts."[26] In August 2011, the Philippines acquired the US Coast Guard Cutter USCGC *Hamilton.* The *Hamilton*, renamed BRP *Gregorio del Pilar*, is expected to patrol disputed waters in the South China Sea.[27] The Philippines expects to take delivery of a second US Coast Guard Cutter and three new Taiwan-manufactured Multi-Purpose Attack Craft in 2012.[28] The Philippines also hopes to purchase six jet fighters.

In June it was reported that the Philippines Embassy in Washington was in the market for excess defence equipment from the US under its Foreign Military Sales (FMS) program including one or more patrol ships.[29] The Philippines also announced a new US training program for its naval forces to enable them to better carry out their mission of providing security for oil exploration activities in the South China Sea.[30]

Lobbying ASEAN Members

On March 8, President Aquino paid an official visit to Indonesia where he met with President Bambang Susilo Yudhoyono. At a joint press conference after their talks, President Aquino expressed his support for Indonesia's leadership role as ASEAN Chair. President Yudhoyono said Indonesia as ASEAN Chair would bring the Spratly Islands issue to the forthcoming ASEAN Summit and East Asia Summit. President Yudhoyono expressed his hope that the South China Sea could become a "zone of possible economic cooperation." President Aquino replied, "With regard to joint exploration [in the area], that is an idea that has been proposed a

---

China Sea," March 28, 2011 and Associated Press, "Philippines to bolster watch in disputed Spratlys," Bloomberg Businessweek, March 28, 2011.

26 Katherine Evangelista, "Philippines eye submarines to boost navy," *Philippine Daily Inquirer*, May 17, 2001. The prospect of the Philippines acquiring submarines is remote.

27 "Philippines set to deploy new patrol ship to Kalayaan Islands," *Manila Bulletin*, April 14, 2011 and AFP, "Philippines to boosts Spratly patrols," Channel News Asia, April 15, 2011. The USCGC *Hamilton*, a Weather High Endurance Cutter, was renamed the BRP *Gregorio del Pilar* and will be the largest ship in the Philippine navy; Marichu A. Villanueva, "Keeping Phl Navy afloat," *The Philippine Star*, May 16, 2011.

28 Reuters, "Philippines says will spend $255 mln on military helicopters, boats," April 13, 2011 and Agence France Presse, "Philippines hopes sea dispute with China should ease," September 3, 2011.

29 Michael Lim Ubac, "Philippines shops for US military gear," *Philippine Daily Inquirer*, June 5, 2011.

30 Shirley Escalante, "Philippines increase security for oil exploration," Australia Network News, April 28, 2011.

few decades past but perhaps we should continue the talks with other claimant countries. There is no room for unilateral action in that particular region."[31]

On June 1, President Aquino paid an official visit to Brunei Darussalam for discussions with Sultan Hassanal Bolkiah. According to Presidential Communications Operations Secretary Herminio Coloma Jr., the two leaders expressed their desire to maintain peace and stability in the South China Sea through a multilateral dialogue among the ASEAN countries, claimant countries and China. Cloma quoted the Sultan as stating "it's best to have good relations with China."[32]

President Aquino told the reporters covering his visit: "We govern ourselves there [Spratly Islands/KIG]. Instead of one country has a bilateral agreement with China and the other has a different bilateral agreement with China. Let's come together as a body. Why do we have to fight or increase all of these tensions when it profits nobody?"[33] Aquino also renewed his call for the immediate adoption of the implementing guidelines on the DOC.[34] The following day, June 12, Eduardo Malaya, a spokesperson for the Department of Foreign Affairs, called for a "more binding Code of Conduct of Parties in the South China Sea" in response to Chinese intrusions into Philippine waters.

During his state visit to Brunei President Aquino revealed that the Philippines was preparing to file a complaint to the United Nations in response to Chinese intrusions into its territory. According to Aquino, "We are completing the data on about six to seven instances since February. We will present it to [China] and then bring these to the appropriate body, which normally is the United Nations."[35] The Aquino Administration is supporting two legislative measures in response to China's assertiveness in the Spratly Islands. The House of Representative is drawing up the Philippine Maritime Zones bill to delineate the Philippines' maritime zones, while the Senate is considering the Archipelagic Sea Lanes bill.[36]

31 Quoted by Adianto P. Simamora, "SBY, Aquino agree on talks over Spratlys," *The Jakarta Post*, March 9, 2011.

32 Regina Bengco, "Peace in Spratlys is all they want," *Malaya.Com*, June 2, 2011; Shirley Escalante, "Philippines, Brunei push for dialogue to settle Spratley Islands dispute," Australia Network News, June 3, 2011 and "China denies incursion into West Philippine Sea," *The Philippine Star*, June 2, 2011.

33 Johanna Paola d. Poblete, "Philippines preparing issues for UN about China 'intrusions'." *Business World*, June 2, 2011.

34 "Adoption of territorial guidelines urged," *Manila Bulletin*, June 2, 2011.

35 Johana Paola d. Poblete, "Philippines preparing issues for UN about China 'intrusions'," *Business World*, June 2, 2011; Amita O. Legaspi, "Palace prepares Spratlys incursions report," GMA News TV, June 3, 2011 and Jim Gomez, "Philippines plans new UN protest as China denies aggressive acts in Spratly Islands," Associated Press, June 3, 2011.

36 GMA News, "DFA: Stronger sea code to prevent 'repeat of Mischief Reef'," GMA News TV, June 2, 2011.

Reaffirming US Ties/Diplomatic Pressure on China

On May 14, President Aquino and several members of his Cabinet flew out to the USS *Carl Vinson* aircraft carrier in the South China Sea as it headed towards the Philippines. The aircraft carrier made a "routine port call and goodwill visit" accompanied by the USS *Bunker Hill*, USS *Shiloh* and USS *Gridley*.[37] In fact the visit by the carrier was a reaffirmation of the alliance relationship on the eve of a visit by China's Defence Minister General Liang Guanglie.

General Liang paid an official visit to the Philippines from May 21–25 for discussions with his counterpart Defense Secretary Voltaire Gazmin. The two ministers agreed to hold regular discussions to promote trust and confidence and find common ground on territorial disputes in the Spratly Islands. A joint statement declared, "both ministers expressed hope that the implementing guidelines of the 2002 Declaration of Conduct would soon be finalized and agreed upon, that responsible behavior of all parties in the South China Sea issue would help keep the area stable while all parties work for the peaceful resolution … Both ministers recognized that unilateral actions which could cause alarm should be avoided."[38]

When Defence Minister Liang met with President Aquino South China Sea issues were discussed in general, but the latter refrained from directly mentioning the Reed Bank incident and the reported intrusion of Chinese aircraft into Philippine air space.[39] President Aquino told General Liang that more maritime incidents in disputed areas of the South China Sea could spark a regional arms race.[40] Immediately after the defence ministers met Sun Yi, Deputy Chief of Political Section at the Chinese Embassy in Manila, announced that China looked forward to an "accelerated dialogue" with the Philippines to resolve the dispute in the South China Sea. "It's a bilateral issue. We repeatedly said that and we believe it's a bilateral issue," Sun Yi stated.[41]

All the major incidents of Chinese assertiveness against the Philippines occurred prior to the annual meeting of the Shangri-La Dialogue held in Singapore

37 Christine O. Avendano, Dona Pazzibugan and Jerome Aning, "Palace sees no terror backlash against Aquino visit to ship," *Philippine Daily Inquirer*, May 16, 2011.

38 Quoted by "China, PH agree to hold regular talks on Spratlys," ABS-CBN News, May 23, 2011; Christine O. Avendano and Dona Z. Pazzibugan, "Peaceful Spratlys resolution reaffirmed," *Philippines Daily Inquirer*, May 24, 2011; Simone Orendain, "Philippines, China Support Discussion on South China Sea," Voice of America News, May 24, 2011; Jim Gomez, "China, Philippines warn rivals on Spratlys," *The China Post*, May 24, 2011 and Jim Gomez, "China, Philippines defense chiefs discuss Spratlys," Associated Press, June 4, 2011.

39 Willard Cheng, "Philippines, China OK South China Sea dialogue," ABS-CBN News, May 23, 2011.

40 AFP, "Philippines warns of arms race in South China Sea," May 24, 2011 and William B. Depasupil, "Philippines Warns of Arms Race in South China Sea," *Manila Times*, May 25, 2011.

41 Pia Lee-Brago, "China welcomes dialogue to end 'Nansha' dispute," *The Philippine Star*, May 25, 2011.

from June 3–5. Defence Ministers raised South China Sea territorial disputes in all plenary sessions at the meeting. In light of recent ministerial discussions, Defense Secretary Gazmin, reportedly watered down comments on the South China Sea in his draft text before delivery.[42] His address began by declaring that, "maritime security is one of our foremost concerns." In an obvious reference to the March 2 Reed Bank incident Gazmin stated that the actions by other states "make … the Philippines worry and concerned. These actions necessarily create insecurity not only to the government but more disturbingly to ordinary citizens who depend on the maritime environment for their livelihood." He then gave details of recent incidents involving Chinese vessels without mentioning China by name.[43]

On June 4, the DFA issued a statement revealing it had lodged a protest with the Chinese Embassy two days earlier over the "increasing presence and activities of Chinese vessels including naval assets in the West Philippines Sea (South China Sea)." The note stated, "These actions of Chinese vessels hamper the normal and legitimate fishing activities of the Filipino fishermen in the area and undermines the peace and stability of the region."[44]

China responded on June 7 with a statement by Foreign Ministry spokesperson, Hong Lei: "Chinese vessels were cruising and carrying out scientific studies in waters under China's jurisdiction and their activities were in line with the law … China asks the Philippine side to stop harming China's sovereignty and maritime rights and interests, which leads to unilateral actions that expand and complicate South China Sea disputes. The Philippines should stop publishing irresponsible statements that do not match the facts."[45]

Liu Jianchao, Chinese Ambassador to the Philippines, responded to complaints by the Philippines government for the first time when he met with reporters in Manila on June 9. The ambassador stated that China had not yet started to drill for oil in Spratly Islands. "We're calling on other parties to stop searching for the possibility of exploiting resources in these areas where China has its claims."[46] In response to a question how China would react if countries went ahead and continued to explore without Beijing's permission, the ambassador said China would use diplomatic means to assert its rights. "We will never use force unless we are attacked," he said. Liang also confirmed to reporters that Chinese forces took

---

42 Confidential source who spoke with Secretary Gazmin at the Shangri-La Dialogue.

43 Voltaire Gazmin, "Responding to New Maritime Security Threats," The 10th IISS Asian Security Summit the Shangri-La Dialogue, June 5, 2011.

44 "Statement of the Department of Foreign Affairs On the Presence of Chinese Vessels In the West Philippine Sea (South China Sea)," June 4, 2011.

45 Quoted by Xinhua, "China rejects Philippine's accusation on South China Sa issue," June 7, 2011; AFP, "China says Philippines harming its maritime rights," ABS-CBN News, June 7, 2011; Reuters, "China scolds Philippines over disputed waters," June 8, 2011.

46 Jim Gomez, "China warns neighbors: Stop oil search in Spratlys," Associated Press, June 9, 2011.

action to keep the exploration vessel from Reed Bank. "That's part of our exercise of jurisdiction. It's not harassment," he claimed.[47]

Zone of Peace, Freedom, Friendship and Cooperation

In response to Chinese assertiveness, President Aquino launched a new initiative calling for the South China Sea to become a Zone of Peace, Freedom, Friendship and Cooperation (ZOPFF/C). Aquino explained "what is our is ours, and with what is disputed, we can work towards joint cooperation."[48] He directed the Department of Foreign Affairs to promote the ZOPFF/C concept through sustained consultations and dialogue.

According to the DFA, the ZOPFF/C provides a framework for separating the disputed territorial features that may be considered for collaborative activities from non-disputed waters in the West Philippines Sea (South China Sea) in accordance with international law in general and UNCLOS in particular.[49] A disputed area could be turned into a Joint Cooperation Area for joint development and the establishment of marine protected area for biodiversity conservation. Areas not in dispute, such as Reed Bank that lies on the Philippines' continental shelf, can be developed exclusively by the Philippines or with the assistance of foreign investors invited to participate in its development.

Chinese Assertiveness and Vietnam (January–June)

During the first half of 2011, Chinese assertiveness directed against Vietnam included the imposition of an annual fishing ban and, more significantly, China's unprecedented action in interfering in the commercial activities of oil exploration vessels operating within Vietnam's Exclusive Economic Zones.

China's Annual Unilateral Fishing Ban

On May 11, the Haikou Municipal Government, Hainan province, issued an announcement imposing China's annual unilateral fishing ban in the South China Sea from May 16–August 1 ostensibly to protect dwindling fish stocks during the spawning season. Vietnam immediately issued a verbal protest: "China's unilateral execution of a fishing ban in the East Sea is a violation of Vietnam's sovereignty over the Hoang Sa [Paracel] archipelago, as well as the country's sovereignty and

47 Jim Gomez, "China warns neighbors: Stop oil search in Spratlys," Associated Press, June 9, 2011.

48 Quoted in "A Rules-Based Regime in The South China Sea By: Albert F. Del Rosario, Secretary of Foreign Affairs," Public Information Service Unit, June 7, 2011.

49 Amita O. Legaspi, "Palace prepares Spratlys incursions report," GMA News TV, June 3, 2011.

jurisdiction over its exclusive economic zone and continental shelf…”.[50] Vietnam also protested the deployment of a Chinese Fishery Administration Vessel, *Leizhou* 44261, to patrol in the waters around the Paracel Islands from May 5–25. Vietnam accused the patrol boat of "causing difficulties for normal fishing activities conduced by Vietnamese fishermen in their traditional fishing ground and making the situation at sea more complicated."[51]

Vietnamese local authorities reported the arrival of Chinese fishing boats in Vietnamese waters in greater numbers that in the past. The head of Phu Yen Province Border Guard Headquarters stated that, "every day between one hundred and twenty and one hundred and fifty fishing boats of China were operated within waters from Da Nang City to the Truong Sa [Spratly] Archipelago … Previously Chinese fishing boats have violated our waters, but this was the first time there were so many boats."[52] The numbers reportedly rose to two hundred on some occasions. Vietnamese fishermen formed groups of five to ten boats for protection from larger Chinese craft that sometimes used weapons to intimidate them. The Vietnamese government is currently considering a proposal by the Ministry of Agriculture and Rural Development to build ten fishery patrol boats at a total cost estimated at US $102 million.

Although Vietnamese fishermen vowed to defy the ban the Vietnamese press has not reported any major incidents of harassment or detention.[53] There were two exceptions. On June 1, it was reported that Chinese military vessels threatened to use their guns against a Vietnamese fishing boat operating in waters near the Spratly archipelago.[54] A more serious incident took place on July 5 when armed Chinese naval troops reportedly beat the skipper of a Vietnamese fishing boat, threatened the crew, and then forced the boat to leave contested waters near the Paracel Islands.[55]

Accosting Vietnamese Commercial Exploration Vessels

On May 26, three China Maritime Surveillance ships accosted the *Binh Minh 02*, a Vietnamese seismic survey ship operating in Block 148, in an incident that lasted three hours. China Maritime Surveillance ship No. 84 cut a cable towing seismic

50 "Vietnam opposes China's fishing ban in East Sea," Voice of Vietnam News, May 14, 2011.

51 'Chinese Ship Violates Vietnam's Sovereignty," Vietnam News Agency, May 13, 2011.

52 "Chinese fishing boats violate Vietnam waters; gov't mulls patrol boats," *Thanh Nien News*, May 29, 2011.

53 Deutsche Presse-Agentur, "Vietnam defiant on first day of Chinese fishing ban," May 16, 2011.

54 An Dien and Minh Hung, "East Sea undercurrents," *Thanh Nien News*, June 10, 2011.

55 "Vietnam: Chinese soldiers attack fishermen," Associated Press, July 13, 2011

monitoring equipment.[56] The next day Vietnam lodged a diplomatic protest with China's Ambassador claiming that the actions of the China Maritime Surveillance ships violated international law and Vietnam's sovereignty.[57] Vietnam also sought compensation for the damage caused. The *Binh Minh 02* returned to port for repairs and resumed its oil exploration activities accompanied by an escort of eight ships.[58]

Some news media erroneously reported that this was the first instance in which the Chinese had cut the cable of a Vietnamese exploration vessel. According to Do Van Hau, a senior PetroVietnam official, "When we conduct seismic survey and drilling operations, the [China] have aeroplanes flying over to survey our activities, they harass us with their vessels, and in extreme cases they cut our [exploration] cables."[59] The Vietnamese press reported that when Vietnamese conduced continental shelf surveys in 2008, "Chinese vessels also cut Vietnamese ships' survey cables ... and further obstructed Vietnam from conducting oil and gas exploration in the East Sea...".[60]

China responded to Vietnam's protest on May 28 with the following statement: "What relevant Chinese departments did was completely normal marine law-enforcement and surveillance activities in China's jurisdictional area."[61] Vietnam retorted on May 29:

> the area where Vietnam conducted exploration activities situates entirely in the exclusive economic zone and the two hundred nautical mile continental shelf of Vietnam in accordance with the 1982 United Nations Convention on Law of the Sea. It is neither a disputed area nor is it an area 'managed by China.' China has deliberately misled the public into thinking that it is a disputed area.[62]

---

56 "Bao Cao Su Co Tau Truong Quoc Cat Cap Thu Dia Chan Cua Tau Binh Minh 02 Vao Luc 5H58' Ngay 26/05/2011," and Reuters, "Vietnam says Chinese boats harassed oil exploration ship," May 27, 2011. The incident took place 116 nautical miles off the Dai Lanh Cape on the coast of Phu Yen province at 12 degrees 48'25" north latitude and 111 degrees 26'48" east longitude.

57 "VN condemns Chinese intrusion," Vietnam News Agency, May 28, 2011.

58 Deutsche Presse-Agentur, "Vietnam stands ground in sea dispute, survey ship takes up work," June 6, 2011; Agence France Presse, "Vietnam complains to China as sea tensions rise," June 9, 2011 and Nicholas Heath and Daniel Ten Kate, "Vietnam Says Chinese Boat Harassed PetroVietnam Survey Ship," Bloomberg Businessweek, June 9, 2011.

59 Ben Bland and Kathrin Hille, "Vietnam and China oil clashes intensify," *The Financial Times*, May 27, 2011.

60 "National, world security closely linked: minister," *Vietnam News*, June 7, 2011. Vietnamese sources told the author the reason Vietnam did not protest the 2008 incident was because the Vietnamese survey vessel was operating beyond Vietnam's EEZ.

61 Quoted in Reuters, "China reprimands Vietnam over offshore oil exploration," May 28, 2011.

62 "Vietnam demands China stop sovereignty violations," *Thanh Nien News*, May 29, 2011.

China responded in kind: "the law enforcement activities by Chinese maritime surveillance ships against Vietnam's illegally operating ships are completely justified. We urge Vietnam to immediately stop infringement activities and refrain from creating new troubles."[63]

On June 9, according to Vietnam's Ministry of Foreign Affairs, a second "premeditated and carefully calculated" incident occurred when Chinese fishing boat No. 62226 equipped with a "cable cutting device" snared the cable of the *Viking II* seismic survey ship operating in survey Block 136-03 in the vicinity of Vanguard Bank (Tu Chinh).[64] *Viking II* is registered in Norway and was operating under charter with PetroVietnam.[65] Two China Maritime Surveillance ships and other Chinese fishing craft came to assist the distressed fishing boat. According to Nguyen Phuong Nga, the official Foreign Ministry spokesperson, "China's systematic acts were aimed at turning an undisputed region into one of dispute, to carry out its ambition to make China's nine-dash line claim a reality."[66]

Earlier the *Viking II* had been involved in separate incidents on May 29 and May 31 in which Chinese boats—the *Fei Sheng* No. 16 and Vessel No. B12549—attempted to approach its rear deck and interfere with its operations. Security escorts with the *Viking II* successfully blocked their approaches.[67]

Chinese authorities claimed that the *Viking II* incident occurred when armed Vietnamese ships chased Chinese fishing boats from the Wan-an (Vanguard) Bank. One of the Chinese boats became entangled in the cable of the *Viking II* ship operating in the same area. The Chinese boat was dragged for more than an hour before the entangled net could be cut. According to the Chinese Foreign Ministry spokesperson, Hong Lei, "The Vietnamese ship put the lives and safety of he Chinese fishermen in serious danger." Vietnamese Foreign Ministry officials lodged a protest with Chinese Embassy on the afternoon of the incident and announced that the Vietnam National Oil and Gas Group would be seeking compensation for damages.[68]

A third cable cutting incident reportedly occurred in June but Vietnam decided not to publicize the matter.[69]

---

63 Quoted by Huy Duong, "The Philippines and Vietnam at the Crossroad," *Manila Times*, June 9, 2011.

64 Ian Timberlake, "Sea spat raises China-Vietnam tensions," Agence France Presse, June 9, 2011. Talisman Energy Inc. a Canadian company based in Calgary announced in April 2011 that it would conduct a major seismic program in this area; Nicholas Heath and Daniel Ten Kate, "Vietnam Says Chinese Boat Harassed Petro-Vietnam Survey Ship," Bloomberg Businessweek, June 9, 2011.

65 Reuters, "Vietnam accuses China of harassing another boat," June 9, 2011.

66 Quoted by United Press International, "Vietnam alleges high-seas interference," June 10, 2011.

67 An Dien and Minh Hung, "East Sea undercurrents," *Thanh Nien News*, June 10, 2011.

68 Ian Timberlake, "Sea spat raises China-Vietnam tensions," Agence France Presse, June 9, 2011 and Reuters, "China accuses Vietnam in escalating sea tensions," June 10, 2011.

69 Carlyle A. Thayer, "South China Sea: Third Cable Cutting Incident?," *Thayer Consultancy Background Briefing*, July 1, 2011. Available at: Scribd.com.

Vietnam's Response to Chinese Assertiveness

During the first six months of 2011, China and Vietnam held four high-level meetings. The first two occurred prior to renewed Chinese assertiveness in the South China Sea. The latter two meetings were held under the shadow of increasing tensions in the South China Sea. Chinese assertiveness impacted on Vietnamese domestic politics and resulted in a stiffening of the government's public stance in response to elite pressure including public demonstrations by students and prominent intellectuals.

Special Envoy to China and Other High-Level Meetings

In February 2011, immediately after Eleventh National Congress of the Vietnam Communist Party, the new Secretary General, Nguyen Phu Trong, dispatched a special envoy, Hoang Binh Quan, to Beijing. Quan met with Hu Jintao, President and General Secretary of the Chinese Communist Party, and briefed him on the outcome of the party congress. Quan also extended an invitation to Hu and other Chinese party and state leaders to visit Vietnam. In return, Hu extended an invitation to Secretary General Trong to visit China.[70] In deference to China, and in light of Chinese assertiveness in the South China Sea, Trong reportedly will visit Beijing first later this year.

In April, Senior Lieutenant General Guo Boxiong, vice chairman of China's Central Military Commission, visited Hanoi at the invitation of General Phung Quang Thanh, Minister of National Defence. Lt. Gen. Guo was also received by Prime Minister Nguyen Tan Dung and party Secretary General Nguyen Phu Trong. Prime Minister Dung "proposed the two sides talk and seek fundamental and long-lasting measures that both sides are able to accept for the East Sea [South China Sea] issue…"[71] The joint press communiqué issued after the conclusion of Guo's visit outlined a number of cooperative military activities, including increasing the scope of joint naval patrols in the Gulf of Tonkin, but no mention was made of the South China Sea.[72]

Immediately after General Guo's visit, Vietnam hosted a meeting of the heads of the government delegations on boundary negotiations between China and Vietnam (April 18–19). These discussions were held at deputy minister level. China's Foreign Ministry reported that the two vice ministers pledged, "to properly handle maritime disputes through friendly consultations and explore

70 "Chinese president vows to further ties with Vietnam," Xinhua, February 18, 2011 and "China's Hu Jintao invites Nguyen Pho Trong," Voice of Vietnam News, February 19, 2011.

71 "Party Leader's Meeting with Chinese General," Vietnam News Agency, April 14, 2011.

72 Li Qiong, "China, Vietnam Issue Joint Press Communiqué on CMC Vice Chairman Guo Boxiong's Visit to Vietnam," Xinhua, April 17, 2011.

solutions with a positive and constructive attitude."[73] A Vietnamese spokesperson revealed that "the two sides agreed they will sign an agreement on the fundamental guidelines to settle the maritime issues" but negotiations are still continuing and no date has been set to sign the agreement.[74]

The fourth high-level meeting took place in Singapore in June on the sidelines of the Shangri-la Dialogue. In his address at a plenary session, Vietnam's Defence Minister spoke in detail about the legal basis for activities at sea "to facilitate cooperation for development and deter actions that risk our common interests, regionally and nationally."

Thanh's sideline meeting with Defence Minister Liang Guanglie took place under the shadow of the May 26 *Binh Minh 02* cable-cutting incident. Thanh expressed the concern of Vietnamese party and state leaders over what he termed a "pressing incident" and then offered the conciliatory comment that "Sometime, regrettable cases happen which are beyond the expectation of both sides."[75] Thanh concluded his remarks with these words, "We truly expect no repetition of similar incidents."[76] Liang replied that China did not want a similar incident to occur in the future. He noted in particular that the People's Liberation Army was not involved in the incident. Nonetheless, four days later a second cable-cutting incident occurred.

Vietnam Stiffens Public Diplomacy

On June 9, Prime Minister Nguyen Tan Dung responded to growing domestic pressure by making an unusually strong statement in defence of national sovereignty. Dung said: "We continue to affirm strongly and to manifest the strongest determination of all the Party, of all the people and of all the army in protecting Vietnamese sovereignty in maritime zones of the country." Dung also reaffirmed "the incontestable maritime sovereignty of Vietnam towards the two

73 "Vietnamese Prime Minister Nguyen Tan Dung Meets with Chinese Vice Foreign Minister Zhang Zhijun," Ministry of Foreign Affairs of the People's Republic of China, April 20, 2011.

74 Quoted in Agence France Presse, "Vietnam, China vow to work on disputed sea pact," April 21, 2011 and Deutsche Presse-Agentur, "Vietnam and China pledge to settle South China Sea disputes," April 20, 2011.

75 "East Sea incident a pressing issue: Vietnamese Defense Minister," *Thanh Nien News*, June 4, 2011. Chinese news media distorted Minister Thanh's remarks by reporting that he agreed to "resolve their differences over the South China Sea through bilateral efforts, and that no third party should be allowed to interfere in such efforts or use the issue to harm the bilateral relations," see: "Chinese DM Meets with Vietnamese Counterpart in Singapore," Xinhua, June 4, 2011.

76 Phung Quang Thanh, "Responding to New Maritime Security Threats," The 10th IISS Asian Security Summit the Shangri-La Dialogue, June 5, 2011.

archipelagos, the Paracel and Spratlys."[77] On the same day, President Nguyen Minh Triet, visiting Co To island off Quang Ninh province near the China border, stated that Vietnam was "determined to protect" its islands and "we are ready to sacrifice everything to protect our homeland, our sea and island sovereignty."[78]

Live-Firing Exercises

On June 9, after the Chinese Ambassador to the Philippines called on Vietnam and the Philippines to cease oil exploration in the South China Sea. Shortly after China announced it would be conducting routine naval exercises in the Western Pacific,[79] Vietnam responded by publicly announcing a live-fire exercise. Vietnam's Northern Maritime Safety Corporation issued a notice that two live firing exercises would be held on June 13 in the waters near Hon Ong Island. The exercises would last for a total of nine hours. The notice further declared, "All vessels are to refrain from engaging in activities in the area during the live-fire period."[80] Hon Ong Island is located approximately 40 kilometres off Quang Nam province in central Vietnam.

Vietnam's Foreign Ministry characterized the live-firing exercises as "a routine annual training activity of the Vietnam navy in the area where the Vietnam navy regularly conducts training [activities] that are programmed and planned annually for units of the Vietnam People's Navy."[81] Vietnam did not specify how many ships would be involved. The first phase of the exercise involved coastal artillery while the second part of the exercise involved missile corvettes firing their deck gun. Confidential Vietnamese military sources report that anti-ship missiles were also fired from Sukhoi jet aircraft. On June 11, the *Global Times*, an English-language newspaper published by the Chinese Communist Party, editorialized that Vietnam's conduct of a live-firing exercises was the

> lowest form of nationalism to create a new enmity between the people of the two countries. Hanoi seems to be looking to dissipate domestic pressure and buck

77 Interview with Thanh Nien quoted by Agence France Presse, "Vietnam PM says sea sovereignty 'incontestable'," June 9, 2011 and Deutsche Presse-Agentur, "Vietnam's top leaders add fire to South China Sea disputes," June 9, 2011.

78 Deutche Presse-Agentur, "Vietnam's top leaders add fire to South China Sea dispute," June 9, 2011.

79 Ben Blanchard and Michael Martina, "China says to hold 'routine' navy drills in western Pacific," Reuters, June 9, 2011.

80 Bảo đảm an toàn hàng hải miền Bắc (Northern Maritime Safety Corporation), "Về việc bắn đạn thật trên vùng biển Quảng Nam," So 107/TBHH-CT.BDATHHMB, June 9, 2011, http://www.vms-north.vn.

81 Quoted by John Ruwitch, "Vietnam welcomes international help as sea dispute escalates," Reuters, June 11, 2011. See also: Margie Mason, "Vietnam plans live-fire drill after China dispute," Associated Press, June 10, 2011; Agence France Presse, "Vietnam to hold live-fire drill as China rift grows," June 10, 2011 and Deutsche Presse-Agentur, "Navy official says live-fire drills well inside Vietnam's territory," June 11, 2011.

> up morale at home, while at the same time further drawing in the concern of international society over the South China Sea dispute.[82]

The editorial stated that China has "never sought to politically blackmail smaller countries. But when a small country turns that around and tries to blackmail China, the Chinese people will on the one hand feel rather angry, while on the other hand find it quite amusing." In conclusion, the editorial opined "If Vietnam insists on making trouble, thinking that the more trouble it makes, the more benefits it gains, then we truly wish to remind those in Vietnam who determine policy to please read your history."

Rising Anti-China Nationalism in Vietnam

China's new wave of aggressive assertiveness provoked a patriotic response among students and a wider section of the Vietnamese community. Using Facebook and other social networking sites they mounted a series of anti-China demonstrations on Sundays over a twelve week period. The demonstrations commenced on June 5 when an estimated three hundred Vietnamese gathered near the Chinese Embassy in Hanoi. On the same day a crowd estimated "at nearly 1,000" to "several thousand" gathered in Ho Chi Minh City.[83] On the following weekend, June 12, 200 demonstrators took to the streets of Hanoi while another three hundred marched in Ho Chi Minh City in a repeat of the previous weekend's protests.[84] The protestors held placards reading "Down with China," "The Spratlys and Paracels belong to Vietnam" and "Stop Violating Vietnam's Territory." On Sunday, June 19, another peaceful demonstrations was held in Hanoi while police intervention prevented a third demonstration from being held in Ho Chi Minh City.

During early June, growing enmity between nationalists in China and Vietnam spilled over into cyberspace. According to Nguyen Minh Duc, director of the Bach Khoa Internetwork Security Centre, more than two hundred Vietnamese websites were subject to cyber attacks. Among the sites affected were those of

---

82 Quoted by Associated Press, "Chine Communist Party newspaper cautions Vietnam," June 11, 2011.

83 "Chinese aggression in the South China Sea persists, says Vietnam Foreign Minister," *IB Times*, June 9, 2011; Reuters, "Vietnam accuses China of harassing another boat," June 9, 2011 and Ian Timberlake, "'Facebook effect' stirs Vietnam-China tensions," Agence France Presse, June 10, 2011

84 Deutsche Presse-Agentur, "Vietnamese demonstrate against China as sea disputes heats up," June 12, 2011; Reuters, "Vietnam allows second anti-China protest in Hanoi," June 12, 2011 and Agence France-Presse, "Protesters rally ahead of Vietnam fire drills," *The Standard*, June 13, 2011. Some Vietnamese universities warned their students not to take part in anti-China demonstrations. A notice at the Industrial University in Ho Chi Minh City, for example, threatened to expel students who took part in anti-China demonstrations; see: John Ruwitch, "Vietnam allows second anti-China protest in Hanoi," Reuters, June 12, 2011.

the ministries of Agriculture and Rural Development and Foreign Affairs where hackers succeeded in posting Chinese flags and slogans.[85]

Second Special Envoy to China

In mid-year there were diplomatic signs that China and Vietnam were moving to contain tensions arising from their territorial dispute in the South China Sea. For example, the navies of both countries conducted their eleventh routine joint patrol in the Gulf of Tonkin on June 19–20.[86] After the patrol was concluded, the Vietnamese ships paid a visit to Zhanjiang, Guangdong, Vietnam's second ever port call to China.[87]

After the second weekend of anti-China demonstrations, Vietnam dispatched deputy foreign minister Ho Xuan Son as a special envoy to Beijing to hold talks on the South China Sea with his counterpart Zhang Zhijun. Significantly, Son was received by State Councilor Dai Bingguo. According to a joint press release issued by Vietnam's Ministry of Foreign Affairs on June 25th:

> The two sides emphasized the necessity to actively implement the common perceptions of the two countries' leaders, peacefully solving the two countries' disputes at sea through negotiation and friendly consultation; employing effective measures and working together to maintain peace and stability in the East Sea [*sic*].
>
> They also laid stress on the need to steer public opinions along the correct direction, avoiding comments and deeds that harm the friendship and trust of the people of the two countries.
>
> The two sides agreed to speed up the tempo of negotiations so as to early sign an "Agreement on basic principles guiding the settlement of sea issues between Vietnam and China," and boost the implementation of the Declaration on Conduct of Parties in the East Sea [*sic*] (DOC) and follow-up activities so that substantial progress will soon be achieved.[88]

---

85 AFP, "Vietnam complains to China as sea tensions rise," June 9, 2011 and Ian Timberlake, "Vietnam to hold live-fire drill as China rift grows," June 10, 2011.

86 Margie Mason, "Vietnam and China hold joint naval patrol amid spat," Associated Press, June 21, 2011 and Agence France Presse, "China, Vietnam hold joint sea patrols near disputed Spratlys," June 23, 2011.

87 "Vietnamese naval ships on friendly visit to China," *Quan Doi Nhan Dan Online*, June 22, 2011; "China, Vietnam engage in Joint naval patrols," *People's Daily Online*, June 22, 2011 and "Vietnamese naval ships wrap up visit to China," *Quan Doi Nhan Dan Online*, June 27, 2011.

88 Socialist Republic of Vietnam, Ministry of Foreign Affairs, "Vietnam-China joint press release," June 26, 2011. http://www.mofa.vn/en. See also: Edward Wong, "China and Vietnam Agree to Talks on South China Sea Dispute," *The New York Times*, June 26, 2011;

Adoption of Guidelines for the Declaration on Conduct of Parties in the South China Sea

In 2004, two years after negotiating the Declaration on Conduct of Parties in the South China Sea, the ASEAN-China Senior Officials' Meeting decided to establish the ASEAN-China the Joint Working Group (JWC) to Implement the DOC. The Joint Working Group held its first meeting in Manila from August 4–5, 2005. The Terms of Reference for the Joint Working Group specified that the JWG was to meet twice a year to formulate recommendations in four areas:

- Guidelines and the action plan for the implementation of the DOC.
- Specific cooperative activities in the South China Sea.
- A register of experts and eminent persons who may provide technical inputs, non-binding and professional views or policy recommendations to the ASEAN-China JWG.
- The convening of workshops, as the need arises.[89]

ASEAN tabled draft guidelines for discussion. It immediately became apparent that point two was a major sticking point. Point two stated, "ASEAN will continue its current practice of consulting among themselves before meeting with China." China objected and insisted that outstanding disputes should be resolved by consultations "among relevant parties" and not with ASEAN. The Joint Working Group did not make any progress for the next six years.

Chinese assertiveness in pushing its sovereignty claims in the South China Sea in 2009 and 2010 provoked an international backlash. South China Sea disputes featured prominently at the ASEAN Regional Forum in mid-year and at the inaugural ASEAN Defense Ministers Meeting Plus in October 2010. China was out maneuvered diplomatically and sought to limit further damage by agreeing to revive the heretofore-moribund ASEAN-China Joint Working Group to Implement the Declaration on Conduct of Parties. In December 2010 the fifth meeting was convened in Kunming China. The sixth ASEAN-China Joint Working Group met in Medan, Indonesia from April 18–20, 2011. At both meetings it became clear that progress was hostage to China's insistence that territorial and sovereignty claims could only be settled bilaterally by the states concerned. China specifically objected to a clause in the draft guidelines, drawn up by ASEAN, that mentioned

---

Brian Spegele, "China Announces Pact with Vietnam on Disputes Sea," *The Wall Street Journal*, June 26, 2011; Dan Martin, "China, Vietnam vow to cool S. China Sea tensions," Agence France Presse, June 27, 2011; and Qin Zhongwei, "China, Vietnam agree on talks to solve sea dispute," *China Daily*, June 27, 2011.

89 "Terms of Reference of the ASEAN-China Joint Working Group on the Implementation of the Declaration on Conduct of Parties in the South China Sea," available at: http://www.asean.org/16886htm.

ASEAN members would gather first to work out a common position before meeting with China.

In July 2011 ASEAN Senior Officials quietly dropped the offending clause and offered drastically revised draft guidelines to their ministers for approval.[90] On July 20, 2011, the ASEAN and Chinese foreign ministers finally reached agreement on The Guidelines for the Implementation of the DOC. These guidelines consist of eight brief points preceded by a three-paragraph preamble. The preamble identifies the DOS as "a milestone document signed between the ASEAN Member States and China," implying this is not an agreement between ASEAN as a group and China. Second, the preamble states that the "effective implementation of the DOC will contribute to the deepening of the ASEAN-China Strategic Partnership for Peace and Prosperity." This is an inducement for China to take concrete action. Finally, the preamble notes that Guidelines "are to guide the implementation of possible joint cooperative activities, measures and projects as provided for in the DOC." This formulation clearly indicates that the Guidelines are tentative and nothing is binding.

The eight substantive points are as follows:

1. The implementation of the DOC should be carried out in a step-by-step approach in line with the provisions of the DOC.
2. The Parties to the DOC will continue to promote dialogue and consultations in accordance with the spirit of the DOC.
3. The implementation of activities or projects as provided for in the DOC should be clearly identified.
4. The participation in the activities or projects should be carried out on a voluntary basis.
5. Initial activities to be undertaken under the ambit of the DOC should be confidence-building measures.
6. The decision to implement concrete measures or activities of the DOC should be based on consensus among parties concerned, and lead to the eventual realization of a Code of Conduct.
7. In the implementation of the agreed projects under the DOC, the services of the Experts and Eminent Persons, if deemed necessary, will be sought to provide specific inputs on the projects concerned.[91]

90 As of this writing the guidelines have not been released. According to a confidential source who attended the ASEAN related meetings in Bali, the new guidelines state, "The parties to the DOC will continue to promote dialogue and consultations in accordance with the spirit of the DOC." Private email received July 22, 2011.

91 The "Guidelines for the Implementation of the Doc" appeared on the ASEAN Secretariat web site under External Relations, China, Cooperation on the South China Sea. They have since been removed.

8. Progress of the implementation of the agreed activities and projects under the DOC shall be reported annually to the ASEAN-China Ministerial Meeting (PMC).

The foreign ministers also agreed to convene the seventh meeting of the ASEAN-China Joint Working Group later in the year in China.

Immediately after the Guidelines were adopted, the Philippines Foreign Secretary Albert del Rosario noted that they would need more "teeth" to make them effective. According to Rosario, "The necessary elements to make the guidelines succeed are still incomplete. We're looking for the participants to be honorable. Beyond that there's not much room for us to exact consequences for misbehavior." This view was echoed by Barry Wain, a veteran commentator, "Hard-headed strategists in Southeast Asia know that adopting the implementing guidelines is hardly a constraint on China's increasingly aggressive behavior in the South China Sea. The real restraint on China is the presence of the U.S. Navy and the need to have stable US–China relations."[92]

China's Relations with the Philippines Post-DOC Guidelines

China Hosts State Visit by President Aquino

After President Aquino assumed office he received an invitation to pay an official state visit to China. His visit was reportedly postponed on one or more occasions because of rising tensions over territorial disputes in the South China Sea. After ASEAN and China adopted the Guidelines on the DOC the Philippines dispatched its foreign secretary to Beijing to organize the state visits. President Aquino paid an official visit to Beijing from August 30–September 3 at the invitation of President Hu Jintao. The joint statement issued at the conclusion of bilateral talks indicated that economic issues featured prominently. For example, it was later reported that Aquino has garnered US $1.3 billion in new investments.[93] The joint statement also made the following reference to the South China Sea near the bottom of the list of topics discussed (point 15 of 17 points):

> Both leaders exchanged views on the maritime disputes and agreed not to let the maritime disputes affect the broader picture of friendship and cooperation

92 Barry Wain, "A South China Sea Charade," *The Wall Street Journal*, August 21, 2011.

93 "Aquino back from 5-day US visit," *Malaya*, September 23, 2011. Manolo B. Jara, "Aquino brings home $13b word of China investments," *The Gulf Today*, September 5, 2011 reports, "Aquino said the Chinese 'goodies' he brought home consisted of $1.28 billion worth of new investments, $3.8 billion in assured investments and $7.9 billion from businessmen who showed interest in investing in the Philippines."

between the two countries. The two leaders reiterated their commitment to addressing the disputes through peaceful dialogue, to maintain continued regional peace, security, stability and an environment conducive to economic progress. Both leaders reaffirmed their commitments to respect and abide by the Declaration on the Conduct of Parties in the South China Sea signed by China and the ASEAN member countries in 2002.[94]

Push for Binding Code of Conduct

On Aquino's return to Manila he revealed that President Hu Jin-tao supported an "implementing agreement" for a South China Sea Code of Conduct. According to Aquino, this was "very significant, because before it was just a general statement of principles. Now there's a desire to really put in the implementing rules and regulations."[95] Nevertheless, President Aquino has continued to press for a multilateral South China Sea Code of Conduct and agreement on demarcating the precise maritime areas in dispute. On September 16, for example, on the eve of an official visit to Japan scheduled for September 25–28, President Aquino stated in an interview with the Japanese media that, "There are lot of claimants to the disputed areas, so for it [code of conduct] to be binding it has to be in an multilateral basis [*sic*]."[96] Press reports indicated President Aquino would raise the South China Sea code of conduct in his discussion with Prime Minister Nado in late September. Japan's Ambassador to the Philippines, Toshinao Urabe, was also quoted at this time as stating that Japan supported a stronger code of conduct.[97]

Further Military Modernization

Significantly, immediately after Aquino's state visit to Beijing, the Philippines announced on September 7th that 4.95 billion pesos (US $118 million) would be allocated to top up the defence budget.[98] These funds would be used to purchase a naval patrol vessel, six helicopters and other military equipment in order to secure the Malampaya Natural Gas and Power Project located fifty miles off the coast of Palawan in waters also claimed by China.

94 Joint Statement of the Philippines and China, Beijing, September 1, 2011 reprinted in *Inquirer Global Nation*, September 7, 2011.

95 Quoted in Bloomberg News, "China Wants "Binding' S. China Code: Aquino," August 31, 2011; see also: Barbara Mae Dacanay, "China and Philippines agree to peace over South China Sea," *Gulf News*, September 2, 2011.

96 Reuters, "Aquino wants multilateral solution to South China Sea disputes," *InterAkysyon*, September 17, 2011.

97 "Japan steps in South China Sea territorial feud," *Indian Express*, September 20, 2011; and "Japan calls for South China Sea code of conduct," *The Economic Times*, September 21, 2011.

98 Agence France-Presse, "Philippines Ups Spending To Guard South China Sea," September 7, 2011.

Zone of Peace, Freedom, Friendship and Cooperation

In July, at the 44th ASEAN Ministerial Meeting, the Foreign Secretary of the Philippines presented his counterparts with a proposal to adopt an agreement entitled, "Zone of Peace, Freedom, Friendship and Cooperation in the South China Sea." The ministers took note of this proposal and referred it to a meeting of ASEAN Senior Officials and legal experts for consideration.[99] In preparation for the ASEAN Legal Experts Meeting, the Philippines Department of Foreign Affairs (DFA) drew up a proposal to create "enclaves" for disputed maritime territory in the South China Sea in order to separate these areas from non-disputed maritime territory. According to the DFA proposal, "(E)nclaving will literally operationalize the 'shelving of territorial disputes' and pave the way for effective and meaningful cooperation among the claimant countries in the West Philippine Sea (or) South China Sea."[100]

ASEAN maritime and legal experts convened in Manila on September 22. Their findings will be passed to ASEAN Senior Officials who in turn will make recommendations to their ministers prior to the convening of the 19th ASEAN Summit in Bali in November.

China's Relations with Vietnam post-DOC Guidelines

Anti-China Protests End

Despite the reference in the joint press release to "steering public opinion" issued by Ho Xuan Son and Zhang Zhijun on June 25th, Vietnamese authorities permitted two further demonstrations to take place on June 26 and July 3. Each involved nearly 100 persons who gathered outside the Chinese Embassy in Hanoi. On the following weekends, July 10 and July 17, the police forcibly intervened and detained a dozen persons including journalists when they gathered outside the Chinese Embassy. On the eighth weekend, July 24, the protesters gathered at Hoan Kiem lake and were permitted to march and display anti-China banners. No protests took place on Sunday, July 31. Organisers and their supporters met in coffee shops to plan strategy on what turned out to be a cold and rainy day.

Anti-China protests were resumed on the weekends of August 7 and August 14. An estimated 100 persons took part in each. On August 18, the Hanoi People's Committee issued a directive banning public protests. When a crowd of up to 50

99 Bea Cupin, "ASEAN, China agree to heed guidelines covering Spratlys," GMA News, July 20, 2011 and Brian Padden, "ASEAN Maritime Specialists Discuss Guidelines to Resolve S. China Sea Dispute," Voice of America, September 22, 2011.

100 Quoted in ELR/VS, "DFA to propose 'enclaving' of disputed areas in South China Sea," GMA News, September 21, 2011 and ELR/VS, "VP Binay pushes for DFA proposal on Spratlys," GMA New, September 22, 2011.

persons gathered at Hoan Kiem Lake on August 21 the police moved in to disperse them. Fifteen were detained.[101] No further public protests have been reported.

Bilateral Discussions Continue

In August, China and Vietnam held the seventh round of bilateral discussions aimed at reaching a settlement of their maritime disputes. The origins of these talks dates back to December 2008 when China and Vietnam agreed to give priority given to developing a set of "fundamental guiding principles" as a framework for settling maritime issues. These confidential discussions began in early 2010 and five sessions were held during the year.

According to Vietnamese Foreign Ministry sources, Vietnam and China agreed to settle their differences "through peaceful negotiation" and "refrain from any action to complicate the situation, violence or threat of use of violence."[102] Significantly, Vietnam and China agreed to bilateral discussions on maters that did not affect third parties, such as the waters at the mouth of the Gulf of Tonkin. Vietnam wanted to include the Paracel Islands in bilateral discussion but China refused. Vietnam and China also differed on the question of multilateral negotiations. According to Vietnam:

> Issues that are related to other countries and parties like the Spratly Islands cannot be settled by Vietnam and China; they require the participation of other concerned parties. For issues that are not only related to countries that border the East Sea such as maritime safety and security, they must be negotiated and settled by all countries that share this common interest.[103]

China and Vietnam have since held two further rounds of working-level discussions. At the seventh and most recent round on August 1st, a Vietnamese spokesperson noted that "the two sides reached preliminary consensus on some principles" and that the eighth round of discussion would be held later in the year.[104]

---

101 "Vietnam issues ultimatum to anti-China protesters," Deutsche Presse Agentur, August 18, 2001 and Marianne Brown, "Vietnam Security Forces Detain Anti-China Protesters," Voice of America News, August 21, 2011

102 "Answer from Vietnam Ministry of Foreign Affairs Spokesperson Nguyen Phuong Nga to Questions by Greg Torode—*South China Morning Post*," December 2010; see: Greg Torode and Minnie Chan, "China refuses to yield on Paracels," *Sunday Morning Post* [Hong Kong], December 12, 2010.

103 Ibid.

104 'Vietnam, China agree to resolve sea dispute through peaceful means," Vietnam News Agency, August 3, 2011.

2nd Defence-Security Strategic Dialogue

On August 28th, China and Vietnam held their 2nd Defence-Security Strategic Dialogue at deputy minister level in Beijing. Lt. General Ma Xiaotian, vice chair of the PLA General Staff hosted his Vietnamese counterpart, Lt. General Nguyen Chi Vinh, deputy minister of national defence. The two generals agreed to step up the exchange of military delegations, open a hot line between the two defence ministries, and expand military training. Lt. General Ma noted that the sovereignty dispute in the South China Sea was the "most difficult and sensitive issue" in bilateral relations. Lt. General Vinh responded by stating Vietnam's readiness "to cooperate for mutual development with China in really disputed areas" in accord with international law and the mutual interest of both sides. General Vinh also stressed that there were three closely related aspects to the East Sea issue: "the declaration of sovereignty by concerned countries, solving issues related to the ties between Vietnam and China, and solving issues at multilateral forums."[105]

5th Meeting of the Joint Steering Committee

On September 6th China and Vietnam held the fifth annual meeting of their bilateral Joint Steering Committee in Hanoi. China was represented by State Councilor Dai Bingguo who met with his counter-part Deputy Prime Minister Nguyen Thien Nhan. The Joint Steering Committee oversees all aspects of their bilateral relations. The two interlocutors, inter alia, discussed conflicting territorial claims in the South China Sea. According to the final communiqué:

> They believe it is critical to properly solve the marine issues in order to maintain the general situation of friendly cooperation between China and Vietnam. They reiterate to abide by the consensus reached between leaders of the two countries, international laws and the spirit of the Declaration on the Conduct of Parties in the South China Sea, solve the marine disputes peacefully through negotiations and friendly consultations and take effective measures to safeguard peace and stability of South China Sea. They will accelerate the process of negotiations and seek fundamental and long-term solutions acceptable to both sides. They agree to strengthen negotiations on the marine issues and sign the agreement on the basic principles guiding the settlement of marine issues between China and Vietnam at an early date. They will boost the implementation of the Declaration on the Conduct of Parties in the South China Sea and follow-up work and try to achieve substantial progress soon.

105 "Vietnam, China hold second defence, security dialogue," Vietnam News Agency, August 31, 2011.

General Political Department Chief Visits Beijing

From September 14–19, China hosted a visit by General Ngo Xuan Lich, head of the VPA's General Political Department and member of the Central Military Party Committee.[106] General Lich held discussions with his counterpart, Li Jinai, who is also a member of Chna's Central Military Commission. Their meeting focused on developing ties between the two militaries. Significantly General Lich was also received by Vice President Xi Jiping, the chairman of the Central Military Commission[107] and heir apparent to the post of state president on the retirement of Hu Jintao in 2013.

Concluding Observations

In the early to mid-1990s, when China began to occupy rocks in the Spratlys including the celebrated Mischief Reef, security analysts described Chinese strategy as "creeping assertiveness" and "talk and take." The events during the first half of 2011 are best described as aggressive assertiveness. China appears to be paying back Vietnam for its role in internationalizing the South China Sea when it was Chair of ASEAN. Chinese actions in the Reed Bank area appear designed to expose ambiguities in the US–Philippines Mutual Security Treaty over whether or not the Kalayaan Island Group is covered by this treaty.

China's aggressive assertion of sovereignty over the South China Sea in the first half of 2001 has raised the security stakes for Southeast Asian states and all maritime powers that sail through its waters. This chapter has drawn attention to three serious incidents involving Chinese state vessels (including one PLAN warship) and Filipino vessels operating with the Philippines' Exclusive Economic Zone. This chapter has also discussed Chinese actions directed against Vietnam, including the imposition of an annual unilateral fishing ban, and deliberate interference by Chinese state vessels in commercial marine activities conducted within Vietnam's Exclusive Economic Zone. Chinese aggressive assertiveness in the South China Sea has now become an international issue that must be addressed multilaterally by all concerned stakeholders.

International diplomatic pressure has resulted in the adoption of Guidelines to implement the DOC. Although these guidelines represent a considerable retreat by ASEAN the offer grounds for cautious optimism that tensions in the South China

106 "Doan can bo chinh tri quan su cap cao nuoc ta tham Trung Quoc," Vietnam TV, September 18, 2011 and Zhous Feng, "Chinese defence official holds talks with Vietnamese counterpart," *PLA Daily*, September 16, 2011.

107 "Phó chủ tịch Trung Quốc tiếp đoàn quân sự cấp cao Việt Nam," *Thanh Nien Online*, September 18, 2011; "Chinese vice president eyes enhanced relations with Vietnam," Xinhua, Beijing, September 16, 2011 and "China, Vietnam pledge to enhance ties amid row in S China sea," Press Trust of India, September 17, 2011.

Sea will abate as the countries concerned adopt positive confidence building and other cooperative measures. There is even the possibility that the DOC may be upgraded into a Code of Conduct.

Dampening tensions may be the first step towards a long-term settlement but lowering tensions are not sufficient to bring about a resolution of unresolved sovereignty claims. At the hear of the matter is the nine-dash line u-shaped map that China submitted to the United Nations Commission on the Limits of Continental Shelf in 2009. On the face of it China's map lays claims to virtually all of the South China Sea over which it claims "indisputable sovereignty." China must now bring its claims into accord with international law and specify just what it is claiming. Does China consider the South China Sea territorial waters? Or is China just claiming all of the rocks and features and surrounding waters within the nine-dash lines and not just the waters surrounding the nine features and rocks that it presently occupies? And, if so, is China claiming that these rocks are in fact islands and thus entitled to a two hundred nautical mile EEZ? If so this is a legal fiction. Islands must be able to sustain human habitation and have an economic function. Rocks, which do not meet these criteria, cannot claim an EEZ or continental shelf.

China's nine dash marks cut deeply into the EEZs that have been declared by Vietnam and the Philippines These EEZs are based firmly in international law. Both states have drawn straight base lines around their coasts and then extended their claim from these baselines seaward out to two hundred nautical miles. Under the United Nations Convention on Law of the Sea littoral states have sovereignty over these waters and continental shelves in terms of exploitation of natural resources such as fisheries and oil and gas deposits on the ocean floor.

Chinese assertiveness has provoked what must be considered a counter-productive reaction from Beijing's perspective. The Aquino Administration is now committed to modernizing its armed forces for territorial defence of its maritme domain. This goal has driven the Philippines to revive defence-security cooperation with the United States under aegis of their 1951 Mutual Security Treaty. Vietnam, while tentatively stepping up defence cooperation with the United State, has meanwhile embarked on a robust program of force modernization including *Kilo*-class submarines, Su-30 multi-role jet fighters, *Gephard*-class guided missile frigates, and a variety of modern anti-ship missiles. It is in the interest of the United States and its allies as well as India to assist both nations in capacity building in the area of maritime security.

ASEAN and the international community, both of which rely on transit through the South China Sea, must continue to diplomatically confront China over its aggressive assertiveness. They should bring collective diplomatic pressure to bear on China to desist from provocative assertions of jurisdiction in the EEZs of South China Sea littoral states. Diplomatic pressure should also be brought to bear on China and other claimant states to faithfully implement the guidelines to implement the DOC.

ASEAN member states and the international community should support Indonesia, in its role as ASEAN Chair, in its efforts to engage China in upgrading the DOC to a more formal (and binding?) Code of Conduct. If China is not forthcoming, ASEAN members themselves should draw up a Treaty on a Code of Conduct in the South China Sea, and after ratification, open it to accession by non-member states along the lines of the ASEAN Treaty of Amity and Cooperation and the Southeast Asian Nuclear-Free Weapons Zone Treaty.

PART III
Major Legal Issues in the South China Sea

Chapter 4
An Analysis of China's Claim to Historic Rights in the South China Sea

Peter A. Dutton

Introduction

In 1947 the Nationalist government of the Republic of China published a map with a U-shaped series of lines delineating its maritime claim in the South China Sea. This map was based on a 1935 internal government report prepared to define the limits of China, many parts of which were dominated by outside powers at the time.[1] Though the exact nature of the claim was never specified by the Nationalist government and has not been clarified by the People's Republic of China either, the cartographic feature persisted in maps published by the Communist Party after it came to power on the mainland in 1949, and today the U-shaped line's nine dashes in the South China Sea remain on maps published both in China and on Taiwan. These maps have been used by scholars and officials in Taiwan and on the mainland to justify claims of historic rights to sovereignty over the islands within the U-shaped line and to some form of historic rights over the waters within the region. These assertions of historic rights, however, have caused considerable friction with Chinese Southeast Asian neighbors and with the United States and others that seek to ensure that freedoms of navigation for all traditional uses of the seas, including military uses, are preserved.

How should China's U-shaped claim and the Chinese understanding of their historic rights be interpreted? This chapter will survey relevant Chinese state practice and authoritative scholarly writings to better understand the nature of China's claim to historic rights within the U-shaped line. It will then survey the relevant international law regarding historic rights to islands and historic rights to water space and draw some conclusions and present key questions for further analysis.

China's Domestic Law and Official Statements

Two laws of the People's Republic of China are relevant to analysis of China's claim to historic rights. The first is the 1992 Law on the Territorial Sea and

1 Li Jinming and Li Dexia, "The Dotted Line on the Chinese Map of the South China Sea: A Note," 34 *Ocean Development and International Law*, 2003, pp. 287–95.

Contiguous Zone of the People's Republic of China. This law specifically claims sovereignty over each of the island groups in the South China Sea, mentioning each in turn and by the name of the group—the Pratas Islands (Dongsha), Paracel Islands (Xisha), Macclesfield Bank (Zhongsha), and the Spratly Islands (Nansha)—rather than enumerating and specifying the various features over which China claims sovereignty. The second is the 1998 Law of the People's Republic of China on the Exclusive Economic Zone and Continental Shelf, which claims an exclusive economic zone emanating from all Chinese coastal territory without distinction. Logically, this suggests that all relevant Chinese territory as specified in the 1992 Territorial Sea Law, which in turn, as noted above, specifically includes each of the island groups in the South China Sea, are entitled to the subject zones. Thus, in combination, these two Chinese laws assert an EEZ and therefore jurisdictional control over nearly the entire South China Sea area within the U-shaped line.

The government of the People's Republic of China further clarified its claims in two submissions to the United Nations Commission on the Limits of the Continental Shelf. In 2009, the Chinese government submitted a letter to the Secretary General of the United Nations in protest of the Joint Submission of Vietnam and Malaysia for an extended continental shelf claim in the South China Sea within the U-shaped line claimed by China.[2] The letter asserted that "China has indisputable sovereignty over the islands in the South China Sea and the adjacent waters, and enjoys sovereign rights and jurisdiction over the relevant waters as well as the seabed and subsoil thereof." The Chinese government also attached a map of the U-shaped claim, with its 9-dashed line in the South China Sea.[3]

After receiving much international criticism for its failure to adhere to the requirement of the United Nations Convention on the Law of the Sea that claims to maritime zones must be based on geography, the Chinese government submitted a second letter, in April 2011, that, without renouncing the historically-based claims presented in the 2009 letter, asserted "under the relevant provisions of the 1982 United Nations Convention on the Law of the Sea, as well as the Law of the People's Republic of China on the Territorial Sea and the Contiguous Zone (1992) and the Law on the Exclusive Economic Zone and the Continental Shelf of the People's Republic of China (1998), China's Nansha [Spratly] Islands are fully entitled to a Territorial Sea, Exclusive Economic Zone (EEZ) and Continental Shelf."[4] Indeed, far from backing off its earlier claims to historic rights, the letter repeated the sentence about China's "indisputable" rights in the South China Sea

---

2 *Letter from the permanent Mission of the People's Republic of China to the Secretary-General of the United Nations*, CML/17/2009, May 7, 2009.

3 It should be noted that on other maps a 10th dash is included in the waters north of the South China Sea and to the east of the island of Taiwan.

4 *Letter from the Permanent Mission of the People's Republic of China to the Secretary-General of the United Nations*, CML/8/2011, April 14, 2011. (For readability, the

and asserted "China's sovereignty and related rights and jurisdiction in the South China Sea are supported by abundant historical and legal evidence."

This was followed up by several official Chinese statements. For instance, on September 15, 2011, a Foreign Ministry Spokesman for the People's Republic of China warned India and other countries not to continue oil exploration projects in the South China Sea off the coast of Vietnam. She stated that "China enjoys indisputable sovereignty over the South China Sea and the islands. China's stand is based on historical facts and international law." She further insisted that the United Nations Convention on the Law of the Sea, when authorizing coastal states to establish jurisdiction at sea beyond territorial waters "did not give any country the right to expand their own exclusive economic zone and continental shelf to other country's territories." The Convention, she said, "Did not negate a country's right formed in history that has been consistently claimed." She held that Vietnam and other countries should therefore not engage in "oil and gas exploration and development activities in waters under China's jurisdiction.[5]

Chinese Scholarly Writings about Historic Rights in the South China Sea

Ge Yongping, a professor of law at Harbin University of Technology, has written that China's sovereignty claim to the Spratlys can be justified either from a historical point of view or from the perspective of international law. He describes the Spratlys as comprising more than 230 islands, shoals and reefs, of which only eleven islands, five shoals and 20 reefs are actually exposed at high tide and therefore susceptible of being claimed as sovereign territory. He argues that Chinese sovereignty over these features is based on "indisputable historic ownership" over all the islands in the South China Sea. He asserts that Chinese explorers first discovered the islands, named them, and managed and developed them. According to Ge, the Chinese government was therefore the first to exercise "administrative jurisdiction over the islands" and as such, he concludes they form "an integral part of Chinese territory."[6]

Ge further develops his perspective that history entitles China to sovereignty over the Spratly Islands by citing Chinese records from as early as the Han Dynasty, which ruled China from 206 BC to 220 AD, and from the 11th through 14th centuries AD when Chinese navy and merchant fleets were the most powerful on the globe. He claims that China's early development as a civilization state entitles it to sovereignty based on these discoveries, since the other claimant

---

italics from original have been removed and the grammar has been slightly improved in the quote above with care taken not to alter the meaning in any way).

5 China Warns on South China Sea Oil, *UPI*, September 15, 2011.

6 Ge Yongping, "Analysis of Spratly Island Sovereignty Dispute, China's Countermeasures," *Taipingyang Xuebao*, September 28, 2009, pp. 71–9 [OSC translation CPP20100111671003].

states—Vietnam, the Philippines, Brunei and Malaysia—were, at this time, "still in the barbaric age with no national independence."[7] Thus, he reasons, China's sovereignty accrued at a point in history when there was no other developed state existed in the region to challenge its position. After acquiring sovereignty, Ge asserts, the Chinese state maintained effective occupation and management of islands. He asserts that Chinese central, regional, and county government records demonstrate that Chinese officials patrolled the waters around the islands, managed sea routes, took astronomical measurements, strengthened coastal defense, punished pirates acting in the areas around the islands, rescued wrecked foreign ships, and prevented foreign intrusions. Finally, Ge observes that as late as the early- and mid-20th century, other states officially recognized China's sovereignty over the islands. British charts from 1901 and 1908, for instance, mark the islands as being Chinese and a 1957 map published in Indonesian geography textbooks similarly acknowledge Chinese sovereignty. He also asserts that the Democratic Republic of Vietnam publicly acknowledged Chinese sovereignty in its maps, newspapers and textbooks up until 1974, after which, he implicitly acknowledges, Vietnam's official position concerning sovereignty changed.

Li Mingjiang, of Singapore's RSIS, has also written that the weight of evidence shows "China was the first country to discover and use the islands and resources in the South China Sea."[8] Like other Chinese scholars, he also dates evidence of Chinese discovery to the Han Dynasty, but adds that a tribute mission to Cambodia during the Three Kingdoms Era in the 3rd century AD also described the existence of both the Paracels and the Spratlys in its official records of the voyage. Li Mingjiang observes, "during the Song and Yuan Dynasties" from the 10th through 14th centuries AD "many official and unofficial Chinese accounts seem to indicate that the South China Sea area was included in the Chinese national boundary." Additionally, he asserts that during the Ming and Qing eras, from 1368–1911, "various official Chinese maps included the Spratlys [within] Chinese territory."

Li Mingjiang notes the activities of the Chinese government during the 20th century to express its sovereignty over these islands and waters. On these bases, he observes, "Chinese analysts maintain that the U-shaped line was publicized long before the emergence of contemporary international law of the sea, including UNCLOS, and that the new international legal regime should not negate China's prior rights in the South China Sea." Echoing China's 1998 Exclusive Economic Zone law, Li Mingjiang concludes that "China should enjoy *both* the EEZ and continental shelf rights stipulated in UNCLOS for the islands *and* at the same time historical rights within the U-shaped line."[9]

---

7 Ibid.

8 Li Mingjiang, "China's South China Sea Policy: Claims and Changing Contexts," Conference Paper Presented at Conference on the South China Sea hosted by the Diplomatic Academy of Vietnam and the Foreign Affairs Institute of the Philippines in Manila, July 6–7, 2011.

9 Li Mingjiang, ibid. (emphasis added).

Another scholar, Li Guoqiang, Deputy Director of the Center for China's Borderland History and Geography of the Chinese Academy of Social Sciences, has provided a more detailed account of historical records from as early as the Eastern Han Dynasty (25 AD to 220 AD) that demonstrate that Chinese maritime voyagers were aware of island features and reefs in the South China Sea. He recounts similar evidence from the Three Kingdoms period (220 AD to 280 AD).[10] It is unclear from Li Guoqiang's account whether the Chinese records from this period refer to the islands in the Spratlys, the Paracels, or to features belonging to some other group of islets in the South China Sea. However, Li discusses the existence of historical evidence from the Sui and Tang Dynasties (589–907) that demonstrates that Chinese "production and operation activities" had extended at that time to the Xisha or Paracel Islands and evidence that by the Song Dynasty (960–1276) the Chinese people had given specific names to islands of the Xisha (Paracel) and Nansha (Spratly) Island groups and included them under the administration and jurisdiction of Guangnan Xilu Qiongzhou, or modern Guangxi province, and conducted "important … naval patrols" and coast guard activities, especially in the Paracels. Without presenting specific evidence, Li Guoqiang concludes that "the Ming (1368–1644) and Qing (1644–1911) Dynasties regarded the South China Sea Islands and the adjacent waters as within their jurisdiction," thus implicitly drawing an unbroken line of Chinese administration over the South China Sea islands and waters from initial discovery more than 2,000 years ago until the beginning of the 20th century.

Li Guoqiang addresses in detail the external competition for dominance over the Spratly Islands from French intrusion during the Republican period. He also discusses the Republic of China's efforts to resume sovereignty over the islands of the South China Sea after World War II, culminating in the publication on December 1, 1947 of the U-shaped line by the Nationalist government's Department of the Interior. The People's Republic of China, he asserts, "continued the established territory of the South China Sea … simultaneously developing and constructing the South China Sea … [and taking] a series of political, military and diplomatic measures to maintain sovereignty." He thus concludes that China's authority over the islands and waters of the South China Sea have been "unique and continuous." This conclusion is strengthened, in his view, in that "[T]he Neighboring countries of the South China Sea knew almost nothing about the South China Sea Islands in the Han, Tang, Song, Yuan, and even the Ming and Qing dynasties. There is no conclusive evidence [he asserts] to show that their ancestors found and named the South China Sea Islands and no historical basis for the jurisdiction of their governments. In the process of historical development, when China had sovereignty over the South China Sea islands and the adjacent waters, no country challenged China's sovereignty and jurisdiction in the South China Sea."

10 Li Guoqiang, "Formation of China's Sovereignty over South China Sea Islands, Origin of South China Sea Issues," *Qiushi Online*, August 1, 2011 [OSC Translation CPP20110801787014].

A fourth Chinese legal expert, Li Anmin, an Assistant Instructor from the Naval Command Academy Strategic Teaching and Research Department, has also picked up on this theme of continuity and written that "China was the first country to discover and name the Spratly [Nansha] Islands, and the one which first exercised sovereign jurisdiction over the Spratly Islands and has continued to do so."[11] The focus of Li Anmin's writing is the period of the 20th century after the end of World War II. "During World War II [Li notes], Japan launched a war of aggression against China, occupying a significant portion of Chinese territory, including the Spratly Islands. … In December 1946, the Chinese government at that time designated senior officials to proceed to the Spratly Islands to take them over. On the island, an acceptance ceremony was conducted, and they also erected a tablet to commemorate this and dispatched troops to defend it."

Li Anmin asserts that after the establishment of the People's Republic of China in 1949, the Chinese government continued to treat "the islands in the South China Sea as an integral part of China's territory" by describing them in the 1958 Declaration by the Government of the People's Republic of China on China's Territorial Sea and claiming a territorial sea around them. In Li Anmin's view, "For a fairly long time [until 1975] after the war, the so-called South China Sea problem really did not exist. Nor did any country in the South China Sea region put forth any objections to the sovereignty exercised by China over the Spratly Islands and the waters near them."

Li Jinming, a professor at the Center for Southeast Asia Studies at Xiamen University, has also written about the events of the 20th century in order to demonstrate that no real dispute existed about China's sovereignty over the Spratly and Paracel Islands until the 1970s.[12] Specifically, he describes an event in 1909 during the Qing Dynasty in which the then-governor of Guangdong and Guangxi ordered the eviction of a Japanese merchant was "was illegally occupying part of the Dongsha [Pratas Reef] Islands. After that, he realized the necessity of defending the other islands in the South China Sea and asked navy commander Li Zhun to patrol the waters off the Xisha [Paracel] Islands with three warships. … Later the Chinese drew charts and made a plan to exploit the islands." Li Jinming cites the existence of a 1938 Royal Navy book, "China Sea Pilot," that describes the islands of the South China Sea as Chinese territory.

The second 20th century event that is the focus of Li Jinming's article is the return of the South China Sea islands to Chinese control after World War II. Adding some details to Li Anmin's account, Li Jinming describes the arrival on November 24,1946 of two Chinese warships to "the main island of the Xisha [Paracel] Islands and the Chinese built a monument there." He further describes the arrival of two additional warships on December 12, 1946 to the "main island" of the Nansha (Spratly) Islands, Taiping Island (Itu Aba). Taiping Island is the

11 Li Anmin, "The South China Sea Problem Yesterday, Today and Tomorrow," Renmin Haijun, November 3, 2009, p. 4 [OSC Translation CPP20100120368017].

12 Li Jinming, "Nansha Indisputable Territory," *China Daily*, June 15, 2011.

largest in the Spratly Island group and remains occupied by the Republic of China today. Li Jinming argues that these acts of occupation of the "main island" in the Spratly and Paracel island groups were sufficient to demonstrate effective occupation and administration over the whole of each respective archipelago.

Two Chinese journalists, Xu Jingjing and Yu Lisha, wrote an article describing the competing claims in the South China Sea since the 1970s as a product of American geopolitics and the American quest for oil.[13] These writers discuss the geophysical surveys conducted by Kenneth Emery and other scientists in the East China Sea and Yellow Sea in 1968 under the auspices of the United Nations Economic Commission for Asia and the Far East (ECAFE) as pivotal to the way coastal states in the South China Sea saw their interests in the resources that might be under the seabed there. These authors comment that "after World War II, geologists represented by Emery in the West took an active interest in the geological structure and sediment distribution of the continental shelf of Southeast Asia's neighboring sea areas. ... In 1967, they published 'Stratigraphy and Petroleum Prospects of the Korea Strait and the East China Sea,' confirming that there may be an abundant reserve of oil in the continental shelves of China's Yellow Sea, East Sea and South Sea." They assert that American oil companies began cooperation with South Vietnam to explore and exploit the offshore energy resources in the 1970s, which was followed by American and international efforts to drill for gas and oil up through the current day.

Additionally, Xu and Yu describe the importance of the South China Sea to the United States in geostrategic and military terms. The strategic location of the South China Sea, they believe is far more important to the United States than even the energy resources that might be available under its waters. They observe, "The Malacca Strait is the main passage for the U.S. Navy to enter the Indian Ocean, and the South China Sea is an important hub linking two oceans and three continents." The importance to the United States of the South China Sea as a region of geographic importance in the Cold War became especially clear in the wake of the Korean and Vietnam Wars, they argue. Their perspective is that American energy and security interests have in part prompted Southeast Asian states to assert sovereignty and jurisdiction claims contrary to China's and that this dynamic continues to propel the disputes in the region.

Shi Xiaoqin, a research fellow in the Department of Warfare Theory and Strategy Studies at the PLA Academy of Military Science, shares this perspective. Shi takes it as a given that "Both from the perspective of historic succession and the perspective of international law, there is sufficient basis for backing up China's traditional maritime area rights, the territorial sovereignty of island-reefs, coastal rights, and continental shelf and exclusive economic zone rights."[14] Shi believes

---

13 Xu Jingjing and Yu Lisha, "International Perspectives on the South China Sea Since 1960s," *Sanlian Shenguo Zhoukan*, November 15, 2010, No. 46, pp. 48–56.

14 Shi Xiaoqin, "Understanding and Dealing with the South China Sea Issue in a Systematic Way," Heping Yu Fazhan, October 20, 2010, pp. 58–63 [OSC Translation

that part of the historical situation that should be considered in understanding China's South China Sea rights is the traditional regional system in which Chinese dominance and territorial rights were upset by western powers. "The South China Sea was a channel for maintaining the smooth communications within this system. … Tribute and trade brought along the development of the regional economy and connected the region into one entity through the links of the sea." Shi describes the loss of Chinese control over the islands and waters of the South China Sea as part of an ongoing problem of western regional influence and currently Shi believes that American geostrategic influence prevents China from exercising its traditional rights over the South China Sea.

In summary, based on the statements of Chinese government spokespersons, correspondence of the Chinese state, Chinese laws and the perspectives of Chinese scholars, what is the nature of China's historic claims? First, it is abundantly clear that China expresses its claim of sovereignty over the islands of the South China Sea in historical terms of discovery and views its history in an unbroken succession of administration and control, if not actual occupation, from perhaps as long ago as two thousand years until the middle of the 20th century. Scholars assert the existence of evidence of patrols, defense activities, scientific research, search and rescue, suppression of piracy, fishing, and administration of resource rights in support of this claim.[15] As late as the first half of the 20th century, other states with authoritative knowledge expressed in maps and other communications Chinese sovereignty over the island features of the South China Sea and this comported with the activities of the government of the Republic of China in 1946 and 1947 to reassert its sovereignty and jurisdiction in the region. Loss of occupation and effective administration and control occurred at some point after the 1949 revolution.

Second, China asserts both historic rights to sovereignty over the islands and historic rights to exercise some degree of jurisdiction over the waters within the U-shaped line. The specific nature of China's claim to authority over the water space remains somewhat ambiguous. Sometimes the term "sovereignty" is used in what seems to refer to broad swaths of the sea within the U-shaped line, as in the statement of the Ministry of Foreign Affairs cited above. At other times a less encompassing historical claim to rights that appear more akin to jurisdiction within the U-shaped line is asserted and is often expressed in terms of the activities of the Chinese state over the span of nearly 2000 years of history in these waters, rather than as a quantified bundle of state authority expressed in terms of the law such as jurisdiction or sovereignty.

CPP20110505671012].

15 It is beyond the scope of this chapter to challenge the quality or quantity of Chinese evidence of its historical rights and for the purpose of analysis this paper will accept as true the evidence as asserted. Obviously, an international tribunal would require sufficient proof of the historic claims asserted.

International Law and Sovereignty over Islands

What does international law say about China's claim to sovereignty over the islands? In the *Island of Palmas Case*, the Permanent Court of Arbitration was called upon by the United States and the Netherlands to determine which country possessed sovereignty over an island situated approximately fifty miles southeast of the Island of Mindanao.[16] At the time, the United States exercised sovereignty on behalf of the Philippines and the Netherlands exercised sovereignty over the Indonesian archipelago. The island of Palmas, or Miangas to the Indonesians, "is a single, isolated island, not one of several islands clustered together. It lies about half way between Cape San Augustin (Mindanao, Philippines Islands) and the most northerly island of the Nanusa (Nanoesa) group (Netherlands East Indies)."

The United States claimed sovereignty over the island based on the historic rights of Spain, which ceded authority over the Philippines to the Americans as a result of the 1898 Treaty of Paris that ended the Spanish-American War. Spain asserted its sovereignty based on the "first rights of discovery" by Spanish explorers in October 1526 and the island's appearance on various Spanish maps and in official Spanish documents during the Spanish colonial period from the 16th through 19th centuries. The court concluded that original title derived from discovery belonged to Spain, since it had first depicted the existence of the island before the appearance of the Dutch in Southeast Asia.

However, in the court's view, "a distinction must be made between the creation of rights and the existence of rights." Additionally, "discovery alone, without any subsequent act cannot … prove sovereignty. … An inchoate title of discovery must be completed within a reasonable period by the effective occupation of the region claimed to be discovered. … [A]n inchoate title could not prevail over the continuous and peaceful display of authority by another State; for such display may prevail even over a prior, definitive title put forward by another State." The court then concluded that it must consider "whether and to what extent the territorial sovereignty of Spain was manifested in or in regard to the island of Palmas." Looking at the evidence of infrequent Spanish contact with the island, the court observed that those Spanish contacts that were proven were largely naval activities presumably in relation to Spain's never fully successful attempts to subdue the Moros people on Mindanao. The Court concluded "the complete absence of evidence as to display of Spanish sovereignty over the Island of Palmas is not due to mere chance, but is to be explained by the absence of interest of Spain in the establishment or maintenance of her rule over a small island lying far off the coast of a distant and only incompletely subdued province."

The Netherlands, on the other hand, asserted its sovereignty based on a series of "conventions entered into with native princes … establishing the suzerainty of the Netherlands over the territories of these princes, including Palmas (or Miangas)."

16 *The Island of Palmas Case (or Miangas)* (United States of America v. the Netherlands), Award of Tribunal, Permanent Court of Arbitration, April 4, 1928.

These contracts between the Dutch government and the local Princes contained clauses regarding the Prince's power internal administration, his exclusion from direct relations with other foreign powers, the use of Dutch currency, and the right of the Dutch to exercise jurisdiction over foreigners among other provisions. Although the court noted that "the acts of indirect or direct display of Netherlands sovereignty at Palmas ... are not numerous, and there are continuous gaps in the evidence of continuous display," the court had before it evidence of Dutch administration over the island in accordance with the provisions of the various agreements including the presence of the Dutch flag flying on the island, the existence of tax records, the existence of occasional Dutch patrols, and the presence of Dutch coats of arms on administrative documents. The court determined that when a contested claim of sovereignty over territory exists,

> what is essential in such a case is the continuous and peaceful display of actual power in the contested region.
>
> ...
>
> [I]t is not necessary that the display of sovereignty should go back to a very far distant period. It may suffice that such display existed in 1898 [at the time of the Treaty of Paris], and had already existed as continuous and peaceful before that date long enough to enable any Power who might have considered herself as possessing sovereignty over the island, or having a claim to sovereignty, to have, according to local conditions, a reasonable possibility for ascertaining the existence of a state of things contrary to her real or alleged rights.

The court concluded that since the Netherlands exercised "open and public ... continuous and peaceful display of State authority" over the island "probably back before the year 1700," the Netherlands was the true sovereign over the Island of Palmas. Two additional points of law from this case are worth observing. First, the court looked with skepticism at evidence of sovereignty based on historical maps, because of their general lack of geographical accuracy and the inherent bias of their creators. Second, the court rejected the idea that title to offshore islands can arise out of simple contiguity of the islands to a larger piece of sovereign territory. It emphasized that actual display of authority over the territory is essential to claim sovereignty.

Not long after the Island of Palmas case, the King if Italy acted as an international arbiter in a dispute decided in 1933 between France and Mexico concerning sovereignty over a small uninhabited (and, for practical purposes, uninhabitable) reef in the Pacific Ocean. The Clipperton Island Case involved competing claims to a "low coral lagoon reef, less than three miles in diameter ... some 670 miles southwest of Mexico."[17] Mexico claimed the island by succession

17 Editorial Comment: The Clipperton Island Case, *American Journal of International Law*, Vol. 27, No. 1 (January 1933), pp. 130–33. The full case can be found at American Journal of International Law, Vol. 26 (1932), p. 390.

from the Kingdom of Spain, though there was no record of Mexican activity on the island until "comparatively recent times." A French naval officer formally proclaimed sovereignty over the island in 1858 and subsequently traveled to the kingdom of Hawaii where the proclamation of sovereignty was published in a Hawaiian journal. In 1897, French inspectors found three Americans on the island gathering guano and made a formal complaint to the U.S. government. The King awarded the island to France, finding no proof either of prior Spanish discovery or of an "effective occupation" by Mexico. He reasoned,

> [T]he actual, and not the nominal, taking of possession is a necessary condition of occupation. This taking of possession consists in the act, or series of acts, by which the occupying state reduces to its possession the territory in question and takes steps to exercise exclusive authority there. ... [I]f a territory, by virtue of the fact that it was completely uninhabited, is, from the first moment when the occupying state makes its appearance there, at the absolute and undisputed disposition of that state, from that moment the taking of possession must be considered accomplished, and the occupation is thereby completed.

Thus, the French notice of occupation was sufficient to perfect its claim of sovereignty over the island and the fact that France did not exercise its sovereignty there "in a positive manner," that is, by physically occupying the coral reef, did not cause it to forfeit its authority. Although discovery gives only inchoate title which must subsequently be perfected by "use and settlement," where islands are incapable of traditional settlement, then the occupation which the law requires is "such an occupation as is appropriate and possible under the circumstances."

Another dispute over sovereignty decided in 1933 was heard by the Permanent Court of International Justice. Similarly to the Clipperton Island Case, the *Case Concerning the Legal Status of Eastern Greenland* dealt with a state's historic claims to "a vast area remaining unoccupied even in the 20th century, [and over which] something other and less than actual administration and control" was evidenced.[18] Greenland was discovered by Europeans in about 900 AD by a Norwegian, Eric the Red, and around 100 years later two colonies were formed toward the southern end of the western coast. These two colonies fell under the sovereignty of the King of Norway, but by 1500 the colonies disappeared in the face of attacks by indigenous tribes and neglect from the Norwegian crown. For more than two centuries afterwards, no colonies existed in Greenland and "knowledge of it diminished," but even so "the tradition of the King's rights lived on and in the early part of the [17th] century a revival of interest in Greenland on the part of both the king and his people took place." Even though diminished, contact

18 *Editorial Comment: The Case Concerning the Legal Status of Eastern Greenland*, American Journal of International Law, Vol. 27, No. 4 (Oct. 1933), pp. 732–8. The full case can be found at *Legal Status of Eastern Greenland (Denmark v. Norway)*, Publications, Permanent Court of International Justice, Series A/B, No. 53, (1933), p. 23.

had not been lost entirely, since the waters surrounding Greenland were regularly visited by Norwegian whalers and maps from this period also demonstrated knowledge of the coast of Greenland. By the 18th century, regular Norwegian commercial activities had resumed in Greenland, new colonies were established, and administrative activities were once again evident.

Historically, the Kingdoms of Norway and Denmark were united under a single crown until 1814, when the Kingdom of Norway was ceded to Sweden by the Treaty of Kiel. The Treaty excepted cession of Greenland, the Faroe Islands and Iceland, which were retained by Denmark. In 1905, Norway resumed its independent status, and a dispute arose between it and Denmark as to how much of Greenland Denmark could claim based on its two small, erstwhile colonies. The court was called upon to decide whether Denmark could claim the whole of Greenland from the two small colonies founded in the southwest and whether Denmark's claim had been extinguished during the period of approximately two centuries of near inactivity such that Norway could claim sovereignty over at least the eastern portion of the island.

From the various administrative activities undertaken by Denmark, the court concluded that "Denmark satisfied the two requisites for the creation of a right of sovereignty to be derived from continued display of authority … namely, 'the intention and will to act as sovereign, and some actual exercise or display of such authority." The court was persuaded that even during the two centuries of inactivity sovereignty had not been extinguished since "there was nothing to show any definite renunciation or voluntary abandonment on the part of the Kings of Norway or Denmark." Instead, "the requisite display of authority was seen in a 'manifestation of state activity' that did not embrace the exercise of administrative control, but expressed itself in large part through bare assertions of state interest in an unoccupied area." The court was persuaded that the intention had always been to exercise the King's authority over the whole of the territory, despite originally having only two small colonial outposts, since in the 10th century "the modern notions as to territorial sovereignty had not come into being [and] it is unlikely that either the chiefs of the settlers in these colonies drew any sharp distinction between territory which was and territory which was not subject to them." Additionally, the king had authorized the imposition of fines upon his subjects for murders "even as far to the North as under the Pole Star."

In analyzing the impact of the case, American commentators noted "It shows not only how very small a part, if any, actual control or possession played in the creation of what was deemed to be an ancient and basic right of sovereignty, but also how small an amount of control, measured geographically or otherwise, sufficed, under the circumstances, to yield to the modern inheritor and existing possessor of that right of sovereignty, a vast and unoccupied and unclaimed island."

Finally, there is a fourth relevant case decided in 1953 and arising from a dispute between Britain and France over the Minquiers and Ecrehos Islands, two small groups of islets and rocks off the northern coast of Normandy and which Britain had treated as part of its Channel Islands possessions appurtenant to the Island of

Jersey.[19] The dispute was largely a factual one in that both "contend[ed] that they have respectively an ancient or original title to the Ecrehos and the Minquiers, and that their title has always been maintained and was never lost." The parties generally agreed on the law, namely that sovereignty should be determined on the basis of as the United Kingdom's brief stated, the "effective possession evidenced by acts which manifest a continuous display of sovereignty," and as France's brief stated, the "effective exercise of ... sovereignty to the extent that the character of these islets and rocks lent itself to such an exercise."

After reviewing historical evidence submitted by the disputants from as distant a period as the Norman conquest of England in 1066, the Court concluded "What is of decisive importance ... is not indirect presumptions deduced from events in the Middle Ages, but the evidence which relates directly to the possession of the Ecrehos and Minquiers groups." The court then focused its attention on the relevant activities of each state in the period leading up to 1886, "when France for the first time claimed sovereignty" over the island groups and the public dispute presumably arose. The court appeared to give events subsequent to that time less weight since it viewed them as measures taken merely to improve the concerned party's position in the looming litigation.

Concerning Minquiers, the Court found that the British authorities on Jersey "have in several ways exercised ordinary local administration ... during a long period of time." Because the United Kingdom had "exercised State functions in respect of this group," it was the sovereign over them. Similarly,

> [T]he Ecrehos group in the beginning of the thirteenth century was considered and treated as an integral part of the fief of the Channel islands which were held by the English King, and that the group continued to be under the dominion of that King. ... The Court further [found] that British authorities during the greater part of the nineteenth century and in the twentieth century ... exercised State functions in respect of the group.

Accordingly, because the United Kingdom had provided the better evidence of its administrative activities and other exercise of state functions over each of the island groups up to the time a dispute arose, and afterward, it was awarded sovereignty in both cases.

In summary, the *Island of Palmas Case* demonstrates that international law regarding sovereignty over territory requires more than mere discovery, which provides only an inchoate title. It requires effective occupation within a reasonable period as manifested through acts of state authority over the territory amounting to the continuous and peaceful display of actual power in the contested region.

---

19 *The Minquiers and Ecrehos Case (France/United Kingdom)*, International Court of Justice, Judgment of November 17, 1953, I.C.J. Reports, 1953, p. 47.

Additionally, it is not necessary that the displays of sovereignty go back to a distant period, but must have been evident before the period in which the dispute arose for a period of time long enough to put other potential claimants on notice.

Where territory is remote and less susceptible or well suited to actual physical occupation, as in the *Clipperton Island Case*, actual possession must still be accomplished by more than merely nominal assertions of authority, but may be achieved by putting the territory under the absolute and undisputed disposition of the claimant state, that is, by the exercise of exclusive power over the territory. However, where ancient claims to inhospitable territory remain inchoate or even dwindle to mere historical memory, the *Eastern Greenland Case* provides that a continuing will to act as sovereign without any definite renunciation or voluntary abandonment of the right is sufficient to assert a continuing claim. Additionally, some reasonable manifestation of state authority in the modern period is sufficient to ensure a continuing claim to sovereignty, especially in light of similar historical activity, taking into account ancient activities that expressed the rights of sovereigns in non-territorial ways.

Observed in the light of international law of sovereignty to islands, the Chinese assertion of sovereignty over each of the South China Sea island groups appears credibly claimed, though many questions remain. For instance, what evidence of similar historical rights do the other claimants raise? Would the historical evidence advanced by each side stand up to unbiased scrutiny? How should China's period of relative inactivity between 1949 and the mid-1970s be viewed? Should it be treated as an abandonment of sovereignty rights such that other claimants could reasonably treat the unoccupied and remote islands as *terra nullius*, as the Dutch were entitled to do with the Island of Palmas after Spain's failure to complete its inchoate authority based on discovery? Or should the islands be treated similarly to Eastern Greenland, in which even two centuries of inactivity by the sovereign did not extinguish its claim where Norway never expressed an intention to abandon the claim, maintained historical memory of its connection to the island of Greenland, and faced limited actual challenge to its authority there?

Law Concerning Historic Rights to State Authority over Water Space

The second assertion of Chinese historic rights in the South China Sea revolves around its authority—sovereign, jurisdictional, or otherwise—to exercise state functions over the waters of the South China Sea within the U-shaped line.

Norwegian Fisheries Case

Perhaps the most authoritative statement of international law on this point was issued in 1951 by the International Court of Justice in the *Fisheries Case*, in which the United Kingdom challenged Norway's claim to sovereignty over waters along Norway's craggy coast line beyond the traditional three-mile territorial sea limit at the time.[20] The Court considered three relevant factors: 1) the close geographical dependence of the territorial sea upon the land domain—the relevant portions of the Norwegian coastline are deeply indented with complex geographic features and an estimated 120,000 minor islands, islets, rocks and shoals; 2) sufficiently close links between the land formations and the sea space to make the region susceptible to a fully-sovereign regime of governance; and 3) unique economic interests belonging to the coastal state based on clear evidence of long usage. Based on its assessment of these factors, the court approved Norway's extension of sovereignty over the sea areas and the features contained within them based on its historic claims.

The United Nations International Law Commission has written on the difficult topic of historic waters that "the concept ... has its root in the historic fact that States through the ages claimed and maintained sovereignty over maritime areas which they considered vital to them without paying much attention to divergent and changing opinions about what general international law might prescribe."[21]

In concluding its analysis, the Commission accepted the existence of historic waters, but observed that

> [A]t least three factors have to be taken into consideration in determining whether a state has acquired a historic title to a maritime area. These factors are: (1) the exercise of authority over the area by the State claiming the historic right; (2) the continuity of this exercise of authority; [and] (3) the attitude of foreign states. First, the State must exercise authority over the area in question in order to acquire a historic title to it. Secondly, such exercise of authority must have continued for a considerable time; indeed it must have developed into a usage. More controversial is the third factor, the position which the foreign States may have taken towards this exercise of authority. Some writers assert that the acquiescence of other States is required for the emergence of historic title; others think that absence of opposition by these States is sufficient.

The Commission also recognized that some authorities suggest the existence of a fourth factor, though it expressed its disfavor in regard to it.

> It has been suggested that attention should also be given to the question whether the claim [to historic rights over the waters in question] can be justified on the basis of economic necessity, national security, vital interest or a similar ground.
>
> ...
>
> The significance of this line of thought is not so much that usage may have to be fortified by other reasons such as geographical configuration or vital interest

20 *Fisheries Case* (United Kingdom v. Norway) Judgment of December 18, 1951, International Court of Justice Reports 1951, p. 116.

21 *Juridical Regime of Historic Waters Including Historic Bays—Study Prepared by the Secretariat*, Document A/CN.4/143, *Yearbook of International Law*, 1962, vol. II, pp. 1–26.

> in order to form a firm basis for a claim to 'historic bays.' It is rather that these other 'particular circumstances' may justify the claim without the necessity of establishing also 'immemorial usage.'

The Commission looked with disfavor on this perspective because the application of the concept of vital interests to one category of waters, for instance to historic bays, without similar application to other categories would certainly be problematic. Additionally, they concluded, the concept of historic waters is just that—about history, not about a state's vital interests. Authorizing coastal states to claim 'vital waters' would destroy the usefulness of any provision of any convention in which limits are set for coastal state authority over maritime space. Accordingly, the Commission concluded that three factors are relevant: the exercise of authority, continuously for an extended period, with the acceptance, or at least acquiescence, of other states.

The requirements established in the Fisheries Case and by the International law Commission for an expansion of coastal state authority over water space will be difficult for China to demonstrate. In particular, there is no close geographical dependence between the sea and the land among any of the island groups in the South China Sea. Indeed, the land features are so insignificant that they have long been seen more as navigational hazards than as productive territory. Additionally, the islets themselves are relatively widely dispersed in comparison with the features along the Norwegian coastline. As such, the lack of sustainable land available to support an indigenous population and the sporadic presence of fishermen and traders strongly suggests that the water space is not susceptible to a fully sovereign regime of governance, as was the case in the waters along the Norwegian coastline.

Additionally, more general historic rights—such as exclusive jurisdiction over fishing, hydrocarbon development, and environmental protection of the waters within the U-shaped line—will also be difficult for China to prove. Although China has asserted such authorities, they have hardly been exclusive, longstanding and continuous, or accepted or even acquiesced in by other states with claims or interests in these waters. Accordingly, China's claim of historic waters would appear to have weak support on these bases.

Concerning the question of unique economic interests and vital security needs, China has had well-documented contacts with the islands of the South China Sea for many centuries by fishermen, traders and the occasional government official. Additionally, the current government and the previous nationalist government both recognized the need for security to be achieved in these waters. However, these bases are disfavored in international law as providing legal protection for coastal state claims or special jurisdictional rights to the coastal state. A stronger basis for the exercise of jurisdiction over the waters in the South China Sea would be based on the assertion of an exclusive economic zone and continental shelf rights from those South China Sea islands eligible to claim these zones, as the government of the People's Republic of China seems to have understood based on its second submission to the Commission on the Limits of the Continental Shelf.[22]

Conclusions

The Chinese claims to sovereignty over the islands of the South China Sea have much strength in light of the relevant law, although questions of law and fact still remain to be clarified, especially in light of the evidence that could be submitted by other claimants. Although the Chinese position in the Paracels is strengthened by the fact that China openly occupies, administers and controls these islands, China's position in the Spratly island group is much weaker. A particular weakness of the Chinese position in the Spratlys is that the substantial majority of islands are occupied, administered and controlled by other countries that dispute Chinese sovereignty. Another weakness is the application of history to a region in which several coastal states have their own version of history and no one state seems to have actually exercised dominant authority to the exclusion of all others. In such a case, whose history dominates? Additionally, were the islands abandoned? Other claimants did not occupy them by force, but took them over at a time when China was unable to prevent them from doing so. Does legal abandonment require an intention to do so? Or is it sufficient to constitute abandonment that the initial sovereign was unable to maintain effective occupation and control over the territory? International tribunals have never reached a decision about the disposition of sovereignty where the islands are remote, difficult to occupy, have been the basis of an ancient claim to sovereignty—albeit a loose interpretation of that concept in the modern sense, are subject to overlapping historical claims, and only relatively recently occupied and administered by the forces of other claimants. Nonetheless, China has at least produced *prima facie* evidence of its rights to sovereignty for other states to rebut if they can.

The strength of Chinese historic claims to sovereignty or jurisdiction over waters within the U-shaped line is on much weaker footing. That China has not in any sense dominated these waters since at least the early 16th century, if it ever did, is manifest from the many European, American and Japanese acts of regional conquest and colonization from the early 1500s until the mid-twentieth century. The current geostrategic dynamic between China and the United States analyzed so well by Chinese authors simply reflects continuity to this trend. That China sees these waters as vital to its economic and security interests is understandable, but not legally protected. Instead, these interests must be articulated through the zones authorized by the various provisions of the United Nations Convention on the Law of the Sea.

22 This chapter makes no observations as to which, if any, of the South China Sea islands would be entitled to an exclusive economic zone and extended continental shelf based on the provisions of UNCLOS Article 121.

Chapter 5

Possibility of US Accession to the LOS Convention and its Potential Impact on State Practices and Maritime Claims in the South China Sea

Yann-huei Song

Introduction

The United Nations Convention on the Law of the Sea (hereinafter LOS Convention),[1] widely considered a "Constitution for the Oceans,"[2] was adopted on April 30, 1982 and opened for signature on December 10 of the same year. The Convention, consisting of 17 parts, nine annexes and 320 articles, entered into force on November 16, 1994. Designed to regulate the use and utilization of 70 percent of the earth's surface, this Convention has been praised as the most comprehensive political and legislative work ever undertaken by the United Nations. As of September 18, 2013, there were 166 parties to the LOS Convention,[3] but the United State—despite being a leading maritime power and possessing the largest exclusive economic zone (EEZ) and one of the longest continental shelves—has not ratified the treaty.

All of the countries involved in sovereignty and maritime disputes in the Spratly Islands of the South China Sea are parties to the LOS Convention except the Republic of China (hereinafter Taiwan).[4] All of the members of the Association of Southeast Asian Nations (ASEAN) have ratified the treaty except Cambodia.

---

1 United Nations Convention on the Law of the Sea, December 10, 1982, 1833 UNTS 397. For the text of the convention with annexed and the agreement to implement Part XI of the convention, visit http://www.un.org/Depts/los/convention_agreements/texts/unclos/unclos_e.pdf.

2 Remarks by Tommy T.B. Koh of Singapore, President of the United Nations Conference on the Law of the Sea on December 6 and 11, 1982 at the final session of the Conference at Montego Bay, Jamaica, available at: http://www.un.org/Depts/los/convention_agreements/convention_overview_ convention.htm (a historical perspective).

3 For table recapitulating the status of the Convention and of the related Agreements, as at September 18, 2013, visit http://www.un.org/Depts/los/reference_files/status2010.pdf.

4 They are the People's Republic of China (hereinafter China), the Republic of China (Taiwan), the Philippines, Vietnam, Malaysia and Brunei.

Thailand became a party to the LOS Convention in May 2011 and is the 162nd member of the treaty.

While the United States is not a party to the LOS Convention, its government has taken actions over the past 20 years to challenge "excessive maritime claims" made by coastal states in different parts of the world that are considered inconsistent with this treaty.[5] Examples of these excessive claims include unrecognized historic waters claims, improperly drawn baselines for measuring maritime claims, archipelagic claims inconsistent with Part IV, EEZ claims inconsistent with Part V, continental-shelf claims inconsistent with Part VI of the LOS Convention, and other claims to restrict navigation and overflight rights as reflected in the LOS Convention.[6]

By relying on naval operations and diplomatic protests, the United States has challenged the "excessive maritime claims" made by countries bordering the South China Sea, which include Cambodia, China, Indonesia, Malaysia, the Philippines, Taiwan, Thailand and Vietnam. The government of the United States does not recognize, in particular, the claims made by these countries that affect freedom of navigation and overflight in their EEZs.[7] However, the actions taken by the United States in support of its maritime rights or freedom can be and have been challenged and considered inconsistent with the terms of the LOS Convention by some South China Sea-bordering countries, in particular China. Examples include the EP-3 and *Impeccable* Incidents that occurred in the Chinese EEZ surrounding Hainan Island in the northern part of the South China Sea in April 2001 and March 2009 respectively. In these two incidents, China protested the United States' action, contending that the US ship and aircraft were operating illegally in its EEZ, in violation of international and Chinese laws. But the United States insisted and asserted repeatedly that its vessel and aircraft were operating lawfully in the Chinese EEZ and that it had the right to conduct survey activities in the area without prior notice or Chinese consent.[8]

---

5 "Excessive maritime claims" are those claims made by coastal states to sovereignty, sovereign rights, or jurisdiction over ocean areas that are inconsistent with the terms of the LOS Convention. See United States Department of State Bureau of Oceans and International Environmental and Scientific Affairs, *Limits in the Seas*, No. 112, United States Responses to Excessive National Maritime Claims, March 9, 1992, p. 7, available at: http://www.state.gov/documents/organization/58381.pdf.

6 Ibid., pp. 7–8.

7 See *Maritime Claims Reference Manual*, DoD 2005.1-M, reissued by the Department of Defense, Under Secretary of Defense for Policy on June 23, 2005, available at: http://www.jag.navy.mil/organization/documents/mcrm/MCRM.pdf.

8 For the incidents, see Margaret K. Lewis, "An Analysis of State Responsibility for the Chinese–American Airplane Collision Incident," 77 NYUL Rev. 1404 (2002), W. Allan Edmiston, III, "Showdown in the South China Sea: An International Incident Analysis of the So-called Spy-Plane Crisis," 16 Emory Int'l L. Rev. 639 (2002), and Jonathan G. Odom, "The True 'Lies' of the Impeccable Incident: What Really Happened, Who Disregarded

In May 1995, in response to rising tension between China and the Philippines in the South China Sea over the ownership of Mischief Reef, the US government issued a comprehensive policy statement on the Spratlys and the South China Sea, which stated, in part, that the United States "view[s] with serious concern any maritime claim, or restriction on maritime activity, in the South China Sea that was not consistent with international law, including the 1982 United Nations Convention on the Law of the Sea."[9] Fifteen years later, in July 2010, when attending the 17th ASEAN Regional Forum, US Secretary of State Hillary Clinton delivered a speech in Hanoi, Vietnam, where she urged claimants in the South China Sea to pursue their territorial claims and accompanying rights to maritime space in accordance with the LOS Convention.[10] This call was reiterated in her remarks made in Bali, Indonesia when attending the 18th ASEAN Regional Forum in July 2011.[11] The Secretary also called on all parties "to clarify their claims in the South China Sea in terms consistent with customary international law, including as reflected in the Law of the Sea Convention."[12] In addition, she stated that consistent with international law, claims made by the parties concerned to maritime space in the South China Sea "should be derived solely from legitimate claims to land features."[13]

The United States' call on all parties concerned in the South China Sea to handle their territorial and maritime disputes in accordance with the LOS Convention has been weakened by its own failure to become a party to the treaty. The credibility of the US as the champion of the international rule of law has also been questioned. Horace B. Robertson, Jr., Rear Admiral, U.S. Navy (Ret.), in his letter to *the Wall Street Journal* in July 2011, pointed out that "[c]ustomary international law, though equally valid with treaty law, is unfortunately imprecise and malleable. Treaty law, on the other hand, provides a solid written and precise basis for assertion of rights."[14] If the United States were a party to the LOS Convention, it would not

International Law, and Why Every Nations (Outside of China) Should Be Concerned," 18 Mich. St. J. Int'l 411 (2010).

9 Spratlys and the South China Sea, Statement by Christine Shelly, Acting Spokesman, May 10, 1995. The statement can be found in US Interest in Southeast Asia, Hearing before the Subcommittee on International Economic Policy and Trade and Asia and the Pacific of the Committee on International Relations, House of Representatives, 104th Congress, 2nd Session, May 30 and June 19, 1996 (Washington, DC: GPO, 1997), p. 157.

10 For Secretary Clinton's remarks made on July 23, 2010, visit the website of the U.S. Department of State at http://www.state.gov/secretary/rm/2010/07/145095.htm.

11 For the remarks made on July 22, 2011, visit the website of the U.S. Department of State at http://www.state.gov/secretary/2011/07/168989.htm.

12 Ibid.

13 Ibid.

14 Horace B. Robertson, Jr., "Sea Treaty Ratification Would Help," *The Wall Street Journal*, July 9, 2011, available at: http://online.wsj.com/article/SB1000142405270230480 3104576428004201354160.html.

have to base its argument on customary international law to challenge China's claim to a large area in the South China Sea.[15]

The dispute over freedom of navigation for U.S. Navy ships off China's coast, according to John Norton Moore, a professor at the University of Virginia Law School, is largely a matter of different interpretations of the LOS Convention, but it is more difficult for the United States to protect its interests given that it is not yet a party to the treaty.[16] Professor S. Jayakumar, former Foreign Minister and Senior Minister of Singapore, also stated that while the United States is a major maritime power "whose engagement with, and presence in, the region is crucial for maintaining stability in the South China Sea,"[17] it is not yet a party to the LOS Convention. He hopes that the current U.S. Senate will give its advice and consent, because accession to the treaty will greatly enhance the role and credibility of the United States in the South China Sea.[18] Caitlyn Antrim and George Galdorisi expressed their view that by becoming a party to the LOS Convention, the United States could not only strengthen its leadership at sea but also serve the interests of all parties in the South China Sea.[19]

Noting that the United States is not a party to the LOS Convention, Secretary Clinton announced at the end of her remarks made in Hanoi when attending the 17th ASEAN Regional Forum that one of the US diplomatic priorities in the year 2011 was to secure the convention's ratification in the Senate.[20] This announcement was followed by the Secretary's comments made at the Commonwealth Club in San Francisco in October 2010, where she stressed that the LOS Convention was one of the most important treaties for the United States to ratify. The accession to the treaty "is critical to our credibility in working with nations in Southeast Asia over questions regarding activities in the South China Sea."[21]

In July 2011, it was reported that the Obama administration and Senator John F. Kerry (D-MA), Chairman of the Senate Foreign Relations Committee (SFRC), are pushing for Senate ratification of the LOS Convention. Interagency meetings on the administration's ratification plans were held, and teams of officials briefed

15 Ibid.

16 "Obama Administration to Push Law of the Sea Treaty in Senate This Year: Prospects look dim for ratification, *Inside the Navy*, February 4, 2011.

17 A copy of Professor Jayakumar's Keynote Address given at the Conference on Joint Development and the South China Sea, organized by the Centre for International Law, National University of Singapore and held in Singapore on June 16–17, 2011, is available at: http://cil.nus.edu.sg/wp/wp-content/uploads/2011/06/CIL_Keynote_Address_16_Jun_11_7.45am-pdf.pdf.

18 Ibid.

19 Caitlyn L. Antrim and Captain George Galdorisi, U.S. Navy (Retired), "Creeping Jurisdiction Must Stop," *Proceedings*, US Naval Institute, April 2011, p. 71.

20 Secretary Clinton's remarks, *supra* note 10.

21 Remarks on Innovation and American Leadership to the Commonwealth Club, Hillary Rodham Clinton, Secretary of State, San Francisco Marriott Marquis, San Francisco, CA, October 15, 2010, http://www.state.gov/secretary/rm/2010/10/149542.htm.

some senators on the drive to approve the treaty.[22] Is it possible for the Senate to consider US accession to the treaty in the 112th Congress (2011–12)? Would the United States become a party to the LOS Convention by the end of President Obama's first term? If the United States indeed becomes a party to the LOS Convention in the years to come, how would the state practices, maritime claims and sovereignty and maritime disputes in the South China Sea be affected? These are important questions that are related to the management of potential conflicts in the South China Sea and deserve careful study.

The purposes of this chapter are twofold. First, it examines the recent development in US efforts to ratify the LOS Convention and assesses the possibility of joining the treaty by the United States during the 112th Congress. Second, it studies the potential impact of US accession to the LOS Convention on state practices and maritime claims in the South China Sea. Part I reviews previous efforts made by the government of the United States to ratify the LOS convention. Part II analyzes the Obama administration's support and attempt to become a party to the treaty. Part III explores the possibility of US accession to the LOS Convention during the 112th Congress. Part IV discusses US interests in the South China Sea and is followed by a brief study of state practices and maritime claims in the South China Sea in Part V. Part VI examines US responses to "excessive maritime claims" made by some countries that border the South China Sea. Part VII comments on the potential impact of US accession to the LOS Convention on state practices and maritime claims in the South China Sea.

I. Previous US Efforts to Ratify the LOS Convention

The LOS Convention has been in force for 18 years and more than 160 nations are party to it. Amazingly, however, as the world's leading maritime and naval power, the United States is not yet a party to this treaty, despite the treaty having received strong support not only from the past Clinton and Bush administrations and the current Obama administration, but also a diverse coalition of US interest groups representing national security, industrial and environmental concerns. One commentator stated that "[n]o other treaty can boast that it is supported by both the American Petroleum Institute and the World Wildlife Fund."[23]

On July 29, 1994, after the adoption of the Part XI Agreement[24] that substantially revised the LOS Convention's original provisions on deep seabed mining, President

22 Bill Gertz, "Sea Law Treaty Push," *The Washington Times*, July 28, 2011, p. A7.

23 Karl Horberg, "Treaty Ratification Meeting," The Connect US Fund, June 15, 2011, available at: http://www.connectusfund.org/blogs/treaty-ratification-meeting.

24 From 1990 to 1994 the United Nations coordinated efforts to revise Part XI of the LOS Convention. On July 28, 1994, the efforts came to fruition in the form of the Implementation Agreement. Forty-one states, including the United States, signed the Agreement on July 29, 1994. The Agreement entered into force on July 29, 1996. As of

Bill Clinton signed the Agreement. On October 7, 1994, the US Senate received the Part XI Agreement and the LOS Convention from President Clinton for its advice and consent, which were then referred to the SFRC for consideration.[25] Between 1994 and 2002, Senator Jesse Helms (R-NC), who chaired the SFRC and opposed almost anything associated with the United Nations, refused all requests to hold hearings on the LOS Convention.

In October 2003, mainly because Senator Helms had retired and Senator Richard Lugar, a strong supporter of the LOS Convention, had become the chairman of SFRC, hearings were held on the Convention and the Agreement.[26] In February 2004, the SFRC considered the two treaties and voted unanimously (19–0) to support US ratification of the two treaties and reported them to the full Senate for its advice and consent. Despite the LOS Convention having been thoroughly reviewed in the Senate hearings and supported by both the Bush administration and a broad coalition of ocean interests, it was held up by a handful of right-wing Republican senators[27] backed by a coalition of national groups who considered the LOS Convention another step toward global government. President Bush himself was worried about alienating his core right-wing constituency, particularly at a time when some members of that group were complaining that his resort to the United Nations for help in Iraq indicated that he had abandoned his unilateralist stance.[28] The then Senate Majority Leader Bill Frist (R-TN) decided not to consider the Convention and the Agreement, and as a result, under the operational rules of the Senate, the two treaties were returned to the SFRC at the end of the 108th Congress. During the 109th Congress, no actions were taken by the SFRC.[29]

July 21, 2011, 141 states were parties to the Agreement. The Agreement Relating to the Implementation of Part XI on the United Nations Convention on the Law of the Sea, with Annex, adopted at New York on July 28, 1994 (the Part XI Agreement) can be found on the UN website at http://www.un.org/Depts/los/convention_agreements/convention_overview_part_xi.htm.

25 See Treaty Doc. 103–39: United Nations Convention on the Law of the Sea and Senate Executive Report 108–10: United Nations Convention on the Law of the Sea, available at: http://foreign.senate.gov/treaties/details/?id=ad607983-5056-a032-52e8-f598c3f7cfca.

26 For floor and committee actions on the United Nations Convention on the Law of the Sea: 103–39, visit the website of the US Senate Committee on Foreign Relations at http://foreign.senate.gov/treaties/details/?id=ad607983-5056-a032-52e8-f598c3f7cfca.

27 Such as Senators James Inhofe (R-OK), Judd Gregg (R-NH), John Kyl (R-AZ) and Jeff Sessions (R-AL).

28 Jim Lobe, "Right-Wing Republicans Sinking Law of the Sea, Again," Inter Press Service, August 27, 2004, available at: http://www.commondreams.org/headlines04/0603-07.htm.

29 In 2006, it was stated in a report by the International SeaKeeper Society that as of the fall of 2005, some 95 of 100 US senators were prepared to vote for the LOS Convention. But a lack of Senate and White House leadership in the face of concerns expressed by a handful of conservatives prevented action on the treaty. See 11 Critical Ocean Issues: with

On February 7, 2007, the Bush administration's treaty priority list for the 100th Congress was attached to a letter sent by the U.S. Department of State to Senator Joseph R. Biden, SFRC chairman, which included the LOS Convention and the Part XI Agreement in the category of treaties currently on the Committee's calendar on which the administration supported Senate action.[30] In May 2007, President Bush publicly urged the Senate to approve the LOS Convention during the 110th Congress. He said that joining the Convention "will serve the national security interests of the United States, including the maritime mobility of [US] armed forces worldwide. It will secure US sovereign rights over extensive marine areas, including the valuable natural resources they contain. Accession [to the Convention] will promote US interests in the environmental health of the oceans. And it will give the United States a seat at the table when the rights that are vital to [US] interests are debated and interpreted."[31] During the 110th Congress, two hearings on the LOS Convention and the Part XI Agreement were held by the SFRC in September and October 2007, respectively. On October 31, 2007, the Committee considered the two treaties, and ordered them favorably reported by a roll call vote of 17–4.[32]

President Bush's support for the Convention, unfortunately, disappeared in October 2008 mainly because Senator John McCain (R-AZ) opposed the LOS Convention during his campaign for the Republican nomination.[33] In November 2008, John B. Bellinger, former legal advisor to the U.S. Department of State, gave his explanation for the failure of Senate's consideration of the LOS Convention. He said: "Opponents were ultimately successful in keeping it from reaching the Senate floor by making it clear that a debate on US accession would trigger every possible procedural maneuver and thereby take up maximum floor time. The Senate Majority Leader decided not to send the treaty forward under these

---

Action Items for Concerned Citizens, 2006, p. 9, available at: http://www.adxhosting.com/seakeepers/oceans11report.pdf.

30 For the letter and the treaty priority list, visit the website of the U.S. Department of State at http://www.state.gov/documents/organization/116355.pdf.

31 President Bush's Statement on Advancing US Interests in the World's Oceans, May 15, 2007, available at: http://www.whitehouse.gov/news/releases/2007/05/20070515-2.html.

32 See Senate Exec. Report 110-09: Convention on the Law of the Sea, December 19, 2007, available at: http://foreign.senate.gov/treaties/details/?id=ad607983-5056-a032-52e8-f598c3f7cfca.

33 Senator McCain supported the LOS Convention for ten years, but changed position as his presidential campaign began late in 2007. In response to a survey from the Iowa Christian Alliance, McCain said he opposed the treaty. See Keith Porter, "Palin Supports Law of the Sea Treaty," About.Com US Foreign Policy, October 15, 2008, available at: http://usforeignpolicy.about.com/b/2008/10/15/palin-supports-law-of-the-sea-treaty.htm. See also Caitlyn Antrim, "UNCLOS needs bipartisan push," IntLawGrrls: voices on international law, policy, practice, December 10, 2010, available at: http://intlawgrrls.blogspot.com/2010/12/unclos-needs-bipartisan-push.html.

circumstances, and the treaty has languished on the Senate calendar in 2007.[34] As a result, once again no actions were taken by the Senate, and the LOS Convention was returned to the SFRC at the end of the 110th Congress.

II. The Obama Administration's Support and Attempt to Join the LOS Convention

During the 2008 presidential election campaign, Senator Barack Obama (D-IL) expressed his strong support for the LOS Convention, stating that "[t]he oceans are a global resource and a global responsibility for which the U.S. can and should take a more active role. I will work actively to ensure that the U.S. ratifies the Law of the Sea Convention."[35] Senator Joseph Biden (D-DE), Obama's running mate and the chair of the SFRC during the 2007 hearings on the Convention, was also supportive of US accession to the treaty. Taken together, the election of President Obama and Vice President Biden, the democratic gains in the Senate[36] and the rising call to protect American Arctic interests[37] created favorable conditions for US accession to the LOS Convention at the very beginning of the 111th Congress.

In January 2009, at her confirmation hearing before the SFRC, Secretary of State Hillary Clinton answered the question raised by Senator Lisa Murkowski (R-AK): "Will ratification of the Law of the Sea Treaty be a priority for you?" Clinton replied: "Yes, it will be, and it will be because it is long overdue."[38] Later in the same confirmation hearing, Senator John Kerry (D-MA), the new SRFC

34 John B. Bellinger, III, Legal Advisor, U.S. Department of State, "Generational Consistency in Law of the Sea," Remarks at the Law of the Sea Institute, Berkeley, California, November 3, 2008, available at: http://www.oceanlaw.org/index.php?module=News&func=display&sid=83&theme=Printer.

35 See Barack Obama's answers to the top 14 science questions facing America, August 30, 2008, available at: http://www.sciencedebate.org/debate08.html.

36 The Democrats gained eight seats in the Senate and with the two independents continuing to caucus with the Democrats, the party held 59 seats in the 111 Congress. The Republicans lost eight seats in the Senate in the 2008 election.

37 The call to ratify the LOS Convention was widely reported in major US newspapers. For example, *The New York Times* reported on June 28, 2007 that "[I] n this battle for Arctic territory, the United States is on the sidelines for the moment, as conservatives in Congress delay ratification of the United Nations Convention on the Law of the Sea, which governs all claims." See Mike Nizza, "Russian Scientists Say the Arctic Is Theirs," *The New York Times*, June 28, 2007, available at: http://thelede.blogs.nytimes.com/2007/06/28/whats-the-russian-for-santas-workshop/. See also "Our view on Law of the Sea treaty: Who owns Arctic's wealth?" *USA Today*, August 14, 2007 and "U.S. Resistance to Sea Treaty Thaws," *The Wall Street Journal*, August 22, 2007.

38 For transcripts of Hillary Clinton's Confirmation Hearing, January 13, 2009, visit the website of Council on Foreign Relations at http://www.cfr.org/us-election-2008/transcript-hillary-clintons- confirmation-hearing/p18225.

chair, confirmed that the Convention would also be a committee priority.[39] In May 2009, the Obama administration's Treaty Priority List for the 111th Congress was sent to the SFRC chair Senator John Kerry, in which the LOS Convention was included in the category of treaties that the administration supported.[40] In October 2009, Secretary Clinton sent letters to the SFRC chair and the committee's ranking member Senator Richard Lugar, offering her strong support for US accession to the LOS Convention, in which the Secretary stated:

> As you are aware, the convention protects and advances the national security, economic, and environmental interests of the United States. In particular, the convention codifies navigational rights and freedoms critical to U.S. military and commercial vessels and secures U.S. economic rights to natural resources off-shore. In addition, as a party, the United States would have access to procedures that would maximize international recognition and legal certainty for U.S. sovereign rights over offshore resources (including minerals) beyond 200 miles of our coastline.

The United States, as a major maritime power, the country with the largest exclusive economic zone, and one of the largest continental shelves, stands to gain more from this treaty in terms of economic and resource rights than any other country. Having a seat at the table as a party would allow the United States to participate more effectively in the interpretation and development of the convention and the ability to participate formally in its institutions.[41]

Despite the Obama administration's expression of strong support for US accession to the LOS Convention and Democratic control of both houses of the Congress, no progress was made during the first session of the 111th Congress. Competing legislative priorities, including health-care reform and climate change issues, were considered main reasons for not being able to move the Convention through the SFRC to a vote in the full Senate in 2009.[42]

In 2010, aside from the LOS Convention's importance in the Arctic, the Obama administration began to prioritize the treaty's role in dealing with rising tensions in the South China Sea and to pursue US geostrategic interests in the region,

---

39 The Senator stated that "we are now laying the groundwork for and expect to try to take up the Law of the Sea Treaty. So that will be one of the priorities of the committee, and the key here is just timing, how we proceed." See ibid.

40 For the list, visit http://globalsolutions.org/files/general/White_House_Priorities_List.pdf.

41 The letters are available at: http://www.oceanlaw.org/downloads/ClintonToKerryLugar-16Oct09.pdf.

42 See Lauren Morello, "U.S. Pushes for Law of the Sea Ratification as New Arctic Mapping Project Begins," *The New York Times*, July 29, 2009, available at: http://www.nytimes.com/cwire/2009/07/29/29climatewire-us-pushes-for-law-of-the-sea-ratification-as-89174.html.

in particular preserving its freedom of navigation and maintaining stability and peace in the Asia-Pacific. In July 2010, when attending the 17th ASEAN Regional Forum, Secretary Clinton stated in Hanoi that the Obama administration wanted claimants to pursue their disputes in the South China Sea in accordance with the LOS Convention rather than through coercion. She also said the United States and every other nation "has a national interest in freedom of navigation, open access to Asia's maritime commons, and respect for international law in the South China Sea." Clinton added one more point at the end of her remarks on the South China Sea issues, saying that the LOS Convention has strong bipartisan support in the United States, and one of the US diplomatic priorities in 2011 was to secure its ratification in the Senate.[43]

On July 19, 2010, upon receiving the final recommendations of the Interagency Ocean Policy Task Force,[44] President Obama signed into law Executive Order 13547, entitled "Stewardship of the Oceans, Our Coasts, and the Great Lake,"[45] which provides that his policy should be promoted by "pursuing the United States' accession to the Law of the Sea Convention."[46] In addition, in carrying out the provision of this order and implementing the Final Recommendations, "all actions of the Council and the executive departments, agencies, and offices that constitute it shall be consistent with applicable international law, including customary international law, such as that reflected in the Law of the Sea Convention."[47] In the Final Recommendations, the Task Force strongly and unanimously supports US accession to the LOS Convention, stating that the Convention "is the bedrock legal instrument governing activities on, over, and under the world's oceans. United States accession to the Convention will further [US] national security, environmental, economic, and diplomatic interest."[48]

The year of 2010 was the mid-term election year, during which the political environment complicated the efforts made by supporters of US accession to the LOS Convention to push for Senate action on the treaty, since moderate senators facing re-election found themselves under pressure from a determined minority of senators strongly opposed to ratification of the Convention.[49] In addition, the

43 *Supra* note 10.

44 For the Final Recommendations, see the White House Council on Environmental Quality, Executive Office of the President of the United States, Final Recommendations of the Interagency Ocean Policy Task Force, July 19, 2010, available at: http://www.whitehouse.gov/files/documents/OPTF_Final Recs.pdf.

45 Executive Order 13547—Stewardship of the Ocean, Our Coasts, and the Great Lakes, *Federal Register*, Vol. 75, No. 140, July 22, 2010, pp. 43023–7.

46 Ibid., p. 43024.

47 Ibid., p. 43027.

48 *Supra* note 44, p. 8.

49 This small group of Senate Republicans, led by Senators James Inhofe (R-OK) and Jim DeMint (R-SC), insist that accession to the LOS Convention would subjugate US sovereignty to the international community. See Josh Rogin, "This Fight Ain't Over," *Foreign Policy*, August 4, 2011, available at: http://www.foreignpolicy.com/

Obama administration prioritized the Strategic Arms Reduction Treaty (START) for ratification in 2010 and devoted all of its political efforts to that task, which was confirmed by a statement made by Secretary Clinton in 2010: "We prioritized the START Treaty this year. We're going to prioritize the Law of the Sea next year."[50] On December 22, 2010, the Senate voted 71 to 26 to ratify START, with 13 Republicans joining 58 Democrats to help the measure pass the two-thirds majority needed for ratification.

The Obama administration made no progress in 2010 on US accession to the LOS Convention, and the results of the mid-term elections further reduced the prospects of LOS Convention ratification. Although the Democrats retained a 53–47 majority in the Senate, the Republicans won control of the House of Representatives and gained six seats in the Senate. As a result of the "worst losses for 62 years,"[51] President Obama had little choice but to work closely with Republicans on his legislative program. While the Senate took no action on the LOS Convention in 2010, ongoing efforts have been made by the Obama administration to push for ratification of the treaty during the 112th Congress.

It was expected that the Obama administration would send its Treaty Priority List to the SFRC at the beginning of the first session of the 112th Congress, and that following ratification of START in December 2010, the LOS Convention would be moved to the top of the list.[52] Although in February 2011 the State Department did not send the treaty priority list to the SFRC, the Convention was included in the list of treaties pending in the Senate that can be found on the website of the Department.[53] In March 2011, the Secretary of the Navy, Ray Mabus, and the Chief of Naval Operations, Admiral Gary Roughead, both testified before the Senate Armed Services Committee hearing on navy posture. In their written testimony, both addressed the importance of the LOS Convention to the U.S. Navy and the country,

---

articles/2011/08/04/this_fight_aint_over?page=0,5. See also Michael A. Becker and Ernesto J. Sanchez, "International Law of the Sea," *The International Lawyer*, Vol. 44, No. 1 (Spring 2010), p. 520.

50 See Rob Huebert, "Canada and the Newly Emerging International Arctic Security Regime," in *Arctic Security in an Age of Climate Change* (Cambridge University Press, 2011), edited by James Kraska, p. 204 and "Obama Administration to Push Law of The Sea Treaty In Senate This Year," *supra* note 16.

51 Tom Leonard and David Gardner, "Republican tsunami: Democrats lose control of the House as voters slam Obama with worst losses for 62 years," *Daily Mail Online*, November 3, 2010, available at: http://www.dailymail.co.uk/news/article-1326053/MID-TERM-ELECTIONS-2010-Democrats-lose-House-Republican-tsunami.html.

52 Andrew Burt, "Obama Administration To Push Law of the Sea Treaty In Senate This Year," *Inside the Navy Newsletter*, February 4, 2011, available at: http://www.InsideDefense.com.

53 Treaties Pending in the Senate (updated as of May 12, 2011), available at: http://www.state.gov/s/1/treaty/pending/.

and strongly recommended US accession to this treaty.[54] On May 12, 2011, when attending the Arctic Council Ministerial Meeting in Nuuk, Greenland, Secretary Clinton reiterated the Obama administration's call to ratify the LOS Convention.[55]

In June 2011, among the 94 advance questions to which Leon Panetta, the nominee to be Secretary of Defense, provided responses during the confirmation process, one was related to the LOS Convention. Panetta wrote: "I support U.S. accession to the Law of the Sea Convention." In response to the question of how being a party to the treaty would help or hinder the US security posture, he stated:

> Being a party to the Law of the Sea Convention would not hinder the U.S. security posture, nor would it have any adverse impact on our sovereignty. In fact, becoming a party would enhance our security posture by enabling the United States to reinforce the Convention's freedom of navigation and overflight rights, including transit passage in strategic straits, and preserve our rights and duties in the Arctic. In addition, becoming a Party to the Convention would support combined operations with coalition partners and support the Proliferation Security Initiative; establish undisputed title to our extended continental shelf areas; and bolster our leadership in future developments in the law of the sea. Accession would also add to DoD's credibility in a large number of Asia-focused multilateral venues where Law of the Sea matters are discussed.[56]

In July 2011, apparently in response to a report on Senator John Kerry's intention to push for US accession to the LOS Convention, interagency meetings on the Obama administration's ratification plans were held, and teams of officials briefed senators on the drive to approve the treaty.[57] As stated in a fact sheet prepared by the US government in support of the LOS Convention, the United States needs to ratify the treaty in order to fully protect its navigation rights/freedom, economic rights and other ocean-related interests. Becoming a party to the treaty, the United States "would have the level of influence in the interpretation, application, and development of law of the sea rules that reflects its maritime status." In addition, the fact sheet provides that for the United States, accession to the Convention "is a matter of geostrategic importance in the Arctic (where

---

54 See Statements of the Honorable Ray Mabus, Secretary of the Navy, and Admiral Gary Roughead, Chief of Naval Operations, before the Senate Armed Services Committee on March 8, 2011, available at: http://armed-services.senate.gov/statemnt/2011/03%20March/Roughead%2003-08-11.pdf, p. 9 and http://armed-services.senate.gov/statemnt/2011/03%20March/Roughead%2003-08-11.pdf, p. 20.

55 Steven Lee Myers, "Cooperation Is Pledged by Nations of the Arctic," *The New York Times*, May 12, 2011, available at: http://www.nytimes.com/2011/05/13/world/europe/13arctic.html?_r=1&partner=rss&emc=rss.

56 See Advance Policy Questions for the Honorable Leon Panetta Nominee to be Secretary of Defense, June 20, 2011, available at: http://armed-services.senate.gov/statemnt/2011/06%20June/ Panetta%2006-09-11.pdf.

57 See Bill Gertz, supra note 22.

all other Arctic nations, including Russia, are parties and can fully secure their continental shelf rights) and the South China Sea (where China is flexing its muscles with respect to maritime claims)."[58]

The Obama administration's support for US accession to the LOS Convention has been stated repeatedly by high-ranking officials from various departments and agencies. At the hearing held by the Senate Subcommittee on Oceans, Atmosphere, Fisheries and Coastal Guard on July 27, 2011, David Balton, Deputy Assistant Secretary for Oceans and Fisheries, U.S. Department of State, Admiral Robert Papp, Commandant, United States Coast Guard, and Rear Admiral David Titley, Oceanographer and Navigator of the Navy, United States Navy, emphasized the importance of US accession to the LOS Convention in their testimonies. Balton stated that action to ratify the treaty has passed through the Senate several times with bipartisan support and the Obama, George W. Bush and Clinton Administrations have all supported it. Papp and Titley explained that when they attend international events related to maritime issues, one of the first questions they are asked is why the United States has not ratified the Convention.[59] In August 2011, US State Department spokesman Mark Toner said that the push for US accession to the LOS Convention remains a treaty priority for the Obama Administration. As the Senate considers the agenda for the remainder of the first session of the 112th Congress, the Department is working with interested Senate offices to explore their views on ratification of the treaty.[60]

In November 2011, President Obama travelled to Bali, Indonesia to attend the 6th East Asia Summit (EAS) and talked about the importance of the summit, the role played by the ASEAN, major issues in the region, including nuclear proliferation, the increase in conventional arms, maritime security, climate change, and the promotion of shared values and civil society, the work being done in other fora, such as the Asia-Pacific Economic Cooperation, the ASEAN Regional Forum, and the ASEAN Defense Ministerial Meeting, and the relationships between the United States and its alliances in the region as well as the relationships between Washington and Beijing, and between the United States and India.

---

58 The fact sheet was prepared by the US Government in July 2011 and posted by the Association for the U.S. Navy on its website at http://ausn.org/Portals/0/pdfs/advocacy/los-info-082011.pdf.

59 See American Geological Institute, Governmental Affairs Program, Summary of Hearings on Water and Ocean Policy, August 1, 2011, available at: http://www.agiweb.org/gap/legis112/waterocean_hearings.html.

60 "Obama Attempts another Sell-out of US Sovereignty under Law of the Sea Treaty," August 7, 2011, available at: http://grendelreport.posterous.com/obama-attempts-another-sell-out-of-us-soverei.

III. Possibility of US Accession to the LOS Convention in 2012

Listed among the five controversial treaties[61] to be wary of in the United States in 2011, the odds of the LOS Convention receiving Senate consideration is 15 percent, according to Steven Groves.[62] In July 2011, Groves further stated that "2011 is beginning to feel a lot like 2007" when the SFRC held hearings on the Convention but it was never brought to the Senate floor for a vote.[63] In March 2011, John Bellinger III, former State Department legal advisor, predicted that suspicion of international treaties will likely be stronger in 2011 because "many conservative Republicans have tended to be skeptical of large multilateral treaties as a general matter." The LOS Convention is considered one of these treaties, and therefore it would be hard to sell during the 112th Congress.[64]

Mike Gravel, former Alaska Senator, suggested that "today's political climate in Washington, DC makes it unlikely that the US Senate will change the federal government's perspective on the Law of the Sea, given the conservative makeup of the US House of Representatives."[65] This view is shared by Mark Helmke, a spokesman for ranking member of the SFRC Senator Richard Lugar, who stated that "this time, you have [fewer] Democrats and it's going to be harder for [Obama] to get the necessary Republicans to support [the LOS Convention]." In addition, he said, the President "may even have a hard chance getting all the Democrats."[66]

---

61 They are: (1) the Convention on the Elimination of All Forms of Discrimination Against Women ; (2) the Convention on the Rights of Persons with Disabilities; (3) the Convention on the Prohibition of the Use, Stockpiling, Production and Transfer of Anti-Personnel Mines and on Their Destruction; (4) the LOS Convention; and (5) the Treaty Between the United States of America and the Russian Federation on Measures for the Further Reduction and Limitation of Strategic Offensive Arms (also known as New START). The New START was signed between President Obama and Russian President Dmitry Medvedev in April 2010. On December 22, 2010, the US Senate voted 71 to 26 to ratify New START treaty. See Mary Beth Sheridan and William Branigin, "Senate Ratifies new U.S.–Russia nuclear weapons treaty," *Washington Post*, December 22, 2010, available at: http://www.washingtonpost.com/wp-dyn/content/article/2010/12/21/AR2010122104371.html.

62 Steve Groves, "Five Controversial Treaties to Be Wary on in 2011," The Heritage Foundation, WebMemo, No. 3069, December 1, 2010, p. 2.

63 Steven Groves, "Law of the Sea Could Cost U.S. Trillions," Commentary, The Heritage Foundation, July 6, 2011, available at: http://www.heritage.org/research/commentary/2011/07/law-of-sea- treaty-could-cost-us-trillions.

64 Rachel Bade, "Americans Have Long Love-Hate Relationship with International Law," The Washington Diplomat, March 29, 2011, available at: http://washdiplomat.com/index.php?option=com_content&view=article&id=7294:2011-03-29-16-23-22&catid=1089:april-2011&Itemid=428.

65 See Ellen Lockyer, "Navy Officials Meet to Plan for Diminished Arctic Ice," alaskapublic.org, June 20, 2011, available at: http://www.alaskapublic.org/2011/06/20/navy-officials-meet-to-plan-for-diminished-arctic-ice/.

66 "Obama Administration To Push Law Of The Sea Treaty In Senate This Year," *supra* note 16.

Andy Fisher, also Senator Lugar's spokesman, predicted that a full Senate vote on the LOS Convention is unlikely. "The chances are slim to none of the Senate seriously addressing this treaty at a time when the nation is rightfully focused on the fundamental issues of jobs, debt and war," he said.[67] Also, according to Julian Ku, there is no chance that the LOS Convention would be ratified in 2011.[68]

After examining a number of statements made recently by key members of the SFRC and other Republican senators, as well as the lack of stronger support from the White House, the possibility of US accession to the LOS Convention during the 112th Congress is indeed very small, if not entirely improbable.

In June 2011, Senator John McCain made remarks on the need for the United States to join the LOS Convention in his keynote address delivered at CSIS Conference on Maritime Security in the South China Sea, stating that it is unpopular among some conservative Republican senators to consider seriously the treaty. "I have had doubts about it myself," he said. For national security reasons, Senator McCain suggested, "the Senate needs to decide whether it is finally time to ratify the Law of the Sea Treaty." A possible interpretation of these remarks is that Senator McCain is avoiding taking a firm position on the LOS Convention. Indeed, in response to a question raised by Caitlyn L. Antrim, Executive Director of the Rule of Law for the Oceans, at the CSIS meeting, the senator said that it was very important to avoid having a vote that would reject the Convention.[69] The implication of the Senator's reply is that the treaty does not have the needed 67 votes in the Senate, and if it is pushed to the full Senate for a vote, it would be rejected.

In order to be ratified, a treaty is submitted by the President to the Senate and then referred to the SFRC, but first the Committee must hold hearings on the treaty. This is to be followed by a vote in the SFRC. If the vote is favorable, the treaty will be sent to the full Senate for advice. At the same time, the SFRC will discuss a resolution on advice and consent of the ratification of the treaty. Then the treaty is placed on the Senate schedule, if the Majority Leader is so inclined. The full Senate will then consider the resolution and begin a vote on the treaty. Sixty-seven votes are required for ratifying the treaty. If no action is taken by the Senate, the treaty will be returned to the SFRC at the end of each Congress in accordance with the operation of the Senate rules.

The LOS Convention was transmitted to the Senate by President Clinton in 1994, but no actions on the treaty had been taken between 1994 and 2002. In October 2003, hearings on the Convention were held by the SFRC, chaired by Senator Lugar (R-IN). In March 2004, the treaty and a resolution of advice and consent to ratification with declarations and understandings were reported to the

---

67 Bill Gertz, "Sea Law Treaty Push," *supra* note 22.

68 Kulian Ku, "The Battle in the U.S. Over the Law of the Sea Treaty," Opinio Juris, July 19, 2011, available at: http://opiniojuris.org/2011/07/19/the-battle-in-the-u-s-over-the-law-of-the-sea-treaty/.

69 Caitlyn Antrim, "Senator McCain's Written Comment on UNCLOS and the Senate," *The Ocean Law Daily*, June 22, 2011.

full Senate. However, no further action was taken when the 108th Congress ended its legislative session on December 20, 2004. Accordingly the LOS Convention was automatically referred to the SFRC. In September and October 2007, again, hearings on the Convention were held, and on October 31, 2007, the SFRC reported favorably on the treaty and referred it to the Senate floor for action. On December 19, 2007, Senator Joseph Biden, the SFRC chair, reported the treaty and moved a resolution of advice and consent for ratification with declarations and understandings, and conditions, to the Senate for floor action. But again, as of January 2, 2009, no further action had been taken at sine die adjournment of the 110th Congress, and accordingly the LOS Convention was automatically returned to the SFRC.[70]

In accordance with the US treaty ratification process, and based on the ratification history of the LOS Convention as described previously, it is clear that the key to ratification of the Convention lies in the position and efforts taken by the following three senators: John Kerry, the SFRC chair, Richard Lugar, the committee's ranking member, and Harry Reid, Majority Leader of the Senate. With the endorsement of these senators, along with stronger support from and priority set by President Obama, it is likely that the United States could become a party to the LOS Convention during the 112th Congress. As of September 2011, unfortunately, a sign of stronger support from both the SFRC and the White House has still not been given. Thus, contrary to expectations, the likelihood of US accession to the LOS Convention has become slimmer, and might now be described as "slim to none."

Senator Richard Lugar is a long-time supporter of the LOS Convention, but is facing a tough re-election primary challenge from Indiana Treasurer Richard Mourdock, who is backed by Tea Party conservatives. It is reported that a vote by Senator Lugar to support the LOS Convention would likely boost Mourdock, who, according to a new Club for Growth-sponsored poll of 500 likely GOP primary voters, holds a slight lead over Senator Lugar, who has represented the state of Indiana over 35 years in the US Senate.[71] It seems that the support of Senator Lugar for US accession to the LOS Convention could be weakened by 2012 Senate election political concerns. This is also true for Senator Kerry, who hopes to move the Convention forward in 2011, but "will meet with folks and see where we are" before taking further action.[72] A senior Senate national security aide has said that

70 For the ratification history, visit the website of the US Senate Committee on Foreign Relations at http://foreign.senate.gov/treaties/details/?id=ad607983-5056-a032-52e8-f598c3f7cfca

71 See "Mourdock leads Lugar in Club for Growth poll," *The Examiner*, July 26, 2011 and Bill Gertz, "Sea Law Treaty Push," *supra* note 22.

72 Allison Winter, "Oceans: Sen. Kerry sees prospects to advance Law of the Sea," Environment and Energy Daily, On the Hill, Vol. 10, No. 9, July 20, 2011, available at: http://www.eenews.net/eed/2011/07/20/.

Senator Kerry does not plan to go forward with a full Senate vote on the LOS Convention unless he is assured of receiving support from at least 67 senators.

In 2007, the SFRC voted 17–4 in favor of sending the LOS Convention to the full Senate for consideration. Eight of the members who remain on the SFRC voted for the treaty, namely John Kerry (D-MA), Barbara Boxer (D-CA), Bob Menendez (D-NJ), Ben Cardin (D-MD), Bob Casey (D-PA), Jim Webb (D-VA), Richard Lugar (R-IN), Bob Corker (R-TN); two current members of the committee previously voted against the treaty: Jim DeMint (R-SC) and Johnny Isakson (R-GA).

In 2011, the current SFRC has 19 members, among whom ten are Democrats, six with a voting record supportive of the LOS Convention, and nine Republicans, two of whom have supported the treaty. The current committee chair, John Kerry, and ranking member, Richard Lugar, are both supportive of the treaty. Three members of the current committee oppose the LOS Convention: James Inhofe, Jim DeMint and Johnny Isakson. Three Democratic members and four Republican members of the current SFRC were elected to the Senate either in 2008 or 2010, and their positions on the LOS Convention are not clear.[73]

Although it is possible for the SFRC to hold hearings on the treaty and vote on whether or not to report it to the full Senate for ratification consideration, the chair of the committee will hesitate to do so unless he is assured that it will receive the votes of at least 67 senators. Among the current members of the US Senate, 112th Congress, it is known that the following senators oppose the LOS Convention: Jeff Sessions (R-AL), Jon Kyl (R-AZ), Johnny Isakson (R-GA), Mitch McConnell (R-KY), David Vitter (R-LA), James Inhofe (R-OK) and Jim DeMint (R-SC). Most Senate Democrats have remained silent on the issue. Unless the SFRC decides to hold hearings and vote on sending the treaty to full Senate for ratification consideration, it is also unlikely that Senate Majority Leader Harry Reid will move the treaty forward in 2011–12.

In September 2011, however, it was announced that a new Senate Oceans Caucus had been established by a bipartisan group of US senators hoping to move forward with US accession to the LOS Convention. Caitlyn L. Antrim, Executive Director of the Rule of Law Committee for the Oceans, suggests that this group "will be a key part of the Senate support for approval of the LOS Convention."[74] The members of this group are Senators Sheldon Whitehouse (D-RI), Daniel Akaka (D-HI), Mark Begich (D-AK), Richard Blumenthal (D-CT), Barbara Boxer (D-CA), Scott Brown (R-MA), Maria Cantwell (D-WA), Ben Cardin (D-MD), Tom Carper (D-DE), Chris Coons (D-DE), Lindsey Graham (R-SC), Daniel Inouye (D-HI), John Kerry (D-MA), Mary Landrieu (D-LA), Patty Murray (D-WA), Lisa

73 Senator Jeanne Shaheen (D-NH) (2009–15), Chris Coons (D-DE) (2011–17), Tom Udall D-NM) (2009–15), Jim Risch (D-ID) (2009–15), Marco Rubio (R-FL) (2011–17), John Barrasso (R-WY) (2009–15), and Mike Lee (R-UT) (2011–17).

74 Caitlyn A. Antrim, "The New Senate Oceans Caucus," *The Ocean Law Daily*, September 7, 2011.

Murkowski (R-AK), Olympia Snowe (R-ME) and Ron Wyden (D-OR).[75] Most, if not all, of the members of the Senate Oceans Caucus are supportive of US accession to the LOS Convention.

While it is believed that the chance of receiving Senate consideration is slim in 2012, the possibility of US accession to the LOS Convention cannot be completely ruled out. In 2010, after signing the treaty in April, the Obama administration decided to prioritize the Strategic Arms Reduction Treaty (START) for ratification and dedicated all of its political resources to the task. President Obama successfully pushed the US Senate to consider ratification of the treaty even after being subject to the "worst losses for 62 years"[76] in the 2010 mid-term elections. On December 22, 2010, the Senate voted 71 to 26 to ratify START, with 13 Republicans joining 58 Democrats to help the measure receive the two-thirds majority needed for ratification.

If the LOS Convention were ratified by the United States in 2012, it could enhance the country's role and credibility in the South China Sea, but it is certain that the United States will meet challenges in the interpretation and implementation of the provisions of the treaty. In addition, ratification of the treaty would very likely be followed by conflicts between the United States and countries bordering the South China Sea due to differing interpretations and applications of the law of the sea rules contained in the treaty.

Before discussing the potential impact of US accession to the LOS Convention on state practices and maritime claims in the South China Sea, it is necessary to examine US interests in the South China Sea and its policy dealing with the sovereignty and maritime disputes in the region. This is to be followed by a brief account of state practices and maritime claims in the South China Sea and US responses to the "excessive national maritime claims" in the region in Part V and Part VI.

IV. US Interests in South China Sea Disputes

The complex disputes in the South China Sea are grouped into three severable categories, "each with its own parties, rule sets, and politics";[77] these are: (1) disputes over territorial sovereignty, in the overlapping claims to the South China

75 See Kristin Mellon, "Media Advisory: Bipartisan Group of Senators to Form Oceans Caucus," Ocean Leadership, September 7, 2011, available at: http://www.oceanleadership.org/2011/media-advisory-bipartisan-group-of-senators-to-form-oceans-caucus/.

76 Tom Leonard and David Gardner, "Republican tsunami: Democrats lose control of the House as voters slam Obama with worst losses for 62 years," *Daily Mail Online*, November 3, 2010, available at: http://www.dailymail.co.uk/news/article-1326053/MID-TERM-ELECTIONS-2010-Democrats-lose-House-Republican-tsunami.html.

77 Peter Dutton, "Three Disputes and Three Objectives: China and the South China Sea," *Naval War College Review*, Autumn 2011, Vol. 64, No. 4, p. 42.

Sea's islands, rocks and reefs; (2) disputes over which coastal states claim rightful jurisdiction over waters and seabed; and (3) disputes over the proper balance of coastal-state and international rights to use the seas for military purposes.[78] All of these disputes involve US national interests and are related to the interpretation and application of international law, in particular the LOS Convention.

The American national interests are defined in *The 2010 National Security Strategy* as:

- the security of the United States, its citizens, and US allies and partners;
- a strong, innovative and growing US economy in an open international economic system that promotes opportunity and prosperity;
- respect for universal values at home and around the world; and
- an international order advanced by US leadership that promotes peace, security, and opportunity through stronger cooperation to meet global challenges.[79]

In accordance with these national interests, it is assumed that US interests in the South China Sea sovereignty and maritime disputes include: (1) exercising freedom of navigation and overflight rights without limitation; (2) keeping security commitments to US allies and partners; (3) maintaining regional peace and stability by opposing use of force and threats; (4) safeguarding sea lines of communication; (5) demanding open commerce and access to maritime commons; and (6) promoting good order at sea by respecting international law. All of these interests are related to the management of potential conflicts in the South China Sea by the six claimants of the Spratly Islands and member states of ASEAN, bilaterally or multilaterally.

Traced back to 1988, when tension in the South China Sea escalated into armed conflict at sea between China and Vietnam over the Spratly Islands, the Reagan Administration responded by stating that while the United States took no position on the merits of competing claims in the South China Sea, it supported a peaceful resolution of the disputes and opposed the threat or use of force by the claimants.[80] In May 1995, concerned about the conflict between China and the Philippines over ownership of Mischief Reef, the Clinton administration issued "the most comprehensive statement on the Spratlys,"[81] which stressed that the

78 Ibid.

79 The White House, *National Security Strategy*, May 2010, available at: http://www.whitehouse.gov/sites/default/files/rss_viewer/national_security_strategy.pdf p. 7.

80 "China's Syndrome: Ambiguity; What Seizing a Tiny Reef Says About Beijing's Soul," *The Washington Post*, March 19, 1995, p. C4.

81 "Dispute Over Islands and China's Gunboats Roiling Asian Waters," *The Washington Post*, June 5, 1995, p. A14. The statement, entitled "Spratlys and the South China Sea," issued by Christine Shelly, Acting Spokesman, on May 10, 1995, can be found in US Interest in Southeast Asia, Hearing before the Subcommittees on International

United States "has an abiding interest in the maintenance of peace and stability in the South China Sea"[82] and the United States "view[s] with serious concern any maritime claim, or restriction on maritime activity, in the South China Sea that was not consistent with international law, including the 1982 United Nations Convention on the Law of the Sea."[83]

More recently, the US interests in sovereignty and maritime disputes in the South China Sea were made clear in the remarks by former Defense Secretary Robert Gates at the Shangri-La security dialogue meeting held in Singapore in June 2010, when the Secretary stated that "the South China Sea is an area of growing concern. This sea is not only vital to those directly bordering it, but to all nations with economic and security interests in Asia."[84] Due to its commitments to (1) free and open commence, (2) a just international order that emphasizes rights and responsibilities of nations and fidelity to the rule of law, (3) open access by all to the global commons of sea, air, space and cyberspace, and (4) the principle of resolving conflict without the use of force, it is US interest and policy that stability, freedom of navigation and free and unhindered economic development in the South China Sea should be maintained, that while not taking sides on any competing sovereignty claims in the area, the United States opposes the use of force and actions that hinder freedom of navigation, and that the United States objects to any effort to intimidate US corporations or those of any nation engaged in legitimate economic activity.[85]

The US interest in the South China Sea was further elaborated by Secretary of State Hillary Clinton when attending the 17th ASEAN Regional Forum in Hanoi, Vietnam in July 2010, where she stated that the United States, "like every nation, has a national interest in freedom of navigation, open access to Asia's maritime commons, and respect for international law in the South China Sea."[86] In addition, the Secretary made it clear that although the United States does not take sides on the sovereignty and maritime disputes over the islands in the South China Sea, "claimants should pursue their territorial claims and accompanying rights to maritime space in accordance with the UN convention on the law of the sea."[87]

US interest in the South China Sea was reiterated in a letter sent by the US SFRC Chairman John Kerry and Senator John McCain to Chinese State Councilor

---

Economic Policy and Trade and Asia and the Pacific of the Committee on International Relations, House of Representatives, 104th Congress, 2nd Session, May 30 and June 19, 1996 (Washington, DC: GPO, 1997), p. 157.

82 Spratlys and the South China Sea, Statement by Christine Shelly, ibid.

83 Ibid.

84 Remarks by Secretary of Defense Robert M. Gates, Shangri-La, Singapore, June 5, 2010, available on the website of the Defense Department at http://www.defense.gov/speeches/speech.aspx?speechid=1483.

85 Ibid.

86 *Supra* note 10.

87 *Supra* note 10.

Dai Bingguo on July 14, 2011, in which the senators wrote: "the United States does not take a position on the overlapping territorial claims in this region, but we do maintain a deep and abiding interest in ensuring freedom of navigation, commerce, and economic exploration; maintaining US commitments to our allies and partners; and supporting peace and security in the Asia-Pacific region."[88] The two senators also expressed US concern about a series of naval incidents that occurred in the South China Sea and raised tensions in the region, and warned that "[i]f appropriate steps are not taken to calm the situation, future incidents could escalate, jeopardizing the vital national interest of the United States."[89]

The most recent statements of the Obama administration concerning US interest in the South China Sea were made by Secretary Clinton on July 22, 2011 when she attended the 18th ASEAN Regional Forum in Bali, Indonesia. In her remarks, the Secretary stated that "as a Pacific nation and resident power we have a national interest in freedom of navigation, open access to Asia's maritime domain, the maintenance of peace and stability and respect for international law in the South China Sea."[90] She urged all parties involved in sovereignty and maritime disputes in the South China Sea to pursue their territorial claims and accompanying rights to maritime space in accordance with international law, particularly as reflected in the LOS Convention.[91] She also expressed US concern about a number of naval incidents in the South China Sea that threaten peace and stability in the Asia-Pacific because these incidents "endanger the safety of life at sea, escalate tensions, undermine freedom of navigation, and pose risks to lawful unimpeded commerce and economic development."[92] In addition, the Secretary asked all of the parties concerned to clarify their claims in the South China Sea in terms consistent with customary international law, particularly as reflected in the LOS Convention. "Consistent with international law, claims to maritime space in the South China Sea should be derived solely from legitimate claims to land features,"[93] she added. On July 24, 2011, in her remarks made at APGWV Soundbite, Nusa Dua, Indonesia, the Secretary stated that:

> The United States takes no position on any claim made by any party to any disputed area. What we want to see is a resolution process that will be aided by the code of conduct that ASEAN is working toward, based on the Declaration of Conduct, and that the principles of international law will govern so that there can be peaceful resolution of all the claims. In order to achieve that, every claimant

88 For a copy of the letter, visit http://media.ft.com/cms/4907a816-b1fd-11e0-a06c-00144feabdc0.pdf.

89 Ibid.

90 *Supra* note 11.

91 *Supra* note 11.

92 *Supra* note 11.

93 Supra note 11.

> must make their claim publicly and specifically known so that we know where there is any dispute.
>
> All of us have a stake in ensuring that these disputes don't get out of control, and in fact the numbers have been increasing of intimidation actions, of ramming, of cutting of cables, the kind of things that will raise the cost of doing business for everyone who travels through the South China Sea, which … is half of all global commons.[94]

US interest in the South China Sea and concerns about rising tensions in the region can also be found in a number of US Congressional resolutions introduced in 2011. On June 13, 2011, Senator Jim Webb (D-VA), chair of the Senate Foreign Relations East Asian and Pacific Affairs Subcommittee, introduced resolution 217, calling for a peaceful and multilateral resolution to maritime territorial disputes in Southeast Asia, along with subcommittee ranking member James Inhofe (R-OK).[95] The resolution, approved by the US Senate on June 27, 2011, supports the continuation of operations by the US military in support of freedom of navigation rights in international waters and air space in the South China Sea. On July 15, 2011, resolution 352 was introduced by Representative Ileana Ros-Lehtinen, calling for a peaceful and collaborative resolution of maritime territorial disputes in the South China Sea. This resolution, referred to the House Committee on Foreign Affairs and the Committee on Armed Services, condemns the use of force by the Chinese naval, maritime security and fishing vessels in the South China Sea.[96]

It is clear that the United States has national interests in the South China Sea and is concerned about the potential impact of rising tension on the maintenance of peace and stability in the region. But what is the current state of the sovereignty and maritime disputes in the South China Sea? How does the United States respond to "excessive maritime claims" made by a number of countries bordering the South China Sea? Before commenting on the potential impact of US accession to the LOS Convention on state practices and maritime claims in the region, Part V describes briefly state practices and maritime claims in the South China Sea and Part VI examines US responses to the "excessive maritime claims" in the region.

---

94 Remarks by Hillary Rodham Clinton, Secretary of State, APGWV Soundbite, Nusa Dua, Indonesia, July 24, 2011, available at: http://www.state.gov/secretary/rm/2011/07/169010.htm.

95 For Bill Summary & Status, 112th Congress (2011–12), S.Res.217, visit http://thomas.loc.gov/cgi-bin/bdquery/Z?d112:s.res,217.

96 For Bill Summary & Status, 112th Congress (2011–12), H.RES.352, visit http://thomas.loc.gov/cgi-bin/bdquery/z?d112:H.RES.352.

V. State Practices and Maritime Claims in the South China Sea

There are 10 countries[97] that border the South China Sea. Of these, eight are members of ASEAN, and the other two are in the process of continuously improving their political relations based on the so-called "92 Consensus"[98] or the principle of "one China, but subject to different interpretations."[99]

All of the countries bordering the South China Sea are parties to the LOS Convention except Taiwan[100] and Cambodia. Five of the 10 South China Sea-bordering countries use the method of straight baselines to measure their maritime zones, and claim both 12 n.m. territorial sea and 24 n.m. contiguous zone: Cambodia, China, Taiwan, Thailand and Vietnam. In addition to their claim to 12 n.m. territorial sea, all of the 11 countries declare a 200 n.m. EEZ by promulgating their respective domestic legislations on the zones. With the exception of Singapore, all claim a 200 n.m. continental shelf (see Table 5.1).

Five of the 10 South China Sea-bordering countries made submissions or sent preliminary information to the Commission on the Limits of the Continental Shelf (CLCS), a body of scientists established by the LOS Convention, to extend their continental shelves beyond 200 n.m. into the South China Sea: Brunei, China, Indonesia, Malaysia, and Vietnam.[101] China objected the submissions made by

97 They are Brunei, Cambodia, China, Indonesia, Malaysia, the Philippines, Singapore, Taiwan, Thailand and Vietnam.

98 The term "92 Consensus" describes the outcome of a meeting in 1992 between the semi-official representatives of the People's Republic of China in mainland China and the Republic of China in Taiwan. The Consensus is that, on the subject of the "One China principle," both sides recognize that there is only one China—both mainland China and Taiwan belong to the same China, but both sides agree to verbally express the meaning of that one China according to their own individual definition. For more information about the consensus, see "1992 Consensus," Wikipedia, the free encyclopedia, available at: http://en.wikipedia.org/wiki/1992_Consensus.

99 Ibid.

100 The Republic of China (Taiwan) was a member of the United Nations before 1972. Since being expelled from the organization in 1972, Taiwan has been barred from participating in the UN and UN-related organizations and meetings, which includes the Third United Nations Conference on the Law of the Sea (1973–82). As a result, Taiwan cannot become a party to the LOS Convention either by ratification, accession or declaration of acceptance. However, the ROC government has expressed its willingness to abide by the provisions contained in the LOS Convention voluntarily.

101 For discussions of these submissions and the preliminary information, see Nguyen Hong Thao and Rames Amer, "Coastal States in the South China Sea and Submissions on the Outer Limits of the Continental Shelf," *Ocean Development and International Law*, Vol. 42, No. 3 (August 2011), pp. 245–63.

Vietnam and Malaysia jointly[102] and by Vietnam separately[103] by sending two diplomatic notes to the UN Secretary-General on May 7, 2009.[104] The Philippines also objected to the joint submission of Vietnam and Malaysia.[105] In response to the map attached to the Chinese *Note Verbale* dated May 7, 2009, which is referred to as the nine-dashed-lines map and is believed to be used by China as an official document to support its claim to sovereignty, sovereign right and jurisdiction in the South China Sea, Vietnam,[106] Indonesia[107] and the Philippines[108] sent official communications to the UN Secretary-General to challenge the Chinese claim. It is stated in Vietnam's diplomatic note that "China's claim over the islands and adjacent waters in the Eastern Sea (South China Sea) as manifested in the map attached with the *Note Verbale* CLM/17/2009 and CLM/18/2009 has no legal, historical or factual basis, therefore is null and void."[109] It is stated in the official communication sent by Indonesia on July 8, 2010 that "the so-called 'nine-dotted-lines map' ... clearly lacks international legal basis and is tantamount to upset the UNCLOS 1982."[110] In its communication sent to the UN Secretary-General on April 5, 2011, the Philippines stated that "the Kalayaan Islands Group (KIG) constitutes an integral part of the Philippines. The Philippines has sovereignty and jurisdiction over the geological features in the KIG." It is also stated that the Chinese claim to sovereign rights and jurisdiction in and under the waters

---

102 Joint Submission dated May 6, 2009 by Malaysia and the Socialist Republic of Vietnam to the CLCS, through the UN Secretary-General, in accordance with Article 76, para. 8 of the LOS Convention, available at: http://.www.un.org/Depts/los/clcs_new/submissions_files/submission_mysvnm_33_2009.htm.

103 Submission by the Socialist Republic of Vietnam to the CLCS, through the UN Secretary-General, in accordance with Article 76, paragraph 8 of the LOS Convention, available at: http://www.un.org/Depts/los/clcs_new/submissions_files/submission_vnm_37_2009.htm.

104 Note CML/17/2009, May 7, 2009 and Note CML/18/2009, May 7, 2009, available on the website of the CLCS at http://www.un.org/Depts/los/clcs_new/submissions_files/mysvnm33_09/chn_2009re_mys_vnm_e.pdf and http://www.un.org/Depts/los/clcs_new/submissions_files/vnm37_09/chn_2009re_vnm.pdf.

105 The Philippines, Note No. 000818, August 4, 2009 and Note 000819, August 4, 2009, available on the website of the CLCS at http://www.un.org/Depts/los/clcs_new/submissions_files/vnm37_09/clcs_ 37_2009_los_phl.pdf.

106 The submission is available at: http://www.un.org/Depts/los/clcs_new/submissions_files/vnm37_09/ vnm_re_chn_2009re_vnm.pdf.

107 The communication is available at: http://www.un.org/Depts/los/clcs_new/submissions_files/ mysvnm33_09/idn_2010re_mys_vnm_e.pdf.

108 The communication is available at: http://www.un.org/Depts/los/clcs_new/submissions_files/ mysvnm33_09/phl_re_chn_2011.pdf.

109 The communication is available at: http://www.un.org/Depts/los/clcs_new/submissions_files/ mysvnm33_09/vnm_chn_2009re_mys_vnm_e.pdf.

110 The communication is available at: http://www.un.org/Depts/los/clcs_new/submissions_files/ mysvnm33_09/idn_2010re_mys_vnm_e.pdf.

Table 5.1 Maritime Zones and claims of countries bordering the South China Sea

STATE	LOS Convention Ratification, Accession Date	Does the legislation provide for straight baselines?	Does the State claim archipelagic status?	MARITIME ZONES					
				Territorial sea	Contiguous zone	Exclusive economic zone	Fisheries zone	Continental shelf, including submissions to the CLCS	
				Breadth of the zone in nautical miles*				Outer limit	Sub.
Brunei	05/11/1996			12		200		CM/200	p/i
Cambodia		Yes		12	24	200		200	
China	07/06/1996	Yes		12	24	200		CM/200	p/i
Indonesia	03/02/1986		Yes	12		200		CM/200	Yes(*1)
Malaysia	14/10/1996			12		200		CM/200	Yes(*2)
Philippines	08/05/1984		Yes	(*3)		200		CM/200	Yes(*4)
Singapore	17/11/1994			12 (*5)		(*5)			
Thailand	15/05/2011	Yes		12	24	200			
Vietnam	25/07/1994	Yes		12 (*6)	24	200 (*7)		CM/200 (*8)	Yes(*9 & *10)
Taiwan		Yes		12	24	200		CM/200 (*11)	(*12)

Source: Tabulated by the author based on maritime space: Maritime zone and maritime delimitation, http://www.un.org/depts/los/LEGISLATIONANDTREATIES/PDFFILES/table_summary_of_claims.pdf.

* The number reflects a claim regarding the breadth of the zone (in nautical miles), measured from the baselines, as contained in national legislation—regardless of whether this legislation contains an additional specific reference to the need for delimitation of maritime boundaries with adjacent or opposite states. However, where the national legislation establishes the limits of a given zone only by reference to the delimitation of maritime boundaries with adjacent or opposite states, or to a median (equidistant) line in the absence of a maritime boundary delimitation agreement, the symbol DLM is used.

*1. With respect to the northwest of Sumatra Island. *2. Joint submission by Malaysia and Vietnam in respect of the southern part of the South China Sea.

*3. Polygon defined by coordinates. Claim extends beyond 12 nautical miles. *4. With respect to the Benham Rise region. *5. "Should the limits of its territorial sea or Exclusive Economic Zone overlap with claims of neighbouring countries, Singapore will negotiate with those countries with a view to arriving at agreed delimitations in accordance with international law." *6. Deposit made in respect of the delimitation with China in the Gulf of Tonkin. *7. Ibid. *8. Ibid. *9. Joint submission by Malaysia and Vietnam in respect of the southern part of the South China Sea. * 10. With respect to the region of the North Area (VNM-N). *11. In accordance with 1958 Geneva Convention on the Continental Shelf. *12. Barred from submitting an application for outer continental shelf to CLCS because of not being a party to the LOS Convention and not a member of the CLCS.

inside the nine-dashed-lines map "would have no basis under international law, specifically UNCLOS."[111]

In response to the challenge from the Philippines, on April 14, 2011, in its *Note Verbale*, China made a statement regarding its claim to maritime zones in the South China Sea, which states that "under the relevant provisions of the 1982 United Nations Convention on the Law of the Sea, as well as the Law of the People's Republic of China on the Territorial Sea and the Contiguous zone (1992) and the Law of the Exclusive Economic Zone and the Continental Shelf of the People's Republic of China (1998), China's Nansha Island [the Spratly Islands] is fully entitled to Territorial Sea, Exclusive Economic Zone (EEZ) and Continental Shelf."[112] This communication was followed by another Vietnamese response sent to the UN Secretary-General on May 3, 2011, in which Vietnam claimed "Hoang Sa (Paracel) and Truong Sa (Spratly) Archipelagoes are integral parts of Vietnamese territory. Vietnam has sufficient historical evidences and legal foundation to assert her sovereignty over these two archipelagoes."[113]

The Philippines and Indonesia are two archipelagic states in the South China Sea and are permitted to draw straight baselines connecting the outermost points of the outermost islands in their archipelago. If all of the geographical features located in the South China Sea are considered "rocks" as defined in Article 121, paragraph 3, of the LOS Convention, all of the waters of this semi-enclosed sea will become EEZ of the bordering countries, except a small area of "donut hole" located in the middle of the South China Sea that is considered high sea under the LOS Convention.

Based on the definition provided in Article 122, the South China Sea is a semi-enclosed sea and therefore the countries that border the sea are required to cooperate with each other in the exercise of their rights and in the performance of their obligation under Article 123 of the LOS Convention. In particular, they are required: (1) to coordinate the management, conservation, exploration and exploitation of the living resources of the South China Sea; (2) to coordinate the implementation of their rights and duties with respect to the protection and preservation of the marine environment in the South China Sea; and (3) to coordinate their scientific research policies and undertake where appropriate joint programmes of scientific research in the South China Sea.

In addition to the conflict over overlapping maritime zones and the problem of maritime boundary delimitation, six of the 10 South China Sea countries are in dispute over the ownership of the four groups of islands situated in the South China Sea, namely the Pratas Islands (Dongsha), the Paracel Islands (Xisha),

---

111 The communication is available at: http://www.un.org/Depts/los/clcs_new/submissions_files/ mysvnm33_09/phl_re_chn_2011.pdf.

112 The communication is available at: http://www.un.org/Depts/los/clcs_new/submissions_files/mysvnm33_09/chn_2011_re_phl_e.pdf.

113 The communication is available at: http://www.un.org/Depts/los/clcs_new/submissions_files/mysvnm33_09/vnm_2011_re_phlchn.pdf.

Scarborough Shoal and Macclesfield Bank (Zhongsha), and the Spratly Islands (Nansha).[114] The Pratas Islands are claimed by China and Taiwan; the Paracel Islands by China, Taiwan and Vietnam; the Scarborough Shoal and Macclesfield Bank by China, Taiwan and the Philippines; and the Spratly Islands by China, Taiwan and Vietnam as a whole and by the Philippines, Malaysia and Brunei partially. The Pratas Islands are under Taiwan's effective control and no territorial disputes exist between China/Taiwan and any members of ASEAN. Since 1974, the Paracel Islands have been under Chinese rule. No military troops are stationed on Macclesfield Bank because it is completely submerged at low tide. It was reported that 21 features of the Spratly Islands are occupied by Vietnam; nine by the Philippines; seven by China; six by Malaysia; but the largest island, Taiping Dao (Itu Aba), is occupied by Taiwan.[115] To help manage the potential conflicts in the South China Sea, an informal workshop has been held since 1990 until present.[116] The 20th workshop was held in Bandung in November 2010, which marked the 20th anniversary of the meeting. The 21st workshop will be held in mid-November this year in Indonesia. All of the countries that border the South China Sea participate in the workshop meetings.

The call to rely on the LOS Convention to make claims to maritime rights and resolve the disputes over sovereignty and jurisdiction in the South China Sea has been repeatedly mentioned in many official statements and political documents issued by ASEAN member states and China since as early as 1995. In August 1995, delegations from the Philippines and China met in Manila for consultations on the South China Sea and on other areas of cooperation, where the two sides agreed, inter alia, to settle their bilateral disputes in accordance with the recognized principles of international law, including the LOS Convention.[117] The Philippines and Vietnam also agreed to resolve their disputes on the basis of the Convention.[118]

---

114 For a good summary of their claims, see Joshua P. Brown, "The US–Japan Security Alliance, ASEAN, and the South China Sea Dispute," *Asian Survey*, Vol. XLV, No. 3, May/June 2005, pp. 419–29. See also Rommel C. Banlaoi, "Clash of sovereignties in the Spratlys," June 30, 2011, PhilStar.com, available at: http://www.philstar.com/Article.aspx?articleId=701324&publicationSubCategoryId=200.

115 See Rommel C. Banlaoi, ibid.

116 See Yann-huei Song, "The South China Sea Workshop Process and Taiwan's Participation," *Ocean Development and International Law*, Vol. 41, Issue 3, 2010, pp. 256–60.

117 Joint Statement, Republic of the Philippines–PRC Consultations on the South China Sea and on Other Areas of Cooperation, August 9–10, 1995. The statement can be found in Yann-huei Song, United States and Territorial Disputes in the South China Sea: A Study of Ocean Law and Politics, Maryland Series in Contemporary Asian Studies, Number 1– 2002 (168), Appendix A, pp. 297–8.

118 Joint Statement on the Fourth Annual Bilateral Consultations between the Socialist Republic of Vietnam and the Republic of Philippines, Hanoi, November 7, 1995. See Yann-huei Song, United States and Territorial Disputes in the South China Sea, ibid., Appendix B, pp. 299–301.

Since December 1995, all of the declarations, chairman's statements and joint communiqués issued at the ASEAN Summit, ASEAN Ministerial Meeting and ASEAN Regional Forum have urged the countries concerned to deal with South China Sea issues in accordance with the recognized principles of international law, which include the LOS Convention. More importantly, the call to rely on this treaty was reiterated in the 2002 Declaration on the Conduct of Parties in the South China Sea that was adopted by the Foreign Ministers of ASEAN and China at the 8th ASEAN Summit on November 4, 2002. In July 2011, the participating foreign ministers of ASEAN member states asked the parties concerned to resolve disputes peacefully in the South China Sea in accordance with universally recognized principles of international law, including the LOS Convention.[119] On July 23, 2011, the Foreign Ministers and Representatives of the participating states made the same statement at the 18th ASEAN Regional Forum.[120]

Some of the maritime claims made by the countries bordering the South China Sea are considered inconsistent with international law, as reflected in the 1982 LOS Convention, and are described as "excessive maritime national claims" and are not recognized by the United States. Examples include historic waters claims, excessive straight baseline claims, territorial sea claims in excess of 12 n.m., archipelagic states or archipelagic waters claims not consistent with Part IV of the LOS Convention, EEZ claims not consistent with Part V of the LOS Convention, continental shelf claims not consistent with Part VI of the LOS Convention, permission or prior notification claims that limit the exercise of the right of innocent passage, and other claims that impede freedom of navigation and overflight.[121] US responses to these claims are examined below.

VI. US Responses to the "Excessive Maritime Claims" in the South China Sea

Over the past three decades, actions have been taken by the United States, through the State Department's diplomatic protests and the Defense Department's operational assertions, to challenge the "excessive maritime claims" made by a number of countries that border the South China Sea. In particular, operational

119 Joint Communiqué of the 44th ASEAN Foreign Ministers Meeting, Bali, Indonesia, July 19, 2011, para. 22, available at: http://www.asean.org/documents/JC44thAMM19JUL2011.pdf.

120 Chair's Statement of the 18th ASEAN Regional Forum, July 23, 2011, Bali, Indonesia, para. 11, available at: http://www.mofa.go.jp/announce/jfpu/2011/7/pdfs/0727_02.pdf.

121 J.A. Roach and Robert W. Smith, *United States Responses to Excessive Maritime Claims*, 2nd edition (The Hague/Boston/London: Martinus Nijhoff Publishers, 1996), pp. 15–16.

assertions have been conducted by US military units against the countries maintaining claims that are considered contrary to international law and impair freedoms of navigation and overflight under the Freedom of Navigation Program established by the Carter administration in 1979.[122]

It was reported in 2010 that the United States diplomatically protested 32 of the excessive straight-baseline claims made by the coastal states and conducted operational assertions against 22 of the claims worldwide.[123] In the South China Sea, the United States challenged straight-baseline claims made by the following bordering countries: Cambodia,[124] China,[125] the Philippines,[126] Taiwan,[127] Thailand[128] and Vietnam[129] (see Table 5.2). The United States also protested or conducted operational assertions against the claims made by Cambodia, China, Myanmar, the Philippines, Taiwan, Thailand and Vietnam.[130]

The United States protested and conducted operational assertions against the requirements made by the following South China Sea-bordering countries for foreign warships to obtain permission or send notification prior to transiting their territorial sea: Cambodia, China, Indonesia, Malaysia, Taiwan and Vietnam (see Table 5.3). Operational assertions were conducted by the United States to challenge the claims made by Indonesia in relation to archipelagic sea lanes passage between 2005 and 2010 and those made by the Philippines between 1994 and 2010.[131] In 1987, the United States protested the historic waters claims made by Cambodia in the Gulf of Thailand. In 1982 and 1987, diplomatic protests were made by the United States against the historic waters claims made by Vietnam in the Gulf of

---

122 For more information about the program, see William J. Aceves, "The Freedom of Navigation Program: A Study of the Relationship between Law and Politics," *Hasting International and Comparative Law Review*, Vol. 19 (Winter 1996), pp. 277–81.

123 See J. Ashley and Robert W. Smith, "Straight Baselines: the Need for a Universally Applied Norm," *Ocean Development and International Law*, Vol. 31, Nos.1–2, p. 48.

124 See Under Secretary of Defense for Policy, *Maritime Claims Reference Manual*, DoD 2005.1-M, p. 90, available at: http://www.jag.navy.mil/organization/documents/mcrm/MCRM.pdf

125 Ibid., p. 126.

126 Ibid., p. 463.

127 Ibid., p. 597.

128 Ibid., p. 605.

129 Ibid., p. 689.

130 See *Maritime Claims Reference Manual*, DoD 2005.1-M, *supra* note 7, pp. 84, 90, 126, 463, 597, 605 and 689 and Steven Groves, "Assessing to the U.N. Convention on the Law of the Sea Is Unnecessary to Secure U.S. Navigational Rights and Freedoms," The Heritage Foundation, Backgrounder # 2599, Appendix (I.S. Navy Challenges to Excessive Maritime Claims, FY 1993–2010), available at: http://www.heritage.org/research/reports/2011/08/accession-to-un-convention-law-of-the- sea-is-unnecessary-to-secure-us-navigational-rights-freedoms.

131 Steven Groves, Appendix, ibid.

Tonkin. In addition, operational assertions were conducted in 1996, 1998, and between 1999 and 2002 to challenge the Vietnamese claims.[132]

In order to preserve and protect its navigational rights and freedoms, as well as the right to conduct military-related survey activities in the EEZ of the South China Sea-bordering countries, the United States also lodged diplomatic protests and conducts operational assertions against claims that it considers inconsistent with international law, particularly as reflected in the LOS Convention. The United States does not recognize the jurisdictional rights claimed by Malaysia to subject freedom of navigation and overflight to broad restrictions, such as the requirement to obtain prior permission for military exercises in EEZ. Operational assertions were conducted by the United States to challenge the claims made by Malaysia to restrict its military activities in the Malaysian EEZ in the periods 1998–2003 and 2007–10.[133] In response to claims made by China to exercise jurisdiction over airspace above its EEZ and to criminalize foreign survey activity in its EEZ, the United States protested and conducted operational assertions between 2007 and 2010.[134]

The United States also acted to challenge the claims made by some countries that border the South China Sea, which include the right to exercise control in the contiguous zone and to prevent, and impose penalties for, activities concerned with security,[135] the requirement for foreign submarines to navigate on the surface and show flag, prohibiting foreign aircraft from being launched from or taken aboard ships, the requirement for foreign ships to place weapons in nonoperative positions before entering the zone, and the right to restrict "stopping, dropping anchor, and/or cruising about without legitimate reason" in high seas "adjoining" Indonesian territorial waters.[136] The United States protested the Chinese claim in 1992 and the Vietnamese claims in 1982 and 2002.[137]

As examined previously, although not yet a party to the LOS Convention, the United States has already acted to challenge the claims made by the South China Sea-bordering countries that are considered inconsistent with international law, including the LOS Convention. The actions taken are based on US interpretations of certain provisions of the Convention in question, which include Article 7 (Straight baselines), Article 17 (Right of innocent passage), Article 33 (Contiguous zone), Article 53 (Right of archipelagic sea lanes passage), Article 58 (Rights and duties of other States in the exclusive economic zone) and Article 87 (Freedom of the high seas). However, except the calls made by Secretary Clinton at the

132 *Maritime Claims Reference Manual*, DoD 2005.1-M, *supra* note 7, p. 90 and p. 689.

133 *Maritime Claims Reference Manual*, DoD 2005.1-M, *supra* note 7, p. 373 and Steven Groves, Appendix, *supra* note 131.

134 Steven Groves, Appendix, *supra* note 131.

135 The United States does not recognize the Chinese claim in its contiguous zone. See *Maritime Claims Reference Manual*, *supra* note 7, p. 126 and p. 689.

136 *Maritime Claims Reference Manual*, *supra* note 7, p. 280.

137 *Maritime Claims Reference Manual*, *supra* note 7, pp. 126 and 689.

Table 5.2 US diplomatic protests and operational assertions against the excessive straight-baseline claims

National claims	Diplomatic protests	Operational assertions
Cambodia		1986, 1989, 1993, 1994, and 1996–2005 and 2010
China	1996	1997
The Philippines	1961, 1969, 1986	1979–92, 1994–2006
Taiwan	2001	2000–3
Thailand	2000	1995
Vietnam	1982, 1987	1996–2003, 2010

Source: Prepared by the author based on *Maritime Claims Reference Manual*, DoD 2005.1-M and Steven Groves, "Assessing to the U.N. Convention on the Law of the Sea Is Unnecessary to Secure U.S. Navigational Rights and Freedoms," The Heritage Foundation, Backgrounder # 2599, Appendix (U.S. Navy Challenges to Excessive Maritime Claims, FY 1993–2010).

17th and 18th ASEAN Regional Fora in July 2010 and July 2011 to respect, and make claims consistent with, international law, including the LOS Convention, specific actions have not yet been taken by the United States to challenge Chinese claims that it possesses historic rights in most of the waters of the South China Sea enclosed by the nine dashed lines as shown in the map attached to its official note to the UN Secretary-General in May 2009, and that the Spratly Islands are entitled to territorial sea, EEZ and continental shelf in accordance with the LOS Convention, and its 1992 Territorial Sea and 1998 EEZ laws. Would US accession to the treaty give rise to legal disputes between the United States and South China Sea-bordering countries? The answer is "Yes", and would be most likely between the United State and China.

VII. Potential Impact of US Accession to the LOS Convention on State Practices and Maritime Claims in the South China Sea

After becoming a party to the LOS Convention, the United States is under a legal obligation to bring its laws and conduct into conformity with the treaty. The United States will be required, also, to interpret, apply and implement the treaty in accordance with the provisions contained in the LOS Convention. However, it is very likely that US accession to the Convention will give rise to legal disputes over the interpretation and application of a number of provisions of the treaty between the United States and some countries that border the South China Sea.

Four reasons can be given in support of this prediction. First, as noted previously, the United States, being a nonparty to the LOS Convention, has already taken a series of actions, in particular through diplomatic protests and operational assertions conducted by the air and sea forces of the U.S. Navy and Air

Force under the Freedom of Navigation Program, to challenge the interpretation and application of a number of the provisions of the treaty by the countries in the region that are considered inconsistent with the LOS Convention and seen to affect US rights and interests in the South China Sea.

Secondly, several South China Sea-bordering countries attached declarations or statements of understanding to express their positions on the interpretation and application of certain provisions of the LOS Convention when signing or ratifying the treaty, which have been challenged by the United States as being not in conformity with the Convention.

Thirdly, the US SFRC included a set of declarations and understandings in the draft Resolution of Advice and Consent to the ratification of the LOS Convention when it reported the treaty favorably to the full Senate for a vote in March 2004 and December 2007. The declarations and understandings included in the two Senate draft resolutions are identical and it is very likely that these declarations and understandings will be included again in the future Senate resolution on advice and consent when the Committee decides to report the LOS Convention to the full Senate for consideration.

Finally, there exist possibilities for some US practices or maritime claims to be challenged as being not in conformity with the provision contained in the LOS Convention by the bordering countries in the South China Sea. Examples include the US to remote Pacific islands, such as Baker Island and Howland Islands, to be entitled the right to generate a 200 n.m. EEZ and continental shelf, and the US claim that its warships and surveillance planes may conduct military-related survey activities in EEZ of foreign coastal states in the South China Sea. In the 2001 EP-3 and 2009 *Impeccable* incidents, China said that foreign ships and planes have to obtain permission before entering its 200-mile EEZ under the LOS Convention, but the US disagreed.

The status of US responses to the "excessive maritime claims," as one of the reasons for a possible rise in legal disputes between the United States and some South China Sea *littoral states* after US accession to the LOS Convention was discussed in Part VI of this chapter and there is no need to elaborate further. Instead, this part comments on the other three reasons, beginning with the declarations and understandings that were made by a number of South China Sea littoral states when they signed or ratified the Convention.

The LOS Convention does not allow states and entities to make reservations or exceptions to the Convention unless expressly permitted by other articles of the Convention.[138] However, the Convention allows states and entities to make declarations or statements regarding the Convention's application at the time of signature, ratification, or accession, which do not purport to exclude or modify the legal effect of the provisions of the Convention.[139] When these declarations,

138 Article 309 of the LOS Convention.

139 Article 310 (Declarations and statements) of the LOS Convention reads: "Article 309 does not preclude a State, when signing, ratifying or acceding to this Convention, from

Table 5.3 US diplomatic protests and operational assertions against the excessive claims related to innocent passage of warships

National claims	Diplomatic protests	Operational assertions
Cambodia		1986, 1989, 1992–2000, 2010
China	1992, 1996	1986, 1991–4, 1996, 1997
Indonesia		1992, 1993, 2000–4
Malaysia	1997	2007–10
Taiwan		2001, 2006
Vietnam	1982	1982, 1983, 1985, 1986, 1998–2003, 2010

Source: Prepared by the author based on Under Secretary of Defense for Policy, *Maritime Claims Reference Manual*, DoD 2005.1-M and Steven Groves, "Assessing to the U.N. Convention on the Law of the Sea is Unnecessary to Secure U.S. Navigational Rights and Freedoms," The Heritage Foundation, Backgrounder # 2599, Appendix (U.S. Navy Challenges to Excessive Maritime Claims, FY 1993–2010).

statements or understandings are made, other contracting parties of the LOS Convention may challenge on the ground that they are not consistent with the treaty and therefore cannot be accepted.

China, Malaysia, the Philippines and Vietnam are the four South China Sea-bordering countries that attached declarations or understandings regarding the interpretation and application of the Convention when they signed or ratified the treaty. On December 10, 1982, the Philippines, when signing the Convention, made eight statements, which include:

- The provisions of the Convention on archipelagic passage through sea lanes do not nullify or impair the sovereignty of the Philippines as an archipelagic state over the sea lanes and do not deprive it of authority to enact legislation to protect its sovereignty, independence and security.
- The concept of archipelagic waters is similar to the concept of internal waters under the Constitution of the Philippines, and removes straits connecting these waters with the economic zone or high sea from the rights of foreign vessels to transit passage for international navigation.[140]

making declarations or statements, however phrased or named, with a view, inter alia, to the harmonization of its laws and regulations with the provisions of this Convention, provided that such declarations or statements do not purport to exclude or to modify the legal effect of the provisions of this Convention in their application to that State."

140 For the understandings, visit the website of the United Nations at http://www.un.org/Depts/los/convention_agreements/convention_declarations.htm.

On June 7, 1996, China made four statements when ratifying the Convention in which it claimed that a foreign state is required to obtain advance approval from or give prior notification to the coastal state when its warships pass through the territorial sea of the coastal state.[141] On October 14, 1996, when ratifying the Convention, the government of Malaysia made eight declarations, in which it stated that the provisions of the LOS Convention "do not authorize other States to carry out military exercises or maneuvers, in particular those involving the use of weapons or explosives in the exclusive economic zone without the consent of the coastal State."[142] In addition, the Malaysian government declared that foreign nuclear-powered vessels or vessels carrying nuclear material or other material of a similar nature must obtain prior authorization of passage before entering its territorial sea.[143] On May 8, 1984, when ratifying the LOS Convention, the government of the Philippines reiterated the eight understandings it made on December 10, 1982 when it signed the Convention.[144]

These declarations or understandings involve interpretations and applications of Article 17 (Right of innocent passage), Article 21 (Laws and regulations of the coastal state relating to innocent passage), Article 22 (Sea lanes and traffic separation schemes in the territorial sea), Article 23 (Foreign nuclear-powered ships and ships carrying nuclear or other inherently dangerous or noxious substances), Article 53 (Right of archipelagic sea lanes passage), and Article 58 (Rights and duties of other states in the exclusive economic zone) and have been challenged by the government of the United States. In January 1986, for example, the United States protested a declaration made by the Philippines,[145] stating that:

> With respect to other States and the nationals of such other states, the rights and duties of states are defined by international law, both customary and conventional. The rights of States under international law cannot be enlarged by their domestic legislation, absent acceptance of such enlargement by affected States.[146]

In addition to the declarations and understandings made by China, the Philippines and Malaysia, the interpretation and application of the provisions of the LOS Convention and the enactment of domestic ocean legislations by other states in

141 For the statements, visit the website of the United Nations at http://www.un.org/Depts/los/convention_agreements/convention_declarations.htm.

142 For the declarations, visit the website of the United Nations at http://www.un.org/Depts/los/convention_agreements/convention_declarations.htm.

143 Ibid.

144 For the statements, visit the website of the United Nations at http://www.un.org/Depts/los/convention_agreements/convention_declarations.htm.

145 The declaration stated that: "The signing of the Convention by the Government of the Republic of the Philippines shall not in any manner impair or prejudice the sovereign rights of the Republic of the Philippines under and arising from the Constitution of the Philippines".

146 See Roach and Smith, *supra* note 121, p. 221.

the South China Sea—Indonesia, Myanmar, Taiwan, Thailand and Vietnam—have been challenged by the United States for exceeding the provisions of the Convention. Accordingly, once the United States becomes a party the LOS Convention, it is likely to see similar disputes occur because of conflicting interpretations of the provisions in question. In particular, the United States will interpret and apply the provisions in accordance with its positions on the law of the sea, ocean policy and national interests as reflected in a set of declarations and understandings included in the Senate resolution of advice and consent to US accession to the LOS Convention drafted by the SFRC in March 2004 and December 2007, and which will surely re-emerge in any future Senate resolution on advice and consent to ratification.

On February 25, 2004, the US SFRC voted 19–0 to send the resolution of the ratification of the LOS Convention to the full Senate for advice and consent. The resolution contains two declarations made in accordance with Article 287(1) and Article 298(1) of the Convention, 24 declarations and statements of understanding made pursuant to Article 310, and five conditions relating to procedures within the United States for considering the proposed amendments to the Convention.[147] While under international law these declarations and understandings are without legal effect, US accession to the LOS Convention is subject to the declarations and policy statements contained in the Senate resolution of advice and consent. Identical declarations and understandings were included in the draft Senate resolution of advice and consent to ratification of the LOS Convention in December 2007.

Among the 26 declarations presumably to be made by the United States in the 112th Congress (2011–12) or in the years to come when acceding to the LOS Convention, two concern the dispute settlement procedure under the Convention. In accordance with Articles 287(1) and 298(1), the United States will choose special arbitration[148] for all the categories of disputes where it may be applied and arbitration[149] for all other disputes. The United States will exclude (1) disputes regarding maritime boundaries between the United States and its neighboring states, (2) disputes between the United States and foreign countries concerning military activities and certain law enforcement activities, and (3) disputes in respect to functions of the UN Security Council assigned to it by the UN Charter from the binding dispute settlement procedures provided for in Part XV of the LOS Convention. In addition, US accession to the Convention will be conditional upon the understanding that, under Article 298(1), each state party has the exclusive right to determine whether its activities are or were "military activities" and that such determinations are not

147 For the text of the 2004 Senate Resolution of Advice and Consent to Ratification, see 108th Congress, 2nd Session, Senate, *Exec. Rpt. 108–10*, March 11, 2004, pp. 16–21 and for the Text of 2007 Senate Resolution of Advice and Consent to Ratification, see 110th Congress, 1st Session, Senate, *Exec. Rept. 110–9*, December 19, 2007, pp. 19–24.

148 In accordance with the procedure provided for in Annex VIII of the LOS Convention.

149 In accordance with the procedure provided for in Annex VII of the LOS Convention.

subject to review.[150] Because of these two US declarations, and the declaration made by China on August 25, 1996, stating that the Chinese government "does not accept any of the procedures provided for in Section 2 of Part XV of the Convention with respect to all the categories of disputes referred to in paragraph 1 (a) (b) and (c) of Article 298 of the Convention," it is unlikely that the United States and China will settle their disputes over the interpretation and application of the provisions of the LOS Convention related to national security in accordance with mandatory dispute resolution mechanisms under the terms of the Convention. This is also true for possible disputes between the United States and other South China Sea-littoral countries, such as Indonesia, Malaysia, the Philippines and Myanmar.

One of the statements of understanding that will likely be included in the draft Senate Resolution of advice and consent to ratification concerns the US position that nothing in the LOS Convention, including any provisions referring to the wording "peaceful uses" or "peaceful purposes"[151] impairs the inherent right of individual or collective self-defense, or rights during armed conflict.[152] This understanding corresponds with the US position taken in 1976 during the fourth session of the Third United Nations Conference on the Law of the Sea (UNCLOS III),[153] at which an American delegate declared:

> The term "peaceful purposes" did not, of course, preclude military activities generally. The United States had consistently held that the conduct of military

150 Sec. 2, Declarations under Articles 287 and 298, Senate Resolution of Advice and Consent to Ratification, *supra* note 148.

151 The wording can be found in the Preamble, Articles 141, 143(1), 147(2)(d), 155(2), 240(a), 242 (1), 246 (3), and 301 of the LOS Convention.

152 Section 3, Other Declarations and Understandings under Article 310, understanding 1, *supra* note 148.

153 The Third United Nations Conference on the Law of the Sea was held between 1973 and 1982 with 11 sessions in total that took place in New York, Caracas, Geneva and Montego Bay. The first session of UNCLOS III was held in New York, December 3–15, 1973, which was devoted to procedural matters such as the election of officers and the adoption of the rules of procedure. The second session was held in Caracas, June 20–August 29, 1974; the third session in Geneva, March 17–May 9, 1975; the fourth session in New York, March 15–May 7, 1976; the fifth session in New York, August 2–September 17, 1976; the seventh session in Geneva, March 28–May 19, 1978 and resumed seventh session in New York, August 21–September 15, 1978; the eighth session in Geneva, March 19–April 27, 1979; and resumed eighth session in New York, July 19–August 24, 1979; the ninth session in New York, March 3–April 4, 1980; and resumed ninth session in Geneva, July 28–August 29, 1980; the tenth session in New York, March 9–April 16, 1981 and resumed tenth session in Geneva, August 3–28, 1981; the eleventh session in New York, March 8–April 30, 1982; resumed session in New York, September 22 and 24, 1982; and final session in Montego Bay, Jamaica, December 6–10, 1982. For more information about UNCLOS III, visit the website of the United Nations at: http://untreaty.un.org/cod/diplomaticconferences/lawofthesea-1982/lawofthesea-1982.html

> activities for peaceful purposes was in full accord with the Charter of the United Nations and with the principles of international law. Any specific limitation on military activities would require the negotiation of a detailed arms control agreement.[154]

This position is likely to give rise to legal disputes between the United States and South China Sea-bordering countries, in particular China, which has been taking the position that the US military-related activities conducted in the Yellow Sea, East China Sea or the South China Sea are in violation of the LOS Convention, because the US military activities targeted at China threatened its national security and therefore are not for peaceful purposes. The Chinese position is reflected in the statements it made during the 2001 EP-3 aerial collision incident and the 2009 *Impeccable* incident.

Several understandings related to the enjoyment of the right of innocent passage in foreign coastal states' territorial sea, transit passage in international straits and archipelagic sea lanes passage in archipelagic waters of archipelagic states, as well as other maritime rights related to intelligence gathering, hydrographic and military surveys in foreign coastal states' EEZs will also be included in the Senate resolution of advice and consent to ratification of the LOS Convention if the SFRC votes to report the treaty to the full Senate for consideration.[155] The United States opposes any coastal states seeking to condition its exercise of the right of innocent passage by any US ships, including warships, on the giving of prior notification to, or the receipt of, prior permission from the coastal states. That said, a number of countries bordering the South China Sea include just such conditions in their respective domestic laws, including Cambodia, China, Indonesia, Malaysia, Myanmar, Taiwan and Vietnam. The United States also claims that its ships and aircraft, including warships and military aircraft, regardless of cargo, armament, means of propulsion, flag, origin, destination or purpose, are entitled to transit passage, and archipelagic sea lanes passage in their "normal move," which includes, inter alia, submerged transit of submarines and overflight by military aircraft in military formation. The United States will interpret the wording of "straits used for international navigation" in the provisions contained in Part III of the LOS Convention as including all straits capable of being used for international navigation. The US positions have been, and will be, challenged by the countries in the South China Sea that border the Straits of Malacca and Singapore and the Taiwan Strait, and the archipelagic states in the region.

---

154 See Summary Records of Meetings Documents, Fourth Session: New York, March 15–May 7, 1976, *Official Records of the Third United Nations Convention on the Law of the Sea*, Vol. V (United Nations Publication, Sales No. E.76. V.8.), paragraph 81, p. 61.

155 Section 3, Other Declarations and Understandings under Article 310, understanding 1, *supra* note 148, understandings 2 and 3.

One of the understandings to be attached to the US Senate resolution of advice and consent to ratification of the LOS Convention is related to the interpretation of Article 58 of the Convention by the United States and states that:

> All States enjoy high seas freedoms of navigation and overflight and all other internationally lawful uses of the sea related to these freedoms, including, inter alia, military activities, such as anchoring, launching and landing of aircraft and craft, operating military devices, intelligence collection, surveillance and reconnaissance activities, exercises, operations, and conducting military surveys.[156]

It is certain that the interpretations and applications of Article 58 by the United States and the countries in the South China Sea, in particular China, will give rise to serious legal disputes in the South China Sea. This prediction can be supported by the US response to the adoption of the guidelines for navigation and overflight in the EEZs of foreign coastal states,[157] which was the product of a series of meetings on the Regime of the Exclusive Economic Zone: Issues and Responses, held from 2003 to 2005, attended by members of EEZ Group 21 and including about 14 ocean law and policy scholars from Japan, Australia, Indonesia, the Philippines, China, South Korea, Vietnam, India, and a judge from the International Tribunal for the Law of the Sea.[158]

The guidelines were adopted for the purpose of dealing with the increasing frequency and intensity of incidents involving foreign military vessels and aircraft in EEZs of the countries in the East Asian seas, such as the 2001 EP-3 and 2002 *Bowditch* incidents.[159] It is reported that the United States refuses to consider accepting the guidelines mainly because of its position that "all States enjoy high seas freedoms of navigation and overflight and all other internationally lawful uses of the sea related to these freedoms," including military exercises, hydrographic and military survey and intelligence gathering.

The United States considers that restrictions or requirements for prior consent or notification to operate military vessels or aircraft in the EEZs of foreign coastal states are inconsistent with the LOS Convention. After becoming a party to the treaty, the United States will continue to challenge the "excessive maritime claims" made by the countries that border the South China Sea through diplomatic protests

156 Section 3, Other Declarations and Understandings under Article 310, understanding 1, *supra* note 148, understanding 4.

157 EEZ Group 21, "Guidelines for Navigation and Overflight in the Exclusive Economic Zone: A Commentary," Ocean Policy Research Foundation, March 2006, available at: http://nippon.zaidan.info/seikabutsu/2005/00817/contents/0001.htm

158 See Appendix, ibid.

159 See Yann-huei Song, "The EP-3 Collision Incident, International Law and its Implications on the U.S.–China Relations," *Chinese (Taiwan) Yearbook of International Law and Affairs*, Vol. 19 (2001), pp. 1–15 and Bill Gertz, "Bowditch fight," *Inside the Ring*, September 27, 2002, available at: http://www.gertzfile.com/gertzfile/ring092702.html.

and operational assertions under the program of Freedom of Navigation, which are related to the interpretation and application of Article 7 (Straight baselines), Article 47 (Archipelagic baselines), Article 121 (Regime of islands) of the LOS Convention, and historic rights or historic title under international law.

While US interpretation and application of Article 7 concerning the use of straight baselines method were not mentioned in the statements of understanding that were included in the draft Senate resolution of advice and consent to ratification to the LOS Convention, diplomatic protests and operational assertions have been made by the government of the United States to challenge the claims made by several South China Sea countries, including China,[160] Taiwan,[161] Cambodia,[162] Vietnam,[163] the Philippines,[164] Thailand[165] and Myanmar.[166] After becoming a party to the LOS Convention and based on its previous interpretation of Article 7 (Straight baselines) and Article 46 (Archipelagic states), it can be expected that the United States will continue to challenge the claims made by South China Sea-bordering countries that use the method of straight baselines to determine their maritime zones in the South China Sea.

The interpretation and application of Article 121 are one source of legal dispute between the countries in the South China Sea. While Vietnam, Malaysia and Indonesia and perhaps the Philippines are taking the position that the Spratly Islands situated in the South China Sea cannot "sustain human habitation" or do not have "economic life of their own" and therefore should be treated as "rocks" as defined in Article 121, paragraph 3 of the LOS Convention, and "shall have no exclusive economic zone or continental shelf," China and perhaps the Philippines disagree. On March 10, 2009, the Philippines enacted an act to define its archipelagic baseline.[167] Section 2 of the Act provides that the Philippines' exercise of sovereignty and jurisdiction over the Kalayaan Island Group located

---

160 See United States Department of State Bureau of Oceans and International Environmental and Scientific Affairs, *Limits in the Seas*, No. 117, Straight Baseline Claim: China, July 9, 1996, and J. Ashley Roach and Robert W. Smith, "Straight Baselines: The Need for a Universally Applied Norm," *Ocean Development and International Law*, Vol. 31, 2000, pp. 62–3.

161 *Limits in the Seas*, No. 127, Taiwan's Maritime Claims, November 15, 2005, and J. Ashley Roach and Robert W. Smith, ibid., p. 67.

162 J. Ashley Roach and Robert W. Smith, ibid., p. 58.

163 *Limits in the Seas*, No. 99, Straight Baselines: Vietnam, December 12, 1983, and J. Ashley Roach and Robert W. Smith, ibid., pp. 59–60.

164 *Limits in the Seas*, No. 33, Straight Baselines: the Philippines, March 22, 1973, and J. Ashley Roach and Robert W. Smith, ibid., pp. 53–6.

165 *Limits in the Seas*, No. 31, Straight Baselines: Thailand, March 24, 1971, and *Limits in the Seas*, No. 122, Straight Baseline Claim: Thailand, September 8, 2000, and J. Ashley Roach and Robert W. Smith, ibid., pp. 56–7.

166 See J. Ashley Roach and Robert W. Smith, ibid., pp. 58–9.

167 The Republic Act 9522 is available at: http://www.lawphil.net/statutes/repacts/ra2009/ra_9522_2009. html.

in the Spratly Islands and Bajo de Masinloc (Scarborough Shoal) located near the Macclesfield Bank of the South China Sea should be determined as "Regime of Islands" consistent with Article 121 of the LOS Convention. The position taken by the Philippines is not clear regarding whether the feature enclosed by a polygon-shaped line in the Spratly Islands, that is, the Kalayaan Island Group, and Scarborough Shoal are considered "rocks" in accordance with Article 121, Paragraph 3, and therefore cannot claim an EEZ and continental shelf, or are treated as "islands" and therefore have the right to do so in accordance with Article 121, paragraph 2. How would the United States respond to the claim made by the Philippines after becoming a party to the LOS Convention?

In another situation, in response to the Philippines' official note sent to the UN Secretary-General on April 5, 2011, China stated in its diplomatic note dated April 11, 2011 that:

> under the relevant provisions of the 1982 United Nations Convention on the Law of the Sea, as well as the Law of the People's Republic of China on the Territorial Sea and the Contiguous Zone (1992) and the Law on the Exclusive Economic Zone and the Continental Shelf of the People's Republic of China (1998), China's Nansha [Spratly] Islands is fully entitled to Territorial Sea, Exclusive Economic Zone … and Continental Shelf.

The United States did not specifically respond to the Chinese claim except for the general statement made by Secretary Clinton in Hanoi and Bali in 2010 and 2011 respectively, indicating that "all parties should pursue their territorial claims and accompanying rights to maritime space in accordance with international law, including as reflected in the 1982 Law of the Sea Convention." However, according to Tommy Koh, the United States "is concerned about the Chinese map[168] and would oppose any attempt by China to assert rights to the waters enclosed by the nine dashed lines."[169]

Once the United States becomes a party to the LOS Convention, it is possible for the countries in the South China Sea, in particular, China, to challenge the state practice and domestic law of the United States, which, in part, claim the right to

168 This map, known as the nine-dashed-lines map, was attached to the Chinese official note to the UN Secretary-General on May 7, 2009, in which China protested the joint submission by Malaysia and Vietnam and the separate submission by Vietnam to the CLCS concerning the outer limits of their continental shelves beyond 200 n.m. in the South China Sea and stated that "China has indisputable sovereignty over the islands in the South China Sea and the adjacent waters, and enjoys sovereign rights and jurisdiction over the relevant waters as well as the seabed and subsoil thereof (see attached map). The above position is consistently held by the Chinese Government, and is widely known by the international community." See *supra* note 103.

169 "Tommy Koh, "Mapping Out Rival Claims To The South China Sea," *The Strait Times*, September 13, 2001, available at: http://www.pressdisplay.com/pressdisplay/zt/viewer.aspx.

generate 200 n.m. EEZ and continental shelf for some of the Pacific remote islands, such as Howland and Baker Islands, which cannot "sustain human habitation" or do not have "economic life of their own" and therefore should be treated as "rocks." This implies that the EEZ coordinates for Howland and Baker Islands contained in the U.S. Department of State's Public Notice No. 2237 of August 28, 1995 are not consistent with Article 121(3) of the LOS Convention,[170] and can be considered an "excessive maritime claim" made by the United States and be used as counterargument if the Chinese claim to sovereign rights over the Spratly Islands is challenged by the United States or other claimants in the South China Sea. While it was commented that "if China claims all the islands in the Spratly group with a view to claiming EEZs and continental shelves from them, then there must be some inconsistency in its position on Article 121, paragraph 3,"[171] a difference must be recognized between some of the larger islands located in the South China Sea, such as Yongxing Dao (Woody Island), Taiping Dao (Itu Aba), Pagasa (Thitu Island) and Dao Hoang Sa (Spratly Island) and Okinotorishima situated in the Western Pacific with a total land area no bigger than a king-size bed, or between some of the Spratly Islands and the Pacific remote islands, in particular Howland and Baker islands.

Although the LOS Convention contains no rules to determine a state's claim to sovereignty over land and the claim to historic waters or historic title, its preamble affirms that "matters not regulated by this Convention continue to be governed by the rules and principles of general international law." The disputes arising from the territorial and historic title claims in the South China Sea cannot be settled in accordance with the provisions of the LOS Convention, but should rely on the rules and principles of general international law. Due to the fact that the United States takes no position on any claim made by the parties to territorial disputes in the South China Sea, the United States, after acceding to the LOS Convention, will not involve itself in the disputes. However, it is possible for the United States to challenge the historic waters and historic title claims made by the countries in the South China Sea.

The position of the United States is that "to meet the international legal standard for establishing a claim to historic waters, a state must demonstrate its open, effective, long-term, and continuous exercise of authority over the body of water, coupled with acquiescence by foreign states in the exercise of that authority."[172] The

170 See *Federal Register*, Vol. 60, No. 163, Department of State Public Notice No. 2237, Regarding US EEZ and Maritime Boundaries, August 28, 1995, cited in *Maritime Claims Reference Manual*, *supra* note 7, pp. 646, 647 and 666. See also Yann-huei Song, "The Application of Article 121 of the Law of the Sea Convention to the Selected Geographical Features Situated in the Pacific Ocean," *Chinese Journal of International Law*, vol. 9 (2010), pp. 689–91.

171 Robert W. Smith, "Maritime Delimitation in the South China Sea: Potentially and Challenges," *Ocean Development and International Law*, Vol. 41 (2010), p. 223.

172 *Limits in the Sea*, No. 112, United States Responses to Excessive National Maritime Claims, March 9, 1992, available at: http://www.state.gov/documents/organization/58381.pdf, p. 8.

United States took actions to protest the historic waters claims made by Cambodia, Thailand and Vietnam in the past.[173] However, so far, no actions have been taken by the United States to challenge the historic waters or historic title claims made by Taiwan and China. In Taiwan's 1993 Policy Guidelines for the South China Sea, it was claimed that "The South China Sea area within the historic water limit is the maritime area under the jurisdiction of the Republic of China, in which the Republic of China possesses all rights and interests."[174] However, these policy guidelines were suspended in December 2005 under the Chen Shui-Bin administration.

As far as China's historic title claim is concerned, it was stated by the former PRC Deputy Foreign Minister Li Zhaoxin, in 1996, that after ratification of the LOS Convention, China "can still preserve and protect its rights and interests in the South China Sea based on the nine-dashed-lines map and the traditional fishing activities conducted by the Chinese fishers in the Spratly Islands, as well as the Convention's specific rules on historic waters."[175] Although the Deputy Foreign Minister referred incorrectly to the Convention's specific provisions that governed historic waters, he did suggest that a claim to historic title or traditional fishing rights can be made by China in the South China Sea. This claim was then incorporated into law on the Exclusive Economic Zone and the Continental Shelf of the People's Republic of China, promulgated by Order No. 6 of the President of the People's Republic of China on June 26, 1998. Article 14 of the law provides that "The provisions in this Law shall not affect the enjoyment of historic rights by the People's Republic of China."[176] Accordingly, the claim made by China on April 14, 2011 to enjoy sovereign rights over its EEZ and continental shelf of the Spratly Islands should not affect China's historic rights in the waters encircled by the nine dashed lines in the South China Sea. At present, it is still not clear whether China is making a claim to historic rights in the area enclosed by the nine-dashed-lines map which was attached to its diplomatic note to the UN Secretary-General on May 7, 2009.

It remains to be seen if any actions, and if so, which, will be taken by the United States to challenge the Chinese historic rights claim in the South China Sea. But the position of the United States is: "Consistent with international law, claims to maritime space in the South China Sea should be derived solely from legitimate

173 Ibid., pp. 10–12.

174 See Kuan-Ming Sun, "The Republic of China's Policy Toward the South China Sea: A Review," *Issues & Studies*, March 1996, p. 43.

175 Explanation concerning the Item that Proposes to Consider the Ratification of the United Nations Convention on the Law of the Sea, Li Zhaoxing, Deputy Foreign Minister, at the 19th Meeting of the Standing Committee of the Eighth National People's Congress on May 15, 1996.

176 Law on the Exclusive Economic Zone and the Continental Shelf of the People's Republic of China, adopted at the 3rd Meeting of the Standing Committee of the Ninth National People's Congress on June 26, 1998 and promulgated by Order No. 6 of the President of the People's Republic of China on June 26, 1998, available at: http://www.asianlii.org/cn/legis/cen/laws/loteezatcsotproc790/.

claims to land features."[177] In addition, no matter whether the United States becomes a party to the LOS Convention or continues to stay outside the treaty, it can be expected that the United States will act to challenge the interpretation and application of Article 58 of the LOS Convention by the countries of the South China Sea, in particular China, because the enjoyment of military-related freedom of navigation and overflight in the EEZs in the South China Sea is considered a vital national interest of the United States.

Conclusion

It is unlikely that the United States will become a party to the LOS Convention in 2012. Due to political considerations, it is less likely that the US administration and Democrats in the US Senate will push for the ratification of any controversial treaty during an election year. Unfortunately, the LOS Convention has been considered a controversial treaty in the United States ever since being transmitted to the Senate by President Clinton in 1994, and has not yet received Senate advice and consent for ratification. However, it is still possible for the country to ratify the Convention if the Obama administration and the US Senate work closely to move the treaty forward.

It is possible for the SFRC to hold hearings on the LOS Convention during the 112th Congress, as it did in 2004 and 2007, provided that President Obama decides to push for the ratification of the treaty and dedicates significant political resources to the task. The recent establishment of the Senate Oceans Caucus, which consists of 18 bipartisan groups of US senators and most of the members of which are in support of the LOS Convention, could bring hope for US accession to the LOS Convention in 2011–12.

The United States has a national interest in the management of the potential conflict in the South China Sea and the maintenance of peace and stability in the region. US interests in the South China Sea sovereignty and maritime disputes include: (1) freedom of navigation and overflight rights; (2) security commitments to US allies and partners; (3) regional peace and stability; (4) sea lines of communication; (5) open commerce and access to maritime commons; and (6) international order at sea. As either a nonparty to the LOS convention or a member of the treaty at some point in the future, the United States will continue to act to challenge what it views as "excessive maritime claims" made by countries bordering the South China Sea. Diplomatic protests and operational assertions will be conducted by the U.S. Department of State and Department of Defense under the 1979 Freedom of Navigation Program to challenge "excessive maritime claims" which it views as in violation of the provisions contained in the LOS Convention.

However, after becoming a party to the LOS Convention, the United States will be asked to bring its laws and conduct into conformity with the treaty. The United States should interpret, apply and implement the treaty in accordance

---

177 Secretary Clinton's remarks in Bali, Indonesia, July 22, 2011, *supra* note 11.

with the provisions contained in the LOS Convention. On the one hand, the legitimacy of the actions taken by the United States to challenge the asserted "excessive maritime claims" in the South China Sea could be underscored. On the other hand, American practices and claims relating to the law of the sea—in particular concerning the interpretation and application of the provisions of the LOS Convention—could be challenged by countries bordering the South China Sea. Examples of such challenges include the possible legal disputes over the interpretation and application of Article 58 and Article 121 of the Convention that govern the right to claim an EEZ and continental shelf for a feature that cannot sustain human habitation or does not have its own economic life, and the right to conduct military-related activities in the EEZ of foreign coastal states.

China's claims in the South China Sea, in particular the claim related to historic rights in the area enclosed by the nine-dashed-lines map that was made public to the international community in May 2009, and the claim related to China's sovereign rights and jurisdiction over its EEZ and continental shelf surrounding the Spratly Islands, will become a main source for possible conflict not only between China and the United States, but also between China and other countries that border the South China Sea.

A question was raised by U.S. Senator David Vitter at a hearing on the LOS Convention held in September 2007: "If the [LOS Convention] is so definitive and clear, then why is there a need for 24 declarations and understandings [that were included in the Senate draft resolution of advice and consent to ratification]?"[178] In addition, Senator Vitter said that the pollution provisions of the LOS Convention would open a "Pandora's box."[179] Would US accession to the Convention open a "Pandora's box" in the South China Sea, where tension has been rising, "excessive maritime claims" are protested and the United States has enduring national interests? The question might be answered when the SFRC decides to hold hearings on the LOS Convention and again votes to send the treaty to the full Senate for a vote on a resolution of advice and consent for ratification that contains the same 26 declarations and statements of understanding that appeared in the 2004 and 2007 Senate draft resolution of advice and consent.

---

178 Cliff Kincaid,"Bush Officials Deceive Senators at Hearing on U.N.'s Law of the Sea Treaty; Sen. Vitter Cites Proof that Pact is a Back-door Global Warming," *USA Survival News*, September 30, 2007, available at: http://www.usasurvival.org/ck09.30.07.shtml.

179 Ibid.

Chapter 6
Maritime Boundary Delimitation, Excessive Claims and Effective Regime Building in the South China Sea

Sam Bateman

Maritime Boundaries

The world was a much simpler place when countries could only claim a three nautical mile (nm) territorial sea. Then maritime boundaries were not required unless countries were adjacent to each other on the same piece of land, or had territories lying within six nm of each other. When the territorial sea was the limit of a country's maritime jurisdiction, boundary differences had little effect on the relative size of jurisdiction that a country could claim and maritime boundary negotiations between neighbouring countries were comparatively straightforward. All this has changed. Countries now require maritime boundaries if they have territory within 400 nm of each other (and more in situations where the countries have an entitlement to an extended continental shelf), and the location of a boundary can have a large effect on the size of a country's maritime jurisdiction. It is little wonder that since the acceptance of the extended maritime jurisdiction allowed by the 1982 UN Convention on the Law of the Sea (UNCLOS), the pace of maritime boundary delimitations has slowed down.

Despite the old adage that "good fences make good neighbors",[1] sometimes it is physically impossible, for a variety of reasons, to build good fences, particularly in the sea. This is the case in East Asia mainly because the complex geography of the region, with its concave areas of coast, numerous islands and archipelagos, and longstanding historic claims, means that many boundaries, or at least their end points or turning points ("tri-points" or "tri-junctions"), will require the agreement of three, or even more, countries. Boundaries are also not an end in themselves. Their purpose is to set limits on sovereignty, jurisdiction and the allocation of resources, and to provide a basis for effective management of regional oceans and seas. Without them, good order at sea is much more problematic.[2]

---

1 Attributed to Robert Frost, *Mending a Wall*, in J.M. and M.J. Cohen, *The Penguin Dictionary of Quotations*, 1st ed., Harmondsworth: Penguin Books, 1960, p. 163.

2 Sam Bateman, "Good Order at Sea in the South China Sea" in Shicun Wu and Keyuan Zou (eds), *Maritime Security in the South China Sea: Regional Implications and*

Further difficulties arise due to liberal interpretations by regional countries of the principles in UNCLOS for drawing straight territorial sea baselines. Coastal States have an incentive to make maximum use of straight baselines as it enables them to maximize the extent of their maritime jurisdiction. Straight baselines may also be advantageous in maritime boundary delimitation negotiations. As Victor Prescott has explained, "States may also use such lines to gain an advantage in negotiating common boundaries with neighbouring states."[3]

Almost all East Asian countries (that is, Cambodia, China, Japan, North Korea, South Korea, Malaysia, Myanmar, Thailand and Vietnam) have used straight baselines. Many of these appear excessive in terms of what is customarily regarded as acceptable under international law.[4] At issue then is whether these straight baselines should be the starting point for boundary determinations or whether it should be the actual coastline. In making their joint submission for an extended continental shelf in the South China Sea, Malaysia and Vietnam accepted each other's straight baselines as the base points for determining the area of continental shelf covered by the submission (see Figure 6.1).[5]

There are two other issues which complicate maritime boundary delimitation that are relevant to the situation in the South China Sea. The first is that the negotiation and adoption of a maritime boundary between two or more States is always "political in nature."[6] There are no firm laws for boundary-making. Two countries may agree whatever boundary they like. Provided an agreement is a bilateral one and there is no impact on a third party, there are few limitations on the type of boundary arrangement that might be reached between two countries.[7] However, it is often the case in the South China Sea that a bilateral boundary agreement will have some impact on a third party. The fundamental point is that each delimitation is different and there is no limit on the factors that might be considered in reaching an equitable outcome.

International Cooperation. Farnham: Ashgate, 2009, pp. 15–34.

3 J.R.V. Prescott, "Straight and Archipelagic Baselines" in Gerald Blake, ed., *Maritime Boundaries and Ocean Resources*. London: Croom Helm, 1987, p. 39.

4 Sam Bateman and Clive Schofield, "State Practice regarding Straight Baselines in East Asia—Legal, Technical and Political Issues in a Changing Environment", Paper for international conference on "The Difficulties of Implementing the Provisions of UNCLOS", International Hydrographic Bureau, Monaco, October 16–17, 2008, http://www.gmat.unsw.edu.au/ablos/ ABLOS08Folder/ablos08_papers.htm.

5 Sam Bateman and Clive Schofield, 'Outer Shelf Claims in the South China Sea: New Dimension to Old Disputes', *RSIS Commentary 65/2009*, Singapore: S. Rajaratnam School of International Studies, July 1, 2009.

6 Division for Ocean Affairs and the Law of the Sea. *Handbook on the Delimitation of Maritime Boundaries*. 2000. United Nations: New York, para 193, p. 42.

7 Bill Campbell, "Maritime Boundary Arrangements in the Timor Sea", in Donald R. Rothwell and Martin Tsamenyi (eds), *The Maritime Dimensions of Independent East Timor*, Wollongong Papers on Maritime Policy No.8, Centre for Maritime Policy, University of Wollongong, 2000, p. 76.

This essentially political flexibility in determining maritime boundaries is particularly apparent when assessing whether EEZ and continental shelf boundaries should be coincident. Different approaches to this issue are evident around the world. While the general trend is to have coincident seabed and water column boundaries,[8] this is not always possible, and states with overlapping EEZ claims may adopt separate boundaries for the EEZ and the continental shelf.[9] This may be the case when a continental shelf boundary was agreed, largely on the basis of geological considerations, prior to wide acceptance of the EEZ regime in the late 1970s and early 1980s. While the two boundaries need not necessarily coincide, as a matter of international order, the use of separate boundaries is desirable in view of the complicated legal regime that might result and the possibility that tensions between the parties could be heightened.[10] This is a relatively new problem of international law with no good experience yet of how the inevitable management difficulties will be resolved. It may become an issue for marine resource development in the South China Sea where overlapping jurisdictions might be an outcome of boundary negotiations.

When the seabed boundary is different to the water column boundary, one State has jurisdiction over fisheries while the other has jurisdiction over the oil and minerals of the seabed and subsoil. This is the situation now with segments of the maritime boundary between Australia and Indonesia. However, in an apparent rebuttal of any Indonesian bid to seek a similar arrangement with Malaysia in the waters east of Natuna Island in the South China Sea, as well as in the northern part of the Malacca Strait, Malaysia made a declaration on ratifying UNCLOS that the Malaysian understanding was these boundaries should coincide.[11] An EEZ boundary coincident with the previously agreed continental shelf boundary in this area would appear inequitable for Indonesia.

The last issue to mention that complicates the delimitation of maritime boundaries is that the principles involved have become more complex. As Ivan Shearer has noted with regard to trends in the delimitation of the continental

8 Robin R. Churchill and A.V. Lowe, *The Law of the Sea*, 3rd ed., Manchester: Juris Publishing, Manchester University Press, 1999, p. 197.

9 For example, the EEZ boundary agreed, but not yet ratified, between Australia and Indonesia in the Timor and Arafura Seas does not coincide with the pre-existing seabed boundary in some parts of these seas. *Treaty between the Government of Australia and the Government of the Republic of Indonesia establishing an Exclusive Economic Zone Boundary and certain Seabed Boundaries*, signed March 14, 1997.

10 David James Attard, *The Exclusive Economic Zone in International Law*. Oxford: Clarendon Press, 1987, pp. 214 and 216.

11 All declarations and statements with respect to the Convention and to the Agreement on Part XI made before December 31, 1996—upon signature, ratification or accession—have been analysed and published in *"The Law of the Sea: Declarations and statements with respect to the United Nations Convention on the Law of the Sea and to the Agreement relating to the Implementation of Part XI of the United Nations Convention on the Law of the Sea"*, (United Nations publication, Sales No. E.97.V.3).

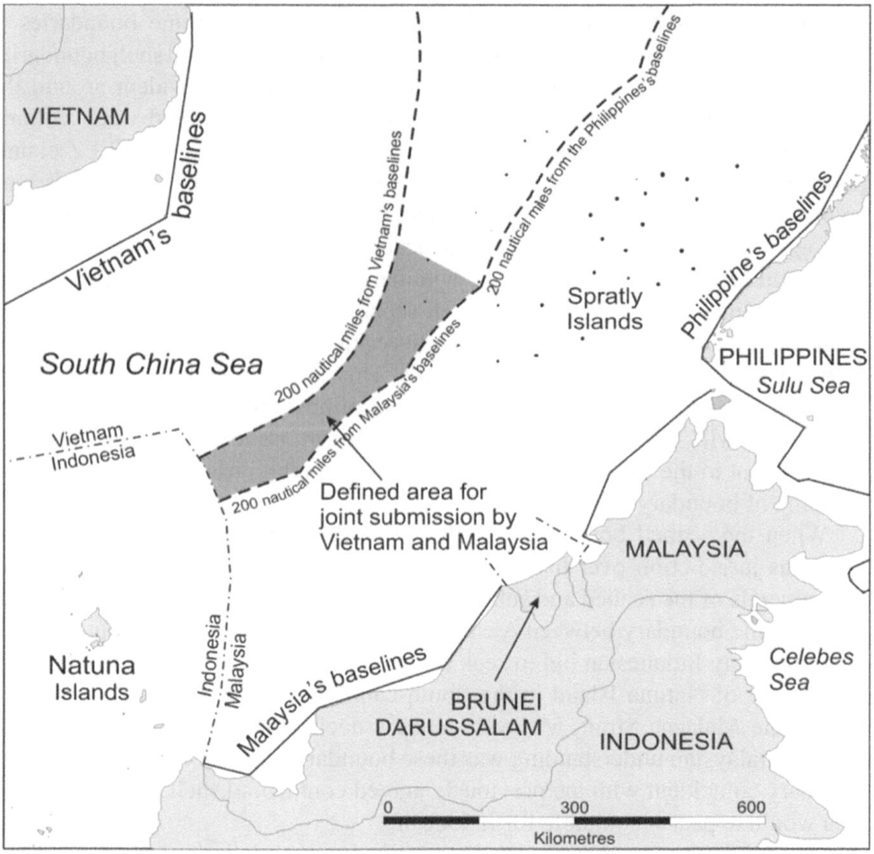

Figure 6.1 Malaysian and Vietnamese Joint Submission

Source: Prepared by I Made Andi Arsana of the Department of Geodetic Engineering, Gadjah Mada University, Indonesia.

shelf and of the EEZ, "Emphasis is now placed not on natural prolongation but on the geography of the immediate area in which delimitation is to take place, on disparity in coastal lengths, and—to a limited extent—economic factors affecting the immediate area."[12]

The International Court of Justice (ICJ) has applied "equitable principles" to judgments relating to the determination of maritime boundaries but has been loath to list or define the factors that will be considered in assessing equity.[13] It is not just a matter of equidistance. Consideration may also be given to geographical

12 Ivan A. Shearer, *Starke's International Law*, 11th ed. London: Butterworths, 1994, pp. 244–5.

13 For a succinct description of the relevant factors considered by Courts and Tribunals in determining maritime boundaries, see Stuart Kaye, *Australia's Maritime*

features, including length of coastline, the shape of the opposite or adjacent coasts (particularly whether they are concave or convex), and the relative weight to be given islands as opposed to mainland, as well as to geological, geomorphological, economic and political factors.[14] Nevertheless, and despite all the learned legal debate on the issue, "the happy fact" is "that nobody has ever really known what an 'equitable principle' of delimitation was or is."[15]

It has been claimed that the equitable principles of greatest importance to the South China Sea are that islands should not generate full maritime zones in relation to adjacent larger land bodies, and that the proportional lengths of coastlines are important in determining whether an allocation is equitable.[16] Another relevant consideration is that, in deliberating on maritime boundaries, the ICJ has given consideration to traditional fishing activities, and the relative impact on the livelihood and economic well-being of the countries concerned, and the political status of the territories involved. In the South China Sea, traditional fishing could be an important consideration, for example, in and around the Paracel islands which have been traditionally fished by Vietnamese fishermen.[17]

The South China Sea

The general width of the South China Sea is in the order of 600–700 nm. This means that when only the claimed territorial sea baselines are taken into account and no weight is given to offshore islands, there is a significant belt of high seas in the middle of the sea beyond national jurisdiction (see Figure 6.2). However, this area outside of national jurisdiction may disappear altogether if extended continental shelves are accepted in the area. The area of high seas is larger if the limits to national jurisdiction are taken from the coastline rather than from the territorial sea baselines, which as has been noted, in the case of some bordering countries appear excessive.

The situation is further complicated by the fact that most of the area beyond 200 nm from the mainland coasts is within 200 nm from the various small islands in

Boundaries, Wollongong Papers in Maritime Policy No.4, Centre for Maritime Policy, University of Wollongong, 1996, pp. 11–26.

14 A useful discussion in the context of the South China Sea of the "equitable principles" that have been used to resolves boundary disputes may be found in Mark Valencia, M.J., Jon M. Van Dyke and Noel A. Ludwig, *Sharing the Resources of the South China Sea*. The Hague: Martinus Nijhoff Publishers, 1997, pp. 50–54.

15 Malcolm D. Evans, "Maritime Boundary Delimitation: Where Do We Go From Here?", in David Freestone, Richard Barnes and David Ong (eds), *The Law of the Sea: Prospects and Problems*. Oxford: Oxford University Press, 2006, p. 144.

16 Valencia, Van Dyke and Ludwig, *Sharing the Resources of the South China Sea*, p. 134.

17 Greg Torode, "Disputed Islands are prized catch", *South China Morning Post*, May 30, 2011, p. A4.

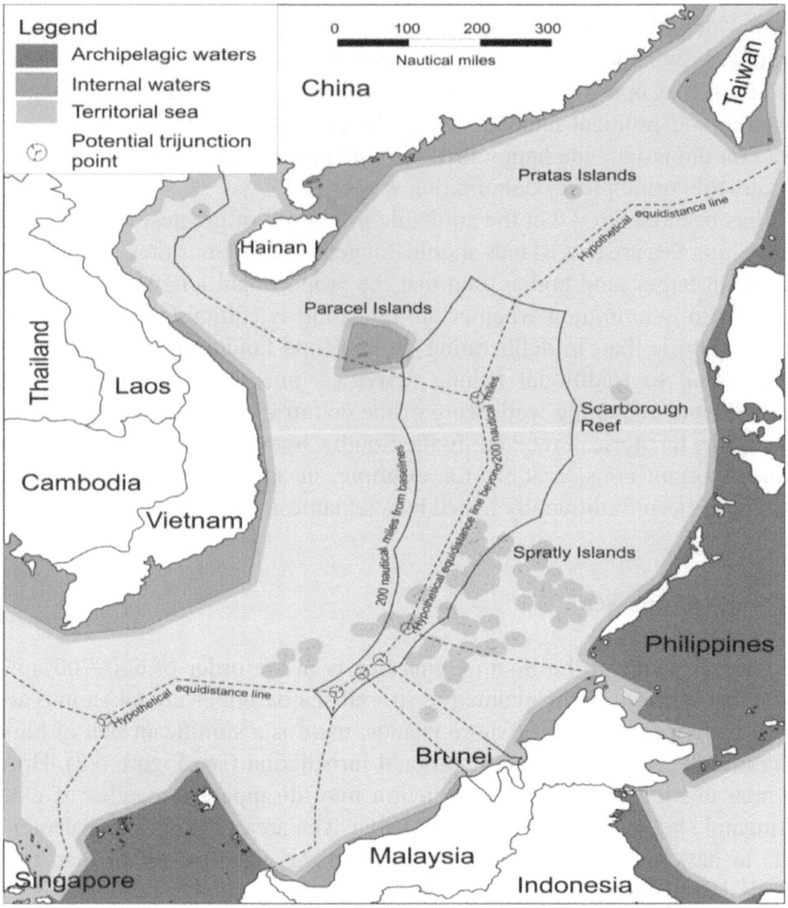

Figure 6.2 Notional Equidistance Lines in the South China Sea ignoring the Islands

Source: Prepared by I Made Andi Arsana of the Department of Geodetic Engineering, Gadjah Mada University, Indonesia.

the South China Sea. This means that if any of the islands within the major groups of the Pratas, Paracel and Spratly islands are recognized as generating a full set of maritime zones, there is no area of the South China Sea that is outside of national jurisdiction.[18] This situation is shown in Figure 6.3 which includes equidistant lines between the various features and the coasts of the bordering countries.

18 Alex G. Oude Elferink, "The Islands in the South China Sea: How does their Presence Limit the Extent of the High Seas and the Area and the Maritime Zones of the Mainland Coasts", *Ocean Development and International Law*, Vol. 32, 2001, p. 169.

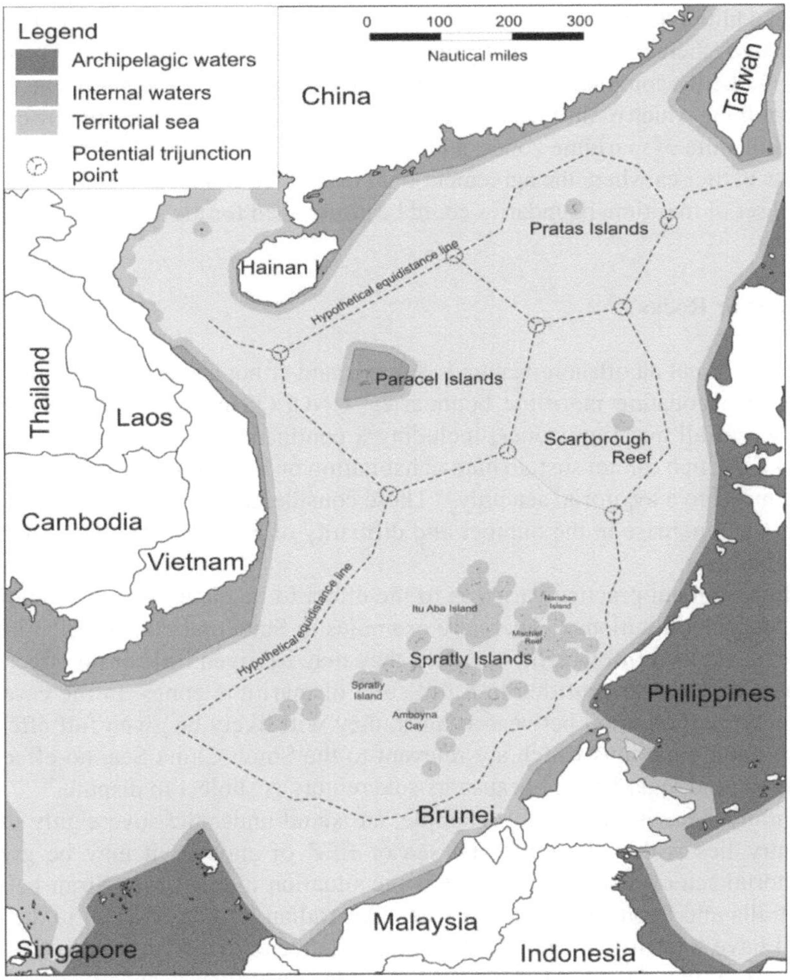

Figure 6.3 Notional Equidistance Lines in the South China Sea including the Islands

Source: Prepared by I Made Andi Arsana of the Department of Geodetic Engineering, Gadjah Mada University, Indonesia.

Other boundary disputes exist in the South China Sea that are independent of sovereignty over the islands. These include the boundaries in the South between Indonesia and Malaysia and in the North between the Philippines and China and Taiwan. Indonesia has enclosed the Anambas and Natuna Islands within its system of archipelagic baselines. The continental shelf boundary agreed with Malaysia in 1969 applies to the east and west of Natuna Island, but there is no EEZ boundary. The Philippines has as yet no maritime boundaries with its neighbors.

In addition to the general problems of maritime boundary delimitation already discussed, there are two other features of the geography of the South China Sea that markedly complicate maritime boundary making in the region. The first is determining which of the many offshore features in the South China Sea are entitled to a full suite of maritime zones, and the second is the existence of numerous tri-points in the sea where the agreement of at least three countries is required before a full set of maritime boundaries could be established for the sea.

Islands or Rocks?

Whether or not an offshore feature is a true island or not can be a vitally important issue in negotiating maritime boundaries. UNCLOS provides that islands are entitled to all maritime zones, including a continental shelf and EEZ, but that "rocks", which cannot sustain human habitation or an economic life of their own, are limited to a territorial sea only.[19] These considerations have contributed to "a dramatic" increase in the number and difficulty of potential maritime boundary delimitations.[20]

International practice varies as to the effect to be given islands in maritime boundary delimitations.[21] There are examples in State practice in which islands have been given full weight, but often they may be given little or no effect even if an island appears entitled to a full suite of maritime zones. In the case of a boundary delimitation between islands, they will likely be given full effect. In some other situations which are relevant to the South China Sea, no effect has been granted to an island because its sovereignty is subject to dispute.[22]

In other cases, where, for example, an island under the sovereignty of one country lies within the territorial sea or EEZ of another, it may be given a territorial sea of reduced size. This is the situation in the Torres Strait between Australia and Papua New Guinea where Australian islands adjacent to the PNG coast have a territorial sea based on equidistance on their landward side and a three nm territorial sea on their seaward side. Australian islands further out in the strait but were given an all round territorial sea of only 3 nm and are enclaves within PNG's EEZ. There are similar situations elsewhere in the world and these provide a potential precedent for the South China Sea.[23]

The tests of human habitation and economic life to determine whether a particular feature is a rock or an island entitled to a full set of maritime zones have attracted considerable attention in the literature. Prescott and Schofield

19 UNCLOS Article 121.

20 UN. *Handbook on the Delimitation of Maritime Boundaries*, para 153, p. 33.

21 Ibid., pp. 33–4.

22 Ibid., para 159, p. 34.

23 Valencia, Van Dyke and Ludwig, *Sharing the Resources of the South China Sea*, pp. 47–8.

claim that these tests should be applied only when it has been established that an insular feature is a rock. They argue that to classify a particular feature as a rock because it cannot sustain human habitation or an economic life of its own is to put "the cart before the horse."[24] The basic test is to decide whether the feature meets the ordinary meaning of a rock, which might include an islet but needs to be distinguished from an island proper.[25] The general conclusion appears to be that the term "rock" in UNCLOS Article 121(3) denotes any type of small islands.[26]

The greater majority of the features in the South China Sea fall short of being fully fledged islands in accordance with UNCLOS Part VIII capable of generating a full suite of maritime zones. Most are classified as submerged features or low-tide elevations.[27] Some, however, are above water at high tide and thus come within the regime of islands in UNCLOS. According to Schofield, "A case can be made that some of the Spratlys at least, are fully fledged islands capable of generating claims to continental shelf and EEZ rights."[28] Itu Aba, Spratly Island and Thi Tu in the Spratlys, Lincoln Island and Woody Island in the Paracels, and Pratas Island have been identified as features in the South China Sea that due to their size and other characteristics appear to be fully fledged islands.[29]

This line of argument tends to make the arguments over the tests of whether a feature can sustain human habitation or an economic life of its own rather semantic. If there are features within the South China Sea that are true islands rather than rocks then these tests do not apply. This at least removes one area of debate that was leading nowhere because the tests could be interpreted so many different ways that it was useless. Even if the tests could be applied so as to provide an answer, it is also the case that the ability of rocks to sustain human habitation might change over time. As Schofield and Prescott observe, "There can be no doubt that future technology will make it easier to occupy rocks and exploit their resources without any habitation if that is desirable."[30]

The size of a feature is an important element in determining whether it is an island or a rock. However, there is no agreement on what the size criterion should be, and attempts to define islands, rocks and islets on the basis of size have failed.[31] A detailed discussion of features in the South China Sea, which may

---

24 Victor Prescott and Clive Schofield, *The Maritime Political Boundaries of the World* 2nd ed. 2005. Leiden: Martinus Nijhoff Publishers, p. 76.

25 Ibid., p. 67

26 Marius Gjetnes, "The Spratlys: Are They Rocks or Islands?", *Ocean Development and International Law*, Vol. 32, 2001, p. 194.

27 Clive Schofield, "Dangerous Ground: A geopolitical overview of the South China Sea", in Sam Bateman and Ralf Emmers (eds), *Security and International Politics in the South China Sea*. Abingdon: Routledge, 2009, p. 13.

28 Clive Schofield, "Dangerous Ground", p. 14.

29 Elferink, "The Islands in the South China Sea", p. 178.

30 Prescott and Schofeld., *The Maritime Political Boundaries of the World*, p. 78.

31 Gjetnes, "The Spratlys", p. 194.

Table 6.1 Relative size of small islands

Island	Occupied by:	Land Size (hectare)
South China Sea.		
Itu Aba	Taiwan	38.4–50
Thitu Is.	Philippines	22–37.2
West York Is	Philippines	16
Spratly Is.	Vietnam	13–30
Woody Island (Paracels)	China	500
Pattle Island (Paracels)	China	30
Duncan Is. (Paracels)	China	48
Pratas Is.	Taiwan	174
Islands Elsewhere		
Okinotorishima	Japan	<1
Rose Island	US (American Samoa)	21.4
Swain Island	US (American Samoa)	186.5
Ashmore Is.	Australia	11.4
Cartier Is.	Australia	1.7
Marotiri	French Polynesia	4.3
Clipperton Island	France	600
Bassas da India	France	20
Theva-I-Ra	Fiji	2

Sources: Various.

Notes: A range of sizes for a particular feature results from the various sources providing different areas.

appear capable of supporting claims to a full suite of maritime zones, is beyond the scope of this chapter. However, Table 6.1 compares the sizes of major features within the South China Sea with other islands in the Indo-Pacific region that have been used to support an extended EEZ. The data in this table supports the view that there is ample precedent for some of the features in the South China qualifying as islands that might support claims to a continental shelf and EEZ. Furthermore, giving no weight at all to these features would seem to run counter to the premises of international law applicable to maritime boundary delimitation.[32]

Notwithstanding the above discussion, it would simplify maritime boundary delimitation in the South China Sea if the claimant states could be persuaded to give up claims for maritime zones beyond a 12 nm territorial sea.[33] Beckman has argued that by making their joint extended continental submission, in effect Malaysia and Vietnam have acknowledged that none of the Spratly islands

32 Elferink, "The Islands in the South China Sea", p. 179.

33 Ibid., p. 171.

is entitled to a full suite of maritime zones.[34] On the other hand, if some of the Spratlys and Paracels, as well the Pratas Islands about which there seems to be less question about their status as islands, could generate a full set of zones, then there would be no areas of high seas or extended continental shelf in the South China Sea. Despite the submission by Malaysia and Vietnam, it is unlikely that other claimants in the South China Sea, particularly China, would accept the position that no features in the South China Sea can generate EEZs and continental shelves.

Third Parties and Tri-points

Many delimitation situations involve the presence of third States and this is certainly the case in the South China Sea. This is a consequence of the geography of the South China Sea with the presence of eight bordering entities (Indonesia, Malaysia, Brunei, the Philippines, Singapore, Taiwan, China and Vietnam). The situation is then complicated by the presence of the islands in the sea, which as has been argued, may be entitled to generate an EEZ and a continental shelf. Depending on any future agreement on sovereignty over these features, we thus have a situation where potentially there are numerous "tri-points" in the sea which require the agreement of at least three countries before a full set of straight-line maritime boundaries might be achieved.

In practical terms, when two countries are negotiating a maritime boundary agreement, they end their delimitation line before it reaches the area of overlapping potential claim by a third State, or at the point equidistant to the coast of the parties to the negotiations and the third State.[35] This is the situation in the eastern and western approaches to Singapore Strait where bilateral boundary agreements have been agreed between the three pairs of parties (that is, Singapore and Malaysia, Singapore and Indonesia, Indonesia and Malaysia), but there are gaps with no agreed boundaries where tri-lateral negotiations would be required to determine the tri-point where the respective pairs of boundaries intersect.

Figure 6.3 circles the possible "tri-points" in the northern part of the South China Sea. The situation is more complicated, however, in the southern part of the sea where, even if the Spratly islands are given no weight, potential tri-points are required as follows between:

- Singapore, Indonesia and Malaysia;
- Indonesia, Malaysia (West) and Vietnam;
- Indonesia, Malaysia (East) and Vietnam; and
- Brunei, Malaysia and the Philippines.

34 Robert Beckman, "South China Sea: Worsening Dispute or Growing Clarity in Claims?" *RSIS Commentary 90/2010*, Singapore: S. Rajaratnam School of International Studies, August 16, 2010.

35 UN, *Handbook on the Delimitation of Maritime Boundaries*, para. 204, p. 45.

The situation becomes much more complicated if some of the Spratlys are recognized as potentially generating EEZ and continental shelf claims, and possibly even under the sovereignty of different nations. The number of "tri-points" then multiplies with the possible creation of points also where the agreement of four nations might be required before a full set of maritime boundaries might be achieved. This remains the case even if the insular features are restricted to a territorial sea only, or as other authors have suggested, they are restricted to a 500-meter safety zone.[36]

Alex Elferink has given extensive consideration to the role of third States in maritime boundary delimitations. After analyzing relevant case law, one of his conclusions is that courts have limited decisions to an area outside the claims of the third States leaving a large part of the bilateral boundary undefined.[37] In the South China Sea, these areas could be very large thus highlighting again the difficulty of developing a full set of straight line maritime boundaries in the area.

Need for Effective Regimes in the South China Sea

Douglas Johnston claimed over a decade ago that the nature of maritime boundaries is affected by two concurrent trends in ocean development and management.[38] The first is the proliferation of "extensive zones of national administrative authority under 'regimes' of functional jurisdiction vested in the coastal state. Such regimes would include resource management, marine environmental protection and marine scientific research. The second trend was toward the building of regional or sub-regional 'regimes' of negotiated arrangements designed to facilitate cooperation in ocean development and management. This he saw as reflecting the "cooperative ethic" of UNCLOS.

Unfortunately, however, this wishful thinking has not been realized generally, or in the South China Sea in particular. Attempts to implement the UNCLOS Part IX obligations to cooperate in the management of enclosed and semi-enclosed seas have not achieved the desired outcomes in the Mediterranean and Caribbean seas, and the experience so far with the East Asian Seas Action Plan steered by

36 Valencia, Van Dyke and Ludwig, *Sharing the Resources of the South China Sea*, p. 133.

37 Alex G. Oude Elferink, "Third States in Maritime Delimitation Cases: Too big a Role, Too Small a Role, or Both?" in Aldo Chircop, Ted L. McDorman and Susan J. Rolston, eds, *The Future of Ocean Regime-Building—Essays in Tribute to Douglas M. Johnston*. Leiden: Martins Nijhoff Publishers, 2009, p. 624.

38 Douglas M. Johnston, *The Theory and History of Ocean Boundary Making*. Montreal: McGill-Queens Press, 1998, p. 227.

the Coordinating Body on the Seas of East Asia (COBSEA) give few grounds for optimism that successful outcomes will be achieved.[39]

As Elferink has observed, case law has moved in the opposite direction to the trend welcomed by Johnston of seeing maritime boundaries as facilitating ocean development and management. As he notes, "instead of an emphasis on the particularistic of any delimitation, the recent case law has contributed to the consolidation of legal norms, emphasizing the centrality of equidistance in the delimitation process."[40] However, it could be argued that the cases considered by Elferink involved areas where the geography was less complicated to that of the South China Sea. A strong case exists for the functionalist approach to the South China Sea although the claimants are still failing to recognize the merits of such an approach.

There is still no effective regime in the South China Sea for cooperative marine management and good order at sea: for the safety and security of shipping; the preservation, protection and conservation of the marine environment; the exploration and exploitation of marine resources; the prevention of illegal activity at sea; and the conduct of marine scientific research. This is despite the obligation of all countries bordering a body of water, such as the South China Sea, to cooperate in accordance with Part IX of UNCLOS, to which convention all the littoral countries are parties.[41] The 2002 ASEAN-China Declaration on the Conduct of Parties in the South China Sea (DOC) is agreed "soft law" that also invites the littoral countries to cooperate on certain marine activities. The DOC was an important confidence-building measure, but it is non-binding and falls short of constituting a successful regime for providing security and cooperative marine management in the South China Sea.

The trans-boundary issues in the South China Sea needing cooperation include the five activities identified in the DOC as requiring cooperation pending a comprehensive and durable settlement of the dispute. These are:

a. marine environmental protection;
b. marine scientific research;
c. safety of navigation and communication at sea;

---

39 Alfred Hu Nien-Tsu, "Semi-enclosed Troubled Waters: A New Thinking on the Application of the 1982 UNCLOS Article 123 to the South China Sea", *Ocean Development and International Law* 41, no. 3 (2010): 281–314.

40 Elferink, "Third States in Maritime Delimitation Cases", p. 638.

41 The Council for Security Cooperation in the Asia Pacific (CSCAP) has produced Guidelines for Maritime Cooperation in Enclosed and Semi-Enclosed Seas and Similar Sea Areas of the Asia Pacific, CSCAP Memorandum No. 13, June 2008, http://www.cscap.org/index.php?page=cscap-memoranda. The guidelines are a set of fundamental, non-binding principles to guide maritime cooperation in the enclosed and semi-enclosed seas of the region, and to help develop a common understanding and approach to maritime issues in the region.

d. search and rescue operations; and
e. combating national crime, including, but not limited to, trafficking in illegal drugs, piracy and armed robbery at sea, and illegal traffic in arms.[42]

Despite the pressing and very obvious importance of cooperation in the South China Sea, very little progress has been made with implementing the required cooperation. Many of the littoral countries to the South China Sea are still not party to the relevant international conventions that provide the framework for good order at sea.[43] Furthermore, the demands for effective management regimes in the South China Sea will become more acute in the future. Volumes of shipping traffic will continue to increase with greater risks of ship-sourced marine pollution and shipping accidents. There will be increased pressure on the resources of the South China Sea, living and non-living, as well as growing concern for the protection and preservation of the sea's sensitive eco-systems and marine biodiversity.[44]

The lack of an effective regime in the South China Sea is due to the several sovereignty disputes over islands and reefs in the sea and the consequent lack of agreed maritime jurisdiction. The littoral countries are committed to a nationalistic approach to their claimed waters and are reluctant to embark on initiatives that may appear to compromise their sovereignty. They are still looking for "fences" in the sea to demarcate the limits of their sovereignty and sovereign rights, and have so far stopped short of effective cooperation or regime building despite the political framework provided by the DOC. Because so many issues of managing ocean space are trans-boundary in nature, fences cannot be established in the sea in the same way as border fences are established on land. As Mark Valencia has succinctly observed:

> Indeed, when countries in Asia think maritime, they think first and foremost about boundary disputes, not protection of the deteriorating marine environment or management of dwindling fisheries. It is these perceptions that must change—and indeed they are changing.[45]

---

42 ASEAN—China Declaration on the Conduct of Parties in the South China Sea (2002), Article 6. This declaration is available at: http://www.aseansec.org/13163.htm.

43 Sam Bateman, Joshua Ho and Jane Chan, *Good Order at Sea in Southeast Asia—Policy Recommendations*, S. Rajaratnam School of International Studies, Singapore, April 2009, Table 5, p. 29. The lack of adherence to the International Search and Rescue (SAR) Convention is particularly noteworthy with only China, Indonesia, Singapore and Vietnam, among the littoral countries to the South China Sea, being parties at present.

44 Yann-Huei Song, 'The Study of Marine Biodiversity in the South China Sea; Joint Efforts Made in the SCS Workshop Process', paper at the international workshop on 'The South China Sea: Cooperation for Regional Security and Development', Ho Chi Minh City, November 2010.

45 Mark Valencia, "Northeast Asia: Navigating Neptune's Neighbourhood" in Benjamin L. Self, and Yuki Tatsumi, *Confidence-Building Measures and Security Issues in Northeast Asia*, Report No.33, Washington DC: Stimson Centre, 2000, p. 20.

Developing Regimes for the South China Sea

Regimes provide benefits and reduce costs in a way that no single country acting on its own could achieve.[46] They reduce the risks of "a tragedy of the commons", where in the short term, individual countries might gain but in the longer term, everyone loses. However, they involve compromises and trade-offs between the different national interests of individual countries. The perceived shorter-term costs of regime participation are often seen as outweighing the longer-term benefits of such participation even though these benefits might greatly outweigh the costs. For example, littoral countries to the South China Sea appear concerned that participation in some maritime regimes might involve a loss of sovereignty and independence, and this outweighs whatever might be the longer-term benefits of regime participation in terms of improved resource management, marine environmental protection, and maritime security.

This attitude reflects the remarkably percipient view of Ken Booth nearly 30 years ago that:

> It may take half a century but unilateralist drives to parcel parts of the ocean will continue and will be legitimised by the territorialist mood of the international community. As this development unfolds, and as state control intensifies over larger patches of the sea, greater meaning will be invested in the new boundaries which are inevitably the outcome of the process. Nations will feel protective and sensitive—indeed patriotic—about these patches of ocean.[47]

This approach was amply illustrated by the joint submission by Malaysia and Vietnam in May 2009 to the Commission on the Limits of the Continental Shelf (CLCS). This was a strongly nationalistic approach to resource allocation in the South China Sea. It amounted to a "zero-sum" claim by these two countries to the seabed resources of the entire southern part of the China Sea to the exclusion of other interested parties, Brunei, China and the Philippines.[48] It could well be argued that this submission was contrary to the spirit of Article 5 of the DOC about self-restraint in the conduct of activities that could complicate or escalate disputes.

It is not hard to identify factors that inhibit progress with the development of a cooperative management regime for the South China Sea. The most intractable are the claims to all features in the sea by China, Taiwan and Vietnam. These mean that there are few prospects for resolving sovereignty in the foreseeable future, but even more seriously, they make functional cooperation more difficult. Other

---

46 Edward L. Miles, "Implementation of International Regimes: A Typology" in David Vidas, and Willy Ostreng (eds), *Order for the Oceans at the Turn of the Century*. The Hague: Kluwer Law International, 1999, p. 327.

47 Ken Booth, *Law, Force and Diplomacy at Sea*. London: Allen & Unwin, 1985, pp. 44–5

48 Bateman and Schofield, 'Outer Shelf Claims in the South China Sea'.

"stumbling blocks" include the desire for countries to see maritime boundaries as "fences in the sea" separating areas of sovereign control; growing concerns over energy security and competition for resources; divisions within ASEAN; and the nationalizing and militarizing of the disputes. Maritime boundary negotiations are always difficult, and essentially political, but they are rendered more difficult in the South China Sea by the geography of the region and the number of parties involved.

There is a need to acknowledge that sovereignty claims in the South China Sea and hence maritime boundaries will not be resolved in the foreseeable future. For the reasons discussed, conventional bilateral maritime boundaries are unlikely in many parts of the sea, and it is not going too far to say that they are not just unlikely but impossible to achieve. The problems discussed above of reaching multilateral agreement on tri-junctions and resolving which islands are entitled to a full suite of maritime zones, as well as all the customary difficulties of maritime boundary negotiations create a hopelessly intractable situation. A changed mindset among the stakeholders, which focuses on common interests and cooperation rather than on national sovereignty, differences and disputes, is the most fundamental requirement.

A cooperative management regime is the only solution. The only acceptable framework for such a regime would appear to be a web of provisional arrangements covering cooperation for different functions and perhaps even with different areas for each function. The functions to be considered might include development of oil and gas resources, fisheries management, marine safety, law and order at sea, and preservation and protection of the marine environment. This would be in line with the "functionalist" approach to maritime boundary making as proposed by the late Douglas Johnston.[49]

None of this is new. Cooperative development and management of the South China Sea has been the theme of many academic papers over the years. It also underpinned much of the work of the South China Sea Workshops that have been hosted by Indonesia since the early 1990s and still continue although they are currently suffering from a shortage of resources.[50] One of the more comprehensive proposals for a cooperative management regime was put forward by Valencia, Van Dyke and Ludwig in the late 1990s.[51] They acknowledged fully the difficulties of allocating the insular features and maritime space of the South China Sea on the basis of sovereign jurisdiction and suggested instead the establishment of a multi-purpose regime to manage the living and nonliving resources and related activities.

---

49 Douglas M. Johnston, *The Theory and History of Ocean Boundary Making*. Montreal: McGill-Queens Press, 1998, Part Three.

50 Clive Schofield, Ian Townsend-Gault, Hasjim Djalal, Ian Storey, Meredith Miller and Tim Cook, "From Disputed Waters to Seas of Opportunity—Overcoming Barriers to Maritime Cooperation in East and Southeast Asia", *NBR Special Report #30*, The National Bureau of Asian Research, July 2011, p. 26.

51 Valencia, Van Dyke and Ludwig, *Sharing the Resources of the South China Sea.*

Conclusions

Building effective regimes in the South China Sea has clearly been hindered by the problems of maritime boundary-making in this area. The geography of the immediate region, with its concave areas of coast (the Gulfs of Thailand and Tonkin), off-lying archipelagos and numerous islands subject to conflicting sovereignty claims, means that conventional straight line maritime boundaries are unachievable in many parts of the area. As has been noted, many boundaries, or at least their end points or turning points ('tri-points') will require agreement of three, or even more, countries. Past experience in Asia and other parts of the world shows that this agreement is very hard to achieve.

It is increasingly necessary to find some other means of managing the South China Sea and exploiting its resources, which is not based on unilateral jurisdiction and sole ownership of the resources. A cooperative management regime is required based on a functional approach that exploits the common interests of claimant countries. To achieve this outcome, work is required by Track One on a multi-lateral basis to promote functional cooperation and joint development. The work involved is not to be under-estimated. It requires identifying the particular functions for cooperation; defining the area for joint management; identifying the specific mission of the joint venture; finding a formula to share costs and resources; and establishing a management body.

The claimant countries must adopt a more cooperative mindset that recognises the futility of pursuing resource rights and management regimes on a national basis. Discussion of modes of functional cooperation in the South China Sea should continue at both Track One and Track Two forums. The claimant countries should fulfil their obligations under both the DOC and UNCLOS Part IX, noting that CSCAP Memorandum No. 13 provides a useful guide to the fulfilment of these obligations. Track Two can provide vital assistance in progressing this work.[52] Rather than establishing new forums, greater support is required for the Workshop process hosted by Indonesia. It is by supporting this process and assisting in developing management arrangements for the South China Sea that non-claimant and extra-regional stakeholders can best contribute to reducing the tensions that are currently evident.

Without more cooperation, the South China Sea will continue simmering away as an obstacle to a stable maritime security regime and good order at sea in Southeast Asia. Occasional surges in tension will occur, such as the separate incidents in March 2011 when Chinese patrol boats disrupted the work of a survey vessel conducting a seismological survey for the Philippines off the Reed Bank in the Philippines claimed area of the Spratly group, and Vietnam protested to

52 Clive Schofield, Ian Townsend-Gault, "Brokering Competition Amidst Competing Maritime Claims: Preventative Diplomacy in the South China Sea" in Aldo Chircop, Ted L. McDorman and Susan J. Rolston (eds), *The Future of Ocean Regime-Building—Essays in Tribute to Douglas M. Johnston*. Leiden: Martins Nijhoff Publishers, 2009, p. 670

China over Chinese military exercises in waters of the South China Sea claimed by Vietnam.[53] Such incidents set back any progress towards cooperation, and only serve to highlight the importance of establishing effective cooperative regimes for managing the South China Sea, its environment and its resources. In the long term, all parties will suffer due to the continued lack of effective arrangements for resource management, marine scientific research, marine environmental protection, the safety and security of shipping passing through the area, and the prevention of illegal activities at sea. Ultimately the national interest of all parties requires greater cooperation, as well as continuity and stability in resource management regimes.

53 Banyan, 'Carps Among the Spratlys—Tensions in the South China Sea', *The Economist (UK)*, March 12, 2011, http://www4.economist.com/node/18332702.

Chapter 7
Bringing the South Pole to the South China Sea: Towards the Establishment of an International Regime for Peace and Security

Keyuan Zou

Introduction

The date of June 23, 2011 marked the 50th anniversary of the entry into force of the Antarctic Treaty.[1] For the celebration, the Antarctic Treaty Consultative Parties (ATCPs) issued a Declaration on the occasion of the 34th Antarctic Treaty Consultative Meeting (ATCM) in Buenos Aires. In that Declaration, the ATCPs reaffirmed "their continued commitment to upholding the Antarctic Treaty and all the other elements of the Antarctic Treaty system that have evolved since the Treaty's entry into force," and "their intention to continue their strong and effective cooperation under the Antarctic Treaty and all the other elements of the Antarctic Treaty system."[2] As we can see, cooperation is a most important keyword in the implementation of the Antarctic Treaty.

Based on the Antarctic Treaty, an international legal regime for Antarctica has been established. I endorse the most popular definition of the term "regime" as that which is "composed of sets of explicit or implicit principles, norms, rules, and decision-making procedures around which actor expectations converge in a given area of international relations and which may help to coordinate their behaviour."[3] For an international regime, in the perspective of international lawyers, the primary elements it should possess are legal principles, norms and rules. It is generally acknowledged that the Antarctic Treaty and its associated legal documents and the institutional arrangements based on them constitute an international regime.

This regime preserves the Antarctic region to be a land of peace, cooperation, science and environmental protection. This chapter is designed to address the

1 The text is available at: http://www.ats.aq/documents/ats/treaty_original.pdf.

2 See the Declaration on Antarctic Cooperation on the Occasion of the 50th Anniversary of the Entry into Force of the Antarctic Treaty, June 20–July 1, 2011. The whole text is available at: http://www.ats.aq/documents/ATCM34/op/atcm34_op031_rev1_e.pdf.

3 S.D. Krasner, "Structural cases and regime consequences: regimes as intervening variables," in S.D. Krasner (ed.), *International Regimes* (Ithaca: Cornell University Press, 1986), p. 2.

essential elements of the Antarctic Treaty and its associated legal documents and discuss whether and to what extent these elements the claimants to the South China Sea can take into consideration for dispute solution. While there is some existing literature discussing the possible application of the "Antarctic model" to the South China Sea, this chapter takes the approach to functionalism by examining relevant legal principles and norms embodied in the Antarctic Treaty System which could be borrowed to apply to other contested regions. More importantly, the topic is worth further exploring, particularly under the current circumstances of high tension and even confrontation in the South China Sea.

Antarctic Treaty System

Antarctica has been legally regulated since 1959. This legal regime is called the Antarctic Treaty System (ATS) which includes the Antarctic Treaty of 1959, the measures in effect under that Treaty, and its associated separate legal documents.

The Antarctic Treaty is the core of the System, and also a pivotal essence for constant development of the System. It realizes the use of Antarctica forever for peaceful purposes only and ensures the freedom of scientific research in Antarctica on the premise of freezing different legal positions of the Treaty Parties on the territorial sovereignty claims. But the Antarctic Treaty is a purpose-limited treaty, mainly regulating scientific research activities without mentioning other matters in detail. The Treaty has no provision directly relating to environmental protection, and in fact no such word as "environment" appears in all its provisions.[4] Nevertheless, for the peaceful purposes, the Antarctic Treaty addresses environmental protection though it does so indirectly: to prohibit certain kinds of activities which would cause significant damage upon the Antarctic environment such as military activity, nuclear explosion and disposal of radioactive waste. Further, Article IX provides that the ATCPs shall consult together on matters of common interest, and formulate measures in furtherance of the principles and objectives of the Treaty, including conservation and preservation of living resources. Accordingly, the ATCPs may at any time conduct consultation and adopt relevant measures for the issues on environmental protection and resource utilization.

More than 50 years of practice have shown that the Antarctic Treaty Consultative Meetings always put the issue of environmental protection on the major agenda, and adopted many recommendations in this respect. Among them, the Agreed Measures for the Conservation of Antarctic Fauna and Flora of 1964[5] has been so far regarded as a most important comprehensive measure on environmental protection. The Agreed Measures prohibit within the Antarctic Treaty Area the killing, wounding, capturing or molesting of any native mammal or native bird, or

4 See Alfred van der Essen, "La Protection de l'Environnement dans l'Antarctique," 18 *Revue Belge de Droit International*, (1984–5), 617–8.

5 See *Handbook of the Antarctic Treaty System*, Seventh edition (1990), Part II, 2402.

any attempt at any such act, and the bringing into the Treaty Area of any species of animal or plant not indigenous to that Area, except in accordance with a permit. In order to effectively implement the Agreed Measures, in the Treaty Area are designated Specially Protected Areas and Sites of Special Scientific Interest to preserve their unique natural ecological system or to prevent a demonstrable risk of interference with scientific research. The ATCPs acknowledged the possibility of resource exploitation and utilization while taking full consideration of the environmental protection. This was reflected in the two subsequent conventions in relation to the Antarctic marine living resources.

The Convention for the Conservation of Antarctic Seals,[6] concluded in 1972, is designed to protect the seals offshore and onshore the Antarctic continent. It prohibits the killing or capturing of three kinds of seals, namely Southern elephant seals, Ross seals and fur seals, and allows the taking of other kinds of seals in accordance with permissible catch quotas for the purpose of scientific research or on other reasonable grounds. In addition, the Convention provides that at any time after commercial sealing has begun, the Contracting Parties may convene to establish necessary regulatory institutions.

The Convention on the Conservation of Antarctic Marine Living Resources of 1980 (CCAMLR)[7] also bases its purpose on the conservation of Antarctic marine living resources. It applies to the Antarctic marine ecosystem as a whole, and establishes the ecosystem standard as its fundamental principle, which contains three basic elements: maximum net recruitment; maintenance of ecological relationships; and the avoidance of nonreversible reductions of any species in the Southern Ocean. On the other hand, the Convention includes rational use in its conservation purposes and objectives. It does not exclude the fishing operations conducted in compliance with the principles and conditions of the ecosystem standard. In order to implement its purposes and principles, the Convention provides that the Commission for the Conservation of Antarctic Marine Living Resources and the Scientific Committee should be established.

The above two Conventions for Antarctic marine living resources came into force in 1978 and 1982 respectively, and have formed a part of the Antarctic Treaty System.

The Convention on the Regulation of Antarctic Mineral Resource Activities (CRAMRA) was adopted in June 1988.[8] The Convention has never come into force and has been put aside for an indefinite period due to the aftermath opposition from Australia and France.

As a result, the ATCPs negotiated and adopted the Protocol on Environmental Protection to the Antarctic Treaty (Madrid Protocol) in Madrid on October 4,

6 See *Handbook of the Antarctic Treaty System*, ibid., Part IV, 4105.

7 Text is reprinted in *Handbook of the Antarctic Treaty System*, ibid., Part IV, 4209.

8 For the whole text, see Antarctic Treaty: Final Report of the Fourth Special Antarctic Treaty Consultative Meeting on Antarctic Mineral Resources (Wellington, 1988), 43–109.

1991. It came into force on January 14, 1998.[9] According to the Protocol, the whole Antarctic area is to be designated as a natural reserve, devoted to peace and science. The protection of the environment and ecosystems and the intrinsic value of Antarctica, including its wilderness and aesthetic values and its value as an area for the conduct of scientific research, in particular research essential to understanding the global environment, shall be fundamental considerations in the planning and conduct of all activities in the Antarctic Treaty Area. Any mineral resource activity shall be prohibited during the operation of the Protocol. While decision making on environmental protection still remains through the ATCM mechanism, the Protocol provides for the establishment of a Committee for Environmental Protection to provide advice and formulate recommendations to the ATCMs in connection with the implementation of the Protocol and its annexes.

Effectiveness of Implementation

International Cooperation and Scientific Research

Scientific activities began in Antarctica much earlier than the emergence of the legal regime and they helped its establishment. According to the Antarctic Treaty, the freedom of scientific investigation and cooperation is reaffirmed, which confers upon any country in the world the right to conduct its scientific research in its capability at any spot in Antarctica. In order to promote international cooperation in this regard, Treaty Parties agree to exchange scientific information and personnel and to encourage the establishment of cooperative working relations with other international organizations which have a scientific and technical interest in Antarctica.

With the legal guarantee of the Antarctic Treaty, the international cooperation of scientific research has worked very well in the Antarctic. The freedom of scientific research greatly promotes scientific investigations in Antarctica. The main resource today exported from Antarctica is just scientific knowledge. In particular, progress in our knowledge of world climate change is largely due to the research carried out in Antarctica.[10] So the Antarctic continent is truly a land of science and international cooperation.

As to individual countries, a typical example can be drawn from Chinese practice. China, as a leading developing country in the world, has benefited a lot from other countries, especially at its first stage of Antarctic activities under the provision of international cooperation in the Antarctic Treaty: Japan offered training to Chinese explorers before the first expedition; the former Soviet Union extended a warm welcome and gave assistance; Chile and Argentina helped

9 ATS Doc., XI ATSCM/2/3/2, October 3, 1991.

10 Roland Dumas, "The Antarctic in World Politics," 10 *International Challenges* (1990), at 5.

China choose a suitable site for its first Antarctic station; and the United States and New Zealand shared their Antarctic experiences with Chinese scientists.[11] Such scientific cooperation, more or less, softened tensions and promoted friendly relations among the countries concerned.

On the international plane, the Scientific Committee on Antarctic Research (SCAR) is a coordinating organization which is subordinated to the International Council of Scientific Unions (ICSU). SCAR is to initiate, promote and coordinate scientific activity in the Antarctic, with a view to framing and reviewing scientific programmes of circumpolar scope and significance.[12]

Legal Arrangements for Territorial Sovereignty

The sovereignty issue on the Antarctic is very complicated and was a major obstacle to international cooperation and scientific research in the Antarctic. Altogether seven countries formally made territorial claims over the Antarctic. The first claim was made by Britain in 1908. Since then, six other countries have also made their claims to Antarctica: New Zealand in 1923, France in 1924, Australia in 1933, Norway in 1939, Chile in 1940 and Argentina in 1942. These claims are pie-shaped, extending from 60° south latitude to the South Pole, except for the undefined northern limit of the Chilean[13] and the northern/southern limits of the Norwegian.[14] The bases of the claims vary, from discovery, historic rights, symbolic act to geographic contiguity, sector principle and so on, but they are not sufficient enough in international law to support the territorial claims in Antarctica. Furthermore, the claims made by Argentina, Britain and Chile overlap each other. All the claims have covered 85 percent of the Antarctic continent, and only about 15 percent was unclaimed (the Marie Byrd Land), which was tacitly reserved for the US.

The US never officially made such claims, nor recognized the claims made by other countries; but it reserved the right to make territorial claims. A similar

11 For details, see Zou Keyuan, "China's Antarctic Policy and the Antarctic Treaty System," 24 *Ocean Development and International Law*, 1993, 237–55.

12 The Constitution of SCAR is reprinted in *Handbook of the Antarctic Treaty System*, Seventh edition (1990), Part 4, at 4401. For reference, see J.H. Zumberge, "The Scientific Committee on Antarctic Research and the Antarctic Treaty System," in Polar Research Board (ed.), *Antarctic Treaty System: An Assessment* (Washington: National Academy Press, 1986), 153–68.

13 One of the reasons was articulated as "Chile is a single geographic unit which extends from Arica (on the northern border with Peru) to the South Pole." Jack Child, "Latin *lebensraum*: The Geopolitics of Ibero–American Antarctica," 10 *Applied Geography* (1990), at 294.

14 For the purpose of avoiding disadvantages resulting from the "sector principle" of her rights or interests in the Arctic. In fact, Amundsen individually claimed for Norway a circular area comprising the plateau around the South Pole and named it "King Haakon VII Plateau." John Hanessian, Jr., "National Interests in Antarctica," in Trevor Hatherton (ed.), *Antarctica* (New York: Praeger, 1965), at 21.

position is also taken by the former Soviet Union. The rest of the members of the world community have never accepted these claims or rights to make claims.

The controversy on the Antarctic territorial sovereignty during the 1940s and 1950s was a serious problem among the relevant countries. However, the tension and rivalry resulting from the territorial claims were softened by the International Geophysical Year (IGY) of 1957–8. There was a gentleman's agreement among the countries conducting scientific investigations in Antarctica that they agreed not to engage in legal or political argumentation during that period, in order that the scientific programme might proceed without impediment.[15] The IGY represented a major turning point for scientific research in Antarctica, and provided a sound foundation for the development of Antarctic scientific research in a wide range of disciplines in natural sciences.[16] Politically, it became a catalyst for the negotiation of the Antarctic Treaty.

The Antarctic Treaty freezes the different legal positions of the Treaty Parties regarding the territorial claims. Article 4 of the Antarctic Treaty provides:

> 1. Nothing contained in the present Treaty shall be interpreted as:
>
> (a) a renunciation by any Contracting Party of previously asserted rights of or claims to territorial sovereignty in Antarctica;
> (b) a renunciation or diminution by any Contracting Party of any basis of claim to territorial sovereignty in Antarctica which it may have whether as a result of its activities or those of its nationals in Antarctica, or otherwise;
> (c) prejudicing the position of any Contracting Party as regards its recognition or non-recognition of any other State's right of or claim or basis of claim to territorial sovereignty in Antarctica.
>
> 2. No acts or activities taking place while the present Treaty is in force shall constitute a basis for asserting, supporting, or denying a claim to territorial sovereignty in Antarctica. No new claim, or enlargement of an existing claim, to territorial sovereignty in Antarctica shall be asserted while the present Treaty is in force.

The provision created an ingenious solution to the delicate issue of the territorial claims which would otherwise cause serious confrontation, even armed conflict in and/or around Antarctica.[17] Thus the status quo of Antarctica maintained by the

---

15 P.C. Daniels, "The Antarctic Treaty," in R.S. Lewis and P.M. Smith (eds), *Frozen Future: A Prophetic Report from Antarctica* (New York: Quadrangle Books, 1973), at 35.

16 For relevant discussion, see Alan D. Hemmings, "Why did we get an International Space Station before an International Antarctic Station?" *The Polar Journal*, Vol.1 (1), 2011, 5–16.

17 Irrespective of the Cold War during the 1950s and 1960s which culminated in the Berlin and Cuban crises, the two superpowers cooperated well in Antarctic affairs; and

Antarctic Treaty has effectively prevented Antarctica from becoming the scene or object of international discord. The bifocalism in Article IV of the Antarctic Treaty is in fact only a modus vivendi, but it after all successfully put aside the tough issue of Antarctic sovereignty, and instead established the basis for international cooperation in the Antarctic continent. In addition, it is to be noted that because of the legal arrangements under Article IV of the Antarctic Treaty, claimant states to Antarctica have exercised self-restraint regarding the extent of the continental shelf generating from the Antarctic continent which they claimed. The typical case is Australia, which requested the Commission on the Limits of Continental Shelf not to take any action for the time being with regard to the information in its submission that relates to the continental shelf appurtenant to Antarctica.[18]

Another question which is closely related to the sovereignty issue over the South Pole is whether the concept of common heritage of mankind (CHM) should apply. It is not possible that the Antarctic could be recognized as CHM in the present time or near future, though it is often categorized as a "global commons."[19] Nevertheless, there is a tendency that the region is advancing towards becoming CHM, but unlike the legal arrangement for the deep seabed in the 1982 UN Convention on the Law of the Sea (LOS Convention), the arrangement as such, if applied to the South Pole, should be oriented to the environment rather than economic development because of its global environmental importance.

Consultative Mechanism

As provided in Article IX of the Antarctic Treaty, the ATCPs meet regularly for the purposes of exchanging information, consulting together on matters of common interest pertaining to Antarctica and formulating measures in furtherance of the principles and objectives of the Antarctic Treaty, including measures regarding:

- use of Antarctica for peaceful purposes only;
- facilitation of scientific research in Antarctica;
- facilitation of international scientific cooperation in Antarctica;
- facilitation of the exercise of the rights of inspection provided for in Article VII of the Treaty;

during the Falkland/Malvinas War in 1982, the delegates respectively from Britain and Argentina sat together, with other Antarctic Treaty Consultative Parties, to negotiate the Antarctic minerals regime.

18 See "Continental Shelf Submission of Australia: Executive Summary," November 2004, available at: http://www.un.org/Depts/los/clcs_new/submissions_files/aus04/Documents/aus_doc_es_web_delivery.pdf (accessed September 30, 2011).

19 For details, see Zou Keyuan, "The Common Heritage of Mankind and the Antarctic Treaty System," 38 *Netherlands International Law Review* (1991), 173–98; and Donat Pharand, "L'Arcticque et l'Antarctique: Patrimoine Commun de l'Humanité," 7 *Annals of Air and Space Law* (1982), 415–30.

- questions relating to the exercise of jurisdiction in Antarctica;
- preservation and conservation of living resources in Antarctica.

In practice, the matters discussed in the ATCM include all those concerned with Antarctic affairs. In these meetings the Treaty Parties negotiate treaties governing Antarctica as well as adopting recommendations. These recommendations have binding force subject to the explicit acceptance of the Treaty Parties, and furthermore all the treaties within the ATS so far have been concluded on the basis of the relevant recommendations.

With the consultative mechanism provided in Article IX of the Antarctic Treaty as a legal guarantee, the ATS maintains its strong vitality. Thereby, ATCM can, if necessary, at any time negotiate and conclude relevant treaties for various Antarctic activities, thus enhancing the constant development of the ATS. Furthermore, this provision ensures an active cooperation instead of passive coexistence among the Antarctic Treaty Parties in dealing with Antarctic affairs. This is also one of the key elements in the rapid development of the ATS in a short period of 50 years.

On the other hand, the mechanism of decision-making process in the ATS consists of a two-tiered system, that is, those countries who have conducted substantial activities in Antarctica can obtain the position of Consultative Parties and have the right of decision making, whereas other Antarctic Treaty Parties have no such right. This system in practice obstructs the developing countries from participating in the Antarctic decision-making process because the financial and technological capabilities of these countries are comparatively weak.[20] Nevertheless, since 1983 the mechanism has been improved, and non-ATCPs are invited to attend the ATCM as observers, thus enabling them to exert some influence over the development of the ATS.

While this institutional structure has been criticized as a closed shop or "rich man's club,"[21] it still has some advantages. Since Antarctica is a unique environment, newcomers without sufficient knowledge would easily cause environmental damage there. Thus the qualification system will ensure safer and more meaningful contributions from new countries.[22]

In September 2004, the ATCPs decided to establish the Antarctic Treaty Secretariat in support of the ATCM. The headquarters of the Secretariat are located in Buenos Aires, Argentina.

20 Zou, *supra* note 19, at 196.

21 Remarks by J.V. Gbeho, Permanent Representative of Ghana to the United Nations, 80 Proceedings Am. Soc. Int'l L. (1986), at 281.

22 See Zou, *supra* note 19, 196–7.

Resource Management and Environment Protection

Ecosystem Principle

As we know, CCAMLR endorsed the ecosystem approach to the management of the entire Southern Ocean. This approach is in contrast to other treaties on fisheries such as the International Whaling Commission (IWC), the Northwest Atlantic Fisheries Organization (NAFO) and the International Commission for South-East Atlantic Fisheries (ICSEAF), where the aim of the treaty is the sustainable yield of the target species and the welfare of the industry dependent upon it.[23] It is based upon the conviction and understanding that the waters surrounding the Antarctic continent form a distinctive marine region. Thus there was the recognition from the outset that the requirements of ecosystem management would demand that the coverage of the treaty should be larger than that of the Antarctic Treaty. As early as 1977 the ATCPs agreed that the agreement should apply not only to the area of the Antarctic Treaty but also should "extend north of 60° south latitude where that is necessary for the effective conservation of species of the Antarctic ecosystem."[24] The application extent of the Convention is up to the Antarctic Convergence or Polar Front, which is a complex transition zone lying between 45° and 60° south latitude within which colder Antarctic waters sink beneath the warmer sub-Antarctic waters to the north.

According to Article 2 of CCAMLR, the ecosystem approach contains three basic elements or conservation principles: maximum net recruitment; maintenance of ecological relationships; and the avoidance of nonreversible reductions of any species in the Southern Ocean.

The first conservation principle requires harvesting and associated activities to prevent a decrease in the size of any harvested population to levels below those which ensure the population's stable recruitment. For this purpose, the size of a population should not be allowed to fall below a level close to that which ensures greatest net annual increment. The level of greatest net annual increment is the ultimate limit on harvest. If a population falls below this level, then harvest must be consistent with recovery to the level of greatest net annual increment or must cease. This ultimate limit on harvesting activities not only applies to krill, fish

23 M. Basson and J.R. Beddington, "CCAMLR: The Practical Implications of an Ecosystem Approach," in A. Jorgensen-Dahl and Willy Ostreng (eds), *The Antarctic Treaty System in World Politics* (Macmillan, 1991), at 54. See also Adriana Fabra and Virginia Gascón, "The Convention on the Conservation of Antarctic Marine Living Resources (CCAMLR) and the Ecosystem Approach," *International Journal of Marine and Coastal Law*, Vol.23, 2008, 567–98.

24 See Tucker Scully, William Brown and Bruce Manheim, "The Convention for the Conservation of Antarctic Marine Living Resources: A Model for Large Marine Ecosystem Management," in K. Sherman and L.M. Alexander (eds), *Variability and Management of Large Marine Ecosystems* (Boulder, CO: Westview Press, 1986), at 282.

and whales, which are principally the subject of harvest, but also to populations of other species that directly or indirectly interact with a harvested population.[25]

The second principle requires harvesting and associated activities to prevent changes or minimize the risk of changes in the marine ecosystem which are not potentially reversible over two to three decades. This principle recognizes that adaptive change may result from artificial selection as well as ecological change, and thus addresses the resilience of the Antarctic ecosystem to harvesting and associated activities. Hence, while the first principle sets limits on the degree to which populations may be altered by human exploitation, the second conservation principle sets a rate at which such changes must be reversible.

The third principle requires Parties to the Convention to maintain the ecological relationships that exist between harvested, dependent and related populations of Antarctic marine living resources, and to restore depleted populations to levels which ensure the greatest net annual increment. This provision provides authorization for designating selected protected areas of sea, where harvest would be prohibited unless it would restore the ecosystem to such a structure and function as it was before harvesting occurred. Establishment of such areas in the Southern Ocean would provide a hedge against uncertainty and the risk of inadvertent exploitation in harvesting elsewhere.[26]

The ecosystem standard provided in CCAMLR was viewed as an important innovation in international arrangements for living resource management.[27] It is designed to protect the marine ecosystem as a whole while conserving the living species. However, due to the absence of an effective enforcement mechanism and comprehensive scientific data about the whole marine ecosystem, there are many difficulties in its implementation.[28] Secondly, the term "rational use" in the conservation principle of CCAMLR is yet to be unambiguously defined, that is, how and to what extent the use is rational. Further, since the entry into

25 Scully et al., ibid., at 283.

26 Scully et al., ibid., at 285.

27 See T. Scully, "The Convention on the Conservation of Antarctic Marine Living Resources—A Case Study," in L.M. Alexander, S. Allen and L.C. Hanson (eds), *New Developments in Marine Science and Technology: Economic, Legal and Political Aspects*, 22 Law of the Sea Institute Proceedings, 1989, at 138.

28 See M.W. Holdgate, "Antarctica: Ice Under Pressure," 32(6) *Environment* (1990), at 9. The ecosystem standard has been criticized that Article II, para.3 (a), which sets as the criterion for the protection of species, that they not be harvested below the level which ensures the greatest net annual increment, is suitable for those predatory species at the top of the food chain, but not suitable for prey species. See J.G. Gardam, "Management Regimes for Antarctic Marine Living Resources—An Australian Perspective," 15 *Melbourne University Law Review* (1985), at 302. Someone even argued that Article II, which sets out the ecosystem approach, was impractical; not enough was known about the Antarctic marine ecosystem to enable it to work if the pressure to take krill increased and it could therefore, become a source of weakness. See J.A. Heap, "Has CCAMLR Worked? Management Policies and Ecological Needs," 10(1) *International Challenges* (1990), at 15.

force of CCAMLR, the ecosystem standard has not been effectively enforced—particular conservation measures coming into being so late that some species and areas have been overexploited.[29] In this context, for the purpose of the effective implementation of the ecosystem standard of CCAMLR, it is necessary to make clear in furtherance of the concept of sustainable development to apply the precautionary principle: the catch of the species of which mankind has collected sufficient scientific data is permissible, but must be sustainable and subject to the total allowed catch which must ensure the greatest net recruitment of the taken species. As to the species for which there is lack of sufficient scientific data, the catch should be strictly controlled or forbidden, waiting for further scientific justifications. In short, fishing activities should be prohibited unless they are conducted in full compliance with the ecosystem standard.

Despite difficulties in implementation and elaborating of conservation measures as well as desires to improve the existing regime, the ecosystem principle has been in fact a legal principle within the ATS, and it has ramifications for other conservation regimes, especially of those regulating marine fisheries.

Madrid Protocol

The adoption of the Protocol represents an essential step towards the comprehensive protection of the Antarctic environment and ecosystems. The Preamble to the Protocol establishes the principle that the instrument developed partly out of the conviction "of the need to enhance the protection of the Antarctic environment and dependent and associated ecosystems." To this end, the Parties "commit themselves to the comprehensive protection of the Antarctic environment and dependent and associated ecosystems and hereby designate Antarctica as a natural reserve, devoted to peace and science."

1. Principles and standards Article 3 of the Protocol establishes the basic environmental principles. It provides in paragraph 1:

> The protection of the Antarctic environment and dependent and associated ecosystems and the intrinsic value of Antarctica, including its wilderness and aesthetic values and its value as an area for the conduct of scientific research ... shall be the fundamental considerations in the planning and conduct of all activities in the Antarctic Treaty area.

In pursuance to this principle, paragraph 2 of the Article states that:

29 See F. Orrego Vicuna, "The Implementation of CCAMLR: Is the Decision-Making Machinery Conducive to Good Management?" 10(1) *International Challenges* (1990), at 9.

> (a) Activities in the Antarctic Treaty area shall be planned and conducted so as to limit adverse impacts on the Antarctic environment and dependent and associated ecosystems.
> (b) Activities in the Antarctic Treaty area shall be planned and conducted so as to avoid:
> (i) adverse effects on climate or weather patterns;
> (ii) significant adverse effects on air or water quality;
> (iii) significant changes in the atmospheric, terrestrial (including aquatic), glacial or marine environments;
> (iv) detrimental changes in the distribution, abundance or productivity of species or populations of species of fauna and flora;
> (v) further jeopardy to endangered or threatened species or populations of such species; or
> (vi) degradation of, or substantial risk to, areas of biological, scientific, historic, aesthetic or wilderness significance.
> (c) Activities in the Antarctic Treaty area shall be planned and conducted on the basis of information sufficient to allow prior assessments of, and informed judgements about, their possible impacts on the Antarctic environment and dependent and associated ecosystems and on the value of Antarctica for the conduct of scientific research.

Any assessments and decisions made are to take full account of whether technology and procedures are available to provide for environmentally safe operations, and whether there exists the capacity to monitor key environmental parameters and ecosystem components so as to identify and provide early warning of any adverse effects of the activity and to provide for such modification of operating procedures as may be necessary in the light of results of monitoring or increased knowledge of the Antarctic environment and dependent and associated ecosystems.

The decisions are further to take account of whether the capacity exists to respond promptly and effectively to accidents, particularly those with potential environmental effects.

Article 3 is one of the key provisions of the Protocol. In many respects, its substance is borrowed from Article 4 of CRAMRA. But it is more comprehensive in that the provisions of it introduce a basis for a uniform standard to assess all human activity on the continent, irrespective of whether the activity is related to mining or to scientific research.[30]

2. Environmental impact assessment The environmental impact assessment (EIA) procedure was first provided in CRAMRA in which it reads that every proposed activity should be judged on its environmental impact before the activity starts.[31]

30 S.K.N. Blay, "New Trends in the Protection of the Antarctic Environment: The 1991 Madrid Protocol," 86 *American Journal of International Law*, 1992, at 389.

31 Art. 41 of CRAMRA.

Annex I of the Protocol sets forth EIA procedures, and in accordance with Article 8 of the Protocol, these procedures apply to all proposed activities in Antarctica. Article 8 separates human activities in Antarctica into three categories based on their possible impact on the environment or on dependent or associated ecosystems: those having (a) less than a minor or transitory impact; (b) a minor or transitory impact; and (c) more than a minor or transitory impact. For the first category, no preventive environmental impact study is required. As to the other two, two measures shall be applied: "initial environmental evaluation" and "comprehensive environmental evaluation." The first measure is a simplified procedure, carried out within the sphere of national competence and intended to clear the way for development of Antarctic activities after determining the endeavors will not produce more than a "minor or transitory impact" on the Antarctic environment. The second measure applies to activities exceeding the level of minor or transitory impact. In addition to requiring a more detailed analysis of the foreseeable environmental impact, it starts a procedure of international verification and control by the other ATCPs.

Article 3 of Annex I requires that the comprehensive EIA be made public and circulated among all the Parties to the Protocol for a 90-day period of observation and comment. The same article requires that the Committee for Environmental Protection (CEP), established under Article 11 of the Protocol, receive a copy of the assessment report at least 120 days before the next ATCM, and the Committee must make its decision about the feasibility within 15 months of the circulation date of the impact assessment document.

Each Party is to ensure that the assessment procedures set out in Annex I are applied in the planning processes regarding any activities undertaken in Antarctica. The mandatory impact assessment procedures for all activities are a strength of the Protocol, but the major weakness lies in the fact that the annex, allowing national authorities to control the procedural guarantees of impact assessment, may carry the risk that they will use these procedures in an instrumental and "cosmetic" manner in order to legitimize, by the observance of procedural formalities, activities intrinsically contradictory to the environmental protection required by the Protocol.[32] In recent years, a call to introduce the strategic environmental assessment to the Antarctic has been made.[33]

32 Francesco Francioni, "The Madrid Protocol on Protection of the Antarctic Environment," 28 *Texas International Law Journal*, 1993, 65–6. For details on the review of the EIA procedure provided in the Protocol, see David Lyons, "Environmental Impact Assessment in Antarctica under the Protocol on Environmental Protection," 29 *Polar Record* (1993), 111–20.

33 See Simon Marsden, "Introducing strategic environmental assessment to the Madrid Protocol: Lessons from international experience," *The Polar Journal*, Vol.1, 2011, 36–50.

3. Specially protected areas The rules regarding the management of specially protected areas are provided for in Annex V to the Protocol, which was later added to during the ATCM in October 1991. The annex improves the previous management to consolidate the five existing categories of protected areas into two: Antarctic Specially Protected Area (ASPA) and Antarctic Specially Managed Area (ASMA). By virtue of the annex, any area in Antarctica, including marine areas, may be designated as an ASPA or an ASMA. Activities in such areas may be prohibited, restricted or managed in accordance with management plans adopted under the annex. The designation of an area may have the objective of protecting crucial environmental, scientific, historic or wilderness values or ongoing or planned scientific research. Any Party, the CEP, the SCAR or the CCAMLR may nominate an area for designation, subject to procedures provided in Article 6 of the annex.

4. Waste management Annex III updates the 1975 Code of Conduct for Antarctic Expeditions and Station Activities. The annex makes waste storage, disposal and removal from the Antarctic Treaty area, as well as recycling and source reduction, essential considerations in the planning and conduct of activities in the Antarctic. An obligation is imposed upon the Parties to reduce as far as practicable the amount of waste produced or disposed of in Antarctica so as to minimize the impact on the environment, and to remove from Antarctica, to the maximum extent possible, any waste they may produce.

The annex classifies wastes generated in the Antarctic through human activity into five groups: sewage and domestic liquid wastes; other liquids and chemicals, including fuels and lubricants; solids to be combusted; other solid wastes; and radioactive material. Parties are obliged to remove Group 1 waste to the maximum extent possible from the Treaty area. Such waste that is not removed must not be disposed of, to the maximum extent practicable, in sea ice, ice shelves or the grounded ice sheet. The annex permits the incineration of combustible wastes that may be classified under Group 3.

5. Marine pollution Annex IV: Prevention of Marine Pollution is based on the International Convention for the Prevention of Pollution from Ships, as amended by the Protocol of 1978 (MARPOL 73/78). It applies, with respect to each party, to the ships entitled to fly its flag and to any other ship engaged in or supporting its Antarctic operations while in the Treaty area. The annex prohibits the following in the Treaty area: the discharge into the sea of oil or oily mixtures except as permitted by MARPOL 73/78; the discharge into the sea of any noxious liquid substance, and any other chemical or other substances, in quantities or concentrations that are harmful to the marine environment; and the disposal into the sea of garbage and plastics.

The major weakness in the annex may be that it grants sovereign immunity from the measures set out in the annex to warships and any state-owned or—operated ships used only on government noncommercial service. In fact, most vessels used in Antarctica are government owned and operated. The exclusion could therefore remove a substantial number of vessels in the Treaty area from the operation of the annex.[34]

6. Conservation of fauna and flora Annex II addresses protecting native wildlife and the introduction of nonnative species to Antarctica, which updates the 1964 Agreed Measures for the Conservation of Antarctic Fauna and Flora. While including the terms of the agreed Measures, the annex extends protection to freshwater and terrestrial plants and invertebrates; requires the removal of dogs from the Antarctic as of April 1, 1994, and no longer allows for the killing of native wildlife to provide "indispensable food for men and dogs." It expands the definition of "harmful interference" to fauna and flora to include significant damage to native terrestrial plants; the seal concentrations; and "any activity that results in the significant adverse modification of habitats of any species or population of native mammal, bird, plant, or invertebrate."

The annex's most significant drawback is the allowance, by permit, of the killing of wildlife and plants as the "unavoidable consequence of the construction and operation of scientific support facilities."

7. Institutional arrangements Concrete measures can only be implemented by appropriate institutional means. According to the Protocol, the substantial power to protect the Antarctic environment rests on the ATCM. However, to enhance the protection management, a Committee for Environmental Protection is established. The functions of the Committee are to provide advice and formulate recommendations to the Parties in connection with the implementation of the Protocol, including the operation of its annexes, for consideration at ATCM. In particular, the Committee is to provide advice on:

- the effectiveness of measures taken pursuant to the Protocol;
- the need to update, strengthen or otherwise improve such measures;
- the need for additional measures, including the need for additional annexes, where appropriate;
- the application and implementation of the environmental impact assessment procedures;
- means of minimizing or mitigating environmental impacts of activities in the Antarctic Treaty area;
- procedures for situations requiring urgent action, including response action in environmental emergencies;
- the operation and further elaboration of the Antarctic Protected Area system;
- inspection procedures, including formats for inspection reports and checklists for the conduct of inspections;

34 Blay, *supra* note 30, at 394.

- the collection, archiving, exchange and evaluation of information related to environmental protection;
- the state of the Antarctic environment; and
- the need for scientific research, including environmental monitoring, related to the implementation of the Protocol.

Inspection procedure is also provided in the Protocol, which should be carried out in accordance with Article 7 of the Antarctic Treaty.

8. Liability regime It is acknowledged that the establishment of a liability regime for environmental damage was a tough task.[35] The ATCPs spent many years finally formulating the legal document on liability as Annex VI to the Madrid Protocol in June 2005.[36]

Essential Components to Build a South China Sea Regime

From the above, we can see that there are many elements which are conducive to the establishment of a legal regime for the South China Sea. The most important ones are peace, science and care for the environment.

It is noted that among all the South China Sea countries, only China is a party to the Antarctic Treaty and also enjoys Consultative status (see Table 7.1). China also acceded to the CCAMLR on October 19, 2006. On the other hand, Malaysia used to be a major opponent of the ATS at the UN forum. However, in recent years, Malaysia has changed its attitude and sent observers to attend the ATCMs.[37]

Peaceful Purposes

The principle of peaceful purposes is not only embodied in the Antarctic Treaty, but also in general international law. Even in the LOS Convention, it is provided that oceans and seas should be used for peaceful purposes, and any threat or use of force against the territorial integrity or political independence of any state, or in

---

35 For relevant discussion before the adoption of the Liability Annex, see Zou Keyuan, "Environmental Liability and the Antarctic Treaty System," *Singapore Journal of International and Comparative Law*, Vol.2 (2), 1998, 596–628.

36 Annex VI to the Protocol on Environmental Protection to the Antarctic Treaty: Liability Arising from Environmental Emergencies, reprinted in Secretariat of the Antarctic Treaty, *Compilation of Key Documents of the Antarctic Treaty System*, Vol.1, 2011, 87–96. For relevant discussions, see David J. Bederman and Soniya P. Keskar, "Antarctic Environmental Liability: The Stockholm Annex and Beyond," 19 *Emory International Law Review*, 2005, 1383–405.

37 For the shift of the Malaysian attitude, see B.A. Hamzah, "Malaysia and the Southern Ocean: Revisiting the Question of Antarctica," *Ocean Development and International Law*, Vol.41 (2), 2010, 186–95.

any other manner inconsistent with the principles of international law embodied in the Charter of the United Nations, shall be prohibited.[38] No country adjacent to the South China Sea will be against this principle.

Following this principle, it is useful to consider whether the South China Sea should be declared as a nuclear weapon-free zone. The Association of Southeast Asian Nations (ASEAN) signed the Treaty on the Southeast Asia Nuclear Weapon-Free Zone in 1995, declaring a Southeast Asia Nuclear Weapon-Free Zone (SEANWFZ).[39] At the annual meeting of ASEAN Foreign Ministers held in July 2011, a working group on the SEANWFZ called for a meeting between ASEAN arms control specialists and representatives of the P-5 countries.[40]

In September 2009, Chinese President Hu Jintao made a statement, "Work Together to Build a Safer World for All" at the UNSC Summit on Nuclear Non-Proliferation and Nuclear Disarmament. According to him, China has adhered to the policy of no-first-use of nuclear weapons at any time and under any circumstances and made the unequivocal commitment that China will unconditionally not use or threaten to use nuclear weapons against non-nuclear-weapon states or nuclear weapon-free zones.[41] China has signed and ratified the Protocol II of the Treaty for the Prohibition of Nuclear Weapons in Latin America and the Caribbean, Protocols II and III of the South Pacific Nuclear-Free Zone Treaty and Protocols I and II of the African Nuclear Weapon-Free Zone Treaty.[42] As China has already expressed its support of the establishment of the ASEAN nuclear weapon-free zone and its readiness to sign relevant protocols as early as possible,[43] there should be little problem in extending SEANWFZ to cover the sea area in the South China Sea in future.

It is to be noted that the Treaty on the Prohibition of the Emplacement of Nuclear Weapons and other Weapons of Mass Destruction on the Seabed and

38 See Art.301 of the LOS Convention.

39 According to the Treaty, the "Southeast Asia Nuclear Weapon-Free Zone" is the area comprising the territories of all States in Southeast Asia, namely, Brunei Darussalam, Cambodia, Indonesia, Laos, Malaysia, Myanmar, Philippines, Singapore, Thailand and Vietnam, and their respective continental shelves and Exclusive Economic Zones (EEZ). See Article 1 of the Treaty. Text is available at: http://www.asean.org/3636.htm. For relevant discussion, see R. Mütsenich, "Nuclear Weapon-Free Zone in Southeast Asia," 48 *Aussen Politik*, 1997, 391–401.

40 See SOUTHEAST ASIA NUCLEAR-WEAPON-FREE ZONE TREATY (TREATY OF BANGKOK), available at: http://www.nti.org/e_research/official_docs/inventory/pdfs/seanwfz.pdf (accessed September 27, 2011).

41 See "Statement by President Hu Jintao at the United Nations Security Council Summit on Nuclear Non-Proliferation and Nuclear Disarmament," September 24, 2009, available at: http://www.china-un.org/eng/hyyfy/t606550.htm.

42 "Nuclear-Weapon-Free Zones," available at: http://www.fmprc.gov.cn/eng/wjb/zzjg/jks/kjlc/hwt/t410744.htm.

43 See ibid.

the Ocean Floor of 1971 is also relevant as it provides that the non-nuclear zone extends seaward from the 12-n.m. territorial sea of its parties.[44]

The countries adjacent to the South China Sea perhaps also like to consider whether they should reach a consensus on the regulation of foreign military activities including intelligence collection and surveillance, military exercises, ordnance testing and firing, and hydrographic and military surveys conducted within the sea areas under national jurisdiction in the South China Sea. It is worth mentioning that the East–West Center once organized several workshops on "military and intelligence gathering activities in the EEZ." The launch of this series of workshops was triggered by the EP-3 incident in the South China Sea between China and the United States. The first one was held in Bali, Indonesia in June 2002, which focused on identifying disagreements and contrasting positions as well as on areas of possible mutual understanding and agreement.[45] Through these efforts, the guidelines for military activities have been prepared.[46] These guidelines could be used as a basis to govern foreign military activities in the South China Sea.

Freedom of Scientific Research

Freedom of scientific research is fully realized in the Antarctic region. Though a considerable portion of sea areas in the South China Sea are under national jurisdiction, marine scientific research should be encouraged. Like the Antarctic, the South China Sea is another important medium for the study of climate change and sea-level rise, and their impact on human societies. The First Assessment Report of the Intergovernmental Panel on Climate Change (IPCC) anticipated that the South China Sea would experience significant climate and ecological change to the detriment of the region's coastal inhabitants, ecosystems and economies.[47]

It is acknowledged that marine scientific research has been organized under the Track II Informal Workshop on Managing Potential Conflicts in the South China Sea. It established several technical working groups and one of them is to promote marine scientific research in the South China Sea. Due to the nature of Track II, there is no significant progress in this respect.[48] There is also Track-I

44 See M. Rosen, "Nuclear-Weapon-Free Zones," 48 *Naval War College Review*, 1996, at 46.

45 For details, see East–West Center, *Military and Intelligence Gathering Activities in Exclusive Economic Zones: Consensus and Disagreement: A Summary of the Bali Dialogue* (East–West Center, 2002).

46 Text of the Guidelines for Navigation and Overflight in the Exclusive Economic Zone, September 16, 2005, is available at: http://www.sof.or.jp/en/report/pdf/200509_20051205_e.pdf.

47 IPCC, First Assessment Report, 1990, available at: http://www.ipcc.ch/publications_and_data/publications_ipcc_first_assessment_1990_wg1.shtml.

48 For details, see Yann-huei Song, "A Marine Biodiversity Project in the South China Sea: Joint Efforts Made in the SCS Workshop Process," *International Journal of*

cooperation, but mainly limited to a few countries, such as the Philippine–Vietnam Joint Oceanographic and Marine Scientific Research Expedition (JOMSRE-SCS I to IV) between 1996 and 2007. Thus much room is left for regional cooperation in marine scientific research. Natural science is also the basis for resource conservation and environmental protection. Politically, the experiences of the IGY mentioned above are insightful.

Marine Resource Conservation and Environmental Protection

As for the marine resources conservation, the viable principle contained in the ATS is the ecosystem approach as discussed above. This approach has actually been endorsed by the countries around the South China Sea. For example, China began to pay attention to the ecosystem approach in the late 1980s and adopted the ecosystem approach in *China Ocean Agenda 21*, which is accompanied by a project proposal on the sustainability and protection of the Yellow Sea large marine ecosystem for the purpose of restoring the degrading Yellow Sea ecosystem, promoting sustainable development of natural resources, mitigating and preventing environmental threats.[49] The real question is how to implement this approach to the management of the marine resources in the South China Sea. In that sense, taking the whole ecosystem into consideration, integrated ocean management is thus required.

In terms of sustainable management of nonliving resources, a moratorium has to be seriously considered by the littoral states. As we know, oil and gas reserves are rich in the South China Sea. In the Spratly area, there are eight sedimentary basins with an area of 410,000 km^2, and 260,000 km^2 are within China's unilaterally claimed U-shaped line.[50] However, unilateral exploration and exploitation activities by individual South China Sea countries have been undertaken for many decades. These competing activities cause conflicts of interest between/among claimant countries on the one hand[51] and accelerate the depletion of nonrenewable

Marine and Coastal Law, Vol.26, 2011, 119–49.

49 Appendix 6: Sustainability and Protection of the Yellow Sea Large Marine Ecosystem, *China Ocean Agenda 21*, in State Oceanic Administration (SOA), *China Ocean Agenda 21* (Beijing: Ocean Press, 1996), 163–7.

50 See Zhao Huanting et al., *Geomorphology and Environment of the South China Coast and the South China Sea Islands* (Beijing: Science Press, 1999) (in Chinese), at 484.

51 Taking the Crestone Concession case as an example, we can see how serious a unilateral act affected the normal relations between the two countries concerned. In May 1992, China signed a contract with US firm Crestone to explore for oil near the Spratly Islands in an area that Vietnam claimed as its continental shelf. In December 1993 Vietnam demanded that Crestone cancel this offshore oil development. In 1994, Crestone joined with a Chinese partner to explore China's Wan' Bei-21 (WAB-21 block). While Vietnam protested that the exploration was in Vietnamese waters in their blocks 133, 134, and 135, China offered to split Wan' Bei production with Vietnam as long as China retained all sovereignty. In August, Vietnamese gunboats forced a Chinese exploration ship to leave an oilfield in a region claimed

oil and gas resources on the other since each country attempts to maximize its production in the overlapping maritime areas without thinking of sustainability. It is recognized that "cooperative measures to address pollution from oil and gas development activities have not yet been considered seriously by the littoral countries in the SCS/Spratly area."[52]

For regional cooperation purposes, joint development for oil and gas resources in the South China Sea has been proposed,[53] and in state practice, the state-owned oil companies of China, the Philippines and Vietnam (CNOOC, PetroVietnam and Philippine National Oil Company) did sign an agreement on joint seismic exploration in a designated area (143,000 km^2) of the South China Sea in March 2005.[54] However, after the first stage of the joint seismic survey, there has been no follow-up activity sponsored by these three countries. Apparently, this preliminary joint development scheme has encountered a political stalemate resulting from distrust and conflict of maritime interests of the three parties.

Moreover, the proposal for joint development is resource-development oriented with the intention of sharing the benefits from the extraction of nonliving resources, thus containing no appreciated moral values. This lack of moral values can also, at least partially, explain why China's constant call for joint development has received little support from other claimants, much less winning the heart of the world community.

While joint development, as a temporary measure, can still be used as a means of diffusing tensions and enhancing regional cooperation, it is obviously not an optimal option for the interests of all the countries adjacent to the South China Sea. The most optimal option for the South China Sea countries to consider is

---

by the Vietnamese. In April 1996, Vietnam leased exploration blocks to US firm Conoco, and ruled out cooperation with US oil firms that signed Chinese exploration contracts in disputed waters. Vietnamese blocks 133 and 134 cover half the zone leased to Crestone by China. China protested. In March 1997, Vietnamese issued a protest after the Chinese Kantan-3 oil rig drills near Spratly Islands. The drilling was conducted offshore Da Nang, in an area Vietnam calls Block 113. The block is located 64 nautical miles off Chan May cape in Vietnam, and 71 nautical miles off China's Hainan Island. The diplomatic protests were followed by the departure of the Chinese rig. In December 1997, Vietnamese protested after the Exploration Ship No. 8 and two supply ships entered the Wan' Bei exploration block. All 3 vessels were escorted away by the Vietnamese navy. In September 1998, Vietnamese protested after a Chinese report stated that Crestone and China were continuing their survey of the Spratly Islands and the Tu Chinh region (Wan'an Bei in Chinese).

52 Yann-huei Song, "The Potential Marine Pollution Threat from Oil and Gas Development Activities in the Disputed South China Sea/Spratly Area: A Role that Taiwan Can Play," *Ocean Development and International Law*, Vol.39, 2008, 163–4.

53 For details, see Zou Keyuan, "Joint Development in the South China Sea: A New Approach," *International Journal of Marine and Coastal Law*, Vol.21, 2006, 83–109.

54 See "China, Philippines and Vietnam sign agreement to explore oil in the South China Sea," *Lianhe Zaobao*, March 15, 2005, available at: http://www.zaobao.com/gj/yx501_150305.html.

joint sustainable development instead of joint development. In this respect, the Antarctic model serves as a good example.

For marine environmental protection, there have been several existing regional cooperative mechanisms such as the East Asian Seas Programme (EAP) as part of the Regional Seas Programme of the United Nations Environment Programme (UNEP). The Coordinating Body of the Seas of East Asia (COBSEA) recently adopted the New Strategic Direction for COBSEA (2008–12) and the Strategic Action Programme for the South China Sea (SAP).[55] The other regional marine environmental program involving both ASEAN members and China is the Regional Programme on Partnerships in Environmental Management for the Seas of East Asia (PEMSEA) jointly sponsored by the International Maritime Organization (IMO), the United Nations Development Programme (UNDP), the Global Environmental Facility (GEF) and the World Bank, with the mission "To build interagency, intersectoral, and intergovernmental partnerships for achieving the sustainable development of the Seas of East Asia."[56] The China–ASEAN cooperation in marine environmental protection is mainly undertaken under the above regional programs. In the ASEAN Plus Three Cooperation Work Plan 2007–17, the ASEAN members, China, Japan and South Korea have agreed to forge closer cooperation among them in the area of biodiversity and natural heritage conservation.[57]

Since the above programs have a wider coverage than specifically for the area of the South China Sea, they may not serve the purpose of effectiveness in marine environmental protection in this sea area. On the other hand, unilateral designation of marine protected areas in disputed areas "is not particularly helpful because it does not necessarily reflect a regionally endorsed common conservation interest."[58] Some calls have thus been made for the introduction of ecosystem-based management into the South China Sea. A call for the establishment of a Spratly Islands International Marine Peace Park is also voiced.[59]

---

55 For details, see the COBSEA website: http://www.cobsea.org/activities/activities_strategic.html.

56 See "PEMSEA at a Glance," available at: http://www.pemsea.org/about-pemsea/pemsea-at-a-glance/.

57 See "ASEAN Plus Three Cooperation Work Plan 2007–2017," available at: http://www.aseansec.org/21054.htm.

58 See Aldo Chircop, "Regional Cooperation in Marine Environmental Protection in the South China Sea: A Reflection on New Directions for Marine Conservation," 41 *Ocean Development and International Law*, 2011, at 349.

59 For details, see John W. McManus, Kwang-Tsao Shao and Szu-Yin Lin, "Toward Establishing a Spratly Islands Marine Peace Park: Ecological and Supportive Collaborative Activities with an Emphasis on the Role of Taiwan," 41 *Ocean Development and International Law*, 2011, 270–80.

Charting a Legal Framework

As pledged in the 2002 Declaration on the Conduct of Parties in the South China Sea (DOC), all signatories "reaffirm their commitment to the purposes and principles of the Charter of the United Nations, the 1982 UN Convention on the Law of the Sea, the Treaty of Amity and Cooperation in Southeast Asia, the Five Principles of Peaceful Coexistence, and other universally recognized principles of international law which shall serve as the basic norms governing state-to-state relations."[60] Therefore the guiding principles can be found in the UN Charter as well as in general international law, including the LOS Convention.

According to Article 123 of the LOS Convention, the states adjacent to a semi-enclosed sea like the South China Sea have the obligation of cooperation "(a) to coordinate the management, conservation, exploration and exploitation of the living resources of the sea; (b) to coordinate the implementation of their rights and duties with respect to the protection and preservation of the marine environment; (c) to coordinate their scientific research policies and undertake where appropriate joint programmes of scientific research in the area; (d) to invite, as appropriate, other interested States or international organizations to cooperate with them in furtherance of the provisions of this article."[61] It is to be noted that cooperation between the South China Sea states and other states is clearly stated in this provision. It is suggested that experiences and lessons from the Mediterranean Sea and the Caribbean Sea can be learnt by the South China Sea states,[62] in addition to Antarctic experience.

The 2002 DOC certainly serves as a basis to formulate the legal regime for the South China Sea. The negotiation between ASEAN countries and China on the adoption of a legally binding Code of Conduct has clearly shown that the parties concerned have made a right direction and taken an essential step forward. Successful experiences in the establishment and maintenance of the ATS for peace and security in the Antarctic region give the littoral states ample insights in their consideration to develop a regional legal regime for the South China Sea.

Conclusion

This chapter has certainly no intention to suggest that the regime established for the Antarctic based on the ATS is totally applicable to the South China Sea. Nevertheless, some elements in the ATS are useful and to some extent necessary for a regional order to be established for the South China Sea. Though at an embryonic

60 Text is available at: http://www.asean.org/13163.htm.

61 See Article 123 of the LOS Convention.

62 See Nien-Tsu Alfred Hu, "Semi-enclosed Troubled Waters: A New Thinking on the Application of the 1982 UNCLOS Article 123 to the South China Sea," 41 *Ocean Development and International Law*, 2011, 281–314.

stage, a regional order based on general international law and the 2002 DOC can be gradually developed so as to maintain perpetual peace and cooperation in the South China Sea.

Table 7.1 Selected parties to the Antarctic Treaty

Country	Entry into force	Consultative status	Environmental Protocol	CCAS	CCAMLR
Australia	June 23, 1961	June 23, 1961*	Jan 14, 1998	✓	✓
China	June 8, 1983	Oct 7, 1985	Jan 14, 1998		✓
India	Aug 19, 1983	Sept 12, 1983	Jan 14, 1998		✓
Japan	June 23, 1961	June 23, 1961*	Jan 14, 1998	✓	✓
Korea (ROK)	Nov 28, 1976	Oct 9, 1989	Jan 14, 1998		✓
Russian Federation	June 23, 1961	June 23, 1961*	Jan 14, 1998	✓	✓
United States	June 23, 1961	June 23, 1961*	Jan 4, 1998	✓	✓

Source: Adapted from http://www.ats.aq/devAS/ats_parties.aspx?lang=e.

Note: [1] Date on which the Treaty entered into force for the Party. In case of the original Parties, this is the date on which the Treaty first entered into force, June 23, 1961; in case of countries acceding later, it is the date in which they deposited their instrument of accession. [2] The consultative status of the original parties, which is permanent, dates from the entry into force of the Treaty: June 23, 1961. They are marked by an asterisk *. For the other Parties, the date listed is the date on which the consultative status of the Party was recognized by the ATCM. [3] Date of the entry into force of the Environment Protocol for that Party. The Protocol first entered into force on January 14, 1998. [4] Countries Party to CCAS or CCAMLR are indicated with a check mark. [5.] North Korea acceded to the Antarctic Treaty in 1987, but is not a Consultative Party. CCAS= Convention for the Conservation of Antarctic Seals. CCAMLR= Convention for the Conservation of Antarctic Marine Living Resources.

Chapter 8

Bringing the North Pole to the South China Sea: Dots and Lines on Maps and their Explanation

Erik Franckx

Introduction

The title of the present contribution may seem somewhat farfetched, for the North Pole and the South China Sea do not seem to have much in common at first sight. There certainly lies some truth in this primary observation, as will be discussed in the first section below. Nevertheless, as far as the development of the legal regime in both regions is concerned, a notable resemblance is to be discerned if one tries to understand how the largest country in the region, that is, the Russian Federation in the Arctic and China with respect to the South China Sea, have both tried to tighten their grip on the areas in question. By means of legal enactments of a rather broad nature and of which the exact juridical implications are not immediately clear, or at least open to interpretation, Russia and China have veiled their respective legal claims over the area in a haze of uncertainty. The following section will focus on the state practice of both countries in this respect. The final section will subsequently try to draw some conclusions from these similar developments in two areas which at first sight bear but few resemblances.

The Arctic Ocean and the South China Sea: Two Worlds Apart

There are many good reasons to doubt the relevance of comparing the Arctic Ocean with the South China Sea. The first that springs automatically to mind is that the Arctic Ocean is cold and ice-covered, whereas the South China Sea is warm and tropical. These two totally different environments directly impact on the natural resources to be found in these areas. Industrial fisheries in the Arctic seems for the time being still to constitute a possible future activity, as indicated by the recent call by scientists to install a moratorium awaiting the gathering of more scientific evidence before such industrial fishing operations actually start.[1] The natural

1 "Arctic Fishing Moratorium Needed, Scientists Say: Loss of Permanent Sea Ice Making Industrial Fishing Viable for the First Time", CBCNews, April 22, 2012, available

conditions prevailing in the South China Sea on the other hand result in what an author has described as "exceptionally favourable conditions for a fertile marine ecosystem.[2] The latter resulted in heavy governmental investment in the fishery sector by the states surrounding this semi-enclosed sea[3] once the international legal regime had granted the coastal states access rights to 95 percent of all commercially exploited fish resources by means of the creation of the exclusive economic zone.[4] And even though marine capture fisheries has been decreasing world-wide since the early 1990s,[5] an increase in landings and especially in value is still to be noted in the South China Sea area.[6]

A similar distinction is to be witnessed with respect to shipping. Using the Arctic as a through route between the Atlantic and Pacific Oceans is on the verge of becoming a reality, especially as far as the Northeast Passage, or the Northern

---

at: http://www.cbc.ca/news/world/story/2012/04/22/arctic-fishing-moratorium-scientists.html.

2 Rosenberg, D., "Fisheries Management in the South China Sea", in *Security and International Politics in the South China Sea: Towards a Cooperative Management Regime* (Bateman, S. and Emmers, R., eds). Abingdon: Routledge, 2009, p. 62.

3 Ablan, C.A. and Garces, L.R., "Exclusive Economic Zones and the Management of Fisheries in the South China Sea", in *A Sea Change: The Exclusive Economic Zone and Governance Institutions for Living Marine Resources* (Ebbin, S.A., Hoel, A.H.H. and Sydnes, A.K., eds). Dordrecht: Springer, 2005, p. 139.

4 Freestone, D., "Fisheries, High Seas", *Max Planck Encyclopedia of Public International Law Online*. Oxford University Press, 2009, p. 2, as available at: http://www.mpepil.com. This notion was codified in the United Nations Convention on the Law of the Sea. Multilateral convention, signed on December 10, 1982, Arts. 55–75, 1833 *United Nations Treaty Series* pp. 397–581. This convention entered into force on November 1994, as available at: http://www.un.org/Depts/los/convention_agreements/texts/unclos/unclos_e.pdf. But even before this convention entered into force and despite the fact that this notion had only taken shape during the negotiations leading up to the adoption of this document, the notion had already become part and parcel of international customary law. Elaborating on the latter point, see for instance Franckx, E. and Van Assche, C., "Contemporary High Seas Fisheries Law", in *Contemporary Regulation of Marine Living Resources and Pollution (Essays written by and in Honour of the International Francqui Chairholder Professor Dermott Devine)* (Franckx, E., ed.). Antwerp: Maklu Publishers, 2007, pp. 30–34.

5 Food and Agriculture Organization, *The State of World Fisheries and Aquaculture 2010*, Rome, FAO, p. 3 Table 1 (2010), as available at: http://www.fao.org/docrep/013/i1820e/i1820e.pdf. This table covers the period 2004-2010 and should be read in combination with earlier FAO reports covering the period from 1990 until 2003, as available at: http://www.fao.org/fishery/publications/sofia/en.

6 Indeed, the latest statistics from the Southeast Asian Fisheries Development Centre (SEAFDEC) indicate that in the South China Sea between 2003 and 2007 there has been an increase by about 6.5 percent in quantity and even by about 31 percent in value of marine capture fisheries. See Southeast Asian Fisheries Development Center, Summary 2007: An Overview of Fishery Sector for the South China Sea Area in 2007, p. 4, as available at: http://fishstat.seafdec.org/statistical_bulletin/download/2007.pdf.

Sea Route as called by the Russians, is concerned. Or as somewhat prophetically stated by one commentator: "When the future history of the Arctic will be written, 2010 will be marked as the breakthrough year for commercial shipping along the Northern Sea Route."[7] The present-day importance of the South China Sea on the other hand can hardly be over-estimated when it comes to shipping:

> The South China Sea is one of the world's busiest international sea-lanes. Over half of the world's merchant fleet (by tonnage) sails through the South China Sea every year. More than half of the world's oil tanker traffic passes through the region's waters. Over half of the top ten container shipping ports in the world are located in or around the South China Sea.[8]

Finally, totally in line with both previous elements of divergence, it has been argued that if the world economy had a geographical centre, it would be the South China Sea.[9] Again, the Arctic has only been projected to become a "spatial point center" somewhere in the future.[10]

The Arctic Ocean and the South China Sea: Striking Similarities

Despite the major differences between the Arctic Ocean and the South China Sea, it is interesting to note that major countries in the region, when trying to expand their control over these vast water expanses, turned to similar types of juridical instruments in order to do so. This part will look into the way in which both

---

7 Nilsen, T., "The Future History of the Arctic is Now", Barents Observer, September 2, 2010, available at: http://www.barentsobserver.com/index.php?id=4814307. For a closer analysis of that particular shipping season, see Franckx, E. and Boone, L., "New Developments in the Arctic: Protecting the Marine Environment from Increased Shipping", in *The Law of the Sea Convention: US Accession and Globalization* (Nordquist, M.H., Norton Moore, J., Soons, A.H. and Kim, H.-S., eds), Leiden, Martinus Nijhoff Publishers, 2012, pp. 187–93.

8 Rosenberg, D., "Governing the South China Sea: From Freedom of the Seas to Ocean Enclosure Movements", 12 *Harvard Asia Quarterly*, 2010, p. 7.

9 Cronin, P.M. and Kaplan, R.D., "Cooperation from Strength: U.S. Strategy and the South China Sea", in *Cooperation from Strength: The United States, China and the South China Sea* (Cronin, P.M., ed.), Washington, D.C., Center for a New American Security, 2012, p. 7.

10 Valsson, T. and Ulfarsson, G.F., "Future Changes in Activity Structures of the Globe Under a Receding Arctic Ice Scenario", 43 *Futures*, 2011, p. 455. These authors project that "[i]n the far future, as the activity has reached a high degree, the new spatial point center of the Arctic can start to compete with the spatial linear center of the ribbon of today's world" (id.). With the "ribbon of today's world" these author refer to the fact that mankind is at present living on a ribbon that surrounds the globe at lower latitudes, thus including the South China Sea area.

countries have formulated their legal claims over the area. By drawing some lines at sea the Republic of China, later followed by the People's Republic of China, and the former Soviet Union, later followed by the Russian Federation, have both tried to expand their legal claims in the region. The former made use of dotted lines in this respect, the latter of full lines as will be seen. Both claims will be treated in chronological order, after which a comparison will be made.

The Soviet Decree of 1926

At a time when the Bolsheviks were very much afraid that other countries would start claiming land features north of the Eurasian continent on the basis of discovery, the former Soviet Union, in an attempt to forestall such foreign claims, enacted a decree containing the following provision:

> The Presidium of the Central Executive Committee of the Union of Soviet Socialist Republics proclaims as territories all lands and islands which are already discovered or might be discovered in the future and which by the moment of the present [decree] do not constitute a territory of any foreign states recognized by the Government of the Union of Soviet Socialist Republics, situated in the Arctic Ocean northwards of the coast of the Union of Soviet Socialist Republics up to the North Pole within the limits between the meridian 32°04'[3]5" [eastern] longitude from Greenwich passing along the eastern side of the inlet Vaida through the triangular marker on [] Cape Kekurskii, and the meridian 168°49'30" western longitude from Greenwich bisec[t]ing the strait separating the Ratmanov and Kruzenstern islands of the group of islands of Diomid in the Bering Strait.[11]

The crucial question when interpreting this decree was whether it should be understood in a literal manner, meaning that only lands and islands were concerned, or rather as construed by certain Soviet authors of that time period who were quick in inferring that the ice formations and waters surrounding these lands and islands had to be included as forming part of the territory of the former USSR. as well.[12] In fact, the 1926 Decree very much resembles the initiative undertaken two decades

11 Decree of the Presidium of the Central Executive Committee of the USSR of 15 April 1926, *On the Declaration of Lands and Islands Located in the Arctic Ocean the Territory of the USSR.*, 32 SobranieUzakoneniiiRasporiazheniiRaboche-Krest'ianskogoPravitel'stva S.S.S.R. (Collected Laws and Decrees of the Workers' and Peasants' Government of the USSR.), 1926, at 203. The present English translation is taken from Koroleva, N.D., Markov, V.I. and Ushakov, A.P., *Pravovoirezhimsudochodstva v Rossiiskoi Arktike* (Legal Regime of Navigation in the Russian Arctic), Moscow, Soiuzmornii proekt, 1995, pp. 87–8 and 105.

12 Korovin, E.A., "SSSR ipoliarniiezemli" (The USSR. and Polar Lands), 5 *Sovetskoe Pravo*, 1926, pp. 43–6.

earlier by a Canadian Senator, Pascal Poirier, who introduced the sector theory before the Canadian Senate in 1907. His motion went as follows:

> That it be resolved that the Senate is of the opinion that the time has come for Canada to make a formal declaration of possession of the lands and islands situated in the north of the Dominion, and extending to the north pole … From 141 to 60 degrees west we are on Canadian territory.[13]

This motion however was abortive and never reached the House of Commons. Nevertheless it has a similar emphasis on lands, islands and territory as the 1926 Decree.

It can therefore safely be concluded that Canadians might well have invented the Arctic sector theory, but it was the former Soviet Union that first applied it in practice by enacting specific legislation,[14] at least in a version strictly limited to lands and islands, not to waters. Even though this appeared to be the official government position from its inception,[15] Soviet and Russian authors have given it different interpretations over time.[16] Whether the issue is at present definitively shelved cannot be affirmed with certainty, for there are still influential Russian authors who look in admiration to the Canadian state practice in this respect[17]

---

13 Canada, Senate Debates, February 20, 1907, p. 266, as reprinted by Head, I.I., "Canadian Claims to Territorial Sovereignty in the Arctic Regions", 9 *McGill Law Journal*, 1963, p. 203.

14 The Canadians nevertheless started to depict these sector lines as boundaries on maps since 1904, but discussions in Parliament and especially positions taken there by members of the Government, tended to indicate that this country only claimed the land and islands within this sector, not the ice or water. For a careful analysis, see Pharand, D., *The Law of the Sea of the Arctic: With Special Reference to Canada*, Ottawa, University of Ottawa Press, 1973, pp. 134–41 and 171–5 and by the same author, *Canada's Arctic Waters in International Law*. Cambridge: Cambridge University Press, 1988, pp. 1–87. In a final revisit of the issue after a lifelong oeuvre devoted to Canadian Arctic matters, this author disposes succinctly of the matter in the following manner: "This [sector] theory has no validity in international law for the acquisition of title, not even for land areas, and there is no clear evidence that Canada has ever officially relied on it to support a claim to Arctic waters." See by the same author, "The Arctic Waters and the Northwest Passage: A Final Revisit", 38 *Ocean Development and International Law*, 2007, p. 10.

15 An article attributed to the legal adviser of the former USSR. Ministry of Foreign Affairs seems to have put the issue to rest by stressing the limited nature of the 1926 Decree. As emphasized by Butler, W.E., *Northeast Arctic Passage*, Alphen aan den Rijn, Sijthoff en Noordhoff, 1978, p. 74.

16 For an overview, see Timtchenko, L., "The Russian Arctic Sectoral Concept: Past and Present", 50 *Arctic*, 1997, pp. 29–35. See also Franckx, E., *Maritime Claims in the Arctic: Canadian and Russian Perspectives*, Dordrecht, Martinus Nijhoff Publishers, 1993, pp. 152–3 and 168–70.

17 Nikolaev, A.V. and Bunik, I.V., "Mezhdunarodno-pravovoe obosnovanie Kanadoi pravna ee arkticheskii sector" (The International Legal Foundation of Canadian Rights over

and would tend to take a position very much akin to the sector theory.[18] The fact remains, that the Government itself, whether Soviet or Russian, has never tried to apply this principle other than for determining its position with respect to maritime boundary delimitation in the area.[19]

Regarding the latter point, the recently concluded maritime boundary delimitation agreement with Norway represents a perfect example. In the course of the 40 years of bilateral negotiations that preceded this agreement, the USSR. started out by attributing more and more importance to the sector line as maritime boundary,[20] a position that this country maintained steadfastly thereafter.[21] That the sector line serves as a fall-back position for the Russian Federation has been implicitly confirmed by the recent Treaty concerning Maritime Delimitation and Cooperation in the Barents Sea and Arctic Ocean concluded in 2010 between both countries.[22] For it is of course one thing to say that the Russian Federation definitively abandoned the sector principle since the delimitation line finally agreed upon does not coincide with this sector line at all because it generally runs much more to the east of it.[23] But if one is of the opinion that sector lines in the Arctic do not find doctrinal justification as maritime boundaries simply because of their northern location,[24] then the logical result should be that the disputed area

---

Their Arctic Sector), 65 *Moskovskii zhurnal mezhdunarodnogo prava* 1 (2007).

18 Bunik, I.V., "Alternative Approaches to the Delimitation of the Arctic Continental Shelf", *International Energy Law Review*, pp. 114–25 (2008).

19 Franckx, *supra* note 16, p. 170, referring to a "fall-back" position to sustain more limited claims if necessary. Just like Russia, also Canada relies on the sector line in its maritime boundary negotiations with the United States. Stressing this latter correlation, see Churchill, R., "Claims to Maritime Zones in the Arctic: Law of the Sea Normality or Polar Peculiarity?", in *The Law of the Sea and Polar Maritime Delimitation and Jurisdiction* (Elferink, A.G.O. and Rothwell, D.R., eds). The Hague, Martinus Nijhoff Publishers, 2001, p. 123. It has recently been argued however that beyond 200 nautical miles, as far as the extended continental shelf is concerned, the claims of the respective parties work counterproductive to their own interests. Baker, J.S. and Byers, M., "Crossed Lines: The Curious Case of the Beaufort Sea Maritime Boundary Dispute", 43 *Ocean Development and International Law*, 2012, pp. 70–95.

20 Østreng, W., "Norwegen und die Sowjetunion in der Barentssee", 35 *Europa-Archiv*, 1980, p. 714.

21 Østreng, W., "Delimitation Arrangements in Arctic Seas: Cases of Precedence or Securing of Strategic/Economic Interests?" 10 *Marine Policy*, 1986, p. 135.

22 Treaty between Norway and the Russian Federation concerning Maritime Delimitation and Cooperation in the Barents Sea and Arctic Ocean, September 15, 2010. This treaty entered into force on June 7, 2011. For the text of the treaty and its two annexes, see for instance Jensen, Ø., "Current Legal Developments, The Barents Sea: Treaty between Norway and the Russian Federation concerning Maritime Delimitation and Cooperation in the Barents Sea and Arctic Ocean", 26 *International Journal of Marine and Coastal Law*, 2011, pp. 159–68.

23 For a visual representation, see ibid., p. 154.

24 See for instance Elferink, A.G.O., "Arctic Maritime Delimitations: The Preponderance of Similarities with Other Regions", in *The Law of the Sea and Polar*

between Norway, basing its claim on equidistance, and Russia, basing itself on special circumstances (not including the sector line for the sake of argumentation), must be much more restricted than the disputed area of about 176.000 km² which is exactly measured between the equidistance and sector lines claimed by the parties.[25] As is often the case, the treaty itself remains silent on the exact method used to arrive at the final maritime delimitation line.[26] Nevertheless, an analysis of the different joint statements issued by government officials leads to the conclusion that the disputed zone was divided approximately in two areas of the same size, with each measuring about 88,000 km².[27] Commentators seem to be in agreement therefore that the disputed zone in question is bordered in the east by the Norwegian equidistance line and in the west by the Russian sector line.[28] But if that is so, it means that the Russian sector line has been given half-effect, as in fact was the fate that also befell the Norwegian equidistant line. To argue therefore that this agreement between Norway and Russia disposes once and for all of the importance of sector lines in the Arctic only constitutes a half-truth.

The Chinese 9-dotted Line[29]

Also China relies on a claim with respect to the South China Sea of which the origins date back to the same *interbellum* period as the just discussed 1926 Decree, namely a map produced by the Land and Water Maps Inspection Committee of the Republic of China, formed in 1933, which was tasked with the surveying and naming of islands

---

Maritime Delimitation and Jurisdiction (Elferink, A.G.O. and Rothwell, D.R., eds). The Hague, Martinus Nijhoff Publishers, 2001, pp. 187–8. This author moreover stresses that there has never been acquiescence by Norway on this point and he very much doubts that the sector line could ever be the result of applying special circumstances to the area in question. For a succinct listing of the different special circumstances which according to the Russians should result in the adoption of the sector line, see Lalonde, S.,"Barents Sea", Max Planck Encyclopedia of Public International Law Online. Oxford University Press, 2009, p. 3, as available at: http://www.mpepil.com.

25 Aasen, P.J., *The Law of Maritime Delimitation and the Russian–Norwegian Maritime Boundary Dispute*, Lysaker, Fridtjof Nansen Institute, 2010, p. 74, as available at: http://www.fni.no/doc&pdf/FNI-R0110.pdf.

26 Art. 1 only provides a list of eight geographical coordinates and the preamble remains silent on this point as well.

27 As mentioned by Henriksen, T. and Ulfstein, G., "Maritime Delimitation in the Arctic: The Barents Sea Treaty", 42 *Ocean Development and International Law*, 2011, pp. 6–7.

28 *Ibid.*, p. 7; Jensen, *supra* note 22, pp. 153–4.

29 This part is based on a previously published article by the present author together with Benatar, M., "Dots and Lines in the South China Sea: Insights from the Law of Map Evidence", 2 *Asian Journal of International Law*, 2012, pp. 89–118. About the denomination "9-dotted line", used by the present article, see *infra* note 34 and accompanying text.

in the South China Sea.[30] However, the first officially endorsed map appeared only after the Second World War, when the Department of the Territories and Boundaries of the Ministry of the Interior of the Republic of China produced a map on which 11 intermittent dashes are to be found.[31] If one considers the land boundary between China and Vietnam to be the starting point, this imaginary line starts in the Gulf of Tonkin, where the first two dashes are situated. It then moves further south separating by two more dashes the coast of Vietnam from the Paracel and the Spratly Islands respectively. The fifth and sixth dashes take the imaginary line in the same general direction close to James Shoal (4° N), its most southern point. The next two dashes bring the imaginary line back up in a northeasterly direction between the Spratly Islands on the one hand and Borneo (Indonesia, Malaysia and Brunei) and the Philippines (Palawan Province) on the other hand. The ninth and tenth dashes further follow the east coast of the Philippines while the eleventh dash finally separates the northern part of the Philippines from Taiwan Island.[32] This claim of the Republic of China was later taken over by the People's Republic of China once the Nationalists were removed from the mainland.[33] Since then, maps containing these eleven dashes have been surfacing on both sides of the Taiwan Strait. These maps have been characterized by one noticeable change as time went by, namely the sudden disappearance of the two dashes in the Gulf of Tonkin, making it at present generally known as the 9-dotted line.[34]

The major problem with these maps, from an international legal point of view, is that they are shrouded in a veil of uncertainty. When analyzed against the backdrop

30 Li, J. and Li, D., "The Dotted Line on the Chinese Map of the South China Sea: A Note", 34 *Ocean Development and International Law*, 2003, p. 289.

31 This map is for instance reproduced in Hu, N.A., "South China Sea: Troubled Waters or a Sea of Opportunity?", 41 *Ocean Development and International Law*, 2010, p. 208.

32 Wang, K.-H., "The ROC's Maritime Claims and Practices with Special Reference to the South China Sea", 41 *Ocean Development and International Law*, 2010, p. 248.

33 Shen, J., "China's Sovereignty over the South China Sea Islands: A Historical Perspective", 1 *Chinese Journal of International Law*, 2002, p. 129, note 122.

34 This change from eleven to nine dashes is said to have happened either during the 1950s (Li and Li, *supra* note 30, p. 290) or the 1960s (Zou, K., "The Chinese Traditional Maritime Boundary Line in the South China Sea and its Legal Consequences for the Resolution of the Dispute over the Spratly Islands", 14 *International Journal of Marine and Coastal Law*, 1999, pp. 34–5). The latter author in a more recent publication, however, also locates this change in the "late 1950s" and indicates that it might be related to the transfer of the sovereignty of an island located there, namely Bai Long Wei in Chinese or Bac Long Vi in Vietnamese, from China to Vietnam. Zou, K., "China's U-Shaped Line in the South China Sea Revisited", 43 *Ocean Development and International Law*, 2012, p. 24. Depending on whether the map in its upper right corner not only includes Taiwan Island but also the Ryukyu group belonging to Japan, a tenth dash is to be found separating these areas. See for instance Chinese State Bureau of Surveying and Mapping, Map World, available at: http://www.chinaonmap.cn/map/index.html. For present purposes this imaginary line will be referred to as the 9-dotted line.

of international case law, it has been argued by the present author elsewhere that "the 9-dotted line would not fare well as evidentiary material in a hypothetical court case":[35] Different versions of the map are incompatible; incoherent or ambiguous cartographic symbols are used; the intent of the maps remains unclear; there is a lack of neutrality; and technical imprecision has to be noted.[36]

Unlike the 1926 Decree, which entrenched the sector lines in national legislation, China has still to pass legislation giving the 9-dotted line effect in its national legislation.[37] These maps showing the 9-dotted line moreover seem for a long time to have had a mere internal use for it was only in 2009 that China submitted such map for the first time to the United Nations.[38]

China did so in reaction to the joint submission by Malaysia and Vietnam[39] and the individual submission by Vietnam in North Area[40] concerning parts of their continental shelves extending beyond 200 nautical miles to the Commission on the Limits of the Continental Shelf in accordance with the 1982 Convention.[41] By means of two separate letters to the Secretary General of the United Nations, both dated May 7, 2009, China for the first time relied on the 9-dotted line at the international level in a state to state dispute. It did so by attaching this map to a "clarification" of its legal position, expressed in identical ways in the two letters and using the following wording:

---

35 Franckx and Benatar, *supra* note 29, p. 115.

36 Ibid., pp. 105–10.

37 Smith, R.W., "Maritime Delimitation in the South China Sea: Potentiality and Challenges", 41 *Ocean Development and International Law*, 2010, p. 224.

38 As stressed by Fravel, M.T., "Maritime Security in the South China Sea and the Competition over Maritime Rights", in *Cooperation from Strength: The United States, China and the South China Sea* (Cronin, P.M., ed.), Washington, D.C., Center for a New American Security, 2012, p. 42.

39 Malaysia-Socialist Republic of Vietnam, "Joint Submission to the Commission on the Limits of the Continental Shelf Pursuant to Article 76, paragraph 8 of the United Nations Convention on the Law of the Sea 1982 in Respect of the Southern Part of the South China Sea, Executive Summary" (May 2009), as available at: http://www.un.org/Depts/los/clcs_new/submissions_files/mysvnm33_09/mys_vnm2009excutivesummary.pdf. As indicated by the letter of the Secretary-General of the United Nations, acknowledging receipt, this joint submission was made on May 6, 2009, as available at: http://www.un.org/depts/los/clcs_new/submissions_files/mysvnm33_09/mysvnm_clcs33_2009e.pdf.

40 Socialist Republic of Vietnam, "Submission to the Commission on the Limits of the Continental Shelf Pursuant to Article 76, paragraph 8 of the United Nations Convention on the Law of the Sea 1982, Partial Submission in Respect of Vietnam's Extended Continental Shelf: North Area (VNM-N), Executive Summary" (April 2009), as available at: http://www.un.org/Depts/los/clcs_new/submissions_files/vnm37_09/vnm2009n_executivesummary.pdf. As indicated by the letter of the Secretary-General of the UN, acknowledging receipt, this submission was made on 7 May 2009, as available at: http://www.un.org/depts/los/clcs_new/submissions_files/vnm37_09/vnm_clcs37_2009e.pdf.

41 1982 Convention, *supra* note 4, Art. 76(8).

> China has indisputable sovereignty over the islands in the South China Sea and the adjacent waters, and enjoys sovereign rights and jurisdiction over the relevant waters as well as the seabed and subsoil thereof (see attached map). The above position is consistently held by the Chinese Government, and is widely known by the international community.[42]

This first ever, triggered an immediate response from the international community. Not only did governments instantaneously react to this Chinese official statement,[43] but this issue was also thoroughly debated at international conferences[44] and in the legal literature.[45]

The Chinese "clarification" of 2009, however, seems to be a fitting illustration of the Latin maxim *ignotum per ignotius*,[46] for the terms used to explain the

42 People's Republic of China, "Letter to the Secretary-General of the United Nations—CML/17/2009" (May 7, 2009), as available at: http://www.un.org/Depts/los/clcs_new/submissions_files/mysvnm33_09/chn_2009re_mys_vnm_e.pdf>; People's Republic of China, "Letter to the Secretary-General of the United Nations– CML/18/2009" (May 7, 2009), as available at: http://www.un.org/Depts/los/clcs_new/submissions_files/vnm37_09/chn_2009re_vnm.pdf. The map was attached to these letters.

43 It will suffice to refer to the direct reactions these two Chinese letters provoked, in chronological order, from countries like Vietnam, Malaysia, the Philippines and Indonesia, some of them triggering further reactions, with respect to the joint submission of Malaysia and Vietnam, as available at: http://www.un.org/depts/los/clcs_new/submissions_files/submission_mysvnm_33_2009.htm, and from Vietnam and the Philippines, triggering themselves further reactions, with respect to the individual submission by Vietnam in North Area, as available at: http://www.un.org/depts/los/clcs_new/submissions_files/submission_mysvnm_33_2009.htm.

44 If one looks for instance at the proceedings of the first and second International Workshop on the South China Sea: Cooperation for Regional Security and Development, co-organized by the Diplomatic Academy of Vietnam and the Vietnam Lawyers Association, the first of which took place in November 2009, the issue of the 9-dotted line featured prominently, as can be inferred from the fact that the two introductory speakers during the first one touched upon it (Till, G., "South China Sea: Just Waiting for the Breeze?", in *Proceedings of the International Workshop on the South China Sea: Cooperation for Regional Security and Development*, Hanoi, Diplomatic Academy of Vietnam, 2009, p. 11; and in the same publication Valencia, M.J., "Whither the South China Sea Disputes?", p. 15) and it formed part and parcel of the part of the second conference dealing with legal perspectives, as indicated by the editor of its proceedings (Tran Truong, T., "Introduction", in *The South China Sea: Towards a Region of Peace, Security and Cooperation* (Tran Truong, T., ed.), Hanoi, The Gioi Publishers, p. 12 (2011)).

45 It is for instance noteworthy that four articles out of a total of six of the first issue of 2012 of the specialized legal journal *Ocean Development and International Law* specifically deal with the 9-dotted line.

46 Translated into English, it reads: "The action of offering an explanation which is harder to understand than the thing it is meant to explain." Oxford Dictionaries online, as available at: http://oxforddictionaries.com/definition/ignotum%2Bper%2Bignotius.

meaning of the 9-dotted map, and especially the status of the waters enclosed by that imaginary line, are not know to the 1982 Convention and thus unintelligible for international lawyers trying to understand the exact meaning of the Chinese "clarification." Indeed, neither "adjacent waters" nor "relevant waters" are notions to be found in the Constitution for the Oceans, to which China is a party. The result is that at international conferences organized on the South China Sea right after the sending of the Chinese letters to the Secretary-General of the United Nations in May 2009, participants took totally different views on the possible meanings of these letters.[47] And this confusion clearly still persists today as evidenced by a diverse group of authors commenting on the 9-dotted line in the early 2012 issue of Ocean Development and International Law.[48] If there is one common conclusion to be drawn from these contributions, it must be that the Chinese claim is at present still in need of clarification.[49]

Conclusions

The Arctic Ocean and the South China Sea do not seem to have much in common at first sight. Nevertheless, some interesting similarities can be discerned as far as the legal constructs are concerned devised by major regional powers in the area in order to try to tighten their grip on the area in general, and with respect to the vast maritime expanses in particular. One of the methods relied upon was the drawing of lines at sea, whether they are called sector lines or 9-dotted line.

The present study has indicated that the Russian Federation, even though this country seems to have relinquished is sovereignty claim to the waters so enclosed, nevertheless still obtains some advantages from its sector lines enacted by means of the 1926 Decree, namely in the field of maritime delimitation. Granted that this does not imply full recognition, a closer analysis of the recently concluded

47 As already emphasized by the present author elsewhere, see Franckx, E., "American and Chinese Views on Navigational Rights of Warships", 10 *Chinese Journal of International Law* p. 196 (2011). Compare note 46 with note 47.

48 As already referred to above, *supra* note 46.

49 In the order in which these articles appeared in the journal: Masahiro, M., "China's 'U-Shaped Line' Claim in the South China Sea: Any Validity Under International Law?", 43 *Ocean Development and International Law* pp. 3–4 (2012) (asking the question "What is China's U-Shaped Line Claim" and coming to the conclusion that the waters on the inside are claimed by China); Zou, *supra* note 35, p. 20 (indicating that "there is no official explanation from China regarding the U-shaped line"); Nguyen-Dang, T. and Nguyen Hong, T., "China's Nine Dotted Lines in the South China Sea: The 2011 Exchange of Diplomatic Notes Between the Philippines and China", 43 *Ocean Development and International Law* p. 47 (2012) (stating that "the status of the nine dotted lines … remains shrouded in obscurity"); and Michael Sheng-Ti, G., "The U-Shaped Line and a Categorization of the Ocean Disputes in the South China Sea", 43 *Ocean Development and International Law* pp. 60–63 (2012) (inferring that China no longer claims historic waters).

maritime boundary treaty with Norway and especially the statements made by politicians at the time of signature seem to justify the conclusion that half effect was given to this sector line after 40 years of negotiations.

The above conclusion might inspire China, for even if this country would not be able to obtain sovereignty over all of the water expanses located on the inside of the 9-dotted line, the prospect of its application in pending delimitation agreements with the other states surrounding the South China Sea, even if only half effect were to be given to 9-dotted line, may still appear rather appealing. But here one needs to add a number of caveats. First of all, the 1926 Decree was by and large never contested in the sense that all the islands located north of the part of the Eurasian continent over which the Russian Federation today exercises sovereignty, and which were not excluded by the 1926 Decree, are today internationally recognized as falling under Russian sovereignty.[50] It is clear that this situation is a far cry from the present-day situation in the South China Sea where the sovereignty over the island features is contested by no less than six different countries all having claims there. Whether China will therefore ever be able to profit from such fall-back in the South China Sea, as Russia was able to rely upon in the Arctic, is highly questionable, if not outright unrealistic.

By retaining what in French is called a *flou artistique*, that is, a desired but nevertheless controlled vagueness that at the same time blurs the picture while retaining its sharp edges, China and the Russian Federation both hope to be able to cash in on their legal constructs one day. Because of their political import and size, these countries are confident they will carry more weight at the negotiation table than most of their regional partners. Russia has been able to draw some profit from this method in its bilateral maritime boundary delimitation with Norway. Due to the fact that the argument can be made that the sector line does not form part of contemporary international law, as mentioned above,[51] the question could be raised whether this is not contrary to the rules of contemporary international law? This question, however, does not really come up for discussion, for if courts and tribunals have to found their decisions on law when parties turn to them to solve their maritime delimitation issues, this does not apply to states when they settle their maritime boundary disputes in common agreement through direct negotiations between themselves.[52] In the latter case parties are indeed totally free

50 Franckx, *supra* note 17, pp. 143–4, indicating that the last country contesting sovereignty over some of the islands north of the Eurasian continent was the United States, but this country seems to have officially dropped its claim over Wrangel and some other smaller islands in the eastern part. A similar conclusion can by the way also be drawn with respect to the Canadian sector claim as far as land is concerned (id., pp. 73–4).

51 See *supra* note 25 and accompanying text.

52 As stated by Charney, J.I., "Introduction", in *International Maritime Boundaries* (Charney, J.I. and Alexander, L.M., eds), Dordrecht, Martinus Nijhoff, Vol. 1, p. xxxvii (1993): "While third party forums are required to apply the law, states are free to negotiate solutions on the basis of any considerations they wish."

to mutually agree on any boundary line they like, based on any considerations they wish, as long as they do not infringe upon the rights of any third state in the area and do not violate peremptory norms of international law in so agreeing.

China, on the other hand, does not have at present undisputed possession of the insular features in the South China Sea in order to try to gain advantage from its 9-dotted line. And to claim the whole water area as falling under Chinese sovereignty is simply incompatible with existing rules of international law, as recently stressed by Tommy Koh, the President of the Third United Nations Conference on the Law of the Sea, which ultimately adopted the 1982 Convention.[53] If there is one lesson to be learned from this Arctic—South China Sea comparison, it would be that China is well guided to continue the efforts it is apparently undertaking at present to brief embassies behind closed doors that the 9-dotted line relates primarily to land features and the maritime zones the latter could generate.[54] By clarifying its legal position on the 9-dotted line a second time *urbi et orbi*—but this time removing the remaining uncertainties surrounding a possible claim over all the waters on the inside of that line based on historic rights once and for all—this country will defuse an issue which has soured relations in the South China Sea area ever since its first maladroit "clarification" attempt in 2009.

---

53 Koh, T., "Mapping Out Rival Claims in the South China Sea", The Strait Times, September 13, 2011, as mentioned by Storey, I., "China's Bilateral and Multilateral Diplomacy in the South China Sea", in *Cooperation from Strength: The United States, China and the South China Sea* (Cronin, P.M., ed.), Washington, D.C., Center for a New American Security, p. 54 (2012).

54 International Crisis Group, "Stirring Up the South China Sea", *Asia Report N° 223*, April 23, 2012, p. 3 (2012). As available at: http://www.crisisgroup.org/~/media/Files/asia/north-east-asia/223-stirring-up-the-south-china-sea-i.pdf.

PART IV
Major Policy Issues in the South China Sea

Chapter 9

Close Encounters of the Maritime Kind: Freedom of Navigation and its Impact on the South China Sea Problem

Geoffrey Till

> The history of the law of the sea has been dominated by a central and persistent theme—the competition between the exercise of governmental authority over the sea and the idea of the freedom of the seas. The tension between these has waxed and waned through the centuries, and has reflected the political, strategic, and economic circumstances of each particular age.[1]

Introduction

The legal dispute over jurisdiction in the South China Sea is already a famously complicated one. It is further complicated by its implications for sea-users who are not in fact parties to the dispute. That they nonetheless have a strong interest in the management and outcome of the dispute was made clear by Secretary Hillary Clinton in July 2010, a point which should in fact have come as no surprise to anyone. The issue has become related to such evidence of developing discord over the freedom of navigation, specifically of warships, in the Exclusive Economic Zone (EEZ) as the *USNS Impeccable* incident of March 2009. This tangential dispute threatens to make the intractable problem of jurisdiction over the South China Sea more intractable yet, and so deserves attention.

This chapter is therefore about the impact of competing conceptions of the freedom of navigation and its likely impact on the problems of working towards a sustainable way of handling the dispute over the South China Sea, whether that aspires to actually resolving the dispute or more immediately to managing away its more dangerous aspects. Simplistically, this is sometimes simply seen as a contest between Chinese and American perceptions of the extent to which the freedom of navigation of other countries may be constrained within another country's EEZ. But in fact, of course other countries share at least some aspects of the 'Chinese' vision, including India, Malaysia and Vietnam to give some local examples, while most other countries tend rather to support what might be called the 'American' position, including some 60 'zone-locked states' who for their own reasons wish

---

1 D.P. O'Connell, *The International Law of the Sea* (Oxford: OUP, 1982)

to see the EEZ as free as possible, and whose position was made clear during the UNCLOS negotiations.[2]

Furthermore, the debate about the freedom of navigation and the exclusive economic zone is not 'just' a legal issue—not simply a question of interpreting and applying the UN Convention on the Law of the Sea. Instead, these interpretations and the manner in which they should be applied in particular circumstances are themselves heavily influenced by much wider considerations about the nature of the sea in general and *the* near seas in particular—which themselves are much more a matter of national philosophy, politics and strategic culture. Context, in fact, is all, and in fact the context determined the terms of UNCLOS back in 1982. So much so, in fact, that this chapter, by way of conclusion, inclines to the view that convergence in this broader area is an indispensable prelude to any final bridging of the 'legal' gap between the two positions on this aspect of the jurisdictional dispute over the South China Sea. And that it is in this broader area, rather than the quarrels of lawyers, that solutions may need to be found.[3] The fact that international law is established not just by formal international treaty [such as UNCLOS] but also by state practice, reinforces this contention.

Although these two positions should *not* simply be seen as a dispute between the United States and China for the reasons stated above it is analytically convenient to treat it as such in this chapter not least because of its implications for the particular problem of the South China Sea.

US Perspective, Objectives and Assumptions

The United States view is that it takes no position on the ownership of the islands of the South China Sea, that it wants to see the matter resolved peacefully but that neither the dispute nor its resolution should interfere with the principle of free navigation in the area.

This is not simply a formulaic re-statement of a long held belief that lawful merchant and naval shipping should be allowed to sail around the world's oceans without interference; it goes instead to the very heart of the United States as a distinctively maritime country[4] and is central to the whole ethos of the U.S. Navy.

---

2 Kraska, James, *Maritime Power and the Law of the Sea: expeditionary operations in World Politics* (Oxford: Oxford University Press, 2011).

3 Perhaps given the lawyers inability to agree what a 'ship' is and the nightmare prospect attendant on any re-negotiation of UNCLOS, this is just as well! Kraska, op cit, pp. 282–3, p 352.

4 The classic formulation of this, written for the Bi-Centennial was C.G. Reynolds, 'The Sea in the Making of America' *Proceedings of the USNI*, July 1976. It is difficult to imagine a similar article being produced for China—and this is an important point.

Freedom of navigation and the fortunes and independence of the new American Republic were intertwined from the start.[5] The defence of this principle was, after all, the reason why the United States almost decided to go to war with France in the so-called Quasi War of 1798–1800 and did go to war with Britain in 1812. The fact that the United States was prepared with its tiny fledgling navy was prepared to take the risk of confronting the world's maritime hyper-power of the time, and for a while did quite well, demonstrates how important the Americans thought this principle was.

Building on the Grotius tradition that the oceans were 'the common property of all' Alfred Thayer Mahan made this one of his basic assumptions in 1890 when he likened the sea to '… a wide common over which men may pass in all directions, but on which some well-worn paths show that controlling reasons have led them to choose certain lines of travel rather than others.'[6] The word 'common,' deeply rooted in Anglo-American historical experience, was well chosen as it denoted an area essential to the well-being of the community[7] but one which is not owned or supervised by anyone—it was the original 'ungoverned space.' And one, of course, which covers over 70 per cent of the world's surface and on which our peace and prosperity can be said absolutely to depend. The analogy was recently taken further by Barry Posen who widened the argument and extended the concept into the other 'commons'—space, cyberspace and so forth. But the central idea remains. In 2006, Admiral Mike Mullen summed it all up like this:

> The maritime domain, the largest manoeuvre area on earth—the global commons that cover two-thirds of the world, including most of the ungoverned and undergoverned parts of our planet.[8]

The American position on the free and untrammeled use of the sea helped determine America's entry into the First World War and, for all their reservations, on Britain's side this time, in 1917. The British, exercising their 'rights of search,' certainly interfered with American shipping but did not sink or capture it. The Germans did. Only 20 of the 847 neutral ships sunk by Germany up to the US Declaration of War in 1917 were actually American but for the United States it was a matter of principle. In January 1918, accordingly, President Wilson made

5 Kraska, *Maritime Power*, op cit, p. 59.

6 Kraska, *Maritime Power*, op cit, p. 47; A.T.Mahan, *The Influence of Sea Power Upon History 1660–1783* (London: Sampson Low, Marston & Co., Ltd, 1890), p. 25.

7 In English historical experience, a 'common' was, and indeed remains, an area of land available for all to use as it was not owned by anyone, and so was a means by which people who did not own land were able to use for grazing, fuel, social events etc. The partial enclosure of England's commons in the 17th and 18th Century was therefore the cause of much economic distress and social conflict.

8 Adm M Mullen, 'Principles for a Free and Secure Global Maritime Network', *Journal of the RUSI*, February 2006, p. 24.

absolute freedom of navigation upon seas outside territorial waters' the second of his Fourteen Points.[9]

But after the First World War, there was continuing discord between Britain and the United States over what Freedom of the Seas actually meant. From the start, the United States had aimed at securing the immunity from capture of private property on the high seas. As A. Garfield Hays maintained in April 1918, 'Freedom of the seas means abolition of the doctrine of contraband and of commercial blockades and of the right of capture and destruction of enemy [merchant] vessels'.[10] Even though they were by far the biggest strategic victims of a *guerre de course* in the First World War, the British fiercely resisted what they regarded as a notion that would emasculate their naval power particularly against land- powers and which they considered, quite correctly as it turned out in the Second World War, in any case unworkable and naively unrealistic.

In the Second World War, of course, the United States in fact adhered to the British position, but in peacetime both have continued to emphasize the sanctity of private property at sea, and its freedom. The freedom of the seas was often described almost in romantic, lyrical terms:

> Here you have an almost limitless expanse and without a barrier, here you have the estranging ocean, what is now Nature's great medium of communication. There are no difficult mountains to cross, no scorching deserts, the way lies open…Imagine then a road which leads everywhere and you have the first clue to the meaning of that majestic thing, sea traffic….Safe in times of peace from all dangers save the natural perils of the sea, the freedom of this, the broadest and busiest of highways, open to all, used by all, vital to the modern structure of civilisation, is unchallenged.[11]

The continued salience of this essential point, based on seeing the world ocean as a 'flow resource' rather than a 'stock resource' becomes clear when one looks at one of the U.S. Navy's most recent doctrinal publications, the *Naval Operations Concept 2010.*[12] This short unclassified publication has the subtitle '*Implementing the Maritime Strategy* and is intended to be an operational follow-up to the 'A

9 R Cranston, *The Story of Woodrow Wilson* 1945.

10 A Garfield Hays 'What is Meant by Freedom of the seas', *American Journal of International Law*, April 1918.

11 Dixon, W. MacNeile, *The Fleets Behind the Fleet* (London: Hodder & Stoughton, 1917), pp. 94–5.

12 General James T. Conway, Commandant US Marine Corps, Admiral Gary Roughead, Chief of Naval Operations and Admiral Thad W. Allen, Commandant US Coast Guard, *Naval Operations Concept 2010.* (Washington: Department of the Navy, July 2010)—hereinafter NOC2010.

Cooperative Strategy for 21st Century Seapower' publication which appeared in October 2007.[13]

The standard and general US view of the freedom of the seas is clearly if briefly stated:

> The *unhindered* movement of energy resources, commodities and durable goods by sea is the foundation of the global economic system and of every nation's prosperity to a large extent.[14]

Threats to the free movement of the shipping on which the peace and prosperity of the world are seen to depend come from a spectrum of threats that range from maritime crime and disorder at one end of the spectrum to inter-state conflict at the other. As far as the passage of commercial shipping is concerned this view is not a matter of much controversy; but more contention arises over the concept of free navigation for warships.

The U.S. Navy tends to think of the 'world ocean' in global rather than regional terms, and is acutely sensitive to the way in which a precedent established in one area could well be applied elsewhere. This is because of the *strategic* dimension of free navigation. The sea is all joined-up, and can be seen as the world's greatest maneuver space. Thus Mackinder: 'The unity of the ocean is the simple physical fact underlying the dominant value of sea-power in the modern globe-wide world.'[15] This means that ships can go everywhere, conferring enormous geopolitical advantage on those countries that can take advantage of this in a globalised world. In peacetime it means countries can exert political influence and trade with advantage; in times of war and crisis they can use the sea to project power ashore and make use of the exterior lines it offers to outflank an adversary's central position, firstly containing its advance and then by posing a variety of strategic threats from a variety of directions enveloping it. This was the approach that characterized the strategic approach of the western allies in the First, Second and Cold wars. But this depends, of course, on freedom of maneuver and at sea this essentially requires global mobility, the ability of ships, both naval and civilian, to go where they need to.

We can drill down a little further to explore exactly *why* in the early 21st century, the United States [and other countries which express similar views] take the position they do on the freedom of navigation for warships and merchantmen.

---

13 General James T Conway, Commandant of the US Marine Corps, Admiral Gary Roughead [Chief of Naval Operations] and Admiral Thad W. Allen Commandant, US Coast Guard, 'A Cooperative Strategy for 21st Century Seapower' [henceforth CS21] (Washington: Department of the Navy, Oct 2007.)

14 NOC21010, p 52. Author's emphasis.

15 Halford Mackinder, *Britain and the British Seas* (London: D. Appleton & Co Ltd., 1914), p. 12.

This boils down to three sets of intersecting requirements, not necessarily in this order of priority:

Maintaining Political Relationships

These requirements themselves come in as two distinct packages. The first is the traditional business for the US of maintaining credible support for its allies especially those who live in dangerous neighbourhoods. This was an important geo-political [not legal] rationale for the forward presence of the U.S. Navy in support of allies such as Norway, Iceland, Greece, Turkey, Japan and the ROK during the Cold War. Arguably at a time now when US naval power, relative to its commitments is more likely to diminish than to increase in the foreseeable future, these geo-political relationships will prove even more important in the future as a means of compensating for it, not least in the Asia-pacific region.[16] US strength, in short, is measured as much by the political and material support of its allies, and in the ability to exploit their facilities, as it is by its order of battle. These relationships, it is likely to be concluded, need to be serviced by maritime access to those allies which is both untrammeled and perceived as such by its political targets.

In 2009, US Secretary of Defence Robert Gates made the essential point that limits on this could undermine the network of alliances and partnerships that underpin American influence in the area:

> When considering the military modernization programmes of countries like China, we should be concerned less with their potential ability to challenge the US symmetrically—fighter to fighter, or ship-to-ship—and more with their ability to disrupt our freedom of movement and narrow our strategic options. Their investments in …anti-ship weaponry and ballistic missiles could threaten America's primary way to project power and help allies in the Pacific—in particular our forward air bases and carrier strike groups.[17]

The second set of geo-political aspirations is more general and less traditional. The US recognizes that it would be increasingly hard pushed to deal with the multiplicity of threats to the global trading system on its own. The U.S. Navy's most obvious problem is the slow reduction of the number of ships that it can deploy at any one time. For all the growth in their individual military power, capable warships can still only be in one place at a time. This reduces day-to-

16 'DoD Braces for $30B cut in' 12 *Defence News*, 5 Sep. 2011; the extent of the likely relative US naval decline is explored in 'Conclusions: Transitions and Futures' in Geoffrey Till and Patrick C. Bratton, *Sea Power and the Asia-Pacific: The Triumph of Neptune ?* (London: Routledge, 2011), pp. 237–68.

17 'Race on for next generation of anti-ship missiles' *The Straits Times*, January 11, 2011.

day coverage and poses a real time-distance problem in getting ships to areas of concern, especially at short notice. As former CNO Admiral Jay Johnson used to say: 'Virtual presence is actual absence.'[18] Admiral Mike Mullen made the same collaborative point back in 2005,

> Today's reality is that the security arrangements and paradigms of the past are no longer enough for the future. And today's challenges are too diverse to tackle alone; they require more capability and more resources than any single nation can deliver.[19]

Because the world ocean, to use the Russian term, is so vast, defending 'the commons' against such threats requires the collaboration of maritime forces [both navies and coastguards] around the world:

> Global maritime security can only be achieved through the integration of national and regional maritime cooperation, awareness and response initiatives.[20]

Hence the even greater stress in recent years on the winning of partners and allies whose ships and bases can, provided they agree with it, bolster the American position.

'Trust and cooperation' says CS21 'cannot be surged.' They have to be built and sustained over time, through the development of increased understanding amongst US maritime forces and the forging of international partnerships. The document's discussion of naval diplomacy accordingly focuses on coalition-building, with the Global Maritime Partnership initiative being its most significant expression.[21] This becomes one of the Navy's six strategic imperatives and is clearly crucial to two of its six core capabilities, namely Maritime Security and Humanitarian Assistance and Disaster Response. It is worth making the point that countries' reluctance to participate in such multilateral, collective system-defence measures can easily be over- or mis-interpreted in Washington.

The resultant emphasis on the development of an all-embracing global maritime partnership is the main theme, indeed, of CS21 and has generally been welcomed around the world, but the tactics of diplomatic compromise and a

---

18 Quoted in Gordon L. Peterson, 'The Tyranny of Geography: Time-Distance Problem, *Naval Forces*, IV/2006, p 6. In the same way the US Coast Guard maintains that id does not have sufficient assets to prosecute all its 'actionable intelligence' in the counter-narcotics campaign.

19 Admiral Mike Mullen, in John B. Hattendorf, *Seventeenth Annual Seapower Symposium: Report of Proceedings* [Newport: Naval war College Press, 2005], p. 5.

20 NOC2010, op cit p. 36.

21 Christopher J Castelli, 'New Maritime Strategy Would emphasize Soft and Hard Power' *Inside the Navy* June 18, 2007; V Adm John G Morgan and Rear Admiral Charles W Martoglio, 'The 1,000-ship Navy Global Maritime Network' *Proceedings* of the U.S. Naval Institute, Nov 2005.

strategy of sensitive political engagement are both needed in order to make this possible. They both depend on forward presence and the free movement of naval ships, however.

Maritime Domain Awareness

The notion of 'Defending the Global Commons' was initially developed in the United States[22] with a pronounced strategic emphasis but has since become much more general. It is now also being actively explored by NATO in parallel with the completion of its *Alliance Maritime Strategy*. The same sense of the vastness of the task increases the need for the capacity to monitor what is going on across the oceans as far as possible, because that will make cost-effective proactive responses to emerging threats more possible. Accordingly,

> A key cooperative initiative to enhance global awareness is the national and international effort to improve maritime domain awareness (MDA) … the effective understanding of anything associated with the maritime domain that could impact the security, safety, economy, or environment of a nation.[23]

Hence, the American stress on all aspects of maritime surveillance because of the overwhelming need to know what is going on at sea that led to such difficulties as the *USS Impeccable* incident in 2009.[24] Maritime Domain Awareness, however, demands free access to as much of the world ocean as possible, even if supplemented by the full exchange of information amongst navies and coastguards.

Sea Control and Maritime Power Projection

Forward presence and free access are regarded as essential preconditions for the assertion of sea control and maritime power projection. Not surprisingly, it is in this much more 'strategic' area that US perceptions are regarded with wariness or outright hostility by some other countries, who may well even be tempted to think that this is the real driver behind American policy on Freedom of Navigation, especially so far as its warships are concerned. With this, then, we get to the heart of what the U.S. Navy really understands to be an essential characteristic of the sea:

---

22 This approach in effect started with Barry Posen, 'Command of the Commons: The Military Foundation of US Hegemony' *International Security* Summer 2003, pp. 5–46.

23 NOC2010, op cit, p. 15.

24 Michael Perkinson, 'Collision Course: China and US make waves in South China Sea' *Jane's Intelligence Review* May 2009. 'China navy criticizes dispatch of US destroyers: state media' AFP electronic report accessed in http://www.spacewar.com/reports 16 Mar. 2009.

> The Naval service uses the sea as maneuver space. Mobility and manoeuvrability constitute the Naval Service's primary operational attributes.[25]

The ability to go anywhere and do anything, consistent with international law, to the extent of their capabilities is what the US believes navies are all about. Operational freedom, flexibility and adaptability are their main advantage over land and air forces but depends absolutely on the untrammeled freedom of the seas. It allows 'sea-basing' for example:

> … the deployment, assembly, command, projection, reconstitution, and re-deployment of joint power from the sea, without reliance on land bases within the operational area.[26]

The world ocean as the world's greatest maneuver space also critically facilitates the kind of forward presence of naval forces that is seen as helping to shape the strategic environment proactively:

> The combination of forward stationed and rotationally deployed forces is a uniquely adaptable means to maintain global military presence while respecting the sovereignty of other nations.[27]

While it remains critically hard to quantify, forward presence is seen as something that facilitates stability and the good order on which the world's economic system is seen to depend.[28] 'We must,' Admiral Mike Mullen has said, 'be able to continue to react quickly in times of humanitarian crises and with resolve in times of conflict.'[29] The kind of forward presence required depends on the circumstances of the particular area. "Globally distributed, mission-tailored forces" are designed to cope with a wide range of lower order missions that 'promote stability, prevent crises, and combat terrorism.' "Regionally concentrated credible combat power" on the other hand is required for the 'harder' tasks of protecting US vital interests; assuring its friends; '… and (to) deter, dissuade, and if necessary, defeat potential adversaries.'[30] One common element between the two, however, is the need to

25 NOC2010, op cit, p. 14.

26 NOC2010, op cit p. 21.

27 NOC2010, op cit p. 29.

28 For a brave effort to quantify the linkages between forward presence and economic success, see Robert E Looney and David Schrady, 'Estimating Economic benefits: A Brief Summary' in Sam J Tangredi and Antonios Clapsis (eds), *Globalization and Naval Forward Presence: Issues and Insights* (Washington: National Defense University, April 2001).

29 'What I believe: Eight Tenets That Guide my vision for the 21st Century' *Proceedings of the USNI*, January 2006, p. 14.

30 NOC2010, op cit, p. 32.

operate in the littorals. Hence the charge that the U.S. Navy is the world's biggest 'coastal navy' in that it is one which needs to operate off other people's coasts.

If maintaining a forward presence is a question of deterring or 'defeating local adversaries', the central requirement for sea control comes into play:

> The ability of U.S. naval forces to establish local and regional sea control is fundamental to exploiting the maritime domain as maneuver space, protecting critical sea lines of communication, and projecting and sustaining combat power overseas.[31]

US strategic policy in the First and Second Wars and the Cold War too, depended heavily on the opportunities provided by the sea for strategic maneuver. Its opponents were first contained at and from the sea and then threatened and assaulted from multiple points before being finally enveloped.

To summarise, the requirements of multinational naval engagement, maritime domain awareness and forward presence are seen by the U.S. Navy to depend to a large extent on free navigation. The freedom of the seas is essential in this understanding of what sea power is and what navies are for. Hence the acute sensitivity within the U.S. Navy to anything that might limit that freedom, whether this derives from unwelcome interpretations of international maritime law,[32] or the appearance of a politically non-permissive environment or the kind of anti-access, area denial (A2/AD) strategies allegedly being prepared by the PLAN.[33]

The importance of this concept in US naval thinking explains why in the past the Americans have engaged in freedom of navigation exercises 'with attitude' in the past, such as the Gulf of Sirte cruises of the mid 1980s and the bumping incident involving the *USS Caron* and a Soviet warship in the Black Sea in 1988.[34] American disputes with the Soviet Union in the Black Sea, or the Libyan 'line of death' in the 1980s, or with Indonesia about its reading of the rights of the

31 NOC2010, op cit, p. 57.

32 For a vigorous statement of the US position on this in regard to the *USNS Impeccable* see James Kraska, 'Sovereignty at sea' *Survival* Vol. 51, No 3, Jun–July 2009, pp. 13–18.

33 Office of the Secretary of Defense, *Military Power of the People's Republic of China, 2009* (Washington D.C.: Department of Defense, 2009), pp. 20–24. See also Andrew S Erickson and David D Yang, Using the Land to Control the Sea? Chinese Analysts Consider the Antiship Ballistic Missile' in US *Naval War College Review*, Autumn 2009, pp. 37–86. This discusses the significance of a number of papers produced to this effect by China's National Defence University. Eric Hagt and Mathew Durnin, China's Anti-ship Ballistic Missiles, US *Naval War College Review* Autumn 2009, pp. 87–115, at 91.

34 This latter was resolved by a Us-Soviet agreement signed September 23, 1989 at Jackson Hole, Wyoming in which the Soviets agreed on the right of foreign warships to transit territorial waters on 'innocent passage' and in return the US undertook not to engage in more of such freedom of navigation exercises. At issue in this case were foreign rights in the territorial sea not the EEZ.

archipelagic state were disputes about freedom of navigation but, at the same time a collision between local and global perspectives on the role of seapower.

These US assertions of what it considered its rights were justified in American eyes by the fact that the sea is indeed 'all joined up' and that accepting constraints on the freedom of navigation in one area would set precedents that could well weaken it everywhere else.

So far as we can tell, China regards the South China Sea dispute as an internal matter in which outsiders, especially ones which admit to having no territorial claim on the area, have no business in becoming involved and further complicating an already complex affair. But the point is that in their concern for the freedom of the seas, the Americans feel they *do* have a major stake in the matter. After all, were the Chinese claim to all the features of the East and the South China Seas to be accepted, were these features reckoned to generate a 200 mile EEZ that anything like approximates the 'nine dash line', and were Chinese interpretations of what foreign military activity is permitted in the EEZ to become accepted, US naval operations in the whole area would be severely constrained. In effect, a great swathe of the Western pacific would be a no-go area for the U.S. Navy at least in Chinese eyes. Reunification with Taiwan would exacerbate this still further.

For all these reasons, what is seen as the Chinese challenge to American concepts of the free seas is neuralgic for today's United States because it could seem to exemplify a major strategic shift from the time when, 16 years ago it was able to revel in its own 'indispensability' and capacity to call the shots in the international system.[35] Since then, terrorist attack, the dragging mainland wars of Iraq and Afghanistan and the 'Great Recession' have sapped the country's self-confidence. Now even the country's long-term dominance of the Pacific Ocean seems under threat as a new rival appears on the scene. China once seen in the US as 'just' a land power [and a rather backwards one at that], is using its industrial and maritime power to move into what America has become accustomed to think its own back-yard—and to dilute American maritime supremacy in the Pacific Ocean. The problem is exacerbated by the fact that China could take more advantage of the United States' maritime vulnerabilities that the United States could of China's territorial ones. Accordingly, Chinese assertiveness over its near seas can easily be seen as a *symbol* of a momentous transition in great power relations, and (over-) reacted to accordingly.

For the United States, then, a good deal is at stake, not least its continuing capacity to dominate the global commons which as Andrew Hart and Bruce Jones have recently remarked '…has been a critical enabler of the US military's pre-eminent position and has under-written America's own economic influence as

35 Charkles Krauthammer, 'America Rules: Thank God' and James Chace 'A Sunlit America Summer' both in *Time*, 4 Aug 1997.

well as that of its allies, and has helped Washington to lessen the influence of its adversaries.'[36]

China's Attitude to the Near Seas: Resource, Territory and Moat

Establishing the Context

Because such detailed statements of American naval thinking are freely available it is relatively easy for others to understand their conceptions of seapower. This is much more difficult when, as in the case of the PLA[N], that doctrinal understanding is not so readily available and when what China thinks about such issues can only be inferred from their apparent processing of their own experience, their actions, or indeed from the views of the growing unofficial but surprisingly diverse naval 'commentariat' now appearing in China, some of whose statements seem different from, and sometimes distinctly hostile to, American conceptions of seapower.[37] This is a point to which this chapter will return.

As is well known, China's reading of the provisions of UNCLOS leads to its conclusion that Freedom of Navigation within the EEZ of another state is more restricted and conditional than does the United States, particularly when warships seek to exercise it. China has repeatedly sought to make clear that the freedom of navigation of commercial vessels in the South China Sea is not an issue. Thus General Chen Bingde:

> In the South China Sea, freedom of navigation has never been a problem. It serves as an excuse to sensationalize the issue.[38]

Indeed during the ARF meeting In July 2011, Chinese officials proposed top host a workshop on Freedom of Navigation. Instead the real issue is about the Freedom of Navigation of warships.[39]

---

36 Andrew F. Hart and Bruce D. Jones, 'How Do Rising Powers Rise?' *Survival*, Dec 2010–January 2011.

37 For an authoritative American view of the impact of strategic culture on Chinese naval thinking see Toshi Yoshihara and James R. Holmes, *Red Star Over the Pacific: China's Rise and the Challenge to US Maritime Strategy'* (Annapolis: Naval Institute press, 2010), pp. 14–43, 154–62.

38 'China warns US to stay out of South China Sea dispute' *Jane's Defence Weekly*, July 20, 2011. Indeed,

39 Michael Parkinson, 'Collision Course: China and US make waves in South China Sea' *Jane's Intelligence Review* May 2009. 'China navy criticizes dispatch of US destroyers: state media' AFP electronic report accessed in http://www.spacewar.com/reports 16 Mar. 2009. For a balanced review of this complex issue see Klein, Natalie, *Maritime Security and the Law of the Sea* (Oxford: OUP, 2011), pp. 217–24. Klein argues that intelligence gathering in the EEZ is legal, but wonders whether this is desirable (p. 221). This was also

This has led in the recent past to ferocious reactions from Beijing to the perceived activities of US warships in areas of particular concern such as the Yellow Sea. The Chinese response to the putative presence of the aircraft carrier USS *George Washington* in the wake of the loss of the ROKS *Cheonan*, even though the US sought to make clear that North Korea was the target of this maneuver not China, is a good example of this. In addition to strong political protest, the PLAN followed the incident up with a coastal defence exercise involving its highly capable *Houbei* missile attack craft which looked to the Americans as a politically charged and quite pointed anti-carrier enterprise. This regrettable incident therefore also demonstrated the potentially destabilizing effect of such differences of opinion. This is especially likely to be troublesome in those areas of the East and South China Seas where jurisdiction, and so the delimitation of disputed EEZs, is in any case currently unresolved.

Chinese attitudes to the EEZ have been thoroughly consistent from the earliest stages of the negotiations that led to UNCLOS. They were informed by three distinctive, though interconnected approaches to the sea which were no doubt partly responsible for their taking the negotiating position they did and which probably continue to support their reading of the agreed outcome to those negotiations.

The Near Seas as a Resource

In common with all other coastal countries, China sees the near seas as an economic resource vital to its future prosperity because it is a source of resources—most especially oil and gas and fish—which are clearly critical to a developing country with burgeoning energy and human needs. This is entirely consistent with the intention outlined in China's 12th Five year Plan of March 2011 to place much more effort on developing the country's marine interests and industries. China's various agencies for maritime law enforcement have accordingly been expanded.

Thus, China sees the EEZ as a 'stock resource' rather than a 'flow resource'[40]—a somewhat different emphasis from that taken by the United States. Accordingly, one country's take from that stock necessarily diminishes the share available to others; this is not the case for a 'flow resource.' Anything that potentially could disrupt the full and effective exploitation of those national economic resources should therefore be opposed. Hence the noticeably more robust attention paid to commercial exploration activities of the Vietnamese and Philippine concerns in

the 2005 view of the regional experts who reviewed the issue in 2005. See Sam Bateman's introduction to 'Prospective Guidelines for Navigation and Overflight in the Exclusive Economic Zone', 144 *Maritime Studies*, pp. 17 and 23. Luyo Yuan, 'PLA General: US engaging in gunboat diplomacy' *People's Daily*, August 12, 2010. Cited in Manicom, op cit.

40 Kraska, *Maritime Power*, op cit, pp. 97, 108.

the early part of 2011.[41] Hence, also, China takes the position that hydrographic surveys in the EEZ [for whatever purpose] are indistinguishable from marine scientific research and accordingly falls within the jurisdiction of China as the coastal state.

The paradox is that the unsettled nature of jurisdiction over the South China Sea—a situation in which the claimants all believe that 'their' resources are being effectively stolen by other nations—reduces the prospect for the marine protection of the area and its resources, with the result that the fish take is unsustainably high, the habitat put at risk and safety considerations neglected, all of which in fact reduce the 'stock' value of the area for all concerned, and indeed for the wider world. China considers this a justification for its annual fishing moratorium, first in the Yellow sea and East China Sea in 1995 and then imposed in parts of the South China Sea from 1999.

The Near Seas as Sovereign Territory

This sense of the critical importance of this particular area of the world's surface is reinforced by a sense of the territoriality of at least some parts of the Near Seas in which there is an element of 'ownership' not just of the sea bed and the resources in the water column above it, but of the waters themselves. Not unnaturally this is reinforced by Chinese conceptions of their ownership of the various disputed islands in the South and East China Sea.

This becomes an acutely important issue for the authorities in Beijing if that quasi-sovereignty is thought to be violated by other countries. It becomes political in the sense that the re-unification of sovereign territory, most obviously through the eventual absorption of Taiwan, is clearly regarded as a core interest, and the South China Seas may be in the same category too. But in the age of the internet-empowered citizen—the netizen—the authorities cannot ignore the growing nationalism of the people, for whom China's campaign to secure what they see as its islands and the maritime jurisdiction those waters are believed to generate become important performance-indicators in the eyes of its own people, of how well the government is doing. Unauthorised foreign activities within national territory have therefore to be regarded with strong disfavor.[42] This may well have been a factor

41 Carlyle A. Thayer, *China's New Wave of Aggressive Assertiveness in the South China Sea* paper to Conference on maritime Security in the South China Sea, CSIS, Washington DC, June 20–21, 2011.

42 'China warns US to Stay Out of Islands Dispute' *New York Times*, July 28, 2010. The 'Netizen Effect' applies as well to the other South China sea claimants of course, not least Vietnam as exchanges over the incidents of early 2011 have made clear. Thomas J. Christensen, 'Posing Problems without Catching Up: China's Rise and Challenges for US Security Policy' *International Security*, Spring 2011, pp. 5–40.

in the *Impeccable* incident.[43] When asked recently by an *Asahai Shimbun* reporter why China was so concerned about the South China Sea, Admiral Wu Shengli, Commander-in-Chief, PLA[N] replied: 'How would you feel if I cut off your arms and legs? That's how China feels about the South China Sea.'[44]

The Near Seas as Defensive Moat

The Chinese approach to the sea is less global and more local than the American. This is a country that seems to spend more on internal security than it does on defence, and which deploys some 300,000 border guards compared to an equivalent figure of 10,000 in the United States. China seems often to see itself as potentially encircled by foreign forces in local seas, a kind of mirror image of the strategic manoevrism approach adopted by the United States and discussed earlier. Accordingly, Chinese commentators regularly and publicly condemn the 'forward presence' of US naval warships, and no longer accept [if they ever did] arguments that it has a stabilizing function that also works to the benefit of China. Thus PLA Major-General Luo Yuan: "the so-called forward presence means that the United States can send its gunboats to every corner of the world…This way, the United States can even claim the Yellow Sea and the South China Sea is covered within its security boundary.'[45] They point out that were the USS *George Washington* to have sailed into the Yellow Sea, its aircraft would have been capable of reaching Beijing. If to this is added a strategic culture deeply affected by the country's historic exposure to threats from the sea, not least in this particular area, and to the disastrous consequences for China of these activities not being deterred, Chinese sensitivity to the unauthorized presence and activity in 'Chinese waters' is entirely understandable.

Accordingly, China maintains that unauthorized foreign naval activity in its EEZ including what the British call 'military data gathering' are a kind of battlefield preparation, and so prejudicial to the security of China.[46] This, it is claimed, is a contravention of UNCLOS Article 301 which requires parties to refrain from threatening the sovereignty of any state when exercising their rights at sea. The opening of the PLAN's new submarine base at Yulin, with its all important access to deep water, will no doubt have strengthened such perceptions. Should China be slowly developing a 'bastion' approach for the deployment of its future SSBNs as the Soviet Union did in the Barents Sea and the Sea of Okhotsk, sensitivity to such

---

43 Mastro, op cit, p. 225. Li Mingjiang, China's new security posture: Non-confrontational assertiveness, *The Straits Times*, May 19, 2011.

44 Quoted in William Choong, 'Mistrust hurts naval cooperation in region' *The Straits Times*, May 27, 2011.

45 Luyo Yuan, 'PLA General: US engaging in gunboat diplomacy' *People's Daily*, August 12, 2010. Cited in Manicom, op cit.

46 Ren Xiaofeng and Cheng Xizhong, 'A Chinese Perspective', *Marine Policy* 29, no 2, 2005, pp. 139–46.

date gathering would no doubt increase still further.[47] The *Impeccable* incident, after all took place a mere 75 nautical miles south-east of the Yulin naval base.[48]

The unexpectedly harsh tone of China's response to the projected but cancelled presence of the US carrier *George Washington* in an exercise with the ROK Navy in the Yellow Sea and by subsequent editorials in the *Global Times* the English language version of the official *People's Daily*, illustrate the point. The latter said:

> China undoubtedly needs to build a highly credible anti-carrier capacity ... Not only does China need an anti-ship ballistic missile, but also other carrier-killing measures...Since US aircraft carrier battle groups in the Pacific constitute deterrence against China's strategic interests, China has to possess the capacity to counterbalance.[49]

It is this context that China has seemingly embarked on a campaign of developing capabilities that would put American forces at risk should they enter the near seas in a manner to which China takes exception. The resultant anti-access area denial [A2/AD] strategy, as this has been dubbed by its prospective victims, is a complex system-based sea denial strategy that makes use of sophisticated and resilient C4ISR facilities to detect and target 'hostile' surface ships, and to threaten them with a range of ballistic and cruise anti-ship missiles, delivered from land bases, land-based aircraft, submarines and medium and small surface combatants; all of this, accompanied, it would seem by a cyber offensive intended to undermine the U.S. Navy and Air Force's electronic capacities to defend themselves and to sustain offensive operations. The United States seems to have been surprised by how rapidly key components of this strategy, such as the anti-satellite capacity revealed in 2009, the initial operating capacity of the DF-21D anti-ship ballistic missile in late 2010 and the J-20 fifth generation fighter that appeared in March 2011, have emerged. But how effective this would be militarily remains an issue of considerable debate, but even its critics accept that A2/AD puts US forward presence in the near seas at significantly greater hazard, and thus may serve the political purpose of such a strategy.

Given the extent to which American naval power has been consolidated and concentrated into ever smaller numbers of warships, given the country's aversion to loss and finally in view of the extent to which its presence in the Western Pacific may be seen by the American public as a matter of choice rather than geography, these kinds of threat, unless countered, may be disproportionately successful in

47 Tetsuo Kotani, What China Wants South China Sea, *The Diplomat*, July 18, 2011.

48 Oriana Skylar Mastro, 'Signalling and Military Provocation in Chinese National Security Strategy' *Journal of Strategic Studies*, April 2011, pp. 219–44. P.220. Mark Valencia, "the Impeccable Incident: truth and Consequences,' *China Security*, Spring 2009.

49 Staff Writers AFP Beijing, September 7, 2010 'China Needs 'carrier-killer missile: press' citing *Global Times*, September 6, 2010. This was unexpected since China did not protest against the presence of the *George Washington* in the Yellow Sea in 2009.

constraining US naval movement in times of crisis and danger. 'The effect of a single Chinese cruise missile's hitting a US carrier, even if it did not sink the ship,' Robert Kaplan has remarked,' would be politically and psychologically catastrophic, akin to Al-Qaeda's attacks on the Twin Towers.'[50]

Whereas it seems fairly clear that China would, in the extremely unlikely event of conflict, pursue a defensive sea denial strategy against a strong external power such as the United States, its attitude to the activities of other foreign naval forces in the near seas is much less clear. In this connection, the reported interception of an Indian amphibious assault ship INS *Airavat* on passage from a visit to Vietnam in July 2011 may indicate a determination to apply the same rule to the presence of any 'foreign' warship in the South China Sea.[51]

All of this supports two notions that are distinctively different from and potentially in conflict with American perspectives. First China takes a local rather than a global approach to the sea; secondly its regards the near seas more as a defensive moat than as a springboard for action elsewhere. For both reasons, naturally enough, China seeks to make its EEZ as secure as it can.

Implications

One result of such differing perceptions of the status of the near seas between China and the United States may be a significant and potentially very dangerous under-estimate of the stake one side or the other, or most likely both, have in this aspect of the resolution of the South China Sea dispute. It may also lead to unwanted tensions in the conduct of normal maritime business elsewhere. When to this is added a whole range of other tensions between the two countries over such things as arms sales to Taiwan, Nobel prize winners and human rights, the valuation of the yuan, rare earth minerals, the projected exercise of the *USS George Washington* in the Yellow Sea and so forth the need for a much closer not more distant mutual understanding becomes clear.[52] Against this background, it is easy to see how the South China Sea issue as a whole could degenerate further.

As remarked above, the South China Sea issue is already complicated enough, with competing claims among the local disputants of their jurisdictional rights, the lines of delimitation, and the extent of the waters and the rights that individual features generate. If to this the freedom of navigation issue is added to the mix, and more countries necessarily become involved, an already complex and potentially dangerous situation becomes worse still. The conflict between the two approaches to freedom of navigation issues in local seas therefore has important implications not just for the relationship between the countries that adhere to one or other of

---

50 Robert Kaplan, 'How We would Fight China' *The Atlantic*, June 1, 2005.

51 "China confronted Indian warship off Vietnam' *Financial Times*, September 1, 2011.

52 'Washington adds China to Clinton's Asia-Pacific Tour', *Global Times*, October 28, 2010.

these approaches, but for the management and future resolution of the South China issue itself.

Future Developments?

The Freedom of Navigation issue is no more static or unchanging as the seas themselves; over the years the debate about it has changed in character in response to a changing international context, and may well do so again. A glance back at its naval history, should after all, show how American attitudes to its potential global role have altered over the years. While the forward exploits of John Paul Jones off the coasts of the UK during the War of American Independence or operations against North African pirates in the early 19th Century are one aspect of American naval history, in fact during the era of the Monroe doctrine, Washington's approach to its near seas was not unlike that of present day China's. Things do, it seems, change quite a lot!

With its troubled economy and the 'rise of the rest, the United States, as remarked above, is facing a new and more challenging future in which it might in future feel in need of constraining its global role and, in some country's eyes at least, assertiveness. This may well lead to a still greater emphasis on partnership with the other rising maritime powers of the Asia-Pacific than already appear foreshadowed in CS21. Its notions of 'forward presence' may accordingly be affected by the prospects and the challenges of a more shared future. Nonetheless, at a recent meeting of the Asia-pacific Round table in Kuala Lumpur, in late May 2011, Admiral Willard said the U.S. Navy aimed to maintain a 'continuous presence' in the South China Sea, something which China might well not particularly welcome, but for which incidents such as that surrounding the USNS *Impeccable* incident may be partly responsible.[53] President Obama's much advertised 'pivot to Asia' is likely to reinforce such a conclusion

In the meantime, there is some recognition in China of the role that the U.S. Navy and Coast Guard do play in helping assure global stability, including in the Asia-Pacific region where its presence might be thought to have some benefits for China, not least in reducing the need for the expansion of other naval powers in the region, and in making a material contribution to the management of such good order problems as piracy, drug and people smuggling and marine pollution.[54] The US presence in the seas near China need not always be seen as a zero-sum game.

The same processes of change may apply to China also, only in a reverse direction, so far as the Freedom of Navigation is concerned. The PLA[N]'s participation in the international counter-piracy effort off the coasts of Somalia and its recent dispatch of the hospital ship 'Peace Ark' around the Indian Ocean may well suggest that it is probably less *when* China will move out from its primary

53 'Not Littorally Shangri-La' *The Economist*, June 9, 2011.

54 Wu Xinbo 'The End of the Silver Lining: A Chinese View of the US-Japanese Alliance', *The Washington Quarterly* 29, no 1, 2005–06.

focus on the near seas since its burgeoning naval power and the spectacular growth of its global rather than merely regional strategic interests and commitments make this inevitable sooner or later; much more to the point, is with what spirit and intent will it do so. As states get stronger, their maritime interests expand, not least in geographic extent. China now has as much at stake in safe transition of the 74,000 or so merchant vessels that ply the Straits of Malacca and the pass through the South China Sea every year as any other major player in the global system. Recent events have shown, moreover, that China, moreover, is as vulnerable as any other country, and more than most, to the illicit activities of the Iranian Revolutionary Guard in the Gulf, the depredations of Somali pirates or indeed to disorder and instability ashore. As a rising maritime power with extensive state interests and a growing diaspora, China seems likely, as an increasingly maritime power, to have an increasing interest in the Freedom of Navigation, the world ocean as a 'flow resource' and in the general 'defence of the system.' Indeed it may not be in China's long-term interest that legitimate naval activities in the EEZ especially in those of failed, failing or rogue states should be unduly constrained. Here, the ultimate *global* nature of Chinese seapower could, perhaps paradoxically, be regarded as the best counterpoint to its current regional focus on the exclusivity of its near seas and so lead to a degree of convergence on the American position, perhaps rather in the manner of the Soviet Union in 1974.[55]

In the meantime, greater transparency and willingness to discuss, identify and work through different interpretations of UNCLOS provisions on the EEZ and closer tactical adherence to safety procedures at sea particularly during close encounters would significantly improve the atmosphere.

To conclude, it may well be that the course of future events will make the Freedom of Navigation issue a less pressing issue than appears likely at the moment, when it has threatened to skew the geopolitical relationship between China and the United States into a competitive dimension that most on both sides do not want. If so, the impact of this matter on the management and resolution of the South China Sea resolution would also be less. Whether this will in fact prove to be the course of future events, however, remains to be seen.

55 Kraska, *Maritime Power and the Law of the Sea,* op cit, pp. 31, 106-7.

Chapter 10

Jockeying for Position in the South China Sea: Cooperative Strategy or Managed Conflict?

Theresa Fallon

China's Evolving Position

China's increasingly assertive behaviour in the South China Sea has been examined and reviewed in recent publications by Carlyle Thayer,[1] and also by Michael Swaine and Taylor Fravel.[2] After a pause by China in assertive behaviour in July, media across the board have focussed on China's possible motivations for the publication of an article in the *Global Times*, a state-owned Chinese newspaper on September 29 with the title, "Time to teach those around the South China Sea a lesson." This rhetorical missile, one part of a two part op-ed series, was picked up by numerous news outlets in both China and around the world. Were these bellicose writings a reflection of interest groups views in China and their desire to influence government policy or are they part of a multitude of voices vying to be heard in the run-up to the government transition?

China's strategy of self-constraint so far has been based on Deng Xiaoping's "24-character strategy" of "Observe calmly, secure our position, cope with affairs calmly, hide our capacities and bide or time, be good at maintaining a low profile, and do something worthwhile." China's peaceful rise narrative was meant to keep a low profile and to reassure neighbors and the world of peaceful intentions. The narrative now is that the more power China gets, the more challenges it faces. As China's status on the international stage increases, it brings more attention and has made China more suspicious of the outside world. The central theme of the low profile strategy was to never take a global lead as it was actually more disadvantageous in terms of trouble and cost than being the world's leader would provide.

---

1 Carlyle A. Thayer, "China-ASEAN and the South China Sea: Chinese Assertiveness and Southeast Asian Responses", Conference Paper, October 2011; and his chapter in this book.

2 Michael Swaine and Taylor Fravel, "China's Assertive Behavior, Part Two: The Maritime Periphery", *China Leadership Monitor*, available at: http://www.hoover.org/publications/china-leadership-monitor.

The *Global Times* op-ed echoes General Liu Yuan's views[3] and seems to break with Deng Xiaoping's strategy. Already on July 1, Zhu Chenghu, a military scholar with National Defense University, published an article in the same paper warning that rival claimants plundered, "China's oil and gas resources without scruple, turning the South China Sea into an ATM machine." The September 29 op-ed made the point even more forcefully. The op-ed is signed by Long Tao, a pseudonym that means 'way of the dragon.'

Long wrote, "China should take part in the exploitation of oil and gas in South China Sea. For those who infringe upon our sovereignty to steal the oil, we need to warn them politely, and then take action if they don't respond. We shouldn't waste the opportunity to launch some tiny-scale battles that could deter provocateurs from going further. Long asked in his piece, "Who'll suffer most when Western oil giants withdraw?" Such punishment should be restricted only to the Philippines and Vietnam, who have been acting extremely aggressive these days."[4]

Such sabre-rattling would seem unwise and counter-productive from a strategic and military point of view, as it is likely to push Vietnam and the Philippines towards the US, as well as towards India or Japan, to form a coalition against China. But the op-ed may have the one more immediate goal: to scare Western oil companies away from Vietnam and from the Philippines and to deter them from concluding deals with them.

A new cache of US diplomatic cables released by WikiLeaks on September 1, 2011 highlighted efforts going back to at least 2006, to pressure oil companies such as Exxon Mobil, BP, Chevron and Petronas after they cut deals with Hanoi. The United States and other international companies with interests in China were convinced to leave. The world's largest oil firm, Exxon Mobil, was threatened repeatedly by Chinese diplomats to end activities in Vietnam but still went forward with their joint-ventures projects in Vietnam.

Two Chinese oil companies are present in the South China Sea: China National Petroleum Corporation (CNPC) and China National Offshore Oil Corporation (CNOOC). Compared to others, the actions of CNPC appear to be much more cautious. China's offshore oil industry originally started in the South China Sea

---

3 In May of 2011, international media outlets reported on the preface to Zhang Musheng's book *Changing Our View of Culture and History*. The preface was written by PLA General Liu Yuan, the son of Liu Shaoqui. General Liu is considered a powerful mentor to Xi Jinping who is expected to take over from Hu Jintao in 2012. For this reason, the preface generated a great deal of attention both inside and outside of China because of its bellicose tone and its depiction of the role of war in China's national development.

4 For original article in Chinese, see http://mil.huanqiu.com/Observation/2011-09/2038708.html. This article was also linked to the homepage of *People's Daily*. Note the difference in pictures which accompany the articles. The Chinese version has 10 photos which include battles and some military hardware. The English version, on the other hand, is accompanied with a cartoon of three fat cats looking at a goldfish in a bowl, available at: http://www.globaltimes.cn/NEWS/tabid/99/ID/677717/Time-to-teach-those-around-South-China-Sea-a-lesson.aspx.

but after the Vietnam War broke out in 1965, the core of China's offshore oil exploration shifted from the South China Sea to Bohai Bay. The exploration in the South China Sea came to a halt. It was not until 1986 that CNOOC built its first oil platform in the South China Sea.

In recent years, almost every year CNOOC would announce a batch of open areas in the South China Sea for foreign companies to cooperate with CNOOC based on the PSC (production sharing contract) model. PSCs are a common type of contract between a government and an energy company which allocates a percentage of oil extracted that each party to the contract will receive. However, the conditions listed by CNOOC were more severe than those offered in Vietnam. For example, CNOOC maintains a minimum 51 percent stake in projects. This year CNOOC announced 19 development zones in the northwest part of the South China Sea, 16 located in the Zhujiangkou basin, two in the Northern gulf, and one in the basin in the Southeast of Hainan province. The 65/24 zone, the furthest from the Chinese coastline, covers 3,080 sq. km^2, 1,000–2,200 m deep. None of these zones belongs to the Spratly island maritime space.

Besides political considerations, there are also commercial and technical reasons explaining why Chinese oil companies have not ventured deep into the South China Sea so far. The distance between the Chinese coastline and the Spratly Islands is between 2,000 and 3,000 kilometers. It is difficult to guarantee manpower and material supply. The cost of exploration is high and the location of reserves uncertain. The figure for total geological reserves is uncertain and estimates vary between 4 and 30 billion tons.

Another difficulty is deep-water operation. The capacity of China's NOCs in offshore drilling is limited. Most of China's companies can only drill in shallow water (122 m. or less). However, CNOOC recently developed the new drilling platform "Hai Yang Shi You 981", also known as the Mega, which can operate in 3000-m deep sea.[5]

A high-level official from CNOOC reportedly suggested that Chinese oil companies should consider a higher degree of openness toward the outside and that the three big oil companies should combine their strength and cooperate to explore the South China Sea.[6] He also thought that China should set up a fund to support these three big oil companies and elevate the competence of deep-sea prospecting in order to explore the South China Sea.

---

5 See CNOOC's 2010 annual report at: http://www.cippe.net/thread-28606-1-1.html

6 See "How to do Away with Embarrassment When Defending Our Rights in the South China Sea: China Tackles Vietnam's Interference", Southern Metropolis, August 17, 2011, available at: http://news.cnyes.com/Content/20110817/KDYM29BRYOIGY.shtml?c=hk_compnews.

Sharing the Cake: Other Players in the South China Sea

Vietnam

Among the neighboring countries, Vietnam is the most active in exploration of the South China Sea. In 1975 Mobil discovered oil in the southern area of the Vietnamese sea. In 2004, the production of oil in Vietnam reached its highest peak, over 400,000 barrels per day. Afterwards, its production lingers over 300,000 barrels per day. In 2009, the net export of Vietnamese oil was 53,000 barrels per day, half of which were exported to America.

Vietnam's oil sector is the most important pillar of its economy and provides 30 percent of the GDP. In order to intensify exploration, Vietnam modified its "Petro Law" in 2000 which made the procedure of competitive bidding more open and transparent. In addition it created more advantageous conditions for international energy companies. The shares foreign investors are allowed to hold in joint venture companies can be as high as 80 percent.

Vietnam's conditions are more generous to energy companies than China's as Vietnam has found it more difficult to attract investors because of the current political environment and frictions with China. Vietnam's conditions are also more favorable to energy companies as the government needs to attract investment to further develop offshore fields in order to improve the serious decline in their oil production. China opposes Vietnam's claims to the South China Sea also through harassment of oil-related activities in disputed areas. For example, China severed the cables laid by a Vietnamese seismic research ship on several occasions in summer 2011. The South China Sea disputes risks overshadowing the whole China-Vietnam relationship.

Philippines

The Philippines is also involved in the exploration of the South China Sea. The hydrocarbons industry is rather underdeveloped with average daily production of oil at only 15,000 barrels in 2009, of which a little less than 1000 barrels was extracted from the South China Sea. In an attempt to further develop their resources at the end of June 2011 the Philippines announced that several zones in the South China Sea were open for international bidding.

In 1995, China moved to occupy Philippino-held Mischief Reef. This incident raised concern over Chinese behavior across the whole region and led to efforts to create a Declaration of Conduct in the South China Sea (see below).

A joint marine seismic project between Vietnam, China and Philippines only completed the first phase of pre-exploration, gathering data. The second phase, which was to lead to a more concrete project has not been discussed as tensions arose over the Reed Reef.

Despite economic and military weakness, the Philippines has been asserting more and more vocally claims to its own part of the South China Sea, which has become a patriotic issue. Some of the islands are less than 50 miles away from its coast. In 2011 the Philippines increased maritime patrols in the area and strengthened its links with Vietnam and Japan, as well as with the US, in an effort to balance China and to contrast its claims.

Malaysia

Malaysia's South China Sea strategy is "talk less about sovereignty and produce more oil." Nevertheless, from 2007 to 2009 the average daily production of oil was 750,000, 727,000 and 693,000 barrels, most of which came from the South China Sea. The daily export of oil is 190,000 barrels. Petronas and foreign investors usually share the benefits at a rate of 3:7.

ASEAN

ASEAN includes ten countries, of which five stake claims over the South China Sea (Brunei, Malaysia, Philippines, Indonesia and Vietnam). The claimant states have a running dispute with China over maritime borders. China and Vietnam fought military conflicts in the Paracel Islands in 1974 and again near Fiery Cross Reef in 1988. After the 1995 incident between China and the Philippines at Mischief Reef, ASEAN and China started the diplomatic consultations leading to the eventual signature of a Declaration of Conduct (DOC) on the South China Sea in 2002. At the same time, China enhanced its trade, investment and cultural cooperation with the ASEAN states.

The DOC was meant to prevent any further occupation of islands in the region and to preserve the status quo. However, this did not prevent further Chinese claims in the area, for instance over Philippine-held Reed Reef, as well as numerous incidents at sea. In response to the latest spate of incidents in 2011, ASEAN and China decided to start a new round of consultations with a view to adopting an upgraded Code of Conduct on the South China Sea.

The communiqué of the July 2011 ASEAN Regional Forum in Bali, which also included China, states that Ministers "encouraged the need to move towards the eventual establishment of a regional code of conduct (COC) in the South China Sea as provided in the DOC." Signatories of the COC would renounce the threat or use of force to settle their disputes over sovereignty. They would be expected to demilitarize the islands and bring their maritime claims into line with international law. This would include international arbitration.

United States

As a Pacific power the US never really left Asia, but it has put more of a focus on the region now. China feels that the US is interfering with China's core interests. In 2009, at the first Sino-American Strategic and Economic Dialogue, China made clear that it expected that both countries would respect the core-interests of the other. Some analysts have debated whether the Spratlys fall under core interests. Senior officials, including Hillary Clinton said they were told by Chinese counterparts last year that the South China Sea was a "core interest" on a par with Taiwan and Tibet. The Chinese government sensed the alarm this raised both in the US and in Asia and officially the position has neither been affirmed nor denied. Xinhua, the Communist Party's official news agency, declared in August 2011 that, "*China has always made itself loud and clear that it has indisputable sovereignty over the [South China] sea's islands and surrounding waters, which is part of China's core interests. That is based on unambiguous and undeniable historical facts.*"[7] The US made a statement at the July 2010 ARF foreign ministers' in Hanoi advocating a multilateral solution to the SCS dispute, against China's preference for bilateral solutions.

The US was also concerned about Chinese pressure on international oil companies to avoid investing in offshore Vietnamese energy projects.[8] In testimony before the US Senate, Deputy Assistant Secretary of State Scot Marciel expressed US government concern about Chinese restrictions on legitimate commercial activity in the South China Sea.[9] In addition, this issue was addressed by US Defence Secretary Robert Gates at the Shangri La dialogue in Singapore in June 2010. Gates stated that the US government objected to any effort to intimidate US oil firms with lawful contracts engaged in the South China Sea region.

Japan

At the end of August 2011, there was an intrusion into Japanese waters by Chinese official vessels. The question of sovereignty remains but Japan and China can still work together and come up with a clever solution from both sides to exploit resources in the region. Starting a mutually beneficial project is important and can be a symbol of cooperation to the region. Japan also holds strategic talks with Philippines, at deputy vice minister level to discuss coast guard training and anti-piracy issues. For the last 15 years they have helped with anti-piracy and training activities.

Russia

In the 1980s, at the time of the Soviet Union, Petro Vietnam and Zarubezhneft established Vietsovpetra. Vietsopol, has been operating successfully for over 30

7 See http://news.xinhuanet.com/english2010/indepth/2011-08/31/c_131086932.htm.

8 Jason Folkmanis, "China Warns Some Oil Companies on Work With Vietnam, U.S. Says," *Bloomberg*, July 16, 2009, available at: http://www.bloomberg.com/apps/news?pid=newsarchive&sid=ak.lQfnkDStU.

9 Testimony of Deputy Assistant Secretary Scot Marciel, Bureau of East Asian and Pacific Affairs, U.S. Department of State before the Subcommittee on East Asian and Pacific Affairs, Committee on Foreign Relations, United States Senate, July 15, 2009, available at: http://foreign.senate.gov/testimony/2009/MarcielTestimony090715p.pdf.

years. Russia is now the biggest partner of the Vietnamese national oil company. According to WikiLeaks, Russian diplomats questioned their US counterparts over the Chinese harassment and pressure tactics. They acknowledged that Russia's own extensive interests in Vietnam had not been affected. An official commented to me that, "China would never put pressure on Russian energy companies because China was too afraid of Russia."[10]

A Role for the European Union (EU)?

Problems in the South China Sea shipping lanes would mean an increase of insurance premiums, which would affect also European ports that have business in the region, for example, Antwerp. Some energy companies from EU member states are active in the South China Sea, for example Total in Vietnam and Indonesia, BP-TNK in Vietnam, Repsol in Indonesia. However, there do not yet seem to have been any complaints from European energy companies about being discouraged and kept out of projects in the South China Sea. Admittedly, such complaints are difficult to detect. Certain EU member states have sold weapons to countries in the region. For instance, the Dutch have recently sold 4 corvettes to Vietnam, and the French have sold submarines to Indonesia.

Despite these economic interests, the EU does not seem to have any clear position or any strong diplomatic or security role to play in the South China Sea. Unlike the US, it does not have any military assets there. At this time of economic austerity, only limited resources are likely to be allocated to the EU Foreign and Security Policy. Furthermore, strategic resolve and consensus are lacking; EU Member States often have different interests and different priorities.

The EU as a whole has two main foreign policy priorities: the immediate neighborhood of the EU, including a response to the Arab Spring, and relations with strategic partners. China is the EU's most important strategic partner and trade partner in Asia. China has also been supporting some weaker EU Member States during the sovereign debt crisis. Simple declarations by China have an impact on the Euro and sovereign debt issued by weaker eurozone members.

The US did not ask the EU to associate itself to its statement on the South China Sea at the 2010 ARF Ministerial in Hanoi. If China decided to make a show of force in the South China Sea, the EU would be reluctant to condemn it.

So far, the EU has only taken a general position in support of a rules-based approach. Here is the EU speaking-point on the South China Sea that was used at the ARF Ministerial in Bali July 2011:

> Regarding the South China Sea, the EU believes that territorial disputes should be resolved in accordance with international law through peaceful and cooperative solutions.

10 Interview with South-East Asian diplomat, September 2011, Brussels, Belgium.

> The EU recalls the great importance of the South China Sea for the EU, in the perspective of promoting the rules-based international system; the principle of liberty of navigation; the risk of tensions impacting on the consistent increase in trade and investment, with negative consequences for all; the energy security background.
>
> We note previous work to build a collaborative diplomatic process at the regional level, and in that context, encourage ASEAN and China to build on this foundation and agree on a Code of Conduct, underlining the importance of using international law, and in particular UNCLOS, as the basis of this collaboration. We encourage all parties to clarify the basis for their claims.

Some voices in the EU point out that the EU could share with ASEAN its experience in solving maritime disputes, for instance in the North Sea and between UK and Ireland. But how would ASEAN view the European role in dispute resolution?

South-East Asian diplomatic sources in Brussels signalled that ASEAN does not want naval vessels, but rather support in certain fundamental areas for the ASEAN position for the peaceful settlement of disputes built on the basis of international law. This is important because many of the tensions have ebbed and flowed and whenever there has been an incident which suggests that it would be settled by force.

It would be useful for Southeast Asian countries if the EU sent stronger messages in order to deter countries from conducting risk taking activities in the South China Sea. Southeast Asian countries would like the EU to send China more regular messages and at a higher level.

The EU High Representative Catherine Ashton has never spoken publicly on this. She has never attended any high level meeting: ASEAN, ARF, ASEM, even surprisingly didn't attend the ASEM summit even when it was held in Brussels. European Council President Herman Rompuy did attend.

The EU is a member of ARF but it has never sent a ministerial level official to a meeting. The UK and France are quite active, an EU minister dealing in foreign policy or security has never been sent. According to South-East Asian diplomats in Brussels, the general problem is that the EU is interested in China but that the rest of Asia is not on the radar. EU is absent about real regional issues. The European External Action Service is in transition.

If EU officials are generally careful not to upset China, the European Parliament has shown that it can be very vocal with China on matters of principle, for instance on human rights. It could be sensitised to this issue through lobbying. Vietnam recently carried out a demarche to the EU on the South China Sea.

Conclusion

On the future, I have more questions than answers. Perhaps three future scenarios could be identified: a cooperative scenario, a conflict scenario and a "benign acquiescence" scenario.

Co-operative Scenario

Increased economic interdependence would argue for cooperation among the regional players. All involved would also have to help create incentives for a co-operative solution.

South China Sea joint development activities would be pursued. This was the principle of the DOC of November 2002, which was confirmed in July 2011 to agree on implementation.

Under this scenario, ASEAN will have to continue its efforts to involve China as both a competitor as well as a partner. This delicate dance reflects the intricacies of an important and complex relationship which must be handled with prudence.

In a co-operative scenario, China's efforts to extract hydrocarbons in their undisputed block in the South China results in gas finds only. China must co-operate with Vietnam in order to land the gas as a pipeline back to China would be uneconomic to build because of the required length. This time, geography provides a reason for cooperation rather than seen as a curse. China and Vietnam create an example of successful co-operation in the South China Sea which acts as a confidence building measure for the rest of the region.

Conflict Scenario

Maritime incidents increase and bellicose statements by some in China damage confidence. Members of China's leadership, particularly in the military, voice concerns that the US is attempting to pull ASEAN or some of its members together with Australia, Japan and South Korea into an alliance in order to constrain/contain China. The US vows to maintain its continued military presence but to increase it in the region and states that it is necessary in order to maintain peace and stability. China perceives this as US attempts to maintain dominance and thwart China's ambitions.

An exploitation/humiliation narrative gains traction in some quarters in China. The interests of hawkish elements in the PLA and of National Oil Companies (NOC) converge. Plans are made for a "limited war." A violent attack on a joint-venture oil field facility leads to a dangerous explosion and oil spill. Part of the South China Sea is turned into "a sea of fire" as was advocated in the Global Times op-ed. Unable to cap the gushing well, the oil polluted water threatens marine life. Dire consequences for region and world as sea-lanes affected. Can there be a "limited war"? Would it lead to involvement of US?

Benign Acquiescence Scenario

China's strategy after the 1995 Mischief Reef incident seems to have been to promote good relations with neighbors and to achieve their "benign acquiescence" to its territorial claims in the South China Sea. Under its Good Neighbour Policy, China launched generous cooperation programmes with its neighbors concerning trade and investment, infrastructure and culture. In the meantime, China has been gradually and discreetly expanding its presence in the disputed areas. Under this scenario, China's neighbors would not object to this presence and tacitly come to accept it.

However, this scenario does not seem likely. The South China Sea claimant states have demonstrated that their attachment to their own sovereignty rights and their economic interests over energy resources are too strong. China will have to adjust its strategy accordingly, and choose more clearly between a conflict and a cooperation scenario.

To conclude, as this paper has outlined, with so many actors, littoral states and interests jockeying for position in the South China Sea, it is difficult to resolve the situation satisfactorily for all who have a stake in the region. The complicated calculus magnified by the amount of variables creates a situation which cries out for clarification of claims as well as a clear Code of Conduct. Although a COC will not resolve the existing tensions, it will hopefully help safeguard the region from calamity.

Chapter 11
Could China and Vietnam Resolve the Conflicts in the South China Sea?

Stein Tønnesson

Introduction[1]

Although the Philippines, Malaysia, Brunei, the Republic of China (Taiwan) and Indonesia all have claims to islands and/or maritime zones in the South China Sea, Vietnam and China are the two main players in a set of complex disputes that time and again have done serious harm both to internal cohesion among the members of the Association of Southeast Asian Nations (ASEAN) and their relations with China. Vietnam occupies more features in the Spratly area than any other state. China occupies the Paracels. Both Vietnam and China claim all of the Spratlys and all of the Paracels. If an armed conflict should break out in the South China Sea, it would most likely pit China against Vietnam.

Yet they are also the countries with the greatest chance to resolve their bilateral disputes and set precedents for how to resolve the whole complex of disputes in the South China Sea. China and Vietnam successfully agreed on their land border in 1999 and finalized its demarcation ten years later, when placing the last of 1,533 boundary markers. In 2000 they agreed on their maritime border in the Gulf of Tonkin, and subsequently signed and implemented a comprehensive fisheries agreement. In 2008, the two governments declared their bilateral relationship to be a "strategic partnership," and in 2009 upgraded it to a "strategic cooperative partnership."[2] Diplomats and maritime experts from the two sides have met repeatedly on a bilateral basis for talks about the South China Sea. They also meet multilaterally within the framework of the joint China-ASEAN talks aiming to arrive at a Code-of-Conduct (CoC) for the South China Sea, in accordance with article 10 of the Declaration on the Conduct of Parties (DoC) from 2002, where the parties concerned reaffirmed that "the adoption of a code of conduct in the South China Sea would further promote peace and stability in the region" and

1 The author would like to thank Erik Franckx and Stephanie Kleine-Albrandt for their critical comments on an earlier version of this chapter. Responsibility for any remaining misunderstandings relies of course entirely with the author.

2 Carlyle Thayer, "The Tyranny of Geography: Vietnamese Strategies to Constrain China in the South China Sea," 33 *Contemporary Southeast Asia*, 2011, 348–69, at 350.

agreed to work, "on the basis of consensus, towards the eventual attainment of this objective."[3]

A special challenge to the two communist regimes is that the disputes in the South China Sea engage not just their national security, but their regime security as well. Public opinion is increasingly vocal in both countries. This also allows the Chinese and Vietnamese Diaspora to make their voices heard. Media focus strongly on national sovereignty issues, and public opinion appears unwilling to tolerate any compromise that is needed for dispute solution. If the Vietnamese and Chinese governments start making concessions to each other with a view to an equitable solution then this might expose them to public criticism and weaken the communist parties. While concern for regime security may prevent conflict resolution, it may also provide an impetus for resolving the disputes in order to remove the danger of a nationalist backlash against the existing regimes. Conflict resolution will, however, require a self-assured and bold political leadership with an ability to explain to the general public the need to make compromises.

This chapter differs from other analyses by arguing that the dispute over sovereignty to the Spratly islands is not the key to conflict resolution. Indeed this sovereignty conflict does not even need to be resolved. The question of who has the superior entitlement to the islets, reefs and rocks in the Spratly area may simply be shelved while more important issues are resolved. On this basis the chapter argues that conflict resolution is possible, on the basis of international law, and that China and Vietnam have a potential for taking the lead in that endeavour.[4]

The chapter discusses the unfolding of the most recent tension from May 2009, when Vietnam submitted to the United Nations its data on the extension of its continental shelf, until the Sino-Vietnamese agreement of October 11, 2011 to resume negotiations and more strictly control expressions of nationalist public opinions. During 2009–11, Vietnam deliberately sought to internationalize its conflict with China by aligning itself more strongly with ASEAN, and inviting the United States, India and other countries to play a more active regional role. Vietnam also allowed public demonstrations to take place repeatedly in front of China's embassy in Hanoi as well as in Ho Chi Minh City. This annoyed Beijing. Yet China and Vietnam agreed on a formula for rapprochement and new talks when the new leader of the Vietnamese Communist Party, Nguyen Phu Trong, visited China in October 2011. Although there were several incidents also in

3 For the text and signatures of the 2002 Declaration on the Conduct of Parties in the South China Sea (DoC), available at: http://www.aseansec.org/13163.htm.

4 Most commentators tend to be pessimistic as to the prospect that the South China Sea disputes may ever be resolved. One prominent example: "… it is clear that if the South China Sea disputes are to be settled, such resolution will derive from a political rather than essentially legal process. Unfortunately, the prospects of such a political settlement seem vanishingly small." Clive Schofield and Ian Storey, *The South China Sea Dispute: Increasing Stakes and Rising Tensions.* Washington, DC: The Jamestown Foundation, 2009, at 42.

2012, notably after Vietnam adopted a new maritime law in June, the most serious incident that year was not between China and Vietnam, but between China and the Philippines in regard to control over Scarborough Shoal. This led the Philippines to request, on the basis of a right codified in the 1982 Law of the Sea Convention, impartial arbitration between itself and China. Vietnam no doubt sympathized with the request, but did not officially support it, perhaps because it hoped to achieve more through bilateral diplomacy than from global dispute resolution mechanisms.

The chapter concludes that the best way forward for China and Vietnam in the South China Sea may be to combine several venues at the same time: bilateral as well as multilateral talks, and active participation in international attempts to clarify certain aspects of the law of the sea, notably the impact of small islands on the delimitation of maritime zones.

Three Disputes

Media often refer to "the dispute" or "the conflict" in the South China Sea, while assuming that the key issue is sovereignty over islands. This is a misperception. In reality there are three kinds of legal disputes in the South China Sea which, in spite of the fact that they are interlinked, affect Vietnam and China in different ways. They may very well be handled separately.

The first concerns the "freedom of navigation" within the Exclusive Economic Zones (EEZs) of coastal states. This is primarily a dispute between China and the USA, with China sharing many coastal states' wish to prevent foreign countries from conducting military reconnaissance or naval exercises inside their 200 nautical mile EEZs. States wanting to conduct such activities must first seek the coastal state's permission.[5] China has long sought to prevent military reconnaissance and exercises not only in its 12 nm territorial water zone but also in its 200 nm exclusive economic zone. In China's view foreign countries need permission from the coastal state if they wish to carry out military maneuver, hydrographic surveys or other kinds of reconnaissance.[6] As a state with a long coast Vietnam intuitively shares the Chinese view and confirmed this in article 37.1 of its new maritime law, which was adopted by the Vietnamese parliament in June 2012. It states that the freedom of navigation in the EEZ does not allow other countries to "conduct any act against the sovereignty, defence and security

5 For a comparison of the Chinese and US legal positions here, see Erik Franckx, "American and Chinese Views on Navigational Rights of Warships," 10 *Chinese Journal of International Law*, 2011, 187–206.

6 At the United Nations Convention on the Law of the Sea 1973–82 (UNCLOS III), China eagerly promoted the right for coastal states to prevent foreign warships from operating in their 12 nm territorial waters under the principle of "innocent passage." Jeanette Greenfield, *China's Practice in the Law of the Sea*. Oxford: Clarendon Press, 1992, at 74.

of Vietnam."[7] However, to the extent that China represents the principal threat to Vietnam's national security, which it will continue to do as long as China seems to claim so much of Vietnam's EEZ for itself, Vietnam will welcome the presence of other naval powers, such as the USA, India, Russia, and Japan. During the Cold War, Vietnam's favoured external power was the Soviet Union, who joined the USA in defending the freedom of navigation at the 1973–82 UN Conference on the Law of the Sea. Since the Russian navy abandoned its role in the South China Sea in 1999–2000, Vietnam has been eager to promote the presence of other navies. Vietnam has thus not publicized or demonstrated its support for coastal states' right to curtail naval operations in their EEZ. However, if the Chinese threat were significantly reduced through a successful resolution of the two countries' maritime boundary disputes, Vietnam would probably become more active in supporting the Chinese view that the freedom of navigation, although sacrosanct in the civilian domain, does not include "harmful" military operations.

The second dispute in the South China Sea concerns the delimitation of overlapping claims to 200 nm EEZs and agreement on the extension of each country's continental shelf. For coastal states this is the most important dispute they have, not just for reason of national prestige but also because the 1982 Law of the Sea Convention (LOS Convention) awards coastal states sovereign rights to all the resources in the sea and under the seabed within 200 nautical miles of their coasts (the EEZ). In accordance with the LOS Convention, which has been signed and ratified by all the claimant states in the South China Sea (except Taiwan, who has not been allowed to sign, yet respects it),[8] each coastal state is entitled to a 12 nautical mile territorial water zone as well as a 200 nautical miles EEZ and continental shelf. Under certain geographic conditions, the continental shelf may even extend to as much as 350 nautical miles (and in a few cases even more). States with an extensive continental shelf have to submit exact data on the geomorphology of the seabed, as well as other information, to the United Nations Commission on the Limits of the Continental Shelf (CLCS), who is responsible for applying the LOS Convention in this area. The law of the sea has specific rules for how to measure maritime zone claims, and there is much international practice to build upon when negotiating boundaries in areas where zone claims overlap. As parties to the LOS Convention, the claimant states in the South China Sea are legally obliged to apply the existing rules.

The point of departure for measuring legitimate claims is base points on the main coasts of coastal states, including such large islands as Hainan, Luzon, Palawan, Natuna and Con Son. Delimitation may also be somewhat affected by

7 Unofficial English translation of the June 22, 2012 Vietnamese maritime law. The Vietnamese text can be found at: Carlyle A. Thayer, "Vietnam Law of the Sea", *Thayer Consultancy Background Brief*, August 5, 2012, available at: http://www.scribd.com/doc/101998223/Thayer-Vietnam-s-Law-on-the-Sea.

8 Cambodia has not ratified the LOS Convention, but its claims extend only to the Gulf of Thailand, not to the main part of the South China Sea.

the presence of small islets like the Paracels, Pratas, Scarborough Shoal and the Spratlys. Submerged reefs or low tide elevations, however, such as Macclesfield Bank, Reed Bank or Mischief Reef, will not have any effect on maritime delimitation (see Figure 11.1). Since submerged reefs do not satisfy the LOS Convention's criterion for constituting an island, legally speaking they are parts of the seabed and thus belong to the continental shelf of the state that has the nearest coast—if nearer than 200 nm.[9] The same goes for low-tide elevations, unless they are situated within the 12 nm territorial sea of an island, in which case they may be used as base points for maritime delimitation.

Small islets like the Spratlys may not satisfy the conditions established in Article 121 (3) of the LOS Convention for having a right to their own EEZ and continental shelf.[10] If they are considered "rocks" that cannot sustain human habitation or an economic life of their own—the Spratlys have never been permanently inhabited—then each islet or group of islets can have only a 12 nm territorial water zone. Islets and low tide elevations form a group only if they are within 12 nm of each other. International practice varies when it comes to the size or other geographic features required in order for an island to generate extended maritime zones. It is imaginable that some of the Paracels or Spratlys will be judged to satisfy the conditions for generating an EEZ of their own. In that case, their effect on the delimitation of maritime zones will still be modest since maritime boundaries are generally established under the principle of proportionality. Proportionality in this context is not based on economic strength or size of population but on the length of the relevant coasts. Since the coasts of small islets are very short, the boundaries between the economic zones of such islands and the EEZs of countries with long relevant coasts will not be equidistant, but run much closer to the islet than the opposite mainland coast.[11] Hence in the Sino-Vietnamese Gulf of Tonkin agreement of 2000, the Vietnamese Bach Long Vi (Nightingale) island, which has a substantial permanent population, was given only a 12 nautical mile zone and an additional 3 nm EEZ and continental shelf (15 nm in total). Four other islets in the Tonkin Gulf were also given only a modest effect on delimitation. Vietnam, because it had more islands and a longer relevant coast than China, received 53.23 per cent of the overall water area while China had to do with 46.77 per cent. In accordance with normal state practice, the main determining factor was distance from the coasts of Vietnam and the Chinese Hainan Island.[12] If one or more of

9 "An island is a naturally formed area of land, surrounded by water, which is above water at high tide." LOS Convention, Article 121.1, available at: http://www.un.org/depts/los/convention_agreements/texts/unclos/part8.htm.

10 "Rocks which cannot sustain human habitation or economic life of their own shall have no exclusive economic zone or continental shelf." LOS Convention, Article 121.3, available at: http://www.un.org/depts/los/convention_agreements/texts/unclos/part8.htm.

11 Clive Schofield and Ian Storey, supra note 3, 18.

12 Zou Keyuan, "The Sino-Vietnamese Agreement on Maritime Boundary Delimitation in the Gulf of Tonkin", 36(1) *Ocean Development and International Law*,

the Spratly islets are given a right to generate more than a 12 nm territorial sea, the only major consequence would be that their EEZ and continental shelf would encompass much of the deep water area north of the Spratlys, which is outside of 200 nm from all main coasts. South China Sea specialists refer to this area as the "doughnut" (see Figure 11.1). The waters in the "doughnut" would otherwise be High Seas, and the seabed underneath belong to "The Area" (LOS Convention, part IX).[13] Its resources would then have to be managed by a global authority as the "common heritage of mankind" or—if the concept of the High Seas should prevail—be left as a zone free for all. However, most of the doughnut is oceanic crust with no hydrocarbon potential.[14]

The correct way of proceeding towards maritime delimitation of the South China Sea, once all the surrounding states have made their precise EEZ and continental shelf claims known, is to first draw a continuous line 200 nm outside of legitimate base points on the main coasts, while waiting for the UN Commission on the Limits of the Continental Shelf to provide its recommendations in those cases where the continental shelf extends beyond 200 nautical miles from a coast. Only at the next stage—when boundaries are negotiated for areas with overlapping zone claims—shall the question of whether the Paracels and Spratly can have a modifying effect be considered.

The delimitation of maritime zones is the most important dispute in the South China Sea. Effective maritime delimitation is a precondition for establishing responsible environmental protection and management of fish stocks, as well as for exploiting oil, gas and mineral resources. Serious energy companies are reluctant to explore for oil and gas in areas under legitimate dispute between two or more countries, that is, less than 200 nautical miles from more than one coast. If companies with a concession from one country were to explore for oil in areas legitimately claimed by another country, then this could lead to strong reactions. If, as happened in 2011, one state (China) tries to prevent other states (Vietnam and the Philippines) from exploring for oil and gas in areas that are less than 200 nm from their main coast and closer to their coast than to any other coast, then this will also lead to strong reactions.

The third and least important dispute in the South China Sea concerns sovereignty to the Spratly and Paracel islets, as well as Scarborough Shoal. While

---

2005, 13–24 (p. 15); and Nguyen Hong Thao, "Maritime Delimitation and Fishery Cooperation in the Tonkin Gulf", 36(1) *Ocean Development and International Law*, 2005, 25–44 (map on p. 26).

13 Articles 136 and 137 of the LOS Convention read: "The Area and its resources are the common heritage of mankind"; "No State shall claim or exercise sovereignty or sovereign rights over any part of the Area or its resources, nor shall any State or natural or juridical person appropriate any part thereof. No such claim or exercise of sovereignty or sovereign rights nor such appropriation shall be recognized."

14 See the map in Nick A. Owen and Clive H. Schofield, "Disputed South China Sea hydrocarbons in perspective", 36 *Marine Policy*, 2012, 809–22, at 814.

Figure 11.1 South China Sea and the "Doughnut"

Scarborough Shoal is claimed by the Philippines, the PRC and ROC (Taiwan), the Paracels are claimed by Vietnam, the PRC and ROC. The Spratly dispute is more complex since Vietnam, the PRC and ROC claim all of them, the Philippines many and Malaysia some, and since none of these claims seem "indisputable." These are claims *to land*, not waters or seabed. Hence they do not depend on the law of the sea. There is a massive body of international law to be used for resolving sovereignty disputes over land. Claims to sovereignty must be based on a documented history of discovery, conquest or cession by another state, and since then occupation and utilization, preferably permanent. If a sovereignty claim is based on conquest, then it must have happened before 1945, since the use of force was thereafter prohibited except in self-defence or when enforcing decisions by the UN Security Council. Occupation by force after 1945 thus does not contribute to a legal entitlement. The most important is to demonstrate a continuous exertion of sovereignty over time. No such continuous exertion of national sovereignty is indisputable as far as the Paracels, Spratlys and Scarborough Shoal are concerned.

If the dispute over sovereignty to the Spratly islets were to be decided upon by the International Court of Justice, each claimant state would need to put together massive historical evidence. A court would have to take into consideration not just the exertion of sovereignty historically by today's claimant states, but also by Japan (in the period when it controlled Taiwan 1895–1945), Great Britain (until Malaysia was established in 1963 and Brunei became independent in 1984), and France (until it was forced to leave South Vietnam in 1956).[15] It would be a travesty if this process should take precedence over the delimitation of maritime zones, since this would produce interminable delays. By contrast to what many commentators say, such delay is really unnecessary since the impact of the Spratlys on maritime delimitation will at any rate be modest. While the principle that "land dominates the sea" runs supreme, it is land with long coasts that dominates most, not tiny islets or rocks. To complicate the dispute over islands further, all of the Spratly islands are under military occupation by one or another state (Vietnam, the Philippines, Malaysia, Taiwan, or China).[16] These countries waste substantial resources on keeping troops in these inhospitable places, with dormitories and defence installations often constructed on submerged reefs. The Spratlys, which used to be called "Dangerous Grounds" on European maps, have little military value since they are virtually impossible to defend.[17] No power could hold them against a determined invader. They may be of some use for submarines practising navigation in difficult waters, and perhaps as military listening posts,

15 France did not leave Vietnam (as is often said) in 1954 as a concequence of its military defeat at Dien Bien Phu and the decisions of the Geneva Conference. At that time France only withdrew from Vietnam north of the 17th parallel. In 1956, however, the French were thrown out of South Vietnam and replaced by American advisors. France subsequently ceased to exert its sovereignty to the Spratlys. However, when France claimed the Spratlys in 1933 it had done it for itself, not on behalf of Indochina, Cochinchina, Annam or Vietnam. France never transferred its sovereignty over the Spratlys to Vietnam. It is thus not evident that the French sovereignty to the Spratlys was taken over by South Vietnam so it could later be transferred to the Socialist Republic of Vietnam. The Paracels, on the other hand, had been claimed by France on behalf of Annam (Vietnam) and half of them were effectively transferred to South Vietnam. See Stein Tønnesson, "Why are the Disputes in the South China Sea so Intractable? A Historical Approach," 30 (3) *Asian Journal of Social Science*, 2002, 570–601, at 583, and "The South China Sea in the Age of European Decline," 40 (1) *Modern Asian Studies*, 2006, 1–57, at 31, 39–40, and 49–51. These articles can be accessed electronically at www.cliostein.com.

16 The People's Republic of China does not occupy any island, but has established a permanent military presence on several submerged reefs or low-tide elevations. Legally speaking they a part of the seabed and they will hence belong to the continental shelf of the country with the nearest coast.

17 The British government concluded a 1950 study of the Spratlys with the following assessment (note the clear distinction between occupying the Spratlys and controlling the South China Sea): "(a) The Spratly Islands are of no appreciable strategic value to the Allies, whose only concern would be to deny these islands to a potential enemy. (b) Occupation of the Spratly Islands by Communist China in peace might be considered a minor Cold War reverse for the Allies. (c) Enemy occupation in war would not, so long as we retain control of the South China Sea, be a serious strategic threat." J.P. (50) 104 (Final) 'Strategic Importance of the Spratley Islands,' 25 Aug. 1950, CO 537/5723, UK National Archives (cited after Stein Tønnesson, *supra* note 15).

but modern satellite-based signal systems have reduced the importance of island-based installations. The islets are also of little economic value, although guano was exploited in the past, and fishermen have been coming on a seasonal basis when fishing, catching turtles, collecting bird nests or precious shells. These resources have been depleted by the presence of military troops and installations, and fishermen using cyanide and explosives.

The intensity of the sovereignty disputes over the Spratlys is largely symbolical or derived from a mistaken assumption that they can serve as basis for substantial EEZ and continental shelf claims. Admiral Liu Huaqing, the former commander of the Chinese Navy, was wrong when asserting in his 2004 memoirs: "Whoever controls the Spratlys will reap huge economic and military benefits."[18] The key to reaping military benefits is to have a strong navy, not to occupy reefs or islets. The key to reaping economic benefits is to gain international recognition for one's EEZ and continental shelf, or gain concession for one's companies to exploit resources in areas where other states hold sovereign rights.

The optimal way to facilitate conflict resolution in the South China Sea is to draw up a 12 nautical mile territorial zone around each islet or group of islets thus creating a system of enclaves A regional authority could be set up to manage them temporarily, perhaps as nature reserve, so no one can continue to destroy the coral reefs. The quarrel over sovereignty to the Spratlys could simply be shelved indefinitely, while the littoral states delimited the rest of the South China Sea in national maritime zones.

The question of the Paracels is somewhat different. Some of the Paracels (notably Woody/Yongxing Island) are larger than the Spratlys, and have enjoyed more human presence in the past.[19] The Paracels are claimed only by Vietnam and China (PRC and ROC).[20] Thus the sovereignty dispute over the Paracels is less difficult to resolve than the dispute over the Spratlys.[21] Since China has been in full control of the Paracels since 1974, it is rather unlikely that these islands will ever be returned to Vietnam. An argument in favour of the Vietnamese claim is the active interest shown by the Nguyen dynasty in the 19th century, long before

---

18 Liu Huaqing, *Liu Huaqing Huiyilu [Liu Huaqing's Memoirs].* Beijing: Jiefangjun chubanshe, 2004: 538 (cited after M. Taylor Fravel, "China's Strategy in the South China Sea," 33(3) *Contemporary Southeast Asia*, 2011, 296.

19 Yet Jeanette Greenfield found in 1992 that "it is difficult to see how the Paracels, tiny islands lying on what might be regarded as the slope of the shelf extending from South China and Vietnam, irrespective of ownership, could be the effective basis of any extensive shelf claims. It may be argued that at best they generate a territorial sea." Jeanette Greenfield, *supra* note 5, 164.

20 The Taiwanese (ROC) claim should be considered the same as that of the PRC, on behalf of "one China."

21 For a discussion of the legal strength of the Chinese and Vietnamese claims to the Paracels, arguing that China has superior rights, see Greg Austin, *China's Ocean Frontier: International Law, Military Force and National Development.* St. Leonards NSW, Allen & Unwin, 1998, 98–130.

the French colonization. An argument in favour of the rival Chinese claim is the French neglect of the Paracels from the establishment of its protectorate over Annam in 1884 until the 1930s. A further argument in favour of the Chinese claim is that Chinese forces took possession of Woody Island in December 1946 shortly before the arrival of a French occupation force.[22] This led to a partition of the Paracels, with China controlling the Amphitrite group around Woody Island and France the Crescent group around Pattle Island. After South Vietnam inherited the French position in the mid-1950s, the Paracels remained divided until 1974, when China took the Vietnamese-held islands by force—in clear violation of international law.[23] Hence, if the matter of sovereignty were left to impartial arbitration or adjudication, it is imaginable that China would gain sovereignty to Woody Island and the other islets of the Amphitrite group while Vietnam would get Pattle Island and the Crescent group. However, the court would also need to consider if a statement made by North Vietnam's Prime Minister Pham Van Dong in 1958 to endorse a new Chinese territorial waters law constituted recognition of China's sovereignty to the Paracels and thus constituted an "estoppel" of all previous Vietnamese claims.

While Vietnam is unlikely to ever voluntarily give up its sovereignty claim to the Paracels, Vietnam might perhaps, on certain conditions, accept a preliminary maritime boundary between the disputed Paracels and the coast of central Vietnam, not equidistant but nearer to the Paracels given the principle of proportionality. Woody Island, if given a capacity to have its own EEZ and continental shelf, could then be used to establish an EEZ claim in the eastern and southeasternly direction, since a claim here would not overlap with anyone else's. This EEZ would consume a substantial part of the northern part of the "doughnut," and include the submerged Macclesfield Bank. Since China controls the Paracels, it could win widespread recognition (although not from Vietnam) of an EEZ and continental shelf significantly larger than the one displayed on Figure 11.1. It would not be unreasonable for China to make an EEZ claim of this kind, measured from Woody Island.[24]

The Continental Shelf

The first deadline for submissions concerning continental shelf extensions beyond 200 nm to the CLCS expired on May 13, 2009. China, the Philippines and Brunei did not make any submission for the South China Sea, although they did provide some preliminary information. Vietnam and Malaysia, however, made

22 Stein Tønnesson, "The Paracels. The "Other" South China Sea Dispute," 26(4) *Asian Perspective*, 2002, 145–69, at 151, note 12; and 156–8.

23 Stein Tønnesson, *supra* note 15, 586–7.

24 An excellent map showing the maximum imaginable EEZs around the Paracels and Spratlys may be found in Sarah Raine and Christian Le Mière, *Regional Disorder: The South China Sea Disputes*. London: International Institute for Strategic Studies, 2013, 7.

full submissions.[25] Vietnam made a separate submission for the northern and a joint one with Malaysia for the southern part of the South China Sea, where their claims partially overlap. The Malaysian-Vietnamese collaboration was something new: Although Brunei did not take part and the Philippines protested, the joint Malaysian-Vietnamese submission represented a move in the direction of more unity of purpose among the ASEAN claimants. The joint submission was also significant in that it disregarded the Spratly islets. Although the submission was purely technical and did not represent a legal claim, the fact that Malaysia and Vietnam refrained from attributing any continental shelf to the Spratlys meant that they implicitly considered them as "rocks" on the basis of Article 121(3) of the LOS Convention (cited above). Since Vietnam and Malaysia both occupy islands in the Spratlys and thus might have argued that these should have their own continental shelf, their decision to disregard them was a significant development. If all the claimant countries could agree on the Malaysian-Vietnamese approach, it would greatly facilitate conflict resolution.[26] Although the Philippines officially protested the Malaysian-Vietnamese submission on the basis of its long-standing claim to Sabah (one of the member states in the Malaysian federation), there are signs that the Philippines may also be moving in the direction of Malaysia and Vietnam's implicit interpretation of the status of the Spratly islets as "rocks" with a right only to 12 nautical mile territorial waters. There has been much talk among Philippines policy makers about "enclaving" the Spratly islets and their territorial waters so the dispute over these enclaves can be shelved while the littoral states get on with delimiting their maritime zones.[27]

China, whose main coasts are too far away to generate any EEZ or continental shelf claim in the Spratly area, also protested the Malaysian-Vietnamese submission, and on April 14, 2011 sent a *note verbale* to the UN Secretary General, protesting a recent Philippines' claim to the "so-called Kalayaan Island Group," which in fact,

25 Nguyen Hong Thao and Ramses Amer, "A New Legal Arrangement for the South China Sea?" 40 *Ocean Development & International Law*, 2009, 333–49. The Philippines made a partial submission for an area east of Luzon and indicated that it would make a full submission later. Brunei submitted preliminary information. China also submitted preliminary information, particularly concerning the East China Sea, and indicated that it would submit later for "other sea areas." Clive Schofield and Ian Storey, *supra* note 4, 22–23, 29, and 37. China made a full submission for the East China Sea in December 2012.

26 "This clarification to Malaysia and Vietnam's claims regarding the disputed islands is potentially significant as such a view, if adopted by all the South China Sea parties, would significantly simplify the dispute overall by substantially narrowing the maritime claims associated with the disputed islands." Clive Schofield and Ian Storey, *ibid.*, at 18.

27 Carlyle Thayer, "China-ASEAN and the South China Sea: Chinese Assertiveness and Southeast Asian Responses," paper to conference on Major and Policy Issues in the South China Sea: European and American Perspectives: co-sponsored by Institute of European and American Studies and Centre for Asia-Pacific Studies, Academia Sinica, Taipei, October 6–9, 2011: 29, note 100, available at: http://www.scribd.com/doc/52106729/Thayer-ASEAN-China-and-the-South-China-Sea.

it said, is a part of the Chinese Nansha (Spratly) Islands. The *note verbale* then let the cat out of the bag: "China's Nansha Islands is fully entitled to Territorial Sea, Exclusive Economic Zone (EEZ) and Continental Shelf."[28] The apparent mistake in writing "Island*s is*" was probably intentional. It reflects a vagueness in the original Chinese text as to whether the Spratlys form one archipelago with a right to a maritime zone around it or consist of many individual features. The latter would be the correct interpretation of international law since there is not a sufficient ratio of land to water to satisfy the requirement for being a part of an "archipelagic state" and since the Spratlys do not anyway form part of an archipelagic state (The two archipelagic states in the area are the Philippines and Indonesia). Each Spratly island must therefore be considered separately when deciding upon its maritime zones, although zones may overlap in those cases where islands and low tide elevations are close to each other. China was correct to argue in its *note verbale* that "land dominates the sea" *(la terre domine la mer)* in international law. Hence the Philippines, Malaysia and Brunei cannot claim sovereignty to the islands in the Spratly area on the basis of distance from their coasts. A "naturally formed area of land, surrounded by water, which is above water at high tide" (LOS Convention 121.1) is not a part of any EEZ or continental shelf but must be appropriated in the same way as any other piece of land. Any feature, however, that is not above water at high tide, and is not a part of a nearby island's territorial water zone, will belong to the EEZ or continental shelf of the nearest coastal state. This includes submerged reefs, shoals and low tide elevations. If all or some of the 1–48 insular features in the Spratlys that qualify as islands (by being above water at high tide)[29]

28 The Permanent Mission of the People's Republic of China to the United Nations to the UN Secretary General, No. CML/ 8/2011, New York, April 14, 2011, available at: http://www.un.org/depts/los/clcs_new/submissions_files/submission_mysvnm_33_2009.htm.

29 The number of Spratly islands is contested. The British Foreign Office replied to a US request for information about the Spratlys in 1956 that either just one (Itu Aba) or perhaps two more (Spratly Island and Amboyna Cay) were large enough to qualify for being appropriated by a state. Confidential note no. D 1081/10, 12.10.55 with a minute and map by South-East Asia Department, CO 1030/396, UK National Archives (cited after Stein Tønnesson, *supra* note 15, 47–48 (note 146). J.R.V. Prescott, *The Maritime Political Boundaries of the World*. London: Methuen, 1985, 218–19, lists 26 islands in the Spratlys, but two of them are cays in the vicinity of an island, so would be part of the same sovereignty. In addition Prescott lists seven reefs or "sets of rocks," which also may be "claimable," so 24 + 7 = 31. The 48 figure is taken from David Hancox and J.R.V. Prescott, *A Geographical Description of the Spratly Islands and An Account of Hydrographic Surveys Amongst Those Islands*, Maritime Briefing 1(6), Durham: IBRU, 1995 (http://www.dur.ac.uk/ibru/publications/view/?id=229). It finds 48 "groups of features," consisting of 148 named individual features. See also Marius Gjetnes, *The Legal Regime of Islands in the South China Sea*, MA thesis, Department of Public and International Law, University of Oslo, 2000: 65–66; Johan Henrik Nossum, *Straight Baselines of Vietnam*. MA thesis, Department of Public and International Law, University of Oslo, 2000, 4; and Clive Schofield and Ian Storey, *supra* note 4, at 11–12, and 17.

end up under the sovereignty of another state than the one with the nearest coast, then they will either form 12 nm territorial sea enclaves within the EEZ of that other state or get their own EEZ outside of the coastal state's EEZ.

The U-shaped Line

In its May 7, 2009 protest note to the UN Secretary General, China for the first time officially attached a controversial map with nine dashes forming a U-shaped line around most of the South China Sea, cutting through the EEZs of Vietnam, Indonesia, Malaysia, Brunei, and the Philippines. This U-shaped line has often been misinterpreted both in and outside of China as a claim to all the waters and the seabed within it as Chinese "historical waters," "internal waters" or "territorial waters." As Daniel Dzurek and M. Taylor Fravel have pointed out, this is logically inconsistent with the fact that China has adopted a law on territorial waters and published baselines along its coasts.[30] The function of baselines is to distinguish internal from territorial waters, and to provide base points from which to measure the EEZ and continental shelf. If the whole area within the U-shaped line were Chinese internal waters, then the U-shaped line would be China's baseline. And if the U-shaped line should constitute a "territorial waters" claim, then the distance between the published baselines and the U-shaped line would have to be 12 nautical miles. Thus the only possible meaning of the U-shaped line (which first appeared in an official Chinese atlas in February 1948 when the EEZ principle did not yet exist and the idea of national continental shelves was new) is that it represents a Chinese claim to all islands inside it and the maritime zones that can be generated from these islands on the basis of the law of the sea.

Among Chinese scholars there are four competing interpretations of the U-shaped line: Some think it is a claim to "maritime sovereignty" (treating the sea as if it were land), others that it is a "historic waters" claim, yet others that the claim is based on special historic rights, while the fourth interpretation sees it as a claim to land features and their maritime zones.[31] Only the fourth interpretation can be reconciled with the LOS Convention and with the wording of China's May 7, 2009 protest note to the UN: "China has undisputable sovereignty over the islands in the South China Sea and the adjacent waters, and enjoys sovereign rights and jurisdiction over the relevant waters as well as the seabed and subsoil thereof (see

30 Daniel Dzurek, "The People's Republic of China Straight Baseline claims," *IBRU Boundary and Security Bulletin* 4, no. 2, Summer 1996: 85 (www.dur.ac.uk/ibru/publications/download/?id); M. Taylor Fravel, "China's Strategy in the South China Sea," *Contemporary Southeast Asia* 33(3), December 2011, 295.

31 Wu Shicun, *Nansha Zhengduan de Quiyuan yu Fazhan [The Origins and Development of the Spratlys Dispute]*. Beijing: Zhongguo jingji chubanshe, 2010: 32–9. Cited after M. Taylor Fravel, *ibid.*, at 315, note 10.

attached map)."[32] The U-shaped line cannot thus be a maritime boundary, only an indicator of a Chinese claim to islands and their "adjacent waters." This has been made abundantly clear in several recent legal analyses of the U-shaped line. A commentary by the Singapore-based legal scholar Robert Beckman interpreted the Chinese *note verbale* as an indication that China with "adjacent waters" might be meaning 12 nm territorial seas and by "relevant waters" EEZs: "The position of China will likely be that it has sovereignty over all the islands and that at least some of them are entitled to an EEZ and continental shelf of their own."[33] The Belgian legal scholar Erik Franckx finds that "the U-line, whether interpreted as a territorial or a maritime manifestation, clearly lacks precision, and thus poses problems if kept as part and parcel of PRC as well as Chinese Taipei's official policy."[34] The Japanese scholar Masahiro Miyoshi finds that the U-shaped line can hardly be a boundary since it is not a continuous line.[35] The two Vietnamese scholars Nguyen Dang Thang and Nguyen Hong Thao examine an exchange of diplomatic notes between the Philippines and China, and note that China fails to clarify the meaning of the U-shaped line: China "has the burden of proof," they say, "and the first step for China in discharging this burden is to clarify the exact meaning of the nine dotted lines."[36] The UK-based Chinese scholar Keyuan Zou summarizes the adverse reactions against the U-shaped line among scholars and representatives

32 The Permanent Mission of the People's Republic of China to the United Nations to the United Nations Secretary General, No. CML/17/2009, New York, May 7, 2009, available at: http://www.un.org/depts/los/clcs_new/submissions_files/mysvnm33_09/chn_2009re_mys_vnm_e.pdf. Two Vietnamese scholars have pointed out, however, that the wording of the Chinese, April 14, 2011 *note verbale* is slightly different and might indicate a switch in Chinese thinking towards an argument based on limited historical rights rather than full sovereignty: "China's maintenance of historical rights might be a fallback option in its bargain with neighboring states in the SCS over the right to control marine resources." Nguyen Dang Thang and Nguyen Hong Thao, "China's Nine Dotted Lines in the South China Sea: The 2011 Exchange of Diplomatic Notes Between the Philippines and China", 43 *Ocean Development & International Law*, 2012, 35–56, at 44–6. For the *note verbale*, see: The Permanent Mission of the People's Republic of China to the United Nations to the UN Secretary General, No. CML/ 8/2011, New York, April 14, 2011.

33 Robert Beckman, "South China Sea: worsening dispute or growing clarity in claims?" *RSIS Commentaries* 90 (August 19, 2010), available at: http://hdl.handle.net/10220/6604. For the same reading of the terms "adjacent" and "relevant," see Michael D. Swaine and M. Taylor Fravel (2011), "China's Assertive Behavior, Part Two: The Maritime Periphery," *China Leadership Monitor* 35: 4, available at: http://www.hoover.org/publications/china-leadership-monitor/by-date.

34 Erik Franckx and Marco Benatar, "Dots and Lines in the South China Sea: Insights from the Law of Map Evidence." 2(1) *Asian Journal of International Law*, January 2012, 89–118, at 115.

35 Masahiro Miyoshi, "China's "U-Shaped Line" Claim in the South China Sea: Any Validity Under International Law?", 43 *Ocean Development & International Law*, 2012, 1–17, at 3.

36 Nguyen Dang Thang and Nguyen Hong Thao, *supra* note 32, at 44–6.

of other nations, and goes through those actions undertaken by China that are difficult to reconcile with a claim to "maritime territory" within the U-shaped line, such as the drawing of baselines around the Paracels. He finds that "China faces a dilemma regarding the line as it is not yet ready to give a reasonable explanation of the line based on international law."[37] In view of the fact that the U-shaped line cannot under any circumstance represent a claim to the whole area within it, we (scholars and media) should stop reproducing maps presenting the U-shaped line as a claim in competition with legitimate national EEZ claims. Instead we should use maps with likely Chinese EEZ claims calculated from base points on its main coasts, and possible EEZ claims calculated from Woody/Yongxing Island and/or Itu Aba/Taiping Dao. Maps convey more powerful messages than words. If we continue to disseminate maps presenting the U-shaped line as a claim to "maritime territory" we shall further fuel unrealistic expectations among the Chinese and unwarranted fears among their neighbors.[38]

The joint Malaysian-Vietnamese submission and the protests by the Philippines and China have contributed to clarifying the legal disputes by focusing attention on the key question: Do the Spratly islets have the capacity to generate maritime zones beyond 12 nautical miles? The ASEAN claimants seem to agree that they do not. China and the ROC (Taiwan) hold the opposite opinion. It is important to notice the conflict between Vietnam and China on this point. Although Vietnam occupies more Spratly islets than any other state it has at least informally adopted the position that they do not satisfy the criterions set in article 121.3 of the LOS Convention.[39] While China still seems to maintain an ambiguous position on how

37 This should have led him to conclude that the line can only mean a claim to islands and their maritime zones. Instead he disingenuously suggests that the line would have been meant in 1948 to indicate the extension of the continental shelf of the Paracel and Spratly Islands. The reason mentioned is that the line follows approximately the 200 m isobath (depth) along the coasts surrounding the South China Sea. If the isobath did play a role when the map was drawn, as is likely, this more likely means that those who drew the map did not want to claim islands sitting on the continental shelf of the surrounding states. When they selected James Shoal as the southernmost feature to be claimed by China, one reason was probably its separation from north Borneo by the Palawan trough (in the first post-WW2 years the outer limit was considered by many to be the 200 m isobath). At the end of Zou's article he asks some deeply revisionist questions, suggesting, that is, that nations with a long history may invoke historical rights preceding and contravening the LOS Convention, even if those same nations are parties to the Convention. Zou Keyuan, "China's U-Shaped Line in the South China Sea Revisited", 43 *Ocean Development & International Law*, 2012, 18–34, at 28.

38 Let me again mention the excellent map in Sarah Raine and Christian Le Mière, *Regional Disorder: The South China Sea Disputes*. London: International Institute for Strategic Studies, 2013, 7.

39 The June 22, 2012 Vietnamese maritime law, however, did not make this clear. The Vietnamese text of the law can be found at: Carlyle A. Thayer, "Vietnam Law of the

to interpret the law of the sea, Vietnam has aligned itself with ASEAN in adopting an approach more firmly based in international law.

From Calm to New Tension

While the second half of the 1990s were characterized by much tension in the South China Sea, the years 2000–2007 were rather calm. In the mid-1990s there was much speculation about a coming naval war. The Philippines discovered in 1995 that China had constructed shelters on Mischief Reef in the eastern Spratlys, a mostly submerged feature with some low tide elevations just 113 nautical miles from Palawan.[40] This caused uproar in Manila, but the Philippines did not try to physically prevent the Chinese occupation in the way Vietnam had done in 1988 in the western Spratlys. Instead the Philippines called upon the ASEAN countries for support. China claimed its installations were just shelters for fishermen. In 1997, as the Asian economic crisis struck, the Philippines discovered that China had been solidifying its structures on Mischief Reef, and feared it could be a military listening post. There were also some incidents between Vietnam and China at the time, not least related to rival concessions for oil exploration in blocs located between the Spratlys and the Vietnamese coast.

US scholar Samuel Huntington dedicated several pages of his controversial 1996 book The Clash of Civilizations to a war scenario in the South China Sea, escalating from a naval clash to a great civilizational war as the U.S. Navy intervened. Huntington warned his compatriots against "intervention by the core state of one civilization (the United States) in a dispute between the core state of another civilization (China) and a member state of that civilization (Vietnam)."[41] The James Bond film Tomorrow Never Dies (1997) featured a media baron trying to provoke a confrontation in the South China Sea between China and a British frigate, which had been lured to steer off course. Two British authors published a novel about the coming war in the South China Sea.[42]

Much of the hype hinged on the Chinese refusal to talk multilaterally with the ASEAN countries. Beijing insisted that it would only talk bilaterally with each claimant state. In 1999–2000, however, China softened its stance, probably in order to prevent the ASEAN countries from seeking US assistance to counterbalance China's rising power. This paved the way for the talks leading to China and

---

Sea", *Thayer Consultancy Background Brief*, August 5, 2012. http://www.scribd.com/doc/101998223/Thayer-Vietnam-s-Law-on-the-Sea

40 A 2009 photo of the Chinese installations on Mischief Reef, see http://bauvinal.info.free.fr/anh/PLAGeneralAdvises.htm.

41 Samuel Huntington, *The Clash of Civilizations and the Remaking of World Order*, New York: W.W. Norton, 1996, 313–16.

42 Humphrey Hawksley and Simon Holberton. *Dragonstrike: The Millenium War.* London: Sidgwick & Jackson, 1997.

ASEAN's joint Declaration on the Conduct of Parties in the South China Sea (DoC) in Phnom Penh 2002.[43] The main aim of the DoC was to prevent further conflict by having everyone abstain from occupying additional features. The intention was furthermore to continue talks between ASEAN and China with the aim to arrive at a legally binding Code of Conduct (CoC). The DoC put a temporary end to fears of violent confrontations in the South China Sea so in the first eight years of the 21st century there was mostly status quo. China seemed to build a long-term strategic relationship with ASEAN based on increasing trade, mutual investments, and also some political and security consultations. The symbol of China's Southeast Asian achievements was the China-ASEAN Free Trade Area, which was announced in 2002 and entered into force in 2010.

It may or may not be a coincidence that the lull in the South China Sea disputes coincided with a period of tension and distrust between mainland China and Taiwan during the presidency of Chen Hsui-bian, whereas the renewed tension in the South China Sea came at a time when Ma Ying-jeou took over the ROC presidency. Ma, a specialist on the South China Sea disputes, enjoyed a certain level of trust in Beijing.

At any rate, by 2008–2009 the tensions came back with a vengeance. This was not just because of the May 2009 Malaysian and Vietnamese submissions to the CLCS, although they were no doubt a factor. It was also because the CoC talks had stalled. ASEAN had gained the impression that China was sabotaging them. Meanwhile China had continued to upgrade its existing structures in the Paracels as well as in the Spratly area. This was done in conjunction with a rapid build-up of the Chinese South Sea Navy with new, more efficient and silent submarines, more advanced Russian built destroyers, and substantially modernized port facilities in Hainan. Just as importantly, China equipped its fishery supervision services and Marine Surveillance Force with new, faster and more efficient vessels.[44] China used these increasing capabilities to enforce fishing bans in waters considered by Vietnam and the Philippines to be theirs. Vietnamese fishing boats were frequently taken under arrest and their catch and fishing gear confiscated. Vietnam did the same with Chinese fishing vessels. The Chinese Navy did not play a direct part in these fishing incidents, but carried out exercises on an unprecedented scale in the southern half of the South China Sea.[45]

The U.S. Navy was eager to monitor the Chinese build-up, follow the movements of Chinese submarines and register their acoustic profiles so each of

43 See note 3 above. See also Kriangsak Kittichaisaree, "A Code of Conduct for Human and Regional Security around the South China Sea", 32(2) *Ocean Development & International Law*, 2001, 131–48.

44 Zou Keyuan, *supra* note 37, pp. 20–21. M. Taylor Fravel, *supra* note 18, 303–7.

45 Geoffrey Till, *Asia's Naval Expansion: An arms race in the making?* London: International Institute for Strategic Studies, 2012.

them could be recognized wherever they sailed.[46] This led to a Sino-American naval incident in March 2009, when China sought to chase away the USNS Impeccable, a marine hydrographic survey ship mapping the seabed 65 nautical miles south of Hainan along routes presumably employed by Chinese submarines when exiting from their ports. Impeccable was forced to pull out but returned the next day with a military escort.

Taken together all of these factors contributed to removing the fragile peace gained by the 2002 DoC. Tension increased in March 2010 when high level Chinese representatives to bilateral talks with the Obama administration ventured the idea that China's sovereignty in the South China Sea might be defined as a Chinese "core interest." This term had previously been used primarily for Taiwan, Tibet and Xinjiang. When the Chinese suggestion was reported in the *New York Times*, it contributed to increased apprehension among China's neighbors. The question of "core interests" had its background in a joint Sino-American statement agreed upon when President Obama visited China in late 2009.[47] China had long wanted each side in the Sino-US relationship to define certain core interests that the other would pledge to respect. Obama allowed this terminology to enter into his and President Hu Jintao's mutually agreed statement, and China saw this as a breakthrough. In actual fact, however, the Obama administration was not the least interested in defining any US "core interests," and even less in seeing China expand the number of interests worthy of special US "respect." This kind of reciprocity had no appeal in Washington. What the Americans wanted was to define common concerns that both parties should take joint responsibility for as global stakeholders. Yet China proceeded with its attempt to define mutual core interests. It was in this context that the idea of including the South China Sea as a Chinese core interest was aired in a confidential meeting between two top officials on each side. The two Americans were appalled. They probably leaked the Chinese suggestion to the press. This caused considerable Chinese embarrassment, and Beijing retracted. China had good reasons

46 Eric McVadon, "Humanitarian Operations: A Window on US–China Maritime Cooperation," in Andrew Erickson, Lyle Goldstein, and Nan Li, eds, *China, the United States, and 21st Century Sea Power*. Annapolis: Naval Institute Press, 2010, 264–5.

47 There has been much debate among outside observers about China's attempt to broaden its "core interests" to include the South China Sea. Michael Swaine has found that the US diplomats who first heard the suggestion may have misunderstood. Michael D. Swaine, "China's Assertive Behavior Part One: On "Core Interests"," *China Leadership Monitor* 34, 2011, available at: http://www.hoover.org/publications/china-leadership-monitor/by-date. Two naval analysts have assumed that "core interest" means the same as military control, and have asked what it would take for the Chinese navy to control the South China Sea: Toshi Yoshihara and James R. Holmes, "Can China Defend a "Core Interest" in the South China Sea?" *The Washington Quarterly* 34(2), 2011, 45–59. Sarah Raine has seen the Chinese debates about the "core interest" question as proof of serious internal disagreements among Chinese policy-makers. Sarah Raine, "Beijing's South China Sea Debate," *Survival: Global Politics and Strategy*, 53:5, 2011, 69–88. http://dx.doi.org/10.1080/00396338.2011.621633.

to backtrack from its own suggestion. One reason was that China had never issued any precise definition of the extension and nature of its South China Sea claims. If China and the United States were to define the South China Sea as a Chinese core interest within the framework of their bilateral relations, then this would give the United States a role in defining what part of the South China Sea that can be seen as Chinese. This is something China has only been willing to discuss in bilateral negotiations with each of the other claimants, and with no external interference. When Hu Jintao visited Washington DC in January 2011, there was no mention of a need for mutually defined "core interests." However, when Xi Jinping addressed a luncheon in Washington, DC as China's Vice President on February 15, 2012, although not mentioning the South China Sea, he spoke of a need for "strategic trust" and respect for "core interests and major concerns."[48]

All of this happened in the period when China refused to condemn the March 26, 2010 sinking of the South Korean vessel Cheonan, apparently by a North Korean torpedo. So when China escalated a dispute with Japan in September 2010 concerning the arrest of a Chinese fishing boat near the Senkaku/Diaoyu rocks east of Taiwan, this was taken as additional evidence of Chinese assertiveness. Observers and admirers of China's successful regional diplomacy in the first half of the 2000s were taken aback by the sudden degradation of China's relations with its neighbors as well as with the USA. The region suddenly reverted to a situation where most regional countries called upon the United States to get back in a more visible role as a counter-balance to China. This should have been the last thing Beijing wanted. Its interests would have been better served by sticking to its strategy of regional confidence building. China suddenly seemed insensitive to the concerns of its neighbors.

Although China's new assertiveness during 2009–2011 did not probably stem from a top level decision, a co-ordinated effort or a change of strategy, it must have deeply worried the leaders in Hanoi, who had been upgrading their economic, military and party-to-party relations with China for a long time. The same neighbour country who had become its principal source of aid, trade, investments and political support and with whom the Vietnamese leaders shared a concern for regime security, was now seen to threaten Vietnam's national security. In both countries the communist regimes were seen to be challenged by so-called "peaceful evolution," stimulated not only by American and European influences, but also by local and trans-national NGOs as well as the examples set by democratic transitions not only in far away countries but also in Indonesia and, from 2011, even in Myanmar.

48 Xinhua, news in English, February 15, 2012, available at: http://news.xinhuanet.com/english/china/2012-02/16/c_122707589.htm. The New York Times heard him say "core interests" but never noticed the "major concerns." Edward Wong, "Chinese Vice President Urges U.S. to Respect 'Core Interests'," *New York Times* February 15, 2012, available at: http://www.nytimes.com/2012/02/16/world/asia/vice-president-xi-jinping-of-china-urges-united-states-to-respect-core-interests.html. Michael D. Swaine, *supra* note 47, at 3.

It remains unclear what led to China's new assertiveness. Change of personnel in Beijing? Marginalization of the Foreign Ministry from top-level decision making until it began to reassert itself in 2010–2011? Bad coordination of various agencies operating on the basis of broad guidelines? Factional struggles in conjunction with preparations for the 2012 Party Congress? Influence from an increasingly nationalist web-based public opinion? Exaggerated self-confidence when China successfully navigated through the 2008 financial crisis, while the USA and Europe suffered? The impact of an apparent modification of Japan's foreign policy in the brief 2008–2009 interlude when a reformist prime minister, Yukio Hatoyama, seemed to distance himself from the USA and move closer to China? Or perhaps increasing pressure from the Chinese oil companies to get on with offshore oil and gas exploration?[49] In an analysis of the Chinese decision-making process Sarah Raine finds two camps. One thinks it is time to push Chinese claims forcefully, while the second is not yet willing to abandon Deng Xiaoping's suggestion to shelve the sovereignty disputes while seeking to establish joint development of resources. She sees "evidence of a growing gap between civilian and military interpretations of Chinese interests."[50] If this is true, then there is no camp advocating conflict resolution on the basis of international law. Yet this is arguably the only possible way for China to realize its aims.

Mainland Chinese commentators have seen no need to explain China's assertiveness. They blame the increased tension on the behaviour of others. This interpretation has received some support from the two American scholars Michael Swaine and M. Taylor Fravel, who see China's increasing activism both as a logical result of increasing capabilities and a response to assertive behaviour by others, notably Vietnam.[51] This is not fully convincing. While it is true that Vietnam has done many of the same things as China in order to pursue its claims, it has done it on a lower scale and only within areas that are less than 200 nm from its coastal baselines. The difference in scale and legitimacy of Vietnam's and China's behaviour makes it awkward to explain Chinese activism as a response to Vietnam's.

There is also a widespread Chinese notion that the US has orchestrated regional defiance of China. Many Chinese commentators think the United States pushed regional countries to oppose China in an effort reaching its apex during Hillary

49 For an examination of many of these factors, see International Crisis Group, "Stirring up the South China Sea" I–II, Asia Reports 223 and 229, March 23 and July 24, 2012.

50 Sarah Raine, *supra* note 47, pp. 77, 81. However, Lyle Goldstein concludes from a survey of Chinese publications that sharply different views are held also by military analysts, ranging from "hawkish" to "practical, cautious and even enlightened:" Lyle Goldstein, "Chinese Naval Strategy in the South China Sea: An Abundance of Noise and Smoke, but Little Fire," 33(3) *Contemporary Southeast Asia*, 2011, 320–47, at 328.

51 Michael D. Swaine and M. Taylor Fravel, China's Assertive Behavior, Part Two: The Maritime Periphery, China Leadership Monitor 35, 2011, at 7, available at: http://www.hoover.org/publications/china-leadership-monitor/by-date.

Clinton's statements at the ASEAN Regional Forum in Hanoi on July 2010,[52] and in President Obama's "pivoting to Asia" address to the Australian parliament on November 17, 2011. Obama spoke about the creation of a new Free Trade Area in the Asia-Pacific, excluding China, and announced the establishment of new base facilities for US marines in northern Australia. On the day before, Hillary Clinton had stood on the deck of a US warship in Manila Bay after the United States had reassured the Philippines concerning the protection of its national sovereignty. There is little to indicate, however, that the backlash against China from its neighbour states in 2010–2011 resulted from a premeditated US policy. The order of events was rather the reverse. President Obama and Secretary of State Clinton had gone out of their way to smoothen US relations with China at the time when they took office in 2009. It was the negative Chinese reaction and the worsening of China's relations with its neighbors that led them to invite a stronger US role and Washington to then see a chance for a US diplomatic "comeback." At a time when its financial situation dictated huge cuts in US military expenditures, Obama went as far as to commit his administration not to cut any US military expenditures in the Asia-Pacific.[53] The new US priorities came in response to developments in the region rather than the other way round. Obama must also have seen a need for a certain level of activitism in one part of the world at a time when he was keen to withdraw from Iraq and Afghanistan and avoid military involvement in other Middle Eastern crisis countries.

In his speech Obama mentioned US cooperation with Vietnam. Both countries see their bilateral relations as closely related to their relations with China. China fears the establishment of US military listening posts on Vietnamese territory. China has noticed that Vietnam is a part of the Trans-Pacific Partnership talks from which China is excluded. This may help Vietnam take over some of the Chinese

52 Hillary Clinton offered US help in mediating talks about the sovereignty disputes, and declared: "The United States has a national interest in freedom of navigation, open access to Asia's maritime commons and respect for international law in the South China Sea." While her statements pleased the Vietnamese hosts, and received support from representatives of many ASEAN Regional Forum members, they angered China. Mark Landner, "Offering to Aid Talks, U.S. Challenges China on Disputed Islands," *New York Times* July 23, 2010, available at: http://www.nytimes.com/2010/07/24/world/asia/24diplo.html.

53 "As President, I have … made a deliberate and strategic decision—as a Pacific nation, the United States will play a larger and long-term role in shaping this region and its future, by upholding core principles and in close partnership with our allies and friends. … As we end today's wars, I have directed my national security team to make our presence and mission in the Asia Pacific a top priority. As a result, reductions in U.S. defense spending will not—I repeat, will not—come at the expense of the Asia Pacific." Remarks by President Obama to the Australian Parliament, November 17, 2011, available at: http://www.whitehouse.gov/the-press-office/2011/11/17/remarks-president-obama-australian-parliament. See also: "We're back. America reaches a pivot point in Asia." The Economist, 19 Nov 2011, available at: http://www.economist.com/node/21538803.

role in producing or assembling products for American companies when the costs in China go up, and take part in the globalization of services.

Diplomatically, Vietnam played out a few cards of its own during 2009–2011. It made a deliberate attempt to internationalize the issue on a semi-official level by organizing a series of scholarly conferences from November 2009 onwards, hosted by the Vietnamese Law Association and the Diplomatic Academy of Vietnam, and with strong international representation, including prominent Chinese academics.[54] Vietnam also cooperated with the Philippines in drawing American attention to the South China Sea. In addition Vietnam ended its practice of treating maritime incidents with discretion. It loudly protested China's fishing bans, and made known how Chinese ships were mistreating Vietnamese fishermen. A Vietnamese fishing boat captain, who repeatedly lost his boat and fishing gear, and spent several periods in Chinese custody, became a hero in Vietnamese media. Then, in March–June 2011 Chinese (civilian) Marine Surveillance ships on three occasions disrupted Vietnamese exploration of the seabed. This led to incidents were seismic cables were cut by Chinese vessels.[55] Vietnam took the risk of providing military escort for its exploration ships, and decided to draw the world's attention to the matter by distributing pictures and other documentation to the media. This caused an international stir. The US Senate unanimously adopted a resolution "deploring" the Chinese use of force in the South China Sea.[56] A number of mutual accusations followed between China and Vietnam, and many public demonstrations were held

54 For books edited by Tran Trong Thuy from these conferences, see http://nghiencuubiendong.vn/en/conferences-and-seminars-/first-international-workshop. See also Stein Tønnesson, "China's Changing Role in the South China Sea: Reflections on a Scholar's Workshop," *Harvard Asia Quarterly* XII (3&4), 2010, 18–30.

55 A summary of these events can be found in Carlyle Thayer, "China's New Wave of Aggressive Assertiveness in the South China Sea," *International Journal of China Studies* 2(3), 2011, 555–83, at 566–71, and Carlyle Thayer, *supra* note 1, p. 361. Ironically the kind of equipment used when exploring for oil and gas is virtually the same that is used by the USNS *Impeccable* to map the seabed in areas where submarines play hide and seek. While the LOS Convention does not contain any prohibition against seismic exploration in another country's EEZ if the purpose is military, the same exploration would clearly be illegal if the purpose were commercial. M. Taylor Fravel suggests that the location of these incidents means they were designed to signal China's maximum EEZ claims since they were near the limits of a hypothetical 200-nm zone measured from the five largest features in the Spratlys. M. Taylor Fravel, *supra* note 18, at 307. If Fravel is right, then China does not seek to enforce any sovereign rights in areas that are more than 200 nautical miles from the Spratlys or Paracels but still within China's U-shaped line. If this is the case, then China still grossly violates the customary rules. Any area that is closer to the Vietnamese coast than to any of the Spratlys or Paracels must belong to Vietnam's EEZ, regardless of who holds sovereignty to those islets.

56 U.S. Senate Unanimously "Deplores" China's Use of Force in South China Sea, June 27, 2011, available at: http://webb.senate.gov/newsroom/pressreleases/06-27-2011.cfm?renderforprint=1.

against China in Hanoi and Ho Chi Minh-City from June 5 to August 18, at which time the Vietnamese government clamped down on them.[57] Chinese media strongly attacked Vietnam, and Chinese blogs were full of threats. A lead article in the Chinese weekly *Global Times* on September 29, 2011 called for a "strike" against Vietnam.[58] It should be emphasized, however, that no military incidents occurred. During the "crisis," the Vietnamese and Chinese navies conducted a joint patrol in the Gulf of Tonkin, and two Vietnamese naval vessels paid a friendly visit to the Chinese port in Zhanjiang.[59]

The tension also did not interrupt Sino-Vietnamese bilateral diplomacy. Several high level delegations went back and forth in efforts to calm the waters. Concerns for both regional and regime security entered the fray. Chinese representatives urged Vietnam to put an end to anti-Chinese demonstrations, and the Vietnamese government complied. Its repression of public opinion led to protests from the Vietnamese Diaspora as well as from domestic activists. They claimed a constitutionally guaranteed right to state their opinion. The key event in repairing bilateral relations and sealing the fate of the patriotic Vietnamese activists was the successful visit by the Vietnamese Communist Party's new Secretary General Nguyen Phu Trong to Beijing October 11–15, 2011. During his visit deputy foreign ministers Ho Xuan Son and Zhang Zhijun signed the six-point agreement cited above, stating that the two countries should solve their maritime disputes "on the basis of legislation and principles enshrined in international law, including the United Nations Convention on the Law of the Sea signed in 1982." Both sides pledged to "fully respect legal principles." They agreed that the two countries' border negotiation teams would have regular meetings twice a year to negotiate their bilateral differences, while also consulting third parties.[60] The effect of this new agreement was felt immediately when Vietnam organized its third international scholarly conference on the South China Sea in November 2011. Whereas the Vietnamese media had broadly covered the 2009 and 2010 conferences, the third conference was carried out in silence. Vietnam took seriously the promise it had

57 Carlyle Thayer, *supra* note 55, 566–8.

58 "... Unfortunately, though hammered by China in the 1974 Xisha [Paracel] Islands Battle and later the Sino-Vietnamese War in 1979, Vietnam's insults in the South China Sea remain unpunished today. ... it is probably the right time for us to reason, think ahead and strike first before things gradually run out of hand ... out there could just be an ideal place to punish them. Such punishment should be restricted only to the Philippines and Vietnam, who have been acting extremely aggressively these days ... We should make good preparations for a small-scale battle while giving the other side the option of war or peace. ..." Long Tao (strategic analyst of China Energy Fund Committee), "Time to teach those around the South China Sea a lesson," *Global Times*, September 29, 2011, available at: http://www.globaltimes.cn/NEWS/tabid/99/ID/677717/Time-to-teach-those-around-South-China-Sea-a-lesson.aspx.

59 Carlyle Thayer, *supra* note 1, at 355.

60 "China, Vietnam sign accord on resolving maritime issues." Xinhua October 12, 2011, available at: http://news.xinhuanet.com/english2010/china/2011-10/12/c_131185606.htm.

given to China to prevent further expression of public opinion. In return China showed restraint. It had already ceased to take Vietnamese fishing boats under arrest, and declared itself willing to engage in more serious talks with ASEAN about a Code of Conduct (CoC).

National and Regime Security

One of the most interesting aspects of the tension in the South China Sea during 2009–2013 is the role of an increasingly vocal public opinion in China and Vietnam, both in the official media and the blogosphere. Domestic and international experts have been interviewed on TV and in the press, and have often expressed strong personal views. Demonstrations were for some time allowed in Vietnam. Hardly any Vietnamese is in doubt that the main threat to Vietnam's national sovereignty comes from China's rising power. From the perspective of regime security, however, the main threat is often seen to come from so-called "peaceful evolution," which in 2011 was associated with the "Arab Spring." This threat perception is shared by the Vietnamese and Chinese Communist Parties.[61] Hence they both prefer to manage their border disputes in ways that do not stir up uncontrollable patriotism. The Socialist Republic of Vietnam (SRV) and the People's Republic of China (PRC) were both founded in wars of national liberation that were also civil wars and class struggles. The Vietnamese communists successfully defeated first France and its client State of Vietnam and later the US intervention to support the Republic of Vietnam (South Vietnam). With Vietnam's successful national unification in 1975 the Republic of Vietnam disappeared. It survives only in the memory of overseas communities. They are numerous, however, and play a significant role for Vietnam's economic development through remittances, knowledge, investments, networking, and travel. The Vietnamese Communist Party and Vietnam's Ministry of Public Security no doubt worry that their regime security is threatened by increasing contact between internal opposition groups and movements in the Diaspora. The Party has long been in a process of seeking to redefine itself not as partisan or class-based but as representing the whole nation, including its business elite. Instead of allowing competing political parties the Vietnamese Communist Party has sought to broaden its social and ideological basis.

The same applies to China, whose Diaspora reside not only in countries far away, but also in a democratized Taiwan and the semi-democratic Hong Kong, whose economies and civil societies have become thoroughly immersed in the mainland's. Influence from Singapore, however, works in the opposite direction. Its small-state government has a pragmatic approach to international politics,

---

61 In 2009, Chinese State Councillor Dai Binguo defined China's core interests in three main points: "1) preserving China's basic state system and national security; 2) national sovereignty and territorial integrity; and 3) the continued stable development of China's economy and society." Michael D. Swaine, *supra* note 47, at 4.

based on balance-of-power and the application of international law. Singapore encourages US counterbalancing while at the same time seeking to persuade China that it must respect and apply international law. The Chinese communists are engaged in much the same endeavour as their Vietnamese brethren, seeking to broaden their social basis to include all social elites, and solidify their position as a dominant national force, while taking care not to unleash a democratic transition of the kinds that have transformed Taiwan, South Korea, Indonesia, and now also Myanmar. The tension between national and regime security in Vietnam and China forms a necessary background for understanding the particular nature of their national sovereignty disputes, and also for the role that Taiwan might play either as a participant in conflict resolution with solid experience and knowledge of maritime affairs, or as a spoiler, appealing to Chinese nationalist sentiments. From the perspective both of Beijing and Hanoi it is preferable to manage or resolve their disputes through bilateral negotiations, with as little interference as possible from external powers and no uncontrollable engagement of domestic public opinion.

The problem is that this does not seem possible in the South China Sea, for at least four reasons: First, the Chinese and Vietnamese claims to islets and maritime zones overlap to such an extent that any compromise requires concessions of such a magnitude that the legitimacy of the two governments could be threatened. Second, the disputes over sovereignty and maritime delimitation do not just concern China, Vietnam and Taiwan, but the Philippines, Malaysia, and Brunei as well, and to some extent also Indonesia. This makes it necessary to combine bilateral and multilateral diplomacy, which is always difficult. Third, while Vietnam's long coast puts it in a favourable position as far as maritime delimitation is concerned, China's naval power is rising so visibly that it may be hard for the Chinese population to accept a solution based on international law. Expectations are that military power can be used to bend or supersede the law. The PLA Navy has become a source of immense pride among the Chinese public. The South China Sea is about to become a test case for China's respect for international law and its treaty obligations in the LOS Convention, which are impossible to reconcile with the apparent claim to "maritime territory" within the U-shaped line that appears on virtually all Chinese maps, even on weather forecasts. Fourth, organized and unorganized opposition movements in Vietnam and China, as well as within the Vietnamese and Chinese Diaspora do not seem interested in contributing to an equitable solution to the maritime disputes. Some of them have a wider purpose when appealing to patriotic sentiments. They seek to demonstrate that the communist regimes are failing in their duty to defend core national interests.

Bilateral Asymmetry

The relationship between Vietnam and China is asymmetric and emotionally difficult. Yet the two countries moved steadily closer over the first fifteen years after the resolution of the Cambodian conflict in 1991. Brantly Womack, in his 2006 book about Sino-Vietnamese relations, said they had developed a "mature asymmetry" and asked what it would take to unravel normalcy and generate new friction or confrontation. He found that the most significant scenario would be a situation of bipolar global hostility between the USA and China. Just like the other states in the region, said Womack, Vietnam would be averse to choosing sides: "In general, the side that tries to force Vietnam into its camp is likely to lose Vietnam's support because the attempt to force Vietnam's position would be evidence of threat."[62] This was perceptive. If China and the USA develop a hostile bipolar relationship, each of them should understand the risk of antagonizing Vietnam if they try to force it into their camp. In situations where China and the USA fight over matters such as the non-intervention principle, democracy or human rights, Hanoi would feel most threatened by the United States. In situations where the Sino-US strategic rivalry is conflated with Vietnam's conflict with China over maritime rights, Hanoi will feel most threatened by China. The tensions in the South China Sea since 2009 provide a glimpse of what this second situation may look like.

China and Vietnam are often compared to an elder and younger brother. Womack does not use this easy metaphor but speaks of the dangers of either inattention or over attention in asymmetric relationships more generally. The weaker power may be over attentive and the stronger power inattentive, in both cases producing misperceptions and misunderstandings.[63] Sino-Vietnamese asymmetry is complicated by a clash between the two nations' perceptions of history. The Viet never tried to conquer the Middle Kingdom in the way of the Mongols or Manchus, but unlike other ethnic groups within the Middle Kingdom they broke out and formed a kingdom of their own around 1000 A.D. In the modern Vietnamese perception the first thousand years A.D., when the lands in and around the Red River Delta were a part of the Middle Kingdom and most of today's Vietnam was populated by Cham and Khmer, form a period of repression by an external power: Zhongguo/Trung Quoc/ Middle Kingdom/China. Ho Chi Minh's long poem "Our History," which was written and disseminated in several versions during the Second World War, tells a story of repeated struggles against northern invaders. This narrative was used to stimulate the struggle of the Vietnamese people during 1941–1945 against a "double Franco-Japanese yoke." Ho Chi Minh's history of past struggles ("Vietnam never lacked heroes") also motivated the sacrifices made in the "wars of resistance" against France 1945–1954 and the USA and its "puppets" 1959–1975. The aim was to restore Vietnam to its

62 Brantley Womack, *China and Vietnam: The Politics of Asymmetry*. Cambridge: Cambridge University Press, 2006, 255.

63 Ibid. 80–85.

perceived historical status as a unified nation from Cap Mau to the Chinese border. In the struggles against France and the United States, the Vietnamese communist nationalists received massive aid from China. In 1974, however, China provoked deep resentment in Hanoi by exploiting the weakened status of South Vietnam after the 1973 Paris peace agreement to take the western Paracels (the Crescent Group) by force. Hanoi intended of course to take over the South Vietnamese positions both in the Paracels and Spratlys, but could not openly criticize China while the war for national unification was the main priority. When realizing that the Paracels had been lost to China, North Vietnam learned its lesson and rushed to take control of the South Vietnamese garrisons in the Spratlys at the earliest opportunity in 1975.

The massive aid provided by China to Vietnam in its struggle for national unification is sometimes conceived as a continuation of the support and protection in the past by the Middle Kingdom to the tributary kingdom of An Nam whenever it was threatened by outside forces or internal rebellion. The Chinese and Vietnamese perceptions of history thus contradict each other. They clashed in 1978–1979, when Vietnam allied itself with the Soviet Union against China, provoked the exodus of several hundred thousand ethnic Chinese from Vietnam, and invaded Cambodia to liberate it from the genocidal Khmer Rouge Regime. The elder brother in the asymmetric relationship, now no longer Mao but Deng Xiaoping, sought to teach the younger brother a lesson through a bloody five-week invasion in February–March 1979. This brought up all of Vietnam's memories of past struggles, provoked staunch resistance, and led to an icy period through most of the 1980s. The Sino-Vietnamese border was sealed completely off. The rails on the railways connecting the two countries were removed, and there were repeated artillery exchanges and small-scale invasions across the border until January 1987.[64]

The railways and roads were opened again at the end of the Cold War, when Vietnam lost its support from the Soviet Union, withdrew its troops from Cambodia, and signed a comprehensive peace agreement for Cambodia in 1991, providing for a temporary UN administration until national elections could be held. In the final phase of the Cold War, when Vietnam's strategic position was weakened by the Soviet Union's cutbacks in its international commitments, China again used its leverage in 1987–88 to push its position forward in the South China Sea by occupying certain reefs and low tide elevations in the Spratly area, close to islets occupied by Vietnam. When Vietnamese forces sought to prevent China from occupying an additional reef in March 1988, they came under fire, and 64

64 Edward C. O'Dowd, *Chinese Military Strategy in the Third Indochina War: The Last Maoist War*. London: Routledge, 2007; Sophie Quinn-Judge, "Victory on the Battlefield; isolation in Asia: Vietnam's Cambodia decade, 1979–1989," in Odd Arne Westad and Sophie Quinn-Judge, eds, *The Third Indochina War: Conflict between China, Vietnam and Cambodia, 1972–79*. London: Routledge, 2006, 207–30.

Vietnamese sailors were killed or drowned when their ship sunk.[65] This was the last military confrontation between China and Vietnam till this day.[66] There has been much speculation that the People's Liberation Army (PLA) was planning to follow up and take over the Vietnamese held islets in the Spratlys during 1989, but these plans were apparently delayed, perhaps because of Soviet leader Mikael Gorbachev's visit to Beijing in June 1989 and the demonstrations on Tian An Men square. Foreign policy as well as domestic concerns may thus have forced the Chinese Communist Party to concentrate on matters of regime security instead of expanding China's national territory.

In 1991, when the peace agreement for Cambodia was signed, China and Vietnam also upgraded their diplomatic and party-to-party relations to a normal level, and in the following decade China pursued an astute "elder brother" policy, paying an appropriate amount of attention to Vietnam. The two countries opened their border to trade, and Chinese products gradually penetrated the Vietnamese market. Investments followed. Based on a well-established policy of enhancing its national security through border agreements with its surrounding states, China's leader Jiang Zemin made a solemn pledge together with his Vietnamese counterpart to arrive at a full border agreement before 2000. Without this top-level promise there would not have been a land border treaty by 1999 or an agreement on the maritime delimitation of the Tonkin Gulf in 2000. All of this contributed to an astounding improvement of Sino-Vietnamese relations.

China rejected a Vietnamese suggestion to form a new "red alliance" at the time when the Soviet Union fell apart. Subsequently, China did nothing to dissuade Vietnam from normalizing its relationship with the United States. Another aspect of Chinese wisdom in the period was that Beijing encouraged instead of blocking Vietnam's accession to ASEAN in 1995. Vietnam was no longer divided like Korea, and was also not squeezed between China and another great power. Vietnam formed instead a kind of bridge between two cultural spheres. Vietnam belonged at one and the same time to the Chinese or "Confucian" sphere and the more culturally diverse Southeast Asia. By encouraging Vietnam's membership in ASEAN China prevented a sharp division between the two spheres so it could uphold and further develop its cooperation with ASEAN. This contributed to China's insertion into various frameworks for regional dialogue: ASEAN+3, ASEAN Regional Forum, East Asian Summit. China further improved its regional status by avoiding to be engulfed in the 1997–98 Asian Crisis, and by providing aid to some affected countries. These persistent improvements in Sino-Southeast

65 Lu Ning, *Flashpoint Spratlys!* Singapore: Dolphin Books, 1995, 90–91. Others say 72 or 74 Vietnamese were killed: M. Taylor Fravel, *supra* note 18, at 298.

66 The most detailed accounts in English of the battle for the Paracels in 1974 and the Sino-Vietnamese clash in the Spratlys in March 1988 are in Lu Ning, *ibid.*, 74–86; and 87–93.

Asian relations were only slightly impeded by the South China Sea tension in the 1995–99 period.[67]

However, repeated attempts to make progress also on the larger disputes in the South China Sea have not carried fruit, in spite of the 2002 DoC. The necessary political will has been missing. Vietnam has wanted to discuss the Paracels, but China refuses. China wants joint development, but Vietnam does not want to share its resources with anyone else in areas that cannot be disputed on the basis of the law of the sea.

Ways Forward

Border agreements are always a long time in the making. They result from arduous negotiations by experts on two or more sides, who enmesh themselves in excruciating detail. Border negotiators should at some point get a peace prize. They save future generations from much unnecessary risk. In addition to the work of the experts, border agreements also need courageous leaders. Negotiators can make the necessary concessions only if their political leaders dare to take responsibility.

Experts working on the South China Sea disputes know that they are difficult, but also that they are not irresoluble. Maritime delimitation may be achieved through a combination of bilateral and multilateral negotiations, and by referring a few issues to arbitration, adjudication or just legal clarification by the International Court of Justice in The Hague, the Law of the Sea Tribunal in Hamburg or a special Arbitration Tribunal. If China and Vietnam could agree on a way forward, this might pave the way for a process of dispute resolution with the Philippines, Malaysia and Brunei as well. A procedure would then also have to be found for the Republic of China (Taiwan) and the People's Republic of China to jointly represent the interests of "one China." From Vietnam and ASEAN's perspective it would be helpful if the PRC and the ROC (Taiwan) could agree to let Taiwanese experts have a role in bilateral talks between China and Vietnam. This would for geographical reasons be even more important in talks between China and the Philippines. Moreover, if Taiwan does not play its part, then any future compromise between China and Vietnam might come under criticism in Taiwan, and this could stimulate nationalist opposition in Hong Kong and mainland China.

Vietnam's EEZ and continental shelf claims in the South China Sea are of such importance for its economy and national security that Hanoi cannot and will not rely solely on its friendly relations with China. Vietnam knows that it has much to gain from a strict application of international law. Unless there is rapid progress in bilateral negotiations, Vietnam is therefore likely to continue to undertake a number of actions to counter China's assertiveness:

---

67 Ian Storey, *Southeast Asia and the Rise of China: The Search for Security*. London: Routledge, 2011, 96–8.

- Invest further in its navy and air force, notably by strengthening its small submarine force, and by maintaining and strengthening its military occupation of the Spratly islets. In 2009, Vietnam purchased six Kilo class conventional submarines from Russia, to be delivered in 2014;[68]
- Demonstrate its claim to a 200 nautical mile EEZ and continental shelf by continuing to fish in zones where China upholds a fishing ban, by exploring for oil, and by trying to induce international oil companies to explore for oil and gas under Vietnamese concessions (India declared that its state owned oil company would defy Chinese warnings and continue their oil cooperation with Vietnam before a November 2011 state visit to Vietnam);[69]
- Protest and perhaps seek to physically prevent any Chinese attempt to fish in Vietnam's EEZ or explore for oil and gas on Vietnam's continental shelf;
- Resist any Chinese proposal to jointly explore for oil and gas in areas claimed by Vietnam;
- Further develop a common ASEAN approach to the South China Sea, notably by seeking to agree on a legally binding code of conduct (CoC) between ASEAN and China, and by solidifying agreement among the ASEAN countries that the Spratly islets shall have no more than 12 nm territorial waters;
- Seek to attract American interest in the South China Sea through public diplomacy, upgrading of political consultations, possibly also by purchasing American arms, and by welcoming the US and other navies more frequently in Cam Ranh Bay and other Vietnamese ports.

In 2012–13 Vietnam and the Philippines alternated in the role as targets of Chinese maritime assertiveness. In April–May the main incident was a stand-off at Scarborough Shoal between Chinese fishing boats and surveillance vessels and an ill equipped Philippines naval vessel. The result was that China took control of the Shoal by barring its entrance and maintaining a quasi-permanent presence. Then, in June–July, it was Vietnam's turn when its National Assembly finally adopted the new Maritime Law, which led to strong Chinese reactions. China first upgraded "Sansha City" on Woody Island to prefecture states, and then the Chinese National Offshore Oil Company for purely political reasons offered Chinese concessions in blocks off the coast of Vietnam, where several international oil companies are already active under concessions from Vietnam. Vietnam and the Philippines were unable to obtain full support from all the other ASEAN countries at its top meetings in Phnom Penh in November 2012, during the Cambodian chairmanship. This soured relations both within ASEAN and between ASEAN and China. Then,

68 Carlyle Thayer, *supra* note 1, p. 352.

69 "PM Manmohan Singh to China's Wen Jiabao: Back off on South China Sea," *The Times of India*, 19 Nov 2011, available at: http://articles.timesofindia.indiatimes.com/2011-11-19/india/30419126_1_asean-summit-south-china-sea-east-asia-summit.

on 22 January 2013, came the Philippines counter-move to its Scarborough Shoal "defeat." It requested that the United Nations establish an Arbitration Tribunal between itself and China to settle certain outstanding issues in the South China Sea, which had been discussed since 1995. China refused to take part in appointing members of the Tribunal but since the LOS Convention does not allow a country to prevent arbitration, this will happen all the same. The President of the International Tribunal of the Law of the Sea (ITLOS) has therefore already appointed a member to represent China. The result of the arbitration is difficult to predict. The Tribunal may find a reason to reject the case. If not, then it could rule so strongly in China's disfavour that China would reject by withdrawing from the Convention altogether. This would be a serious setback for international law. It is also conceivable that the Tribunal could reach a verdict that would help China clarify and realize its interests on the basis of international law even without itself participating. The Philippines' request to the UN may be seen as a clever move since it moved the dispute from the military and political to the legal domain, and since this may force China to clarify its maritime claims. On the other hand there is a risk that other processes, such as the CoC negotiations and also bilateral talks between China and Vietnam, may now be put on hold for a long time until the result of the arbitration is known. There is little doubt that the Vietnamese government sympathizes with the Philippines move.[70] Yet Vietnam has not come out openly in support of it. Vietnam is not, like the Philippines, a US ally. Perhaps the Vietnamese leaders also still have a faint hope that there will be some little remnant of socialist solidarity in Xi Jinping and his future successors, or a taint of Confucian benevolence deep down in the heart of the growing Chinese dragon.

All of Vietnam's moves seem dictated by a rational perception of Vietnam's national interest. Since it does not have any ally, Vietnam must resort to a kind of "hedging strategy," using all kinds of opportunities to increase the cost to China of an assertive policy. Any Vietnamese government would most probably have pursued this strategy, although a non-communist leadership might perhaps have gone further in soliciting US and Japanese help. It would seem that Vietnam runs a greater risk than the Philippines of becoming involved in a military confrontation with China, since a Chinese attack on the Philippines would be more likely to provoke a forceful US reaction than an attack on Vietnam.

The ideological affinity between Vietnam and China could be a diplomatic advantage for Hanoi. The shared concern of the two communist parties for regime security, their shared interest in keeping US influence at bay, the intimacy of their party-to-party relations, and the recent history of successful improvements of economic, cultural and political ties could provide a basis for constructive bilateral negotiations, running in parallel with the more cautious behaviours summarized

70 Carlyle Thayer, "The Philippines' Claim to the UNCLOS Arbitral Tribunal: Implication for Vietnam" Presentation to International Workshop on the Sovereignty Over Paracel and Spratly Archipelagoes—Historical and Legal Aspects. Pham Van Dong University, Quang Ngai City, April 27–28, 2013.

above. Vietnamese negotiators would wish to impress on China the need that both countries feel for a stable international environment in order to continue their economic development. The negotiators would remind each other of how successfully they negotiated the land border and the maritime border in the Gulf of Tonkin.

The two countries agreed in December 2008 to conduct talks about a number of issues, including a possible prolongation southward of the existing maritime boundary at the mouth of the Gulf of Tonkin. Seven discussion sessions were held between the two countries' teams of negotiators during 2010. In 2011, the South China Sea was a topic in many high level meetings between Vietnamese and Chinese representatives.[71] Then the two countries reached their October 11 agreement, on the first day of Secretary General Nguyen Phu Trong's visit to China. In this agreement the two sides basically repeated what they had already agreed upon in 2008. There would be a hotline between the two countries' leaders so as to avoid misunderstandings. There would be co-operation in several "less sensitive" areas, including marine environmental protection, scientific research, search and rescue, disaster reduction and prevention. And there would be further talks about the bay mouth in the Gulf of Tonkin.[72] New talks have since taken place between the two countries' specialists. One option they may have been discussing is to define those areas where China does not dispute Vietnam's EEZ and continental shelf claim, and vice versa. This would help companies, fishermen and government branches to know where they can operate without any risk of interference from the other side.

The negotiations about the Gulf of Tonkin bay mouth are more important than one might think. The boundary inside the Gulf, as agreed in 2000, is a median line between Hainan and the coast of central Vietnam (with some effect being given to Con Co, a small island off the coast of Vietnam).[73] The question is now if the two sides can manage to prolong this line in a southeasterly direction into the South China Sea. This may be tricky, for two reasons:

First, if the principle of equidistance from the two coasts is followed, then the line will point directly towards the Crescent group of the Paracels. At some stage it should therefore bend eastward if the Paracels are Vietnamese, and southward if they are Chinese. The question then becomes how far the line can be drawn without prejudicing the dispute over the Paracels. If Vietnam allows the line to bend southward, this would not necessarily imply that it abandons its sovereignty claim. A possible solution might be to create an agreed zone around the Paracels, similar to the 15 nm zone that was created around Bach Long Vi in the Gulf of Tonkin, and shelve the question of who has sovereignty to resources inside the zone. (China would then continue to control the Paracels and their recognized

71 Carlyle Thayer, *supra* note 1, p. 350.

72 "China, Vietnam sign accord on resolving maritime issues." Xinhua October 12, 2011, available at: http://news.xinhuanet.com/english2010/china/2011-10/12/c_131185606.htm.

73 Zou Keyuan, *supra* note 12, p. 15 and Nguyen Hong Thao, *supra* note 12, p. 26.

zones.) Yet it might be difficult for the two sides to agree on the extension of the zone if they have not decided who has sovereignty to the islands. In order to decide upon the size of the zone the two sides must first agree on whether or not the Paracels shall be treated as a group or as a number of individual islands. Normal practice would be to give each island a separate effect while taking islands in the vicinity into consideration, but China has drawn highly controversial baselines around the whole group as if it were an archipelago.[74] These baselines could complicate the issue.

The second reason why the bay mouth talks are tricky is that a prolongation of the existing maritime border between Hainan and central Vietnam will approach the first of the nine dashes of the Chinese U-shaped line. Vietnam can under no circumstance allow the border to bend so much southward that it co-insides with the dash, which is close to the Vietnamese coast. A boundary line along the dash would violate all existing rules of maritime delimitation. However, if China allows prolongation of the existing boundary in a direction outside of the dash, then this will further clarify that the U-shaped line is not a claim to "maritime territory" or "historic waters" but a way of signalling China's claim to the islands inside it and their maritime zones. While such clarification is highly desirable from the point of view of conflict resolution in the South China Sea as a whole, it would most likely be opposed by those Chinese who persist in interpreting the U-shaped line as a kind of national border. On the other hand, it might be possible for China to clarify the legal meaning of the U-shaped line in bilateral talks with Vietnam and in that way obviate the need for a UN Arbitration Tribunal to undertake this clarification on China's behalf.

The Sino-Vietnamese negotiations on the mouth of the Gulf of Tonkin could set some important precedents for how to delimit maritime zones in the rest of the South China Sea. This is likely to make the negotiations difficult. If against all odds China and Vietnam's negotiators were to reach an agreement based on international law, it could have some highly beneficial effects for the two countries as well as for the rest of the region, and somewhat reduce the importance of the Philippines request to the United Nations.

Conclusion

Both Vietnam and China have a vested interest in resolving their sovereignty disputes in the South China Sea in ways that contribute to facilitating agreements with other claimants as well. One such interest is strategic: If China wants to realize its aim to reduce the US military presence and establish its own naval supremacy, then it must either become a trusted partner of the dominant superpower in the

74 The Paracels cannot legally speaking be an archipelago since China is not an archipelagic state and also because the ratio of land to water in the Paracels does not satisfy the criterion established for archipelagic states in the LOS Convention.

way the United States became a British partner in the late 19th century, or reassure its own neighbors—and not just Russia. If Japan, India, Australia and ASEAN all seek US help as a counter-balancer, then China can give up its dream of a peaceful and secure home region.[75] It is moreover an illusion to think that China can use a strong navy to force its neighbors to give up maritime claims if these claims have a solid basis in international law. Attempted use of force would lead to strong reactions, even from lesser powers. There is little in the history of Vietnam to indicate that it can be forced by China to give up what it sees as its obvious rights. Even if Vietnam were to stand alone, it would be likely to fight for a long time. In order to remove the prospect of such tragedies, Vietnam on its side has a strong strategic interest in reducing the northern threat by resolving its border disputes.

Economically, both Vietnam and China are engaged in efforts to protect remaining fish stocks from overfishing and explore for oil. Fishery management and oil exploration both presuppose a well-defined legal regime. Yet Vietnam and China's oil interests are somewhat different. Vietnam is used to gaining revenue from exporting its raw oil and pay a high price for imported refined oil. Vietnam's economic growth is now, however, so high that it may soon be at the stage that China reached in 1993 when for the first time it became a net oil importer. This may generate a sense of energy insecurity, as has happened elsewhere, and Vietnam will be eager to boost its income by finding more oil and gas. From a Chinese energy security perspective, the main concern is not the revenue from exporting oil but to get oil and gas from production fields in its vicinity. The main point for China is not national sovereignty to the resources, but how soon it can start drilling in areas with good prospects of finding oil. The best geological conditions are not in the main Spratly area, but in eight areas nearer to the coasts of the surrounding states. Hence a quest for oil does not dictate a focus on the Spratly area as such, but calls for recognizing the EEZs of the other coastal states so concessions can be awarded on a sound legal basis. Once the Philippines, Malaysia, Brunei and Vietnam gain recognition for their EEZ and continental shelves, Chinese oil companies can compete for concessions with companies from other countries, or form joint ventures with the companies of the host states. As long as the dispute remains, Vietnam and the Philippines will be adverse to awarding any concession to a Chinese company or enter any kind of "joint development," but will instead favour American, Indian, Japanese or European companies.[76]

75 For a sober assessment of how costly and difficult it would be for China to gain naval supremacy in the South China Sea, and how this could draw resources away from other important areas, see Toshi Yoshihara and James R. Holmes, "Can China Defend a 'Core Interest' in the South China Sea?", 34(2) *The Washington Quarterly*, 2011, 45–59. http://dx.doi.org/10.1080/0163660X.2011.562082. If China should wish to gain permanent control of events in the South China Sea, say Yoshihara and Holmes (p. 52), "it must dramatically accelerate its naval build-up, factoring in the likelihood of U.S. intervention."

76 The Philippines entered into a Joint Marine Seismic Undertaking (JMSU) with China in 2004, and Vietnam joined it in March 2005. However, Manila got second thoughts

It should be emphasized that the oil prospects in the South China Sea are not so promising that they are likely to significantly improve China's energy security. As Nick Owen and Clive Schofield say in a recent analysis of the hydrocarbon potential, even "an optimistic estimate for disputed South China Sea oil reserves does not have the capacity to significantly improve regional energy security." Although oil finds could provide significant contributions to the energy security of small import dependent economies like the Philippines and Taiwan, "the capacity of South China Sea reserves to bridge [the] gap [between China's oil consumption and production] is negligible."[77]

The experience of the 2009–11 tensions could conceivably lead to a reassessment of Chinese and Vietnamese policies in the South China Sea. Their October 11, 2011 agreement to prevent further conflict and keep talking may reflect a realization that they must find a way forward. It seems that the top leaders in Beijing have reigned in their most activist government agencies, asking them to soften their approach, and that the foreign ministry has taken up a more prominent role in handling the South China Sea disputes. The same thing is not necessarily the case on the Vietnamese side, where it seems that the Ministry of Public Security has expanded its powers and taken up a new role in matters of foreign policy. Just like in China, the Vietnamese Foreign Ministry has in general a weak position in top-level decision-making. By contrast, Minister of Public Security Lieutenant-General Tran Dai Quang is one of the most powerful Vietnamese leaders, seemingly working in a close partnership with Prime Minister Nguyen Tan Dung. They seem to grasp the challenge of combining policies needed to protect national and regime security. The Chinese and Vietnamese Communist Parties both need to reduce the challenge represented by domestic opposition groups who seek to exploit nationalist sentiments in order to weaken public support for the communist regimes. Historically the Chinese and Vietnamese Communist Parties gained a high level of national legitimacy by establishing themselves as the leading forces within national liberation and unification movements. Nationalist sentiments have since turned against the communist regimes. This makes it difficult for them to move decisively in the direction of negotiated compromises, since domestic adversaries will exploit this.

When China and Vietnam negotiated their land border and their boundary in the Gulf of Tonkin in the 1990s, they failed to prepare domestic public opinion for the need to make concessions. This led to protests, acrimony and even arrests and

---

about it afterwards when realizing the risks of conducting joint exploration activities with other states in areas that are close to the Philippines. Such areas cannot be under legitimate dispute, but are part of the Philippines EEZ and continental shelf. After a political scandal, where President Glora Macapagal Arroyo was accused of having sold out of the Philippines national interest in return for financial aid, the Philippines let the JMSU lapse in 2008, without much having been accomplished. Nguyen Hong Thao and Ramses Amer, *supra* note 25, p. 343. Clive Schofield and Ian Storey, *supra* note 4, 28.

77 Nick A. Owen and Clive H. Schofield, *supra* note 14, at 820.

prison sentences. Bilateral negotiations over territorial disputes must of course be conducted in secrecy. Still, if the Chinese and Vietnamese leaders commit themselves to a process of serious bilateral negotiations, they need to prepare their public opinions for the necessity of making concessions in the interest of peaceful development. Thus it is not just reprehensible, but also unwise for either of the two regimes to forcefully repress or prevent protest movements.[78] The way forward is to engage with public opinion, explain the benefits of peace and warn against the crudest forms of nationalist impulses.

At some point, the two parties need to approach the two main obstacles to conflict resolution: the Vietnamese claim to the Paracels and the Chinese claim to "relevant" waters around the Spratlys. Twelve years ago, the present author suggested that these obstacles might be overcome through a "big bargain." Vietnam could retract its historical claim to the Paracels, while China could accept that the Spratly islets can have only 12 nm territorial waters. Such a "big bargain" could follow a "small bargain" of the same structure between China and the Philippines concerning Scarborough Shoal.[79] China would not need to abandon its formal claim to the Spratly islets as such, and if the "one China" principle were applied, the claim of the Republic of China (Taiwan) to the largest of the Spratly islets, Itu Aba/Taiping Dao, which has been strengthened by a long period of occupation, could reinforce China's legal position. China would also not need to give up its U-shaped line, just confirm that it means a claim to the islands within it and their maritime zones. The concession China would have to make was to join up with Vietnam's view that the Spratly islets shall have no other effect on maritime delimitation than to generate 12 nm territorial water enclaves around each island or group of islands and reefs. Such a bilateral bargain would open up the venue to full maritime delimitation between all claimants in the rest of the South China Sea. This would allow the littoral states to establish responsible management regimes for fish and other living resources, as well as for oil and gas exploration. Once the maritime borders have been established between Vietnam and China, there will no longer be much objection to cooperation between Chinese and Vietnamese oil companies in developing hydrocarbons. Once the bargain has been made, the threat of a military confrontation will dissipate, so China and Vietnam can join up

78 Carlyle Thayer, "Vietnam: Bad News for Activist Bùi Thi Minh Hang," Thayer Consultancy ABN # 65 648097123, 2012 relates the sad destiny of activist Bui Thi Minh Hang. She engaged herself strongly in protesting China's actions in the South China Sea. After party leader Nguyen Phu Trong had been to China in October 2011, she and others were told to stop demonstrating. She did not comply. Since, says Thayer, she "could not be slapped with the standard charge of conducting propaganda against the state," she was "bundled off under a detention order issued by the Hanoi municipal authorities and sent to a drug rehabilitation camp to undergo two years of hard labor and re-education" instead.

79 Stein Tønnesson, "China and the South China Sea: A Peace Proposal", 31(3) *Security Dialogue*, September 2000, 307–26. The article may be accessed on www.cliostein.com.

with other nations in seeking to curtail military exercises, hydrographic surveys and naval reconnaissance inside the EEZs of coastal states.

The big bargain was not a realistic prospect in 2000, and remains unrealistic today. Vietnamese friends have often told the author how inconceivable it is for any Vietnamese leader to ever give up sovereignty to the Paracels. Conversely, Chinese friends have asked why China should give anything in return for a Vietnamese recognition of Chinese sovereignty to the Paracels, which are already under Chinese control. It has not helped to answer that a sign of strong leadership is to make big concessions in the interest of one's country. General Charles de Gaulle gave up French sovereignty in Algeria in the face of threats and even rebellion from leading French generals, and gained such respect domestically that he was re-elected several times to the presidency. However, Xi Jinping is perhaps not likely to become another de Gaulle. To make concessions in negotiations is risky. However, what could perhaps be possible is to not just disregard the question of ownership to the Spratlys but to the Paracels away. China and Vietnam could jointly draw a maritime boundary around the whole of the Paracels, with no prejudice for the question of sovereignty. Both sides would tacitly know that the western part of that boundary would become the de facto boundary between China and Vietnam, but this would not be mentioned anywhere, and Vietnam could uphold its formal claim to the Paracels.

The best way forward for Vietnam and China may thus be to combine bilateral negotiations and multilateral consultations in a process that disregards the highly emotional matter of sovereignty to islands, while instead focusing on drawing up maritime boundaries.

The question of whether or not the Spratlys are islands with a right to an EEZ of their own is key. The optimal Chinese legal strategy could be to co-operate with the ROC (Taiwan) in seeking to convince other claimants that at least the Taiwan-occupied Itu Aba/Taiping Dao is big enough to sustain human habitation or an economic life of its own, so it can have a substantial EEZ and continental shelf in the southern part of the "doughnut." At any rate China must prepare itself to swallow the bitter but necessary pill of allowing the Philippines, Malaysia, Brunei and Vietnam to assume sovereignty to the resources in the areas west, south and east of the Spratlys—including areas within the U-shaped line—where the prospects of finding oil and gas seem better.

The South China Sea has become a test case for the application of international law. If China and Vietnam can continue to respect and use the law in the way they did when resolving their land border and maritime border in the Gulf of Tonkin, then this would help prove their will to further peaceful development.

Chapter 12
The South China Sea: A Piece in the Global Naval Encirclement Strategy of Taiwan by Mainland China

Daniel Schaeffer

Introduction

The following three facts must be taken into account for the purpose of assessing the situation in the South China Sea:

1. China–US relations are not confident at all. Mistrust between the two countries could be the master word, even if both are trying to do their utmost to keep a kind of dialogue, including in the field of defense, in order to avoid incidents that could degenerate into clashes.
2. It is quite normal that any country in the world wants to ensure its defense as best as possible. However, it may happen that the defensive concerns may become aggressive towards one's neighbors, because the concerned country feels itself obstructed in the implementation of the general scheme it has elaborated to organize its defense.
3. This is the case for China which, beyond the exchanges of courteous visits and good occasional words, considers the US as a potential hostile party, just as the US is not confident at all in future Chinese peaceful behavior.
4. Except North Korea, all the neighboring countries of the two China seas are deeply concerned by the Chinese rising military power.

Japan just recently expressed it in measured words in its yearly white paper on its defense, disseminated on August 2, as noticeable in the following abstracts: "in regards to the issues on conflicting interest with the surrounding countries, including Japan, China's response has been criticized as assertive, and there is a concern over its future direction." "China has been expanding and intensifying its activities in its surrounding waters. Lack of transparency in its national defense policies and its military activities are referred to as a matter of concern for the region and the international community, including Japan, which should require prudent analysis." But, because of such writings, China considers that Japan is spreading the "Chinese threat theory." Because of that, the Japanese white paper was greeted with a strong but expected rebuff from China on August 4.

Southeastern countries, because of the conflicting territorial interests existing in the South China Sea, are afraid that China wants to impose its own solutions by force to solve the problem in order to satisfy its own interests only. The countries directly involved in the dispute, such as Vietnam, Philippines, Malaysia, Brunei, or those which feel genuinely concerned, such as Indonesia and Singapore, are trying to resist the Chinese hegemonic ambitions in seeking peaceful solutions to the situation without giving up their own, even sometimes conflicting, interests. Such a situation helps to create a division between the Southeast Asian countries involved, a division from which China is trying to draw profit. And it partly succeeds in that since Thailand, Cambodia, Laos and Myanmar, even if they do not disapprove of their other partners in their confrontation with China, stay mute on the question of the South China Sea. They do not want to displease China.

In such conditions one of the problems that make the Southeast Asian nations feel not quite so easy is that, if on one hand China is aggressively defending what it considers its sovereign rights in the South China Sea, on the other hand it is meanwhile forwarding apparently peaceful proposals. Among them, as Professor Su Hao demonstrated in Ho Chi Minh City in November 2010, are Chinese proposals for huge multifarious common economic development schemes, among them the Nanning–Singapore corridor development, Greater Mekong Subregional cooperation program, the Pan-Beibu Gulf Economic Cooperation promoted to make the South China Sea a lake of harmony. All of these programs genuinely sound interesting. But behind them is the Chinese will to bind the different countries involved to China in the same way as, in the imperial era, some of them were vassals of the emperors of the Kingdom of the Middle. We might call that the Kingdom of the Middle syndrome.

Another example is the sudden acceptance in principle by China, last year, to negotiate in order to change the ASEAN–China Declaration on the Conduct of Parties (DOC 2002) into a Code of conduct. Presently the very question is why such a sudden change when we know that, when negotiating the DOC, the Chinese never wanted to hear anything about building a code. And if we consider that up to now, in the East China Sea, the frame agreement that was passed in June 2008 between China and Japan to exploit in common the Chunxiao/Shirakaba gas field has not yet been followed by implementation programs (unless I missed some pieces of information), we may imagine how long the negotiations between China and the Southeast Asian nations shall be supposed to last before finally reaching a code of conduct. This question was indirectly answered by Mr Yang Jiechi, the Chinese Minister of Foreign Affairs, on the occasion of the discussions that occurred with the Foreign Ministers of the ASEAN countries in Bali at the end of last July when he said: "when the conditions are ripe, we are willing to discuss with ASEAN to set up the code of conduct on the South China Sea." Such a declaration cuts short the speculations according to which some analysts think that the Bali guidelines issued on July 29 are a start towards negotiations for a

Code of Conduct. As a matter of fact the guidelines only aim "at ensuring concrete implementation of the Declaration on Conduct of Parties in the South China Sea (DOC)."[1]

All these introductory words stress the fact that, in order to ensure its full defense scheme against the presumed hostile forces that could be those of the US and its allies, especially Japan, China absolutely needs to make the South China Sea a sanctuary. But, in the Chinese full general strategic scheme to ensure the defense of China, the South China Sea appears to be only one piece, a major one certainly, but still only one piece, on the wide board of the "play of go" (Wéiqí /围棋) that China is playing to encircle Taiwan and make it later fall back into the fold of the motherland. The purpose of such an encirclement, not so visible presently, is that, if the reunification does not occur peacefully, China remains free to use military force to succeed in its aim while keeping the US away and preventing it from supporting Taiwan. Beyond the official speech advocating the coming back into the fold of the motherland, the main reason that leads China to the recovery of Taiwan is that China wants to enjoy a full access, without any restraint, to the blue waters of the Pacific Ocean. The aim is to enable its navy to be near to the US territories of Hawaï and CONUS, as close as possible. Therefore it is the reason why the US, in contrast, in order to ensure its own security against a presumed threat from China, absolutely needs Taiwan to remain independent. How to justify all these points?

Making the South China Sea a Chinese Sanctuary

As far as making the South China Sea a Chinese sanctuary is concerned, I demonstrated last November 2010, in Ho Chi Minh City, how, by leaning on the nine-dashes line, China is artificially building a justification of its ambitions on the area. Let me resume that here.

The departing point is that China is interpreting the United Nations Convention on the Law of the Sea (UNCLOS) in its own way. As a matter of fact, the Chinese are applying the rule of the straight baselines to the different archipelagos they are claiming, even though such a rule applies to archipelagic States only (Part IV of the UNCLOS) and never to any other kind of archipelago. Any country which would be recognized as the final genuine sovereign over any of these claimed archipelagos should apply the only available regime to them, namely the regime of the islands (Article 121 of UNCLOS).

But, in the present case, we can see that China is applying the regime of the archipelago states to the disputed archipelagos. It does so in the following way:

- concretely to the Paracel islands, as it is described in the Declaration of

1 Dr Jian Junbo, *China averts collision in South China Sea*, available at: http://www.atimes.com/atimes/China/MG29Ad01.html.

the Government of the People's Republic of China on the baselines of the territorial sea, made public on May 15, 1996;

- virtually to the Spratlys, for the time being;
- virtually too to the Macclesfield Bank that China is claiming, even though not any single country may voice any right on the Macclesfield Bank because it is a shoal, a feature permanently submerged at any time of the tide. But claiming sovereignty over a shoal is contradictory with UNCLOS since UNCLOS does not establish any statute for shoals but only for "low-tide elevations" (Article 13). Macclesfield Bank is not a "low-tide elevation." China knows that. It is the reason why, to circumvent the difficulty, China has elaborated the Zhōngshā Qúndǎo (中沙群岛) concept.[2] How does it do that?

In order to do so, China is simply encompassing the following features in a single entity: the geographical Macclesfield Bank; Truro Shoal, which never emerges either; and Scarborough Reef, which is a feature made of four small rocks emerging at low tide. And it is thanks to Scarborough Reef, by the way disputed with the Philippines, that China considers such an intellectual gathering of disparate features as an archipelago around which, for the moment, it virtually draw straight baselines. This is the Zhōngshā Qúndǎo concept. Moreover, what it adds to the inconsistency of this concept is that there is not any single geomorphologic continuity linking the three features. As a matter of fact the Macclesfield Bank and Truro Shoal are separated by a trough which is around 4,000 meters deep.

This is the first series of points or elements to be taken into account.

The second element to be taken into account relates to the rules of crossing the territorial waters and the exclusive economic zones (EEZs) of one country by foreign navies. As far as the crossing of its territorial sea is concerned, China, contrary to Article 17, Part II, Section III of UNCLOS, denies the innocent passage to foreign navies unless the foreign ships first get agreement from Peking. By the way, Vietnam and Indonesia apply the same kind of rules to foreign navies before they are allowed to cross the territorial waters of these two countries.

Moreover China develops some tendencies to apply to its EEZs the rules normally dedicated to territorial waters only. At least one incident with the United States provides some proof of this. The incident happened on April 1, 2001. It involved a US EP-3 Orion surveillance aircraft. On that day, two Chinese J-8 interceptors harassed the American plane by dangerous maneuvers which led to the loss of one J-8 and to the damage of the American plane which was compelled to make an emergency landing on Hainan Island. The incident occurred some 70 miles off the southern coast of Hainan Island, that is to say, not over the Hainan territorial waters but over the Hainan EEZ. That means that the incident was

2 Keyuan Zou, "Scarborough Reef: a new flashpoint in Sino–Philippine relations?" International Boundaries Research Unit, *Boundary and Security Bulletin*, Vol. 7, no 2, (Summer 1999), 71–81.

deliberately provoked by the Chinese fighters, exactly as if they were performing their task of forbidding illegal entry of a foreign plane into Chinese airspace. That means that the Chinese consider that the rules of navigation in their EEZs must be identical with those applying to military navigation in their territorial waters. That is a distorted interpretation of the law of the sea, since the part of sovereignty that one country may enjoy in its EEZ is related only to exclusive economic rights and law enforcement attaching in respect of these economical rights.

As a matter of fact, Article 56 says:

1. In the exclusive economic zone, the coastal State has:
   a. sovereign rights for the purpose of exploring and exploiting, conserving and managing the natural resources, whether living or non-living, of the waters superjacent to the seabed and of the seabed and its subsoil, and with regard to other activities for the economic exploitation and exploration of the zone, such as the production of energy from the water, currents and winds;
   b. jurisdiction as provided for in the relevant provisions of this Convention with regard to:
      (i) the establishment and use of artificial islands, installations and structures;
      (ii) marine scientific research;
      (iii) the protection and preservation of the marine environment;
   c. other rights and duties provided for in this Convention.

And Article 73.1 says:

> The coastal State may, in the exercise of its sovereign rights to explore, exploit, conserve and manage the living resources in the exclusive economic zone, take such measures, including boarding, inspection, arrest and judicial proceedings, as may be necessary to ensure compliance with the laws and regulations adopted by it in conformity with this Convention.

In these texts, there is nowhere a question of any kind of restrictions opposed to foreign navigation in the EEZ of one country, including when the ships are military ones. Therefore the overflight of the EP-3 Orion was not, in any case, performed in contradiction to UNCLOS. The Chinese considered the contrary.

From the two main elements here analyzed, we may draw the following conclusions:

1. From the application of the straight baselines to the disputed archipelagos (that are not archipelagic states), China draws the fact that the nine-dashes line is the median line between what it considers as its insular territories and the adjacent countries of the South China Sea. Wang Xiguang, a researcher who participated in 1947 in the compilation of maps at the Geography

Department of the Ministry of Internal Affairs of the then Republic of China, under the Kuomintang rule, said: "the dotted national boundary line was drawn as the median line between China and the adjacent states."[3]

2. The area encompassed inside the nine-dashes line is considered by China either as an EEZ or as a territorial sea. China is claiming the latter interpretation by following two different schools of thinking. One considers the area as a territorial sea. Another considers it as a historical sea under the pretext that the nine-dashes line is now more than 60 years old and nobody had expressed any opposition to its existence since the Geography Department of the Ministry of Internal Affairs of the then Republic of China, under the Kuomintang rule, printed the Location Map of the South China Sea Islands (*Nanhai zhudao weizhi tu*) in 1947.[4]

By the way it must be remembered here that until May 7, 2009 China never introduced any genuine official claim over the area delineated by the nine- dashes line. The first genuine Chinese official gesture was that of May 7, 2009, when China extended a verbal note to the Commission on the Limits of the Continental Shelf (CLCS) to protest against the two claims that Malaysia and Vietnam introduced to the CLCS for extended continental shelves in the South China Sea. Malaysia and Vietnam extended their common claim on May 6, 2009 for an extended continental shelf situated in the southern part of the sea. Vietnam extended its own one on May 7, 2009 for a second area lying south of the Paracel Islands.

Whatever the interpretation, it shows that China wants to rule the whole area as its own territorial waters, even though, for the time being, China has not yet really the military means nor the political power to definitely forbid foreign navies, especially the US one, to cross the area. It is the reason why presently China is only performing from time to time naval maneuvers in the contentious area and is trying to exert full police operations all over the area such as the yearly unilateral moratoria it imposes on the fishing activities, such as leading police patrols as the Maritime Surveillance Agency did recently with the *Haixun 31*. Between June 15 and 23, 2011, this ship went on sea patrol in the disputed maritime area before paying a

3 Li Jinming and Li Dexia, "The Dotted Line on the Chinese Map of the South China Sea: A Note," *Ocean Development and International Law*, 2003, pp. 287–95. In their paper the authors say that for the purpose of specifying China's territorial sphere in the South China Sea, the Geography Department of the Ministry of Internal Affairs (of the then Republic of China under the Kuomintang rule) printed *The Location Map of the South China Sea Islands* (*Nanhai zhudao weizhi tu*) in 1947. On this map, the Pratas Islands, the Paracel Islands, the Macclesfield Bank, and the Spratly Islands were shown as being part of China with the use of an 11-dot line. The southernmost boundary was marked at 4° northern latitude. According to Wang Xiguang, who participated in the compilation of maps at the Geography Department of the Ministry of Internal Affairs, "the dotted national boundary line was drawn as the median line between China and the adjacent states."

4 Ibid.

six days' courtesy visit to Singapore. It is also the reason why China resorts to relentless verbal pressure against the US to deter it from meddling in the litigation over the South China Sea.

3. Should China one day succeed in having these different interpretations internationally recognized:

    - It would mean that a country might therefore exert claims over the high seas, contrary to Article 89 of UNCLOS, which clearly stipulates that "no State may validly purport to subject any part of the high seas to its sovereignty."
    - It would confer upon China the capacity to forbid foreign navies to sail over that sea since, in such conditions, the part of the sea encompassed inside the nine-dashes line would be considered as the Chinese territorial sea.
    - Consequently it would give China the possibility to forbid the crossing of a Paracels–Zhōngshā Qúndǎo line to foreign navies so that its submarines, following an east-oriented route from Sanya, could safely sail to their deployment areas, either in the deeper northern part of the sea or in the deeper southern parts of the South China Sea, in this case crossing through the Macclesfield Bank–Truro Shoal trench.
    - In the northern part of the South China Sea which, according to the International Hydrographical Organization, includes the Taiwan Strait, it would mean, since mainland and Taiwanese EEZs are connecting, that China could also forbid foreign navies to sail through the Taiwan Strait if it does not want to deliver the authorization for these navies to proceed.

Going farther, we must consider that, even if China should succeed in securing the South China Sea for itself only, its overall strategic security disposition facing the presumed US threat would be a lame one. It is the reason why the South China Sea is only a piece, certainly a major one, but only one, in the Chinese general strategy of the naval encirclement of Taiwan.

The South China Sea: Only One Piece in the Encirclement of Taiwan

In its strategic project, China has to manage two difficulties: the resistance of Taiwan and the presumed US support of Taiwan in the event of aggravation of the relations between Taiwan and mainland China. In this overall configuration, the main problems that China and the US are respectively facing are the following: for China, it is how to contain the US from approaching and from threatening the Chinese territory; for the US it is how to contain the Chinese strategic expansion ambitions and moreover to prevent China from advancing its naval forces too close to the American territories.

In that prospect, the global Chinese strategy is:

- To ensure its forward defense by leaning on the blue line as defined in 1985 by Admiral Liu Huaqing, the former commander of the People's Liberation Army Navy (PLAN), this blue line roughly stretching along the Mariana island chain.
- Consequently, to be able to bring its naval means, especially its ballistic missile submarines, presently two units at least (when they genuinely have come of age), five in the near future, within possible reach of the American territory.
- To prevent the U.S. Navy from approaching too closely the Chinese territory. Therefore, to answer this last point, that is to say how to prevent the U.S. Navy to come at reach of the Chinese territory, including Taiwan, China has, among other means as nuclear attack submarines, started building up aircraft carrier capabilities and an anti-access/area-denial capacity. This anti-access/area-denial capacity partly rests on the use of the aircraft carrier killer missiles DF-21C, the range of which is in excess of 1,500 km, is guided onto the mobile targets by mean of an overhead and over-the-horizon targeting system to locate and track the moving ships.

But that is not enough. As a matter of fact, to ensure its forward defense by leaning on the blue line and consequently enjoy the capability to push its naval means farther enough from China and close enough to the American territory, China must enjoy the most secured accesses to the high sea.

This is one of the reasons why China wants to make the South China Sea and ensure a secured deployment of its submarines from Sanya up to the deepest part of the South China Sea, as I have already explained.

But this is also one of the reasons, and this is certainly the point, the main one, why China at all costs wants to reunify Taiwan to the mainland. It does want it because Taiwan is the bolt which closes the two China seas, two semi-closed seas structurally barred by chains of islands that constitute as many obstacles for navigation and compel ships to cross passes between the islands:

- The East China Sea is closed by the Ryukyus chain (Nansei in Japanese), up to the Senkakus which, morphologically, do not belong to the Ryukyus.
- The South China Sea is closed by the Philippines, Borneo and Indonesia.
- Therefore, when we look at the morphology of this area, any navy which wants to leave one of these two seas to reach the Pacific Ocean is compelled to cross the different straits that are as many holes into the string of these marginal islands. Some of these straits are large, such as the Okinawa–Miyako Strait, which is roughly 150 miles long. But most of them are narrow. Therefore, in crisis time or in wartime, all these different passes may be easily blocked or ambushed provided the number of submarines and of the other naval means are enough to fulfil the task. This is the

> problem with which the Chinese navy is presently confronted when it wants to sail to the blue waters of the Pacific Ocean. And in peacetime, the Chinese navy cannot move without being spotted on any occasion of its crossings through these chains of small islands. Peter Dutton has already described this better than I can in his February 2009 booklet titled *Scouting, Signaling, and Gatekeeping.*

That island morphological dispositions explain why China is so keen in getting back Taiwan, with the Senkaku islands attached. Because recovering Taiwan would provide the PLAN with secure genuine Chinese territorial waters, those around Taiwan, since these waters would have become under its full control, in the north of Taiwan up to the Senkakus, as well as in the south through the Strait of Bashi. The Chinese navy would consequently enjoy a free way to the Pacific Ocean through what would have become its territorial waters. If these passages would be free in peacetime, that would not, in an atmosphere of declared hostilities, prevent hostile forces from displaying an exit-denial strategy in order to forbid the Chinese navy means to sail to the free waters of the Pacific Ocean.

All this indeed clearly explains why, in its global strategy of counter containment of the US, China absolutely wants to recover Taiwan, the bolt which closes or opens access to the high sea.

And this is the reason why China has started a large-scale strategy of naval encirclement of Taiwan, a strategy in which the making a sanctuary of the South China Sea is only one piece, as I already said, on the board of that huge wéiqi, the game of which has already started. The other pieces, some strong, some less convincing, however, are the following:

- The aggressive Chinese behavior in the South China Sea in order to settle its full domination on the area.
- The aggressive Chinese behavior over the sovereignty of the Senkaku Islands.
- The multifarious passages of the Chinese navy through the Japanese straits, the Chinese naval exercises conducted in waters close to Japan, or the Chinese monitoring of Japan–US naval exercises. The 2011 white paper on the defense of Japan relates ten Chinese activities of this type between November 2004 and June 2011. Before that, Peter Dutton, in his February 2009 booklet titled *Scouting, Signaling, and Gatekeeping*, relates some of these activities, but also two similar crossings, in May 2000 and in November 2003, by Chinese ships through Japanese straits other than Okinawa–Miyaki.
- The Chinese naval reconnaissance activities around Guam.
- The Chinese opposition, on February 6 and August 24, 2009 to the Japanese request introduced on November 12, 2008 to the Division of Ocean Affairs and of the Law of the Sea of the United Nations for an extended continental shelf around Okinotori Island, midway between Okinawa and Guam. The

Chinese fear is, should the Japanese claim be accepted, that Japanese and therefore Americans consequently enjoy largest possibilities of checking the PLAN movements on their way up to the blue line and to Guam.

- Finally, when we put all these Chinese naval activities altogether, we cannot help but determine that the general aim is to isolate Taiwan, to exert a strong indirect pressure on the island so that it finally falls into the mainland nets without offering too much resistance and without suffering too much damage, if possible.

This strategic hypothesis and prospective view I have proposed needs of course to be verified, consolidated, deepened or, conversely, denied by proofs other than those I have brought. Through such a presentation, I just wanted, in the general scheme presently under elaboration by China to prepare its overall defense against a presumed hostile posture from the United States and its allies, especially Japan, to bring the strategic reasons why China absolutely needs to recover Taiwan. And in this scheme, this is why China consequently absolutely needs the South China Sea for itself alone. That is why, despite some peaceful proposals from China dedicated to temper the mistrust against it in the region, the international community as a whole, not only the United States, must remain aware that, unless a huge common diplomatic and political pressure is exerted on China, China will firmly want to extend and reinforce its grasp over the South China Sea.

Fortunately, I am not alone in thinking this. Professor Tetsuo Kotani, *Special Research Fellow at the Okazaki Institute in Tokyo*, reached largely the same conclusions and published them on July 18 of this year in the magazine *The Diplomat* in an issue titled "Why China Wants the South China Sea."[5]

We may, of course, understand the Chinese concerns for its defense. But these concerns cannot be the reasons dedicated to make the South China Sea a Chinese sea, as Mussolini tried to make the Mediterranean Sea a *mare nostrum* during the Second World War. The South China Sea is an international waterway and such a statute must remain as such in its full integrity and not under the control of a single nation only.

5 http://the-diplomat.com/2011/07/18/why-china-wants-the-south-china-sea/.

PART V
Taiwan's Participation in the South China Sea Dialogue Process

Chapter 13
Confidence-Building Measures in the South China Sea and Implications for US–Taiwan–China Relations

Cheng-yi Lin

Introduction

Since the naval clashes in Yongxing Island (Woody Island) in the Xisha (Paracel Islands) in 1974, and at Chigua Jiao (Johnson South Reef) in the Nansha (Spratly Islands) in March 1988, military battles have disappeared in waters of the South China Sea. Nevertheless, tensions over national sovereignty and maritime interests have been lingering since then, despite great attention which has been paid to prevent potential conflicts in the Spratly Islands. Starting from 1990, Indonesia, a non-claimant to the Spratly Islands, has initiated an annual Workshop on Managing Potential Conflicts in the South China Sea (hereinafter the SCS Workshop) with the purpose of exchanging views and building confidence among the parties concerned surrounding the South China Sea region. Other Track-II conferences initiated by respective claimant states have been held frequently as tensions re-emerged since 2009. Taiwan is a claimant to the South China Sea Islands but problems of diplomatic recognition have handicapped Taiwan's participation in the solution of territorial disputes in both bilateral and multilateral forums. Where Taiwan stands in its basic positions over sovereignty claims or in a military confrontation embroiled between China and other claimants and non-claimants has become a Catch-22 situation for decision makers in Taipei. Taiwan's siding with the People's Republic of China (PRC) asserting Chinese historical claims in the South China Sea could change power games in the region, but Taiwan's dependence on the US for security protection might also be endangered.

Confidence-building Measures in the South China Sea

Before the establishment of the Council for Security Cooperation in Asia Pacific (CSCAP) in 1993 and the ASEAN Regional Forum (ARF) in 1994, six original ASEAN members, namely Brunei, Indonesia, Malaysia, the Philippines, Singapore and Thailand, issued a declaration on the South China Sea in 1992, urging all parties concerned to exercise restraint for the "eventual resolution of all disputes," and to "explore the possibility of cooperation in the South China Sea relating to the safety of maritime navigation and communication, protection against pollution of the marine environment, coordination of search and rescue operations, efforts towards combating piracy and armed robbery as well as collaboration in the campaign against illicit trafficking in drugs." This declaration was in response to the Chinese Territorial Sea and Contiguous Zone Law, which lays claim to all Spratly islands. More importantly, the declaration called for "a code of international conduct over the South China Sea."[1] This code of conduct partially materialized in the form of a Declaration on the Conduct of Parties in the South China Sea reached between China and ASEAN members in 2002.

There were also talks of confidence-building measures (CBMs) in the SCS Workshop, which inaugurated its first meeting in 1990 and drew government-endorsed participants from China, Taiwan and Vietnam starting from 1991. The SCS Workshop is regarded as the second-track forum, even though most of the participants, including those from Taiwan, are government officials. Taiwan since then has garnered experiences in talking about CBMs with other parties concerned. The SCS Workshop itself is a talk shop to certain observers, but the process is CBMs in a broader sense. Nevertheless, discussion on CBMs "with regard to military activities" has slowed down when met with reluctance from Beijing.[2] Outside powers such as the US and Japan are deliberately excluded from the very beginning. This might partly explain why achievements of the SCS Workshop have centered on functional matters.[3] In the first several years of the SCS Workshop, military CBMs were on the agenda, and in August 1993, Ambassador Hasjim Djalal of Indonesia summarized the proposals of CBMs previously raised in the SCS Workshop, including as follows:

a. non-expansion of existing military presence;
b. no new occupation of islands and reefs which so far are unoccupied;
c. transparency in military presence, military activities and other activities;
d. exchange of visits to each other's facilities either directly, or through the Workshop Group mechanism;
e. organized visits by the participants of the Working Group to the various occupied islands in the Spratly group, in order to increase transparency;

1 ASEAN Declaration on the South China Sea, Manila, Philippines, July 22, 1992, available at: http://www.asean.org/5233.htm.

2 Hasjim Djalal, "The South China Sea: The Long Road towards Peace and Cooperation," in Sam Bateman and Ralf Emmers (eds), *Security and International Politics in the South China Sea: Towards A Cooperative Management Regime* (London: Routledge, 2009), p. 187.

3 Ian Townsend-Gault, "The Contribution of the South China Sea Workshop: the Importance of a Functional Approach," in Bateman and Emmers (eds), ibid., pp. 194–6.

f. freedom of navigation, passage and overflight through the waterways of the Spratly Islands (at least beyond three nautical miles from the islands).[4]

Ironically, Chinese occupation of Mischief Reef in January 1995 ran contrary to the wishes of the above-mentioned CBMs and unleashed a series of conflicts between China and the Philippines. In March 1995, ASEAN Foreign Ministers were prompt to issue a statement, urging "countries in the region to undertake cooperative activities which increase trust and confidence and promote stability in the area."[5] Amidst the heightened tension, Taiwan's maritime police went on a patrol mission and then were forced to return after departure from Dongsha (Pratas) Islands on their way to Taiping (Itu Aba) Island.[6] The aborted mission was badly timed and also pinpointed Taiwan's dilemma in a dispute between China and other claimants. To settle the Mischief Reef dispute and move Sino–Philippines relations forward, Beijing and Manila signed an eight-point agreement in August 1995 committing to undertake CBMs without resorting to the use of force and affirming that the dispute should be settled by countries directly concerned "without prejudice to freedom of navigation in the South China Sea."[7] In March 1996, China and the Philippines also decided to establish three governmental working groups covering fisheries, marine environment protection and CBMs in

---

4 *The Fourth Workshop on Managing Potential Conflicts in the South China Sea*, Surabaya, Indonesia, August 23–25, 1993, p. 32. Other non-traditional security CBMs include: (A) Freedom of scientific research in the waterways of the Spratly Islands (at least beyond three nautical miles). (B)Cooperation of all the involved parties in resource exploration and exploitation of the waterways and their seabed resources (at least beyond 12 nautical miles off the Islands and reefs). (C) Preservation of the areas within 12 nautical miles off each Island and reef in the Spratly group as a marine park, particularly for marine scientific research and eco-tourism. (D) In case there is no specific cooperation proposed on scientific research, freedom of entry and visit of scientists of and certified by the South China Sea participants to the Spratly Islands for scientific programs and purposes. (E)The participating claimants should begin information dialogue, albeit in personal capacities, to discuss the conflicting territorial claims in the MCA with a view to seek ways and means that could be recommended to arrive at a solution to the disputes. They should also discuss the various CBMs outlined above. The Chairman of the Workshop should take initiative in this direction.

5 "Recent Developments in the South China Sea (1995), March 18, 1995," available at: http://www.asean.org/ 5232.htm; Lee Lai To, "ASEAN and the South China Sea Conflicts," 8 (3) *The Pacific Review*, 1995, p. 539; Greg Austin, "Unwanted Entanglement: The Philippines' Spratly Policy as a Case Study in Conflict Enhancement?" 34 (1) *Security Dialogue*, March 2003, pp. 45–6.

6 Cheng-yi Lin, "Taiwan's South China Sea Policy," 37 (4) *Asian Survey*, April 1997, p. 330.

7 "China Assures RP on Spratlys," *Manila Bulletin*, August 12, 1995, p. 6; Kerry Dumbaugh, David Ackerman, Richard Cronin, Shirley Kan, and Larry Niksch, *China's Maritime Territorial Claims: Implications for U.S. Interests,* Congressional Research Service, November 12, 2001, pp. 11–12; Shee Poon Kim, "The South China Sea in China's Strategic Thinking," 19 (4) *Contemporary Southeast Asia*, March 1998, pp. 383–4.

the South China Sea.[8] Coincidentally, Beijing launched the Taiwan Strait missile crisis to threaten voters of Taiwan in their first ever direct election of the national president. Confronting Taiwan and the US in the Taiwan Strait, Beijing simply had no interest in thinking of cross-Strait CBMs in the South China Sea.

In conjunction with the reckless Chinese actions in the Taiwan Strait, it was detected, by the Philippines, that Malaysia had started building structures in 1997 and then occupied Yuya Ansha (Investigator Shoal) and Boji Jiao (Erica Reef) in 1999.[9] Taiwan joined with other claimants such as China, the Philippines and Vietnam in protesting the Malaysian moves. According to Taiwanese sources, Vietnam increased its occupation of islands and reefs from 24 in 1994 to 27 in 2002.[10] In the meantime, expansion of military presence in the Spratly Islands took place on the islands occupied by China, from about 260 in 1996 to 600 troops in 2002, as well as on those occupied by Vietnam, from 600 in 1996 to 2,000 troops in 2002.[11] The PRC and Vietnam are the only two claimants which have taken active measures to strengthen their military presence in the Spratly Islands. Partly due to tensions in the Taiwan Strait from 1996 onwards and partly due to Sino–Vietnam negotiations leading to two agreements on the Delimitation of the Territorial Seas, Exclusive Economic Zones and Continental Shelves in the Beibu Gulf (Gulf of Tonkin) and on Fishery Cooperation in the Beibu Gulf respectively in December 2000, China tried to project an image of constraint and moderation in its South China Sea policies after the occupation of Mischief Reef.[12]

In May 2000, China and the Philippines issued another statement expressing "their determination to follow through the work of the China–Philippines Working Group on Confidence-Building Measures to enhance peace and stability in the region" and pledging that "they will contribute positively toward the formulation

8 Aileen Baviera, *Bilateral Confidence Building with China in Relation to the South China Sea Disputes: A Philippine Perspective* (Ottawa: Canadian Department of Foreign Affairs and International Trade, 2000), available at: http://www.international.gc.ca/arms-armes/isrop-prisi/research-recherche/intl_security-securite_int/baviera2001/section9.aspx?view=d.

9 "KL Deceived Us in Pawikan Shoal—RP," *Manila Times*, June 25, 1999; "Manila, KL Told: China Owns Shoals," *Philippine Daily Inquirer*, June 30, 1999; "ROC Ministry of Foreign Affairs Statement," July 13, 1999.

10 *ROC National Defense Report 1994* (Taipei: Ministry of National Defense, 1994), p. 31; *ROC National Defense Report 2002* (Taipei: Ministry of National Defense, 2002), p. 24.

11 *ROC National Defense Report 1996* (Taipei: Ministry of National Defense, 1996), p. 26; *ROC National Defense Report 2002*, p. 24.

12 Stein Tønnesson, "Sino-Vietnamese Rapprochement and the South China Sea Irritant," 34 (1) *Security Dialogue*, March 2003, pp. 62–5; Keyuan Zou, "the Sino-Vietnamese Agreement on Maritime Boundary Delimitation in the Gulf of Tonkin," 36 (1) *Ocean Development and International Law*, 2005, pp. 14–15.

and adoption of the regional Code of Conduct in the South China Sea."[13] This led to Beijing's signing of an agreement with ASEAN on the Declaration on the Conduct of Parties in the South China Sea (hereinafter DOC) in November 2002. Although the DOC falls short of legally binding status, it is a partial ASEAN way victory to hold China responsible for its policies in the South China Sea. For example, China agreed in the DOC to cooperate with ASEAN on related matters such as marine environmental protection, marine scientific research, safety of navigation and communication at sea, search and rescue operations, and combating transnational crimes. More importantly, China and ASEAN are committed in the DOC to:

- resolve their territorial and jurisdictional disputes by peaceful means, without resorting to the threat or use of force, through friendly consultations and negotiations by sovereign states directly concerned, in accordance with universally recognized principles of international law, including the 1982 UN Convention on the Law of the Sea;
- exercise self-restraint in the conduct of activities that would complicate or escalate disputes and affect peace and stability including, among others, refraining from action of inhabiting the presently uninhabited islands, reefs, shoals, cays, and other features and to handle their differences in a constructive manner;
- intensify efforts to seek ways, in the spirit of cooperation and understanding, to build trust and confidence between and among them, including: (a) holding dialogues and exchange of views as appropriate between their defense and military officials; (b) ensuring just and humane treatment of all persons who are either in danger or in distress; (c) notifying, on a voluntary basis, other Parties concerned of any impending joint/combined military exercise; and (d) exchanging, on a voluntary basis, relevant information.[14]

Taiwan's Ministry of Foreign Affairs immediately issued a statement expressing "its protest and discontent to ASEAN and the PRC" for not inviting Taipei to participate in the discussion of the DOC. The statement also mentioned that since 2000, Taipei has adopted a series of CBMs in the South China Sea, for example, "staff of the Coast Guard Administration, instead of the Armed Forces, are stationed there to enforce the law," so it urged other parties concerned "to seek

---

13 "Joint Statement between China and the Philippines on the Frame Work of Bilateral Cooperation in the Twenty-First Century," November 15, 2000, available at: http://www.mfa.gov.cn/eng/ wjb/zzjg/yzs/gjlb/2762/ 2763/t16139.htm.

14 "Declaration on the Conduct of the Parties in the South China Sea," November 4, 2002, available at: http://www.aseansec.org/13163.htm; See also Aileen S.P. Baviera, "The South China Sea Disputes after the 2002 Declaration: Beyond Confidence-Building," in Saw Swee-Hock, Sheng Lijun, and Chin Kin Wah (eds), *ASEAN-China Relations: Realities and Prospects* (Singapore: Institute of Southeast Asian Studies, 2005), pp. 351–2.

the peaceful development of the region."[15] President Chen Shui-bian committed that Taiwan was willing to accept the spirit of the DOC and he advocated peaceful means of resolving territorial and jurisdictional disputes.[16] On March 15, 2005, China, Vietnam and the Philippines reached a tripartite agreement for joint marine seismic undertaking in the South China Sea, while Taipei was preoccupied with responding to Beijing's adoption of the Anti-Secession Law on the same day.

Maritime conflicts in the South China Sea have erupted from time to time between China and ASEAN claimants even with the conclusion of the DOC and the tripartite agreement. Beijing has continued its efforts to reduce the chance of coordination between ASEAN and the US in the South China Sea. It has also turned out that ASEAN alone cannot shoulder "responsibility for conflict prevention mechanism" without US involvement.[17] China and ASEAN created a Joint Working Group on the Implementation of the DOC, which was designed to hold meetings twice each year, but they were suspended in 2007 and 2009 (see Table 13.1). The guidelines for the implementation of the DOC became a source of contention.[18]

Table 13.1 ASEAN–China Joint Working Group on the Implementation of the DOC

1st meeting	August 2005	Manila
2nd meeting	February 2006	Hainan, China
3rd meeting	March 2008	Brunei
4th meeting	April 2010	Hanoi
5th meeting	December 2010	Kunming, China
6th meeting	April 2011	Medan, Indonesia

Source: Compiled by the author.

15 "Statement of the Ministry of Foreign Affairs concerning the Declaration on the Conduct of Parties in the South China Sea signed by the Association of Southeast Asian Nations (ASEAN) and the People's Republic of China (PRC) in Cambodia on November 4, 2002," ROC Ministry of Foreign Affairs, November 5, 2002, available at: http://www.mofa.gov.tw/webapp/ct.asp?xItem=2357&ctNode= 1902& mp=6.

16 President Chen Shui-bian's remarks at Taiping Island, see ROC Office of the President, *News Releases*, February 2, 2008, available at: http://www.president.gov.tw/Default.aspx?tabid=131&itemid= 13462&rmid=514&word1=%e5%8d%97%e6%b2%99.

17 Lisellotte Odgaard, "The South China Sea: ASEAN's Security Concerns about China," 34 (1) *Security Dialogue*, March 2003, p. 23; Lee Lai To, "China, the USA and the South China Sea Conflicts," 34(1) *Security Dialogue*, March 2003, p. 37.

18 Nguyen Hong Thao, "The Declaration on the Conduct of Parties in the South China Sea: A Vietnamese Perspective, 2002–2007," in Bateman and Emmers (eds), *Security and International Politics in the South China Sea*, p. 218.

Even though the strategic value of the islands in the Spratlys is debatable, the US government has maintained that its adamant interest is in freedom of navigation, and indicated a neutral position on the claims of disputants on specific islands or reefs in the Spratlys.[19] In 2007, one observer argued that the likelihood of the US and the PRC becoming embroiled "in a military showdown" over freedom of navigation is "extremely remote."[20] However, starting in the summer of 2007, the US has constantly lodged its protests to China over Beijing's attempts to stop US and foreign oil and gas firms from working with Vietnam in the South China Sea.[21] A series of standoffs in the South China Sea between China and the US erupted in 2009. In March 2009, the USNS *Impeccable* was harassed by five Chinese ships in the South China Sea and accused of conducting illegal activities in the Chinese exclusive economic zone; this forced the USS *Chung-Hoon* (DDG-93) to be dispatched to protect the *Impeccable*.[22] A second close encounter happened in June 2009, when a sonar array being towed by the USS *John McCain* (DDG-56) near Subic Bay collided with a Chinese submarine off Subic Bay. The US again protested Chinese attempts "to place limits on the exercise of high seas freedom within an exclusive economic zone (EEZ)" and established high-level defense policy dialogue with Vietnam and Malaysia in 2009 to safeguard maritime security in the South China Sea.[23] The Pentagon issued a warning that "a stronger regional military presence would position China for force projection, blockade, and surveillance operations to influence the critical sea lanes in the region."[24]

US Secretary of State Hillary Clinton indicated that the Obama Administration has resumed a focus on Southeast Asia by signing the ASEAN Treaty of Amity and Cooperation, and she raised the South China Sea issue at the ARF in July 2010 by offering to facilitate moves to create a Code of Conduct in the region. She also said to other members that "legitimate claims to maritime space in the South China Sea

---

19 Dumbaugh, Ackerman, Cronin, Kan, and Niksch, *China's Maritime Territorial Claims*, Congressional Research Service, November 12, 2001, p. 9; Geoffrey Till, "The South China Sea Dispute: An International History," in Bateman and Emmers (eds), *Security and International Politics in the South China Sea*, pp. 36–7.

20 Ian Storey, *The United States and ASEAN-China Relations: All Quiet on the Southeast Asian Front*, October 2007, Strategic Studies Institute, U.S. Army, p. 32.

21 Testimony of Deputy Assistant Secretary Scot Marciel, Bureau of East Asian and Pacific Affairs, U.S. Department of States, before the Subcommittee on East Asia and Pacific Affairs, Committee on Foreign Relations, United States Senate, July 15, 2009, available at: http://foreign.senate.gov/imo/media/doc/MarcielTestimony090715p1.pdf.

22 Chris Rahman and Martin Tsamenyi, "A Strategic Perspective on Security and Naval Issues in the South China Sea," 41 *Ocean Development and International Law,* 2010, p. 326.

23 Testimony of Deputy Assistant Secretary of Defense Robert Scher, Asian and Pacific Security Affairs, Office of the Secretary of Defense, before the Subcommittee on East Asia and Pacific Affairs, Committee on Foreign Relations, United States Senate, July 15, 2009, available at: http://foreign.senate.gov/imo/ media/doc/ScherTestimony090715p1.pdf.

24 Office of the Secretary of Defense, *Military and Security Developments Involving the People's Republic of China 2010*, August 2010, p. 51.

should be derived solely from legitimate claims to land features."[25] In a statement posted on July 25, 2010 on a Chinese government website, Foreign Minister Yang Jiechi sharply criticized the US for internationalizing the South China Sea issue, which he claimed would only make matters worse and complicate the situation. For Beijing, the best way to solve the disputes is through bilateral negotiations between China and individual claimants without interference from non-claimants including the US and Japan.[26]

In addition to US objection to Chinese effort to intimidate American oil companies, Vietnam registered its protest to Beijing for putting pressure on British Petroleum to abandon a joint project with Vietnam in the Spratly Islands in 2008. Hanoi is also concerned about the Chinese sending their fishing regulation cruisers and coast guard ships into the waters of the Paracel and Spratly Islands regularly starting from 2009, and therefore decided to purchase six Russian kilo 636-class submarines to counterbalance China's growing military presence in the region.[27] Vietnam has continued to protest a Chinese tourism plan to the disputed islands and the Chinese moratorium on fishing for three months each year in the South China Sea.[28]

In March 2011, Filipino oil exploration vessels were harassed by China's ships in waters near Reed Bank occupied by the Philippines, which later sent UN Secretary-General Pan Ki-wen a note protesting China's sovereignty claims within the nine dotted lines in the South China Sea. On May 26 and June 9, 2011, Vietnamese oil exploration ships were harassed by Chinese National Marine Surveillance Ships and Fishing Administration Ships in waters closer to Vietnam than to Hainan Island. These two incidents resulted in growing anti-Chinese sentiment in Vietnam, where hundreds of people staged a rare protest over the activities of Chinese ships in disputed waters. This led to Vietnamese government issuance of rules on conscription in war times on June 15, 2011 and dispatch of its Vice Foreign Minister Ho Xuan Son to Beijing to calm the waters in the

---

25 John Pomfret, "U.S. Takes a Tougher Tone with China," *Washington Post*, July 30, 2010.

26 "Foreign Minister Yang Jiechi Refutes Fallacies on the South China Sea Issue," July 26, 2010, available at: http://www.fmprc.gov.cn/eng/zxxx/t719460.htm; Edward Wong, "Beijing Warns U.S. About South China Sea Disputes," *New York Times*, June 22, 2011.

27 Lucy Hornby, "China May Boost Patrols in South China Sea," *Reuters*, March 19, 2009; John Pomfret, "Concerned about China's Rise, Southeast Asian Nations Build up Militaries," *Washington Post*, August 6, 2010; "Navy to Have Submarine Brigade in 5–6 Years: Minister," August 3, 2011, available at: http://en.www.info.vn/society/facts/32377-navy-to-have-submarine-brigade-in-5-6-years-minister.html.

28 " VN Opposes Plan for China Tourism," *Vietnam News*, June 25, 2010, available at: http://vietnamnews.vnagency.com.vn/Politics-Laws/200891/VN-opposes-plan-for-China-tourism.html; "VN Opposes China's East Sea Fishing Ban," *Vietnam News*, May 14, 2011, available at: http://vietnamnews.vnanet.vn/Politics-Laws/211289/VN-opposes-Chinas-East-Sea-fishing-ban-.html.

Spratly Islands.[29] Chinese harassment of US, Vietnam and Philippine ships also led to Senator Jim Webb (D-VA) initiating Senate Resolution 217 (June 2011) to condemn repeated use of force by naval and maritime security vessels from China in the South China Sea and to support "the continuation of operations by the United States Armed Forces to assert and defend freedom of navigation rights in international waters and air space in the South China Sea."[30]

After Secretary Clinton's remarks at the ARF meeting in Hanoi in 2010, China and ASEAN decided to conduct intensive discussions leading to the agreement on DOC implementation guidelines right before the ARF meeting in Bali in July 2011. These implementation guidelines are also flexible and provide room for different interpretations; they indicate a new phase of development in the South China Sea because China and ASEAN, particularly those claimants, will carry out the provisions of the DOC "in a step-by-step approach," "on a voluntary basis" and "based on consensus among parties concerned, and lead to the eventual realization of a Code of Conduct." After repeated incidents and military skirmishes in the South China Sea since 1974, China and ASEAN members once again have determined to target CBMs in their initial cooperative activities, but progress of the implementation "shall be reported annually to the ASEAN–China Ministerial Meeting (PMC)."[31] While the US welcomes the implementation guidelines agreement, Taiwan again was left outside the negotiation process, therefore it refuses to recognize any agreements regarding the South China Sea without its participation in the process.[32]

Taiwan's Participation in South China Sea Workshops

Compared to other claimants to Spratly Islands, Republic of China (ROC) on Taiwan has exercised the longest period of jurisdiction in the South China Sea. Taiwan has been moderate in its South China Sea policy from the very beginning in 1949 and took no concrete actions when its claimed islands were occupied by other claimants. Due to the lack of diplomatic relations with any ASEAN

29 "Vietnam Issues Rules on Conscription in War Times," June 13, 2011, available at: http://en.www.info.vn/society/more/28621-vietnam-issues-rules-on-conscription-in-war-times.html; Edward Wong, "China and Vietnam Agree to Talks on South China Sea Dispute," New York Times, June 26, 2011.

30 "Senators Webb, Inhofe Introduce Resolution Condemning China's Use of Force in South China Sea," June 13, 2011, available at: http://webb.senate.gov/newsroom/pressreleases/06-13-2011-02.cfm; See also William Lowther, "US Resolution Calls for Freedom to Navigate Strait," *Taipei Times*, July 17, 2011, p. 1.

31 "Guidelines for the Implementation of the DOC," July 20, 2011, available at: http://big5.fmprc.gov.cn/gate/big5/ www.mfa.gov.cn/chn/gxh/tyb/wjbxw/t844329.htm; Yu Yan, "Bridge over Troubled Water," *Beijing Review*, Vol. 54, No. 31 (August 4, 2011), pp. 10–13.

32 ROC Ministry of Foreign Affairs, *News Releases*, July 20, 2011, available at: http://www.mofa.gov.tw/webapp/ ct.asp?xItem=53456&ctNode=1547&mp=1.

members and long duration of cross-Strait relations, Taiwan has been handicapped in participating in multilateral institutions such as the ARF or becoming a dialogue partner of ASEAN. ASEAN Spratlys' claimants have indicated concern over Taiwan's presence in the region but they fall short of negotiating with Taipei over the South China Sea issue. The main reasons for not doing so are probably that Taiwan is not a source of tension or problems for ASEAN, and there is no need to provoke reactions from Beijing over a government-to-government negotiation with Taiwan. Even in the Taiwan–ASEAN ISIS annual dialogue, the South China Sea has hardly become a major theme for this Track-II forum. The PRC is also successful in blocking the discussion of Spratly Islands disputes by the CSCAP, in which Taiwan has participated since the mid-1990s in the capacity of "other participants."

In 1991, Taiwan and China began their participation in the South China Sea Workshop and maintained a tacit partnership in the process before cross-Strait relations turned sour in 1995. Taiwan's participation was not due to Beijing's unilateral and turnaround policy of giving Taiwan a say in the South China Sea, but rather was under the context of cross-Strait secret envoy dialogue (1991–5) approved by Presidents Lee Teng-hui and Jiang Zemin. Both Taiwan and China insist that islands and reefs within the nine dotted (U-shaped) lines belong to the ROC or the PRC. With the basis of identical sovereignty claims in the South China Sea, China and Taiwan can easily treat each other as a natural ally vis-à-vis other ASEAN claimants. It is hard to imagine Taiwan publicly protesting against Chinese claims in the South China Sea or vice versa. When cross-Strait relations were calm from 1991 to 1995, participants from Taiwan and China had some form of coordination on the sidelines of the SCS Workshop.

Before the missile crisis in the Taiwan Strait in 1996, Taiwan's participants spoke in a tone similar to that of the Chinese. For example, Taipei was opposed to the internationalization and institutionalization of the SCS Workshop for fear of being excluded if the Workshop turned into an intergovernmental organization. Taiwan had some reservations about inviting non-claimants to attend the South China Sea Workshop.[33] Taipei also showed a negative position regarding military transparency, the freeze on the number of stationed troops and the prohibition of military exercises in the South China Sea.[34] In the eyes of other ASEAN claimants, Taiwan acted like a junior partner of China in the SCS Workshop. Participants from Taiwan were designated "Taiwan, China" and "Taipei, China," before modification into "Chinese Taipei."

Taiwan supports the idea of temporarily shelving the sovereignty dispute in order to explore ways of joint development in the South China Sea. Taiwan

33 Steven K.T. Yu, "Institutional Mechanism for Cooperation," in *The Third Workshop on Managing Potential Conflicts in the South China Sea*, Yogyakarta, June 28–July 2, 1992, p. 243.

34 *The Fifth Workshop on Managing Potential Conflicts in the South China Sea*, Bukittinggi, Indonesia, October 26–28, 1994, pp. 20–1.

is always prepared to cooperate with other claimants with respect to marine environmental protection, marine scientific research, safety of navigation and communication, exploration and exploitation of resources, search and rescue operations, and combating transnational crime such as piracy and armed robbery at sea. Taiwan also actively participated in Technical Working Groups (TWGs) on Legal Matters, Marine Scientific Research, on Marine Environment Protection, on Navigation, Shipping and Communication, on Resources Assessment and Ways of Development, and Study Group on Zones of Cooperation under the process of the SCS Workshop before these working groups ceased to function upon termination of Canadian government sponsorship in 2001. However, Taiwan's offer to sponsor TWG activities, particularly Navigation, Shipping and Communication meeting, or Groups of Experts meetings (GEMs) was never actualized, due to the opposition from Beijing.[35] Nevertheless, Taipei has continued to serve as a generous donor since its first participation in the SCS Workshop.

As cross-Strait relations deteriorated starting from 1996, President Lee Teng-hui set the guidelines of not cooperating with Beijing on the South China Sea issue, and initiated a long period of cool interactions between participants from both sides of the Taiwan Straits in the SCS Workshop. Beijing was opposed to Taiwan's proposal to hold Southeast Asia Ocean Network for Education (SEAONE) meeting from 2004 to 2007, and instead suggested an initiative of Education, Training Course and Exchange on Marine Science and Technology.[36] The impasse was resolved when President Ma came to power on May 20, 2008 through accepting the 1992 Consensus, or one China with different interpretations, and cross-Strait tacit coordination re-emerged in the SCS Workshop. In the November 2008 SCS Workshop, participants from Taipei and Beijing agreed to cooperate in the later approved project of the South East Asia Network for Education and Training (SEA-NET). For the very first time, delegates from Taiwan and China agreed to take turns in sponsoring a training seminar for South China Sea experts. The Chinese (Taiwan) Society of International Law, under the sponsorship of Taiwan's Ministry of Foreign Affairs, conducted the training program in August 2010, discussing issues such as regional cooperation, joint development and marine environmental protection in the South China Sea.[37] As cross-Strait relations have become warmer and warmer, participants from Taipei and Beijing even extended their cooperation into entertainment activities via singing the same folk song in front of other participating parties at the SCS Workshop in 2010.

35 Ibid., pp. 14–16; ROC Office of the President, *News Releases*, September 1, 1997, available at: http://www.president.gov.tw/Default.aspx?tabid=131&itemid=4618&rmid=514&word1=%e5%8d%97%e6%b5%b7.

36 Yann-huei Song, "The South China Sea Workshop Process and Taiwan's Participation", 41 *Ocean Development and International Law*, 2010, p. 262.

37 "Statement of the 20th Workshop on Managing Potential Conflicts in the South China Sea," Bandung, Indonesia, November 1–3, 2010, pp. 5–7.

In addition to the SCS Workshop, which deliberately avoided the sensitive sovereign and security issues, Taiwan was also heavily involved in other Track-II South China Sea seminars and workshops, particularly the one initiated by Pacific Forum CSIS in the US and the Institute of Strategic and Development Studies (ISDS) in the Philippines (see Table 13.2). These two think tanks held four rounds of workshops on the South China Sea, attracting more participants from non-Spratlys claimant countries starting from November 1995.[38] The initiative was suspended in April 2001 with the publication of two volumes of reports related to CBMs on the South China Sea. Taiwan dispatched participants and made financial contribution to the initiative, and sponsored the fourth workshop in Taipei in April 2001 discussing the theme "CBMs in the South China Sea and Taiwan's Involvement." Taiwan's predicament in not being able to join the negotiation of the code of conduct in the South China Sea became one of the pertinent issues, and Taiwan joining and signing the document as a "cooperative entity" was suggested. The report also argued that "unless China and ASEAN devise a way to bring Taiwan into the Code of Conduct discussion in some meaningful way, the Code will be ineffective and perhaps even counterproductive or destabilizing."[39]

Table 13.2 South China Sea Workshop Conducted by Pacific Forum CSIS and ISDS, Philippines

Security Implications for Conflict in the South China Sea, Manila, November 1995
Promoting Trust and Confidence in Southeast Asia: Cooperation and Conflict Avoidance, Manila, October 16–19, 1997
South China Sea Workshop on Confidence-Building Measures, Jakarta, March 2000
CBMs in the South China Sea and Taiwan's Involvement, Taipei, April 2001

Source: Compiled by the author.

To reduce Taiwan's animosity towards China for being excluded from deliberation of a regional code of conduct in the South China Sea, Beijing started an annual cross-Strait South China Sea Workshop in November 2001 (see Table 13.3). This series of workshops has turned out to be the longest academic but policy-oriented exchanges between Taiwan and China. The Chinese Ministry of Foreign Affairs has designated the National Institute for South China Sea Studies (NISCS) in Hainan as the focal point for bilateral cooperation and contacts with the Taiwan counterpart, the Institute of International Relations (IIR), National Chengchi

38 Carolina G. Hernandez and Ralph Cossa (eds), *Security Implications of Conflict in the South China Sea: Perspectives from Asia-Pacific* (Manila: Institute for Strategic and Development Studies, 1997), pp. 3–7.

39 Scott Snyder, Brad Glosserman, and Ralph Cossa, "Confidence Building Measures in the South China Sea," *Issues and Insights*, No. 2-01 (August 2001), pp. 17–18.

University over the South China Sea issue. This asymmetrical style of cooperation has demonstrated China's strategic plan in dealing with Taiwan and ASEAN along two different tracks. It has served more as a forum to convey the concerns of one side to the other than as a platform to dig for common ground and close cooperation. However, this dialogue process to a certain extent could be regarded as practice of cross-Strait CBMs in the South China Sea; on the other hand, it might also be perceived as a balancing act vis-à-vis a third party.

Table 13.3 IIR/NISCS Cross-Strait SCS Workshop Series, 2001–11

November 14–15, 2001	Taoyuan, Taiwan
September 27–29,2002	Haikou, Hainan, China
January 10–12, 2004	Bo'ao, Hainan, China
May 21, 2005	Taipei, Taiwan
November 28, 2006	Haikou, Hainan, China
November 22, 2007	Taipei, Taiwan
January 12–13, 2009	Haikou, Hainan, China
November 30–December 1, 2009	Taipei, Taiwan
January 14–17, 2011	Bo'ao, Hainan, China

Source: Compiled by the author.

The government in Taiwan has simply given little attention to these Track-II activities under the Chen Shui-bian Administration or little support under that of Ma Ying-jeou in order to avoid a perception of cross-Strait government-to-government cooperation in the South China Sea. On the tenth anniversary of the cross-Strait South China Sea Workshop, an assessment report was produced with the recommendations, from two heads of the project, Professors Fu-kuo Liu from Taiwan and Shicun Wu from China, calling for setting up a cross-Strait South China Sea management and coordination commission, and more surprisingly a military coordination mechanism to handle a South China Sea crisis. They also argued that, if necessary, both Taiwan and China should create positive conditions for joint patrol of the South China Sea.[40] This proposal is common and popular in China but for sensible scholars and practitioners in Taiwan seems to go too far and thus arouses criticism and suspicion within the island. It will be misleading if Beijing or other interested observers perceive this joint academic study as evidence representing the thinking of the Ma Ying-jeou government.

40 *An Assessment Report of the South China Sea Regional Situation in 2010* (Taipei: Institute of International Relations and National Institute for South China Sea Studies, 2011), pp. 100–2.

Implications for US–China–Taiwan Relations

When cross-Strait relations were sour from 1996 to 2008 under the Lee Teng-hui and Chen Shui-bian governments, Taipei ruled out the option to cooperate with the PRC as Beijing in the Diao-yu-tai (Senkaku) Islands in the East China Sea.[41] The basic stand is still upheld by the Ma Ying-jeou government, even with the improvement of cross-Strait relations. Taiwan has consistently been somewhat ambivalent about cross-Strait cooperation in the South China Sea. It was impossible for President Chen or the Democratic Progressive Party (DPP) government to side with China vis-à-vis other ASEAN claimants in the South China Sea while Beijing continued to apply coercive measures against Taiwan.[42] However, Taipei has never expressed explicitly and clearly as it does in the Diao-yu-tai issue that it will not cooperate with the Beijing in the South China Sea. Taiwan's Chinese Petroleum Corporation continued its joint exploration contract with the mainland Chinese counterpart in northern waters near Dongsha Island as cross-Strait tensions lingered in the 1990s. Taiwan has been hesitant to apply a similar practice in waters near the Diao-yu-tai to avoid antagonizing Japan.

As tensions between Taipei and Beijing persisted during the Chen Shui-bian government, Taipei was concerned about the possibility of Beijing's use of force or other forms of coercion in the South China Sea, in addition to the main front facing the Taiwan Strait. According to the US Pentagon annual report on the PRC military and security developments, it has continued to warn of a scenario of a Chinese amphibious invasion of Taiping Island and Dongsha Island since 2008.[43] While facing tensions in the Taiwan Strait, President Chen constantly emphasized the importance of maritime interests, which are regarded as one of the nine major security threats to the country. The *2006 National Security Report* urged the government to elevate the status of maritime affairs' decision making and to "utilize oceanic resources for sustainable development, interact with other democratic maritime countries, and together respond to threats from the sea."[44] In addition to establishing Dongsha Island as a sixth national park of Taiwan in 2007, the DDP government completed building an airstrip on Taiping Islands in 2008. President Chen Shui-bian visited Dongsha Island on three occasions, first in December 2000, second in July 2005 and third in February 2008. The readjustment of control from the Ministry of National Defense to the Coast Guard

41 See ROC Statement on Diao-yu-tai, Ministry of Foreign Affairs, March 2011, available at: http://www.mofa. gov.tw/webapp/ct.asp?xItem=40531&ctNode=2038&mp=1.

42 J. Michael Cole, "DPP Issues Statement on South China Sea Tensions", *Taipei Times*, July 25, 2011, p. 3.

43 Office of the Secretary of Defense, *Military Power of the People's Republic of China 2008*, pp. 43–4; Office of the Secretary of Defense, *Military and Security Developments Involving the People's Republic of China 2010*, p. 51.

44 *2006 National Security Report* (Taipei: National Security Council, 2006), p. 93.

Administration might help smooth further infrastructure development of Dongsha Island and Taiping Island. However, the airstrip in Taiping Island is deemed by other claimants as having military ramifications.

It is unimaginable that the PRC will consider a coercive option against Taiping Island and Dongsha Island while the KMT (Chinese Nationalist Party) government retains power in Taiwan. This does not imply that the US is relieved, because the possibility of cross-Strait cooperation in the South China Sea has been widely discussed among observers. If there is a peaceful cross-Strait relationship, Taipei and Beijing might have more chance to explore realms of cooperation both in the Taiwan Strait and in the South China Sea.[45] Facing global financial crisis and high gasoline prices, President Ma was eager to order studies of cross-Strait joint oil exploration in the South China Sea soon after he seized power from the DPP. Cross-Strait cooperation projects in oil exploration in the northern part of the South China Sea were revived in December 2008, when oil corporations from both sides of the Taiwan Strait signed an MOU to extend exploration surveying into December 2010. The Bureau of Energy under Taiwan's Ministry of Economic Affairs even drafted a cross-Strait energy cooperation agreement with China covering areas of the Taiwan Strait and the South China Sea, but it has not been implemented as studied.[46] Cross-Strait joint exploration of oil and natural resources might not be as sensitive as a united front in countering ASEAN claimants in their activities within the waters of the U-shaped lines in the South China Sea. While the Obama administration has been challenging Chinese legal claims in the Spratly Islands, it is also implicitly opposed to Taiwan's similar legal perspectives on the South China Sea waters. Simply put, identical legal claims of Taiwan and China run counter to the US position that not all islands and reefs belong to either China or Taiwan, even though the US has maintained a neutral position on the legal merits of the various territorial claims.

Facing pressure from the US and ASEAN, Beijing has been more eager to enlist Taiwan to jointly assert Chinese sovereignty in the South China Sea. Beijing has been appreciative of Taiwan's contribution in safeguarding Taiping Island, while China was absent before 1988 in the region. As cross-Strait relations become warmer and warmer, military analysts in China have been anxious to propose joint cooperation, studies, development, patrol and defense of the sovereignty in the South China Sea.[47] If China could utilize Taiping Island as a logistics base in

---

45 Bonnie S. Glaser, "China's Approach to CBMs with Taiwan: Lessons from China's CBMs with Neighboring Countries," in Roger Cliff, Philip Saunders, and Scott Harold (eds), *New Opportunities and Challenges for Taiwan's Security* (Santa Monica: RAND, 2011), p. 21.

46 "A Study of Cross-Strait Energy Cooperation Agreement," Ministry of Economic Affairs, ROC, December 14, 2008, available at: www.open.nat.gov.tw/OpenFront/report_download.jspx?sysId=C09702767.

47 See Major General Luo Yuan's remarks in the *China Review*, March 15, 2010, http://www.chinareviewnews.com/doc/1012/6/0/0/101260078.html?coluid=7&kindi

any potential military conflicts, Beijing believes that it could further consolidate Chinese sovereignty in the South China Sea.

Some analysts in the US are worried that collaboration between China and Taiwan in the South China Sea will complicate the US's own relations with Southeast Asian countries.[48] Better cross-Strait relations might symbolize the disappearance of Taiwan as a buffer between ASEAN and China over the Spratly disputes. These kinds of observations are not groundless for several reasons. Cross-Strait CBMs initiated by Taiwan have been under study, not only in the Taiwan Strait, but also in the South China Sea including "exchange of monitoring information on activities taken by other claimants" and "setting up hotlines or notification mechanisms to assist stationed military and coast guard personnel."[49] As mentioned above, participants from Taiwan and China agreed in the SCS Workshop in 2009 that Taipei and Beijing could take turns to sponsor a marine scientific research training seminar in 2010 and 2011. Taipei and Beijing reacted strongly in March 2009 over Filipino legislation that defines the archipelagic baselines of the Philippines as including the disputed islands and reefs in Kalayaan (Spratly) Islands and nearby Scarborough Shoal.[50] In May 2009, Taiwan and China respectively issued a protest to a joint submission of claims by Malaysia and Vietnam to jurisdiction over their continental shelf beyond 200 nautical miles to the Commission on the Limits of the Continental Shelf (CLCS).[51] Retired generals and think tanks closely affiliated with the KMT in Taipei were publicly proposing cooperation with Beijing in the South China Sea.[52]

ASEAN claimants to the Spratly Islands, particularly Vietnam and the Philippines, do not want to see better cross-Strait relations leading to Taipei–Beijing collaboration in the Spratly Islands.[53] For them, direct negotiation with China rather than dissuading Taiwan from forging a tacit alliance with China is a

d=0&docid=101260078; Li Mingjiang, "South China Sea: Emerging China-Taiwan Cooperation," *RSIS Commentaries*, April 19, 2010, p. 2.

48 Richard Pearson, "Taiwan and the South China Sea," *Taipei Times*, July 1, 2011, p. 8.

49 Yann-huei Song, "Cross-Strait Interactions on the South China Sea Issues: A Need for CBMs," 29 (3) *Marine Policy*, May 2005, p. 279.

50 Joel D. Adriano, "China, Philippines Stoke Island Tensions," *Asia Times*, March 27, 2009.

51 See Taiwan's Ministry of Foreign Affairs statement, May 11, 2009, available at: http://www.mofa.gov.tw/webapp/ct.asp?xItem=38046&ctNode=1548&mp=1; Kuan-hsiung Wang, "The ROC's Maritime Claims and Practices with Special Reference to the South China Sea," 41 (3) *Ocean Development and International Law*, 2010, p. 247.

52 Taiwan's retired army general Ying-chuan Fu's article, see *Want Daily* (Taipei), July 14, 2011; Yung-kuang Kao, "An Analysis of Cross-Strait Cooperation in the South China Sea," *NPF Commentary*, January 7, 2010, available at: http://www.npf.org.tw/post/1/6923.

53 Michael A. Glosny, "Deeper Cross-Strait Rapprochement and PLA Modernization: Implications for China's Relations with Asia and the United States," in Cliff, Saunders, and Harold (eds), *New Opportunities and Challenges for Taiwan's Security*, p. 114.

better approach to defusing the potential conflicts in the South China Sea. Vietnam together with the US took up the issue in the ASEAN Regional Forum in July 2010. Abandoning a competitive security approach to the South China Sea vis-à-vis China's position, the Ma government knows the sensitivity of the issue and understands that the possible misperception of Taiwan's actions might complicate Taiwan's standing in the region. President Ma has chosen not to redeploy marines back to the islands, instead letting the coast guard receive military training from marines for six weeks and then dispatching them to Dongsha Island and Taiping Island in order to strengthen Taiwan's defense capabilities. The Ma government has also opened up these two islands for graduate students from Taiwan's universities to study maritime affairs.

Facing tensions in the South China Sea, particularly in 2010 between China and the US, the Ma government has maintained a neutral position, not taking side with either of them. A bilateral CBM arrangement between Taiwan and China implies not only cross-Strait cooperation in avoiding any conflicts but also a joint stand in countering other sovereignty claims taken by others. A bilateral cross-Strait CBM might also pinpoint the difficulties and awkwardness of not having similar arrangements in the Taiwan Strait. Beijing's refusal to rule out the use of force to settle its dispute in the Taiwan Strait might also imply the inconsistency of having a CBM arrangement in the South China Sea. A Taiwan joining hands with China in asserting Chinese legal claims to counter other ASEAN claimants, which have subtle sympathy from the US, while the US continues providing arms to Taiwan, seems incompatible in the eyes of US policy makers. For the US policy toward Taiwan, the South China Sea issue is less critical than the cross-Strait tension. Responding to a PRC military action against Taiwan-controlled islands in the South China Sea also falls beyond the boundary of the Taiwan Relations Act.

Taipei has kept quiet in responding to rifts between China and Vietnam in May–June 2011 over the exploration of oil in waters of the Spratly Islands. The Ma government has criticized neither China nor Vietnam but has watched closely the increase in the number of military exercises in the South China Sea since 2010. In addition to the Chinese maritime patrols and PLA military exercises, the US conducted a series of naval exercises, from June to July 2011, with the Philippines, with Japan and Australia, and then with Vietnam in the South China Sea.[54] Taiwanese scholars and experts have actively participated in Track-II South China Sea meetings in the region, but Taiwan has been excluded from US-initiated military exercises in the South China Sea for fear of antagonizing China. Beijing has urged Taipei to conduct joint maritime patrols in the South China Sea, but Taipei ironically has declined for not alienating the US defense community.

54 Barbara Demick, "Chinese Naval Maneuvers Seen as Warning to Vietnam," *Los Angeles Times*, June 18, 2011, available at: http://articles.latimes.com/2011/jun/18/world/la-fg-china-vietnam-20110618; Michael Wines, "Joint Chiefs Chairman Meets Chinese Counterpart," *New York Times*, July 10, 2011, available at: http://www.nytimes.com/2011/07/11/world/asia/11china.html.

An interesting development has been under way in Ma's government's South China Sea policy: Taipei has started to express more explicitly its stand regarding cross-Strait collaboration in the South China Sea. In July 2011, Philip Yang, the Director-General of Taiwan's Government Information Office, stated in New York City that while Taiwan and China have the same legal claim to the region, Taipei has "no intention to cooperate or talk with the Beijing government whatsoever," as Taiwan does not yet want to turn its "economic alliance with the mainland into a political one."[55] This position is also supported by the Ministry of National Defense and has helped clarify Taipei's formerly ambiguous position.[56]

Conclusion

Taiwan's awkward international status has kept it from actively being involved in multilateral security forums, not to mention the participation in the ASEAN-related activities in an official capacity. For Taiwan, CBMs regarding the South China Sea have more chance to work out with China than with ASEAN, which has shied away from negotiating political and security issues with Taiwan. Even though there was no overt and confirmed cross-Strait security cooperation in the South China Sea, Taiwan and China are natural partners because of their identical legal sovereignty claims leading them to stand opposite ASEAN. Nevertheless, when Taiwan was facing Chinese military coercion from 1995 to 2008, no implicit or explicit security coordination existed between Taiwan and ASEAN. Taiwan's security concerns come mainly from the Taiwan Strait instead of the South China Sea. The US has paid little attention to a Taiwan contingency from the direction of the South China Sea.

A crisis in the Taiwan Strait could trigger tensions in the South China Sea. For example, the PRC could consider launching a long-distance blockade of the sea lines of communications southwest of Taiwan to teach Taiwan independence elements a lesson. Beijing might even adopt hit-and-run tactics against Dongsha Island or Taiping Island to embarrass Taiwanese and American leaders as the Pentagon report suggested. And if, as some fear, Taiwan is absorbed by Beijing, the PRC could then occupy the two largest islands in the South China Sea and then change the status quo and complicate the US strategic posture in the region. Taiwan's neighbors in the region may not appreciate that Taiwan or its military presence in the South China Sea is, in fact, a buffer between them and China's military.

---

55 Bryan Le, "Negotiations with a Giant: Taiwan's 'Win-Win' Strategy," Asia Society, July 12, 2011, available at: http://asiasociety.org/policy/strategic-challenges/intra-asia/negotiations-giant-taiwans-win-win-strategy.

56 Emmanuelle Tzeng and Deborah Kuo, "Taiwan Will not Consult China on Spratly Issue: MND," Central News Agency (Taiwan), August 5, 2011, available at: http://focustaiwan.tw/ShowNews/WebNews_ Detail.aspx?ID=201108050042&Type=aIPL.

As tensions in the Taiwan Strait have abated since President Ma took office, Beijing might have some flexibility to reconsider its missile deployments opposite Taiwan, which then might create a window of opportunity for cross-Strait cooperation in the South China Sea. For the KMT government and the PRC, any islands and reefs inside the U-shaped boundary line belong to Chinese people. Other ASEAN claimants will find no support or sympathy from Taipei in their maritime dispute with the PRC. President Ma is trying to walk a tightrope, not tilting toward China in any joint military actions against other claimants. On the other hand, the Ma government knows the sensitiveness of tilting toward the US in a Sino–American confrontation in the Spratly Islands. Cross-Strait CBMs in the South China Sea cannot be dealt with separately from the situation in the Taiwan Strait. While encouraging cross-Strait CBMs in the Taiwan Strait for some time, the US has no justifications for blocking similar arrangements in the South China Sea. However, the US has remained vigilant because cooperation between China and Taiwan often has security ramifications for ASEAN and the US, be they in the Taiwan Strait or in the South China Sea.

Chapter 14
The South China Sea Workshop Process and the Need for Taiwan's Continuing Involvement in Regional Ocean Initiatives

Ian Townsend-Gault

Introduction

This chapter examines several aspects of the past, present, and future role of Taiwan in a variety of South China Sea issues. It begins by considering the objectives and accomplishments of the track-two informal diplomacy initiative "Managing Potential Conflicts in the South China Sea." It goes on to investigate the appropriate role for Taiwan in the larger question of South China Sea ocean governance, and concludes with suggestions as to how all governing authorities bordering those waters should proceed in the interests of human security, marine environmental protection and preservation, the preservation of biological diversity, and the appropriate exploitation of living and non-living resources.

My approach to the subject of this chapter is apolitical, insofar as this is possible. That is to say, I have no wish to be seen to be intruding into the vexed question of "one China" or its alternatives. Rather, I take the pragmatic view that, *de facto*, there is a government in Taipei making laws and policies relevant to the South China Sea and exercising supervision of certain activities there, and it must therefore be accounted as one of the "authorities" active in that marine area. This stance is dictated with regard to what I take to be the primary imperatives: the preservation and protection of the marine environment, and the sustainable development of fisheries and other biological resources. Other approaches might accord with political dictates, but some appear to me to verge on the ecologically irresponsible. Given the acute human security issues alive and well in the South China Sea—a point to which I shall return—approaching the issues arising here following political paths and ignoring other considerations seems almost irresponsible.

The Workshops on Managing Potential Conflicts in the South China Sea and the Role of Taiwan

What has become known as the South China Sea Workshop Process began with a series of conversations between Ambassador Hasjim Djalal and myself in early 1989. Put briefly, Ambassador Djalal suggested that, unless something was done to prevent it, the security situation in the South China Sea was bound to deteriorate, and this would have unfortunate implications for Southeast Asia as a whole.[1] There could be no question of implementing a process for the resolution of what was largely seen as "the" problem—disputed sovereignty over the Spratly and Paracel islands. The received wisdom at that time was that these disputes, and that pertaining to the Spratlys in particular, encompassed "the key" to the South China Sea. The reasoning was that sovereignty over the islands brought with it jurisdiction over extensive areas of adjacent oceans and continental shelf. This was important because it was generally accepted that there were significant hydrocarbon resources in the subsoil of the South China Sea, access to these untold riches would flow from sovereignty over the disputed islands.

It should be emphasised that, in 1989, and to some extent to the present day, commentators have been exceedingly generous in their predictions as to the hydrocarbon resources of the South China Sea area. There have been references to "the new Saudi Arabia." I think I can say without fear of contradiction that I tended to treat such predictions with a certain degree of healthy scepticism. This is because of my background in natural resources law and policy, subjects which where at least as important as international law to me at one point in my career. This inevitably brought me into close contact with oil industry personnel, from whom there was much to learn. First, the oil industry is undoubtedly geared to "go where no man has gone before", and to brave the hardships in virtually any part of the world in the search for hydrocarbons. But this is accompanied with a fairly strong dose of common sense and realism summarised by the phrase "oil is where you find it." This means that predictions notwithstanding, at the end of the day, the only statistic that matters has to do with the presence or absence of the resource. If it is found, then a series of other questions arise, such as the percentage that can be recovered at the end of the day (this is a reference to the often overlooked distinction between predictions as to the volume of resources, and the volume of reserves, the latter meaning the amount that can actually be won at the end of the day. As regards oil, the latter might not be more than 10 percent of the former, and it is impossible to know until a substantial amount of drilling and testing has been done). I shall return to this point later.

Once the physical geography of the South China Sea is understood, however, the issue or issues regarding the importance of sovereignty over the islands as stated above appear somewhat unlikely. While it is true that any coastal land generates a zone of maritime jurisdiction of some sort, international lawyers have long known that islands are unlikely to be entitled to an area of particular

---

1 The background to the process, its *modus operandi* and accomplishments from 1989–1999 can be found in Hasjim Djalal and Ian Townsend-Gault, "Managing Potential Conflicts in the South China Sea: Informal Diplomacy for Conflict Prevention", in Crocker, Hampson and Aall, eds, *Herding Cats: Multiparty Mediation in a Complex World*, Washington, D.C., United States Institute of Peace Press, 1999, pp. 107–134.

significance when facing an mainland (or much larger island) coast. One thinks in this connection of the decision of the Court of Arbitration established by France and the United Kingdom with respect to the maritime entitlement of the Channel Islands—British islands lying just off the coast of France—and the effect on the course of the continental shelf boundary to the south of the Isles of Scilly.[2] This is a group of islands lying to the South West of England with a population of around 3,000. The United Kingdom contended that they should be given full effect when determining the course of the boundary from the English Channel into the Atlantic. France contended that they should have no effect at all, and the Court, in effect, split the difference. The Channel Islands were given an enclave of territorial sea. In addition to this judicial decision, there was abundant state practice by 1989 showing that states understood that islands could have a distorted effect on the course of an ocean boundary, leading to an inequitable result.[3]

Accordingly, it seemed inconceivable to the objective observer that features as insignificant as the Spratly Islands could possibly generate significant zones of maritime jurisdiction, especially when opposed to a zone measured from a mainland or large island. They would certainly be entitled to a territorial sea, but significant questions would arise as regards their entitlement to anything beyond this. It goes without saying that features which were "rocks"—and a number of features in the South China Sea are nothing more—could not generate zones of jurisdiction beyond the territorial sea.[4] But even those features which are not mere rocks might be similarly treated. Looking back, one wonders why the debate was phrased as it was. I think we see here the extra ordinary influence generated by the mere rumour of extensive deposits of oil and gas. Those who doubt this should examine the sorts of commentaries appearing with respect to the possibility of hydrocarbon activities in the Arctic. Once again, estimates of resources are being bandied around with considerable freedom. It is fair to say that public expectations are high as a result. This, taken with the possibility of generating continental shelf areas well in excess of 200 nautical miles, stokes the unhelpful but inevitable fires of intense nationalism. In such an atmosphere, rational policy-making, and objective discernment of true priorities, tends to be pushed aside.

The South China Sea workshop process has often been criticised for not engaging with the issue of sovereignty over disputed islands. The decision to exclude such debates was taken at the outset. The thinking was: what purpose would such a

---

2 *Decision of the Court of Arbitration between France and the United Kingdom of Great Britain and Northern Ireland on the Delimitation of the Continental Shelf* (1977), 54 I.L.R. 6.

3 There are other examples where inequity would have resulted from equal treatment: *Continental Shelf (Libyan Arab Jamahiriya/Malta), Judgment, I.C.J. Reports 1985*, p. 13.

4 Applying the provisions of Article 121(3) of the United Nations Convention on the Law of the Sea, 1982: *United Nations Convention on the Law of the Sea*, Montego Bay, December 10, 1982, in force November 16, 1994, in UNTS vol 1833, p. 3, also available at: http://www.un.org/Depts/los/convention_agreements/convention_overview_convention.htm.

discussion serve? How could any way forward be found through rehearsing and repeating well known and deeply entrenched stances on the part of the claimant governments? Indeed, the workshop process wanted to side-step these issues, not encourage them. The aim instead was to consider modes of cooperation between not only the littoral states, but all the authorities of the region of the South China Sea. It was not particularly difficult to identify ocean activities where such cooperation would be highly desirable, if not absolutely necessary. These would include marine scientific research, environmental issues, transportation and communications, and resource management, living and non-living. There was an emphasis on setting goals which were achievable and at the same time served a functional (that is, useful) purpose, as opposed to devoting time and effort to reaching targets which were not unimportant, but out of reach for all practical purposes.

Today, we would tend to regard such discussions as part and parcel of the Regime of Enclosed and Semi-enclosed Seas as set forth in the United Nations Convention on the Law of the Sea of 1982.[5] It should not be forgotten, however, that the Convention was not in force in 1989, and some South China Sea littorals or regional states had yet to ratify it.[6] Be this as it may, the Regime of Enclosed and Semi-enclosed Seas calls for cooperation on the part of littoral states in (and this is not a definitive and closed list) marine scientific research, environmental protection, and living resources conservation.

The precise nature of the legal obligation is entailed here has naturally drawn the attention of scholars and researchers. It has been characterised as "weak", meaning that the language appears to encourage cooperation as opposed to requiring it absolutely, or unambiguously. To my mind, such an approach risks ignoring a highly salient point: the framers of the Convention singled out enclosed and semi-enclosed seas as the subject of a discrete regime. The purposive approach to the interpretation of legal instruments suggests that this is, in and of itself, highly significant. Littorals of enclosed and semi-enclosed seas are subject to obligations however defined that are not applicable to others. The purposive approach would require one to consider why this is. The answer is that optimum management of enclosed and semi-enclosed seas requires levels of cooperation on the part of the states concerned not necessarily applicable to other ocean neighbors.

The South China Sea workshop process began modestly with the First Workshop on Managing Potential Conflicts in the South China Sea convened in Bali, Indonesia, in February 1990. The participants were drawn from the then six countries of the Association of Southeast Asian Nations.[7] The thinking behind this was very simple: if the ASEAN countries could not agree on the need for South China Sea cooperation, there was little point in attempting to solicit the participation of their neighbors to the North and West. Once again, it is necessary

5 *Ibid*, Part IX.

6 At the commencement of the Workshop Process, the Convention had yet to be ratified by: Cambodia, China, Laos and Thailand.

7 Brunei Darussalam, Indonesia, Malaysia, the Philippines, Singapore, and Thailand.

to appreciate the geopolitics of the region as they were in 1990. Vietnam had yet to emerge as a regional player, though it managed to perform this role very much more quickly than many had anticipated. Laos was, on the whole, an unknown quantity. Cambodia was still plagued by surviving units of the Khmer Rouge. Free and democratic elections were some years in the future, and in the opinion of many in the region and beyond, the country did not have a legitimate government at this point.

The First Workshop succeeded in its relatively modest purpose—showing that participants saw some value in maritime cooperation not only as a confidence building measure, but for its own sake. I believe this point can bear some elaboration. Inter-state collaboration, when successful, can be an excellent means of building a relationship. This is true especially when the authorities concerned have not had much of a record of working together, for whatever reason. At one level, the workshop process wished to encourage cooperation purely as a confidence building measure. My own perspective was always rather different. I need hardly say that I was in favour of confidence building between South China Sea littorals, but always aware, at the same time, of the functional element, the fact that cooperation was an absolute requirement in order to achieve certain goals. My perspective was comparatively limited: my graduate work had concerned the legal regime governing oil and gas fields divided by a continental shelf boundary. In particular, I had made an in-depth study of the complex set of public law and private law arrangements governing the exploitation of cross–boundary fields in the North Sea.[8] Optimum recovery of the resources of such deposits is usually possible only when there is absolute cooperation between all interest holders. This can only be brought about when the boundary line is ignored for certain purposes. Oil wells should be drilled and installations positioned according to the dictates of good oilfield engineering practice, and no other consideration. If the engineers determine that, let us say, five wells should be drilled into an oil or gas field, and that all of them are on the same side of the boundary, then so be it. The crucial point is that, if the deposit is to be exploited according to the principles of the technique known as "unitization", costs and revenues should be shared in proportion to the percentage of the resources located on each side of the boundary. Other approaches are possible, such as equal shares, or a fixed percentage agreeable to the parties, but the sophistication of oilfield engineering and resource assessment renders this unnecessary. The result of my research, therefore, led me to an understanding of the non-negotiable importance of certain forms of maritime cooperation.

To return to the rough chronology of the workshop process and its development, the success of the First Workshop of 1990 was crowned, for its organisers, by the unanimity with which participants called for a broadening of the initiative, and

8 The role of the oil companies has often been overlooked, but it was crucial, and should be more broadly recognized and its significance considered; see Ian Gault, "The Frigg Gas Field—Exploitation of an International Cross-Boundary Petroleum Field", *Marine Policy*, 1979, p. 302.

the inclusion of as many South China Sea authorities as possible. The months following the First Workshop saw the organisers engaged in precisely that. Ambassador Djalal secured the participation of Beijing and Taipei, while it fell to me to solicit the interest of Vietnam. This was not especially difficult: by 1990, Hanoi had decided that its future lay in no small measure with its neighbors in Southeast Asia, as opposed to the then Soviet bloc. It should be remembered that the Soviet Union was still in being, but economic determinants had made it less relevant to the development of allies such as Vietnam than hitherto. In short, Hanoi had launched a series of diplomatic initiatives with its immediate neighbors, and countries in East Asia with which it had had comparatively little to do (including Taiwan). It was soon evident that its neighbors in East and Southeast Asia welcomed such overtures, and this was soon evidenced by ever–increasing levels of direct foreign investment on their part.[9]

The Second Workshop on Managing Potential Conflicts in the South China Sea was convened in Bandung, Indonesia, in 1991. While the inclusion of participants from Taiwan appeared to pose no problems, especially as the label of "Chinese Taipei" was adopted, there was clearly some uneasiness between participants from the island and those from mainland China. This was despite the very clearly enunciated ground rules to the effect that everyone attending the meeting, no matter what position they held, was present in their personal capacities. There was nothing to suggest that they were in any way representatives of either their governing authorities or any other institution. It was, therefore, something of a pity that everyone was seated as if they were members of national delegations, as opposed to citizens in their private capacity attending a meeting exploring the possibilities of maritime cooperation. This was probably inevitable: the "personal capacities" label could only be carried so far. So while the official designation of the whole initiative was that it was essentially "track–two", more than one observer concluded that it was really "track one-and-a-half", a label which has now achieved general recognition for initiatives involving participants drawn from the public and private, governmental and non-governmental spheres.

Although the record of the meeting produced jointly by staff members of the Research and Development Agency of the Indonesian Ministry of Foreign Affairs and rapporteurs drawn from the ranks of students at my university does not reflect this, the underlying tensions between Taiwan and mainland China surfaced from time to time. Looking back on meetings which took place 20 years ago, one feels free to remark that undue amounts of time were spent—wasted, in the view of

9 Vietnam's emergence as a regional player, and it is willingness to build productive relations with its Southeast Asian neighbors (culminating in membership of ASEAN) rendered regional meetings on ocean affairs infinitely more relevant. Until this point, such meetings (for example, held under the auspices of SEAPOL (Southeast Asian Programme in Ocean Policy and Law) virtually pretended that the country did not exist. Since it is a littoral of both the South China Sea and the Gulf of Thailand, this introduced a certain note of artificiality into the proceedings. For its part, Vietnam's ocean law and policy was not in the healthiest state.

some—in wrangling about nomenclature which was of interest to only a few participants, and wholly irrelevant to the purpose for which everyone had been gathered together. In my view, these dialogues exacerbated a difficult situation, and did nothing whatever to generate the sort of environment necessary for the discussion of the ostensible agenda for the meeting. But these exchanges were very much the product of their day, and I certainly have not seen their equivalent in recent meetings convened under the aegis of the workshop process, and otherwise.

It was always recognised that the "personal capacities" and "Chinese Taipei" designations would serve the purpose of the informal workshop process. I think I speak for Ambassador Djalal and myself when I say that we thought that the transformation of our work from track two to track one was essentially an issue for others. We hoped, of course, that the cooperative spirit of the workshop process would carry forward into the formal sphere. We knew, of course, that there were many ways in which functional solutions to the Beijing/Taipei situation had been found.

These matters may be said to have come to a head when it was clear that a number of South China Sea authorities were ready to enter into the Declaration of the Conduct of Parties in the South China Sea in 2002. Although this instrument is not a treaty, and was never intended to bear that character, it is closer to the formal than the informal agenda. Furthermore, it was seen essentially as an agreement between South-East Asia represented by ASEAN, and China, meaning Beijing. No role was found for Taipei. The end-result would be perplexing to the independent observer. Myanmar, which has no interest of any sort whatsoever in the South China Sea is a party to the Declaration, while Taipei, whose interests need no elaboration, is not. Whatever the politics behind this result may be, from the functional perspective, this is highly regrettable. It "pretends" that a certain situation prevails, but everyone knows that it does not. From my perspective, which is wholly focused on the overriding principles of sustainable development and the preservation and protection of the marine environment and biological diversity, this is a dysfunctional state of affairs. It also ignores the strong participation of Taipei in every aspect of the workshop process. Whatever the politics might be, there can be no doubting that South China Sea Workshop participants from Taiwan have rendered excellent service not only in the annual workshops themselves, but also the various technical working groups and groups of experts meetings where the detailed contributions of the initiatives have been most manifest.[10]

10 Attention tends to focus on the annual Workshops, held in Indonesia. Less notice has been paid to the extraordinary proliferation of technical meetings on a wide range of topics (including Marine environmental and ecological protection, Marine scientific research, transportation and communication matters, including regional hydrography, living and nonliving resource management, and a variety of legal matters including alternative approaches to zones of cooperation) which took place in between them. For further details, see Djalal and Townsend-Gault, *supra* note 1. For another view of the Taiwanese contribution to South China Sea issues, see John W. McManus, Kwang-Tsao Shao and Szu-Yin Lin, "Toward Establishing a Spratly Islands International Marine Peace

Functional Maritime Cooperation

I take functional cooperation to mean a circumstance where a desired end can only be achieved or an undesirable result averted only though cooperative as opposed to unilateral action.[11] The best example of relevance here is where an oil or gas field is divided between more than one interest-holder, for example, by a continental shelf or maritime boundary. If the parties fail to cooperate, it is likely that the resource cannot be optimally exploited. This is because the successful recovery of those reserves which are in fact recoverable depends on the implementation of a host of production techniques, not to mention the location of wells and the placement of installations. All of this must be done according to sound petroleum engineering principles the implementation of which renders artificial boundaries totally irrelevant (if not actually a potential threat to optimum recovery). This approach, treating an oil or gas field as a single unit, is termed unitization, and is described briefly below.

Cooperation is the theme of the Regime of Enclosed and Semi-Enclosed Seas as it appears in Part IX of the 1982 Convention. But it is really a regime in embryo. Its provisions are exiguous, largely because state practice during the 1970s, when the bulk of the Convention was drafted, had not been particularly well developed or evolved into rules of customary international law, and the wording agreed upon in the Convention was as far as states were willing to go. Environmentalists, ecologists and marine managers understood the principles of ecosystem management, but the best they could do in terms of influencing the wording of the Convention was the regime that we have to this day. I think it is fair to categorize that regime as a "law of the sea" development. It is very much in keeping with the development of public international law, pure and simple. If the nature of the legal obligations arising here were phrased in cautious language, that was the spirit of the times, and our understanding of why cooperation was necessary at all had not spread far beyond the ranks of the technical experts.

Ten years after the conclusion of the Third United Nations Conference on the Law of the Sea saw the convening of the United Nations Conference on Environment and Development in Rio de Janeiro in 1992. In the interim, the Brundtland Commission's report, "Our Common Future", had introduced the world at large to the concept of sustainable development.[12] It seems to me that at that conference, classic public international lawyers took second place to the functional experts on issues such as environmental protection and preservation, biological diversity preservation, issues arising from climate change, and the like. This is reflected in instruments such as the Convention on Biological Diversity, a

Park: Ecological Importance and Supportive Collaborative Activities with an Emphasis on the Role of Taiwan", 41 (3) *Ocean Development and International Law*, 2010, 270–280.

11 My favourite example is the international system of air traffic control, and its standardised and universally accepted rules and procedures.

12 Report of the World Commission on Environment and Development: Our Common Future, 1987.

treaty the elaboration of which appears to be wholly in the hands of environmental scientists and similar experts.[13] Accordingly, it is not unlike the more technical treaties developed by entities such as the International Maritime Organization and other specialised agencies of the United Nations. If the 1982 Convention on the Law of the Sea was important for putting the seal on the basic principles maritime jurisdiction and responsibilities, then the results of the Rio Conference, and I am thinking here in particular of Chapter 17 of *Agenda 21* (which deals in detail with the preservation and protection of the marine environment), gave us the substance upon which to develop and elaborate norms of science-based ocean governance for our times.[14] It should be remembered that the 1982 Convention, important as it is, is not the only multilateral instrument relevant to the "law of the sea."

The parallels with domestic law and policy development are obvious: we have moved into an era where science—based decision making takes pride of place. I hope I am not stretching the analogy too much, but the parallels with the resource–based and derived rules for the unitization of divided oilfields are readily apparent.[15] It is the nature of the resource, or the challenge of environmental or biological preservation, that drives the law. This means that unless one is fully aware of the need to grasp the purposive approach to the interpretation of legal instruments, one cannot understand the true purport and intention of the treaty, or statute.

We should not underestimate the demands that this places on contemporary international lawyers. We have moved away from classic legal territorial encapsulated by nostrums such as "the land dominates the sea", where we impose essentially Westphalian–derived notions of governance of ocean space. Instead, we are required to think much more broadly and indeed generously, according to the dictates of large ecosystem management, and similar concepts. Once such concepts are understood and accepted, and it appears to this international lawyer that this is certainly happening, albeit not necessarily in all parts of Southeast Asia, the governance burden placed on authorities responsible for areas of ocean space become clearer. It requires, *inter alia*, that objective and functional approaches to maritime cooperation be adopted: allowing other concepts to dominate might well suit political agendas, but will do nothing to assist optimum ocean governance.

---

13 *Convention on Biological Diversity*, Rio de Janeiro, June 5, 1992, in force December 29, 1993, Article 18.

14 Chapter 17 is to be found in Section Two of *Agenda 21*—Conservation and Management of Resources for Development: the text is available at: http://www.un.org/esa/dsd/agenda21/index.shtml.

15 Unitization, treating the divided field as a single unit for operational purposes and dividing costs and revenues according to the percentage of the resource found on each side of the dividing line, is the standard oil industry response to such deposits. It was introduced into international practice in the North Sea in the 1970s, but a cooperative approach as mandated by continental shelf boundary treaties of the time (and indeed today). See Ian Gault, *supra* note 8, p. 302.

We know that some seven hundred million people derive by far the greater part of their daily protein requirements from the South China Sea. If there is a serious interruption in the fishery, or the harvesting of other marine resources, the consequences will be dire. Recent research suggests that the South China Sea is very unlikely to provide the means whereby the energy security needs of the East and Southeast Asian regions will be satisfied. Research has shown that significant areas of the seabed this ocean space simply are not comprised of the continental crust required for the development of hydrocarbon resources over the millennia.[16] If oil is indeed where you find it, then it follows that it will not be found in locations with oceanic crust. The speculation with respect to hydrocarbon resources should be seen against the background of what we know of the human security challenges facing the coastal populations of the littorals. There is little in the way of speculation here.[17]

Conclusions

It seems to me that the functional (as opposed to political) realities of the South China Sea argue powerfully for the full engagement of Taipei in any arrangements for cooperative ocean governance of any sort whatsoever. For commentators such as myself, the formal nature of that involvement is largely irrelevant. For those that do not have that luxury, I would add my voice to those who urge that the cooperative imperatives are irresistibly powerful, and their functional necessity has long been demonstrated. Despite innumerable meetings and initiatives, marine regionalism in East and Southeast Asia is not in a happy state. It compares badly to equivalent areas such as the Caribbean, the Baltic, the Mediterranean, and the Black Sea. Is it too late to pose the question to governing authorities of the region as to why this is? It is to be hoped that it is not too late to pose the question, and not too late for the said authorities to take the actions that only they can take in the discharge of the obligations which go hand in hand with the rights they are so eager to enjoy.

16 These issues are explored in papers published by the National Bureau of Asian Research as part of its Marine Energy Resources in Asia project, and a forthcoming collection on joint development options in the South China Sea, Beckman, Schofield and Townsend-Gault, eds, Edward Elgar publishing, expected in 2013. No-one addressing hydrocarbon issues in the South China Sea should ignore either. Together, they offer a strong challenge to the blithe and unsubstantiated predictions of the natural resource bonanza which appears to have played a leading role in the shaping of national ocean policies: it may be time for such policies to be radically re-thought.

17 For a comprehensive examination of some of the ecological issues arising here, see Wilkinson et al, Global International Waters Assessment 54—South China Sea, United Nations Environment Programme, 2005.

PART VI
Conclusion

Chapter 15
Conclusions and Further Reflections

Yann-huei Song and Keyuan Zou

All chapters in this book contributed by lawyers and legal studies experts, political scientists, scholars in security/defense and maritime studies, former navy and military officers, and area study experts are revised and updated based on the comments and suggestions from the peer reviewers. Although the chapters have been revised and updated, it is impossible for them to accommodate every development in the South China Sea as the editors of the book set a deadline for the submission of all the contributing chapters. And since April 2012, when the government of the Philippines dispatched its warship to detain fishing vessels from China in the waters near the disputed Scarborough Shoal, tensions in the South China Sea have been on the rise again. A number of new developments that have potential impact on future dispute settlement or conflict management in the region were not covered in these chapters. It is the editors' view that the value of this volume would be affected if these new developments were not addressed in the book. For that reason, we present to the reader this concluding chapter.

We attempt to discuss and examine a number of new trends of development in the South China Sea, as a supplement to as well as prospect for further thinking about the issues existing there. They include, inter alia: (1) increasing Chinese assertive moves in the South China Sea; (2)increasing US concern with and involvement in the South China Sea issue; (3) increasing the European Union's role in the South China Sea dispute; (4) continuing call for the adoption of a regional Code of Conduct in the South China Sea; and (5) American and European support for international arbitration to resolve the South China Sea dispute.

Increasing Chinese Assertive Moves in the South China Sea

Since April 2012, there has been a new wave of Chinese assertiveness in the South China Sea, which arguably speaking is part of China's response to the provocative actions taken by other claimant countries, in particular the Philippines and Vietnam. As stated by Li Mingjiang, a scholar from Singapore's Nanyang Technological University, at the 4th International South China Sea Workshop held in Ho Chi Minh City, Vietnam, in November 2012, when the Philippines or Vietnam or any other claimant country "kicks China once, China will kick back twice." The decision taken by the Japanese Noda administration to nationalize the disputed Diaoyu/Senkaku Islands inthe East China Sea in September 2012 was also considered by China as a very bad and serious "kick," and therefore Beijing must kick back hard.

The developmental trend in the South China Sea region moved from maritime cooperation to conflict escalation during the period between July 2011 and April 2012. Having reached an agreement between China and the ASEAN member states in July 2011 by adopting the Guidelines for the implementation of the 2002 DOC, it seems that the developmental trend in the South China Sea was moving toward cooperation again and tensions in the region gradually decreased. In November 2011, at the 14th ASEAN–China Summit in Bali, Indonesia, the then Chinese Premier Wen Jiabao announced the establishment of a RMB 3 billion (US$474 million) maritime cooperation fund between China and ASEAN. In addition, he stated that China was ready to work actively with ASEAN member states to fully implement the DOC, enhance practical cooperation and begin discussions on a Code of Conduct in the South China Sea. This was followed by two cooperative activities between China and ASEAN member states that took place in China. On December 12, 2011, the Workshop on the Regional Oceanography of the South China Sea was held in Qingdao, which is the first cooperation project of all parties under the framework of the DOC.

On December 14–15, 2011, a workshop on "Implementing DOC: Maintaining Freedom and Safety of Navigation in the South China Sea" was held in Haikou, Hainan. In January 2012, senior officials of ASEAN member countries and the PRC gathered in Beijing for their fourth meeting (SOM) on the implementation of the DOC. At the meeting, among other things, they considered proposals on holding symposiums on experience sharing and cooperation in marine environment, search and rescue, risk mitigation and research on maritime ecosystem and biodiversity, as trust-building measures. In March 2012, China and Indonesia signed a memorandum of understanding on maritime cooperation and agreed to establish a Committee on Maritime Cooperation and to start a bilateral maritime cooperation fund.

This positive development trend of maritime cooperation between China and ASEAN member states was interrupted by the actions taken in particular by the Philippines and Vietnam. In April 2012, the Philippine government dispatched its warship to detain fishing vessels from China in the waters near the disputed Scarborough Shoal. The Chinese fishing vessels were accused of violating the Philippine Fisheries Code and the Convention on International Trade in Endangered Species of Wild Flora and Fauna (CITES). This was followed by the action taken by Vietnam to pass its Ocean Law that defines the country's maritime territories and sovereignty over them, including the Paracel and Spratly Islands.

In response, in June 2012, China established Sansha City to govern the Macclesfield Bank (Zhongsha), the Paracel Islands (Xisha) and the Spratly Islands (Nansha) in the South China Sea and gave police permission to board and seize unauthorized foreign ships in the territorial waters surrounding the Chinese claimed islands in the area by amending the "Regulations for the Management of Coastal Border Security and Public Order in Hainan Province" in November 2012.

The Regulations entered into force on January 1, 2013. The amended Chinese maritime security regulations aim to strengthen its territorial and maritime claims in the South China Sea.

Also in November 2012, China included a map of its territorial and maritime claims inside its passport. India, the Philippines, Taiwan and Vietnam lodged protests against the Chinese act. Hanoi and Manila interpreted it as a new sign of Beijing's assertive moves in the South China Sea. Taiwan responded by stating that the Republic of China is a free and sovereign state and is not part of the People's Republic of China. In January 2013, Sinomaps Press published the new vertical-format maps of China, which include more than 130 islands and islets in the South China Sea. In the same month, China announced that regular patrols over the waters in the South China Sea will be carried out to secure the country's maritime rights and interests. A Chinese submarine flotilla of the South China Sea Fleet cruised in the South China Sea. In addition, the Chinese government appropriated $1.6 billion to fortify its controlled islands in the South China Sea, including the plan to construct airports, piers and other facilities that could have both civilian and military uses. China also conducted naval exercises in the Shansha and Spratly areas in January and February 2013. It is expected that China will continue to behave assertively in the South China Sea after Xi Jinping, who took charge of the Chinese Communist Party in November 2012, became the president of the country in March 2013.

Increasing US Concerns with and Involvement in the South China Sea Issue

China's increasingly assertive moves in the South China Sea and rising tensions in the region have caused concern from the United States. In response, the Obama administration has increased its involvement in the South China Sea issue since April 2012.

In June 2012, when attending the annual Shangri-La Dialogue conference in Singapore, US Defense Secretary Leon Panetta stated that the Pentagon would shift more navy warships to the Asia-Pacific region over the next several years and by 2020 about 60 percent of the fleet was to be assigned there as part of a new strategy to increase US presence in Asia. The United States was also concerned about the rising tensions between the Philippines and China caused by the disputes over the Scarborough Shoal in the South China Sea and the strategy used by China in promoting ASEAN disunity. Two of the key components of the American strategy of "rebalancing toward Asia" are: (1) deepening and broadening US alliances with Japan, Korea, Australia, Thailand and the Philippines; and (2) building new partnerships with a range of emerging players like China, India, Indonesia, Malaysia, New Zealand, Singapore and Vietnam. Although the US officials state that the strategy is not aiming at China, Chinese and international maritime security experts are taking the view that the key strategic aim of the "pivot to Asia" policy is to contain China's maritime assertiveness and protect the freedom of navigation in the Asia-Pacific region, including the South China Sea.

In July 2012, for the first time in its 45-year history, ASEAN's foreign ministerial meeting (AMM) failed to issue a joint communiqué following their annual consultations in Phnom Penh, Cambodia. The main reason for the failure was the differences among the ASEAN members in dealing with the South China Sea issue. In order to help ASEAN "back to business as usual," Indonesia's Foreign Minister Marty Natalegawa conducted an intense round of shuttle diplomacy, visiting Cambodia, Vietnam, the Philippines, Singapore and Malaysia. As a result of his efforts, on July 20, 2012, ASEAN foreign ministers issued a statement of "six-point" principles on the South China Sea, which include the full implementation of the 2002 DOC, the support for the 2011 Guidelines, the need for an early conclusion of a regional code of conduct in the South China Sea, the full respect for the universally recognized principles of international law including the United Nations Convention on the Law of the Sea (LOS Convention), the continued exercise of self-restraint and non-use of force by all parties, and the peaceful resolution of conflicts in accordance with universally recognized principles of international law including the LOS Convention. The United States welcomed the adoption of the six-point principles. At the same time, Washington expressed its concern about the increasing Chinese assertive moves in the South China Sea and its strategy of "buying the loyalties of some Asian states" and dividing the association.

The US concern was reflected in a number of important statements made by Secretary of State Hillary Clinton and other high-ranking government officials in 2012. The US Congress also took action to express its concern about the South China Sea situation and asked the Obama administration to take actions to support the American allies and to protect the American national interests in the region.

In July 2012, when attending the 19th ARF meeting, Secretary Clinton, while not mentioning any country, stated that "the nations of the region should work collaboratively and diplomatically to resolve disputes without coercion, without intimidation, without threats, and without use of force."This was followed by a number of statements made by U.S. Senators in the same month.

On July 26, 2012, U.S. Senator Jim Webb, chair of the Senate Foreign Relations East Asian and Pacific Affairs Subcommittee, stated that China's actions to unilaterally assert control of disputes territories in the South China Sea via the establishment of Sansha City may be a violation of international law. He urged the US State Department to clarity this situation with China and report back to the Congress. In August 2012, a resolution was passed in the US Senate, which inter alia reaffirms the US commitment: to assist the nations of Southeast Asia to remain strong and independent; to help ensure each nation enjoys peace and stability; to broaden and deepen partnership with ASEAN and its member states; and to support enhanced operations by the US armed forces in the Western Pacific in support of freedom of navigation, the maintenance of peace and stability, respect for international law, including the peaceful resolution of issues of sovereignty, and unimpeded lawful commerce.

In August 2012, the U.S. Department of State issued a statement on the South China Sea, urging that "the nations of the region should work collaboratively and diplomatically to resolve disputes without coercion, without intimidation, without threats, and without the use of force."In September 2012, Kurt Campbell, Assistant Secretary, Bureau of East Asian and Pacific Affairs, U.S. Department of State, stated that"[a]s the United States pivots to the Asia Pacific region, the recent spate of disputes in the South China Sea … are sending reverberations throughout the region, threatening instabilities that could undermine U.S. interest."[1] In November 2012, when attending the 7th East Asia Summit, President Obama encouraged the parties concerned to make progress on a binding Code of Conduct in the South China Sea to provide a framework to prevent conflict, manage incidents when they occur and help resolve disputes. In February 2013, a bill (HR 772) entitled "To promote peaceful and collaborative resolution of the South China Sea" was introduced in the House of Representatives, US Congress, in which the new US Secretary of State John Kerry is asked, among other things, to reaffirm the strong US support for the peaceful resolution of maritime territorial disputes in the South China Sea and pledge continued efforts to facilitate a collaborative peaceful process to resolve the dispute; to condemn the use of threats or force by naval, maritime security and fishing vessels from China in the South China Sea that would escalate tensions or result in miscalculations; to note that overt threats and gunboat diplomacy are not constructive means for settling the maritime disputes in the East Asian seas; to welcome the diplomatic efforts of ASEAN and the US allies and partners to amicably and fairly resolve the disputes; and to support the continuation of operations by the US Armed Forces in support of freedom of navigation rights in international waters and air space in the South China Sea.

A number of actions have been taken by the United States since April 2012, which demonstrate further increasing American concern and involvement. In April 2012, a joint statement by the United States and the Philippines reaffirmed the Manila Declaration the two countries signed in November 2011, ensuring that the US–Philippines alliance remains robust, agile and responsive in order to meet changing global and regional dynamics. Washington and Manila agreed to address common strategic and security objectives. In December 2012, at the 3rd US–Philippines bilateral strategic dialogues, the two sides discussed the increase in the number of US military ships, aircraft and troops rotating through the Philippines. The United States agreed to provide a second coast guard cutter to the Philippines, which will be delivered in 2013. It was also agreed in 2012 that the United States

1 Maritime Territorial Disputes and Sovereignty Issues in Asia, Testimony of Kurt Campbell, Assistant Secretary, Bureau of East Asian and Pacific Affairs, U.S. Department of State, before the Senate Foreign Relations Committee Subcommittee on East Asian and Pacific Affairs, September 20, 2012, available at: http://www.state.gov/p/eap/rls/rm/2012/09/197982.htm.

will deploy up to four littoral combat ships (LCB) to Singapore, and the first LCB, USS *Freedom*, is expected to arrive at the citystate in mid-April 2013 for its inaugural ten-month deployment.

In January 2013, when John Kerry spoke at his confirmation hearing to become US Secretary of State, he seemed to back away from a key aspect of President Obama's strategy of "rebalancing" toward Asia. Secretary Kerry said that he wanted to "grow the rebalance" toward China. In addition, although Mark Lippert, US Assistant Secretary of Defense for Asian and Pacific Security Affairs, stated in a conference held in February 2013 that there is a strong sense within the Obama administration that the strategy of "rebalancing toward Asia" is a priority and the government will work to make that continue, the rebalance is not a zero-sum game with Beijing and it is not a contain-China strategy. In fact, a strong bilateral relationship with China is part of the rebalance, he added.

Arguably speaking, these statements are considered the Obama administration's response to an argument that the American strategy of "rebalancing toward Asia" is one of the main reasons for the claimant states taking provocative actions against China in the South China Sea. It is also considered a key factor for triggering China's assertive moves that escalated tensions in the South China Sea and increased the possibility of the US being dragged into armed clashes in the region.

Increasing EU Concern about the South China Sea Situation

In the past, the European Union neglected the development in the South China Sea region. It was observed that Brussels tried to stay out of the South China Sea dispute as much as possible. The lack of EU interest in the South China Sea issue was reflected in the decision by Catherine Ashton, the EU High Representative for Foreign Affairs and Security Policy, not to attend the ARF meetings held in Hanoi in 2010 and in Bali in 2011. The impression of EU indifference to the South China Sea situation has changed after the United States announced its "pivot" toward Asia policy in 2011. In many respects, 2012 is called a "Year of Asia" for the EU.

In June 2012, the Council of the European Union adopted the Guidelines on the EU's Foreign and Security Policy in East Asia, in which Brussels took note that the rising tensions in the South China Sea could have implications for security and stability in the South China Sea region, including more broadly for the freedom of navigation and commerce. Accordingly, the EU and its member states need to recall the importance of the South China Sea for the EU in the perspective of promoting the rules-based international system, the principle of freedom of navigation, the risk of tensions impacting on the consistent interest in trade and investment, with negative consequences for all, and energy security. In addition, the EU and its member states should continue to encourage the parties concerned in the South China Sea region to resolve their disputes through peaceful and cooperative solutions in accordance with international law, in particular the LOS Convention, while encouraging all parties to clarify the basis for their claims.

Moreover, the EU and its member states should recall previous work to build a collaborative diplomatic process on the issues related to the South China Sea at the regional level, and encourage ASEAN and China to build on this foundation and agree on a Code of Conduct. Finally, if welcomed by the relevant parties, the EU and its member states should offer to share their experience in relation to the consensual, international law-based settlement of maritime boundary issues, and to the sustainable management of resources and maritime security cooperation in sea areas with sovereignty or maritime disputes.

In July 2012, Catherine Ashton and Hillary Clinton met in Phnom Penh to exchange views on the developments in the Asia-Pacific region. On the South China Sea issue, they stated that the EU and the United States would continue to encourage ASEAN and China to advance a Code of Conduct in the South China Sea, and to resolve territorial and maritime disputes through peaceful, diplomatic and cooperative solutions. Also in July 2012, the EU High Representative for Foreign Affairs and Security Policy signed the Accession Instrument to the Treaty of Amity and Cooperation, which enables the EU to participate in the East Asia Summit and to work together with the 18 participating members of the Summit, including the ten member states of the ASEAN, Australia, China, India, Japan, New Zealand, Russia, South Korea and the United States, to address some of the security and political concerns of the region. In November 2012, in a meeting with the Philippine President Aquino III, the EU's leaders declared support for an ASEAN approach to the territorial disputes in the South China Sea, namely a peaceful resolution of the territorial conflicts based on international law. However, the South China Sea issue was not included in the Chair's Statement of the 9th Asia–Europe Summit, held in Vientiane, Laos, November 5–6, 2012. In March 2013, the European Parliament adopted its report on EU–China relations, in which it urges China unequivocally to commit itself to observing the UN Charter and international law in the pursuit of its goals abroad. It also asks China to dispel growing international concerns about its non-transparent military budget. In addition, the Parliament underlines the global importance of the South China Sea, expresses its concern about the rising tension in the region and appeals to all the parties concerned to refrain from unilateral political and military actions, to tone down statements and to settle their conflicting territorial claims in the South China Sea by means of international arbitration in accordance with international law, in particular the LOS Convention, in order to ensure regional stability.

Continuing Call for the Adoption of a Regional Code of Conduct in the South China Sea

At the 20th ASEAN Summit in April 2012, the ten leaders of the ASEAN member countries agreed to move for the eventual realization of a regional Code of Conduct (COC). In July 2012, however, ASEAN foreign ministers ended a meeting in Cambodia without issuing a joint statement on the South China Sea issue for the first time in its 45-year history. The ASEAN member states were divided by the key elements contained in the ASEAN draft COC. At the same time, China shifted its priority to the implementation of the DOC and agreed to talk about the COC "when the time is ripe." In order to maintain ASEAN unity on managing the South China Sea issue, ASEAN foreign ministers issued the Statement of ASEAN Foreign Ministers on ASEAN's Six-Point Principles on the South China Sea on July 20, 2012, in which the ASEAN foreign ministers reiterated and reaffirmed their commitment to an early conclusion of a regional COC in the South China Sea.

In November 2012, the heads of state and government of ASEAN member states attended the 21st ASEAN Summit that was chaired by the Prime Minister of the Kingdom of Cambodia. The Chairman's Statement issued after the summit did not mention the need to adopt a regional COC in the South China Sea. The COC issue was not mentioned in the Chairman's Statements of the 15th ASEAN–China Summit and the tenth Anniversary of the DOC held in November 2012. In comparison, during the 18th, 19th and 20th ASEAN Summits, it was urged repeatedly to move for the eventual realization of a regional COC in the South China Sea. The COC matter was also included in the Chairman's Statement of the 13th (2010) and 14th(2011) China–ASEAN Summits as well as the joint statement of a summit commemorating the 20th anniversary of the China–ASEAN dialogue relations held in November 2011.

Both the United States and the European Union are in support of the conclusion of the COC in the South China Sea. Most, if not all, of the US official statements that touch upon the South China Sea issue since 2009 have included a remark that the United States encourages the parties to reach agreement on a full COC. In August 2012, the U.S. Department of State issued a statement on the South China Sea, in which the United States encourages ASEAN and China to make meaningful progress toward finalizing a comprehensive COC. At the 4th leaders' meeting between ASEAN member states and the United States, held in November 2012 in Phnom Penh, the United States and the participating heads of state and government stated that they looked forward to the early conclusion of the COC.

In early February 2013, Admiral Samuel J. Locklear III, the head of US Pacific Command, when visiting Brunei, stated that the United States pledged its support for Brunei to conclude a legally binding COC, while also urging closer relations between ASEAN and China. This was followed by the remarks made by the US Ambassador to ASEAN David Carden, who visited Brunei on February 15, 2013 that "[i]t is deeply understood by all concerned that the South China Sea is an issue that needs to be managed by ASEAN properly" and that "[i]t is my hope this year that we will make progress on a code of conduct."

Also in February 2013, a bill (HR 772) entitled "To promote peaceful and collaborative resolution of the South China Sea dispute" was introduced in the House of Representatives, US Congress, in which Secretary John Kerry is asked, no later than 180 days after the date of the enactment of this Act, that he "shall" submit to the House Committee on Foreign Affairs and Senate Foreign Relations

Committee a report on the COC and other peaceful measures for resolution of the SCS territorial dispute.

It is clear that the European Union is also in support of the conclusion of a COC in the South China Sea. The Guidelines on the EU's Foreign and Security Policy in East Asia, approved by the Council of the European Union in June 2012, state that the EU and its member states encourage ASEAN and China to agree on a COC. In July 2012, European Union High Representative for Foreign Affairs and Security Policy Catherine Ashton and Secretary of State Hillary Clinton met in Phnom Penh to exchange views on developments in the Asia-Pacific. On the South China Sea issue, the Secretary and the High Representative stated that they would continue to encourage ASEAN and China to advance a COC and to resolve territorial and maritime disputes through a peaceful, diplomatic and cooperative solution.

After taking over the ASEAN chairmanship from Cambodia on November 20, 2012, Brunei expressed its intention to push forward the ASEAN–China dialogue and drafting process of a COC in the South China Sea. Thailand, as the coordinator of ASEAN–China relations (July 2012–July 2015), will seek a common ASEAN position on the disputed waters for the bloc talks on the issue with China. In February 2013, it was reported that Thailand would spare no effort to push for the full implementation of the DOC and an early signing of the COC. In January 2013, Le Luong Minh, the new ASEAN Secretary-General, also stated that he wanted to finalize a legally binding COC aimed at easing tensions in the South China Sea. In February 2013, according to a report in *The Economist*, Brunei hopes to conclude a COC by October 2013.

It seems less likely for the conclusion of the COC in the South China Sea in 2013, given that China does not consider "the time is ripe." In addition, Myanmar, to take over the 2014 ASEAN chairmanship from Brunei in November 2013, traditionally maintains close economic, political and security ties with China. However, the trend of development indicates that China will face political pressure not only from the ASEAN but also the United States and the European Union to begin the negotiation process that aims to conclude a regional COC for the South China Sea.

American and European Support for International Arbitration Initiated by the Philippines against China

In February 2013, the Chinese Ambassador in Manila rejected and returned the *Note Verbale* and the attached Philippines' notification of arbitration and statement of claim. The notification was sent to the Chinese Ambassador in Manila on January 22, 2013, notifying China that the Philippines is bringing the dispute in the South China Sea before an arbitral tribunal in accordance with Article 287 and Annex VII of the LOS Convention. The Philippines asks the arbitral tribunal to issue an award that, among other things, "Declares that China's maritime claims in the South China Sea based on its so-called 'nine dash line' are contrary to [the

United Nations Convention on the Law of the Sea] and invalid." Beijing accused Manila of violating the consensus in the 2002 DOC, because the declaration states that disputes should be solved through friendly talks and negotiations by sovereign states directly concerned. In addition, the Chinese government pointed out that there were factual and legal mistakes and unfounded accusations against China in the Philippines' notification and statement of claim. Despite the fact that China returned its notification of arbitration, the Philippines claims that the arbitral procedure will continue.

China is facing an increasing pressure from not only the Philippines but also other members of the international community, which include the United States and the EU and its member states. In January 2013, US Representative Ed Royce, chairman of the House Foreign Affairs Committee, stated in Manila that China should agree to face the Philippines before a UN arbitral tribunal to avoid a possible crisis over their long-raging territorial disputes in the South China Sea. This was followed by support from US Secretary of State John Kerry, the German Foreign Minister and a group of EU lawmakers in February 2013. In March 2013, it is included in a report on EU–China relations approved by the European Parliament, stating that it "urgently appeals to all the parties involved to refrain from unilateral political and military actions, to tone down statements and to settle their conflicting territorial claims in the South China Sea by means of international arbitration in accordance with international law, in particular the UN Convention on the Law of the Sea, in order to ensure regional stability."

China needs to respond to the Philippines' request for arbitration in accordance with the LOS Convention and agrees to appoint its arbitrator after consultation with the President of the International Tribunal for the Law of the Sea (ITLOS) before the deadline set as March 21, 2013. Despite the refusal from China, the ITLOS President has appointed ITLOS Judge Stanislaw Pawlakas Arbitrator representing China. On April 24, 2013, the ITLOS President appointed the remaining three arbitrators. It is interesting to note that among the five arbitrators, four are Europeans and one a long-term European resident.[2] The arbitration raises two important questions: (1) to what extent this development could help clarify a number of legal issues that are related to the status of the nine-dashes line and a number of land features located in the South China Sea; (2) whether the existing complicated and complex South China Sea situation would become more difficult to tackle with between China and the other claimant states. Clearly this development needs to be watched closely.

In summary, it is well perceived that the South China Sea remains a hot spot in international relations at present and in the near future. Unless ASEAN member states and China can reach a legally binding COC, unilateral activities will continue in the South China Sea, which would become a barrier to regional cooperation and a disturbing factor to regional peace and stability as well.

2 For details, see http://www.itlos.org/fileadmin/itlos/documents/press_releases_english/PR_191_E.pdf.

Index

For Product Safety Concerns and Information please contact our EU representative GPSR@taylorandfrancis.com Taylor & Francis Verlag GmbH, Kaufingerstraße 24, 80331 München, Germany